TEACHING STRATEGIC PROCESSES IN READING

Teaching Strategic Processes in Reading

SECOND EDITION

Janice F. Almasi
Susan King Fullerton

GOVERNORS STATE UNIVERSITY
UNIVERSITY PARK, IL

THE GUILFORD PRESS
New York   London

© 2012 The Guilford Press
A Division of Guilford Publications, Inc.
72 Spring Street, New York, NY 10012
www.guilford.com

Printed in the United States of America

This book is printed on acid-free paper.

Last digit is print number: 9   8   7   6   5   4   3   2   1

Library of Congress Cataloging-in-Publication Data
Almasi, Janice F.
  Teaching strategic processes in reading / Janice F. Almasi, Susan King Fullerton. — 2nd ed.
    p. cm.
  Includes bibliographical references and index.
  ISBN 978-1-4625-0642-2 (hardback) — ISBN 978-1-4625-0629-3 (paper)
  1. Reading. 2. Reading comprehension. 3. Word recognition. I. Fullerton, Susan King.
II. Title.
  LB1050.42.A44 2012
  372.41—dc23
                                                                        2012016840

In memory of Michael Pressley,
our mentor, colleague, and friend,
who continues to inspire and challenge us
to become better teachers of strategic processing

About the Authors

Janice F. Almasi, PhD, is the Carol Lee Robertson Endowed Professor of Literacy Education at the University of Kentucky, where she teaches courses in literacy research and theory. She is a former elementary school teacher and reading specialist and a former member of the Board of Directors of the Literacy Research Association and the International Reading Association. Dr. Almasi's research, which has been recognized with several awards, has examined the contexts in which children learn from text, particularly in terms of strategic processes and peer discussion environments. She has published several books, including *Teaching Literacy in Third Grade* and *Lively Discussions!: Fostering Engaged Readers*, and her research articles have appeared in journals such as *Educational Psychologist*, *Elementary School Journal*, *Journal of Educational Psychology*, *Journal of Literacy Research*, *Reading Psychology*, and *Reading Research Quarterly*.

Susan King Fullerton, PhD, is Associate Professor in Literacy and Teacher Education at Clemson University, located in Clemson, South Carolina, where she teaches undergraduate and graduate courses in literacy methods, literacy research and theory, and the roles of the literacy specialist and coach, and clinic practicum courses related to assessment and instruction of struggling readers. She was also formerly a teacher of the deaf, a reading specialist, a Reading Recovery teacher, a Title I staff developer, and a literacy coach, and she continues to work in classrooms collaboratively with teachers. Her research interests and publications have focused on the issues faced by struggling readers, strategic processes in reading, comprehension, the literary responses of young children, and literacy acquisition and instruction for deaf children. She is a principal editor for the *61st Yearbook of the Literacy Research Association*.

Acknowledgments

We would both like to acknowledge the talented staff at The Guilford Press, especially our editor, Natalie Graham, for her patience and guidance throughout the process.

We would also like to acknowledge our mentors with whom we studied at the University of Maryland: Linda B. Gambrell, Michael Pressley, Peter Afflerbach, John Guthrie, John O'Flahavan, Jean Dreher, Beth Davey, Ruth Garner, and Bob Wilson. Their research and insights inspired the theoretical connections contained throughout the book.

From Janice: I am most gratefully indebted to my former graduate students who taught me so much while I was writing the first edition of this book. Without their help and inspiration, the first edition would not have become a reality. They also remain the heart and soul of the second edition: Angela Bies, Anita Brocker, Erin David, Renee Danielewicz, Sheila Ewing, AnnaMaria Figliomeni, Chastity Flynn, Keli Garas-York, Patty DiLaura George, Liz Graffeo, Renee Guzak, Jill Hatfield, Bob Hirsch, Jennifer Izzo, Krista Jaekle, Eileen Ludwig, Jaime Quackenbush, Jody Rabinowitz, Mike Rock, Kathy Sadowski, Summer Sciandra, Donna Von Hendy, and Kristin Zahn. Please continue to challenge yourselves.

I would like to thank my coauthor, Susan King Fullerton. Your unparalleled expertise related to early literacy and struggling readers is a much-needed addition to this book. It seems that our best work together has always happened in the summer—from our days as graduate students in the University of Maryland Summer Reading Clinic to our time spent working together these past two summers. Thank you, dear friend, for pushing, challenging, critiquing, and, most of all, supporting me.

I am grateful to Keli Garas-York, who provided critical feedback on the second edition and generously shared photos from the summer reading clinic she directs at Buffalo State College. I am grateful to my dear friend and colleague Rachel Brown at Syracuse University, whose work in strategies instruction I admire greatly and whose chats stimulate my mind in challenging ways and constantly remind me of Mike Pressley's influence. I would also like to acknowledge the editorial assistance of Nicki Shelton at the University of Kentucky, who quickly and doggedly tracked down references.

Although we wrote the second edition during the hot, humid Kentucky summers, the individuals who shaped, informed, and provided assistance during the writing of the first edition in the cold winter months in Newfoundland, Canada, are, to some extent, still present.

For this, I would like to thank my Newfoundland relatives, who selflessly became my tour guides, translators, historians, and cultural brokers on a daily basis. I am especially grateful to my aunt Susie (Spencer) Barbour; my uncle George Spencer; and my aunt Maisie (Hodder) Spencer, who shared so much of their lives and their love with me. I thank my cousins, Don and Roberta Hogan, Paulette Spencer and Ken Andrews, Chris and MD Spencer, Stephen Spencer, Eileen (Spencer) Staples, Sheila and Fabian O'Brien, Tina and Doug, and Dick and Maisie Hardy, who have since passed away.

In addition, I would like to thank the wonderful friends I met in Victoria Cove and Gander Bay, Newfoundland, who welcomed me into their community, entertained me with their stories, taught me about life in Newfoundland, and often provided me with safe haven: Lynn, Barry, and Nick Torraville, Joy Hodder, Margaret Elliott, the late Don Elliott, Netta French, Bill and Annie Harbin, Marvin and Dianne Hodder, Melvin and Gertie Hodder, Harry and Susie Thompson, Flo Torraville, and Les and Marjorie Vivian. I am also indebted to Reverend Yvonne Thistle, who provided spiritual guidance throughout my stay.

I would like to thank my first teachers and mentors—my mother, Jessie Spencer Almasi, and my father, John Almasi. The warmth of a home filled with unconditional love is the greatest gift a child could ever want. Thank you for that most special gift. I would like to thank my brother, John, who helps me view the world in new ways. Finally, I am grateful to my sisters, Judy L. Downing and JoAnn M. Suchko, who are my first and forever friends and my heroes.

From Susan: I am indebted to my coauthor, Janice, my anchor during the time we earned our doctorates at the University of Maryland and a dear friend and colleague for many years. I am so grateful for the opportunity to work on the second edition with her, and I will treasure the learning and life experiences we have shared over these many months, not least for the many wonderful meals and hospitality during my stays in Lexington. Janice, please know that these few words cannot convey the tremendous wealth of learning and friendship that this endeavor provided.

In addition to my wonderful mentors at Maryland, I must thank my mentors and colleagues at The Ohio State University (Carol Lyons, Gay Su Pinnell, Diane DeFord, Emily Rodgers, Mary Fried, and Rose Mary Estice) and those at other Reading Recovery university training centers (Billie Askew, Salli Forbes, and Trika Smith-Burke) who guided me. To all my Reading Recovery colleagues, too numerous to mention, I remain grateful for the many years of learning and collegiality you have offered. I will be indebted forever to Marie Clay, who pushed my thinking in print and in person. I treasure the memorable opportunities I had to discuss teaching and learning as well as research with her. I would also like to acknowledge my literacy colleagues at Clemson University, Linda B. Gambrell, C. C. Bates, Pamela Dunston, Kathy Headley, and Jonda McNair, who have contributed to this book by sharing their knowledge and expertise.

Without the many wonderful graduate students at Clemson, I would not have been able to collaborate on this book. Their influence on my teaching and understanding of literacy instruction and reading processes over the past 5 years have contributed immensely to this edition. Special thanks must go to the cohorts in our graduate program from the

Anderson and Oconee School Districts in South Carolina, who allowed me to try out ideas from the first edition while I worked on this revision during the clinic courses and beyond. Their professional and personal support motivated me to collaborate on a book that would be useful for wonderful teachers like them.

Even though both my parents, Faye and Calvin King, have been gone for much too long, their desire to see me succeed remains with me and, as always, their examples of strength and perseverance guided me throughout the book's completion. I ask for forgiveness from two dear friends—my brother, Jim King, and Joanne Pfeil Ferguson (my sister since our days at Maryland)—for my neglect as I worked on the book, and thank them for giving me the love and support that I needed, even when it wan't fully reciprocated. To the three most important people in my life—my husband, Steve Fullerton, and my children, Rachel and Mitchell Fullerton—I love you and thank you for your love, support, and patience. In spite of sometimes not giving you my full attention, I hope that you feel a part of this accomplishment. Finally, thank you, Steve, for all the tasks that you completed, both large and small, so that I could work on the book. You have always supported me in following my bliss!

Preface

The first edition of *Teaching Strategic Processes in Reading*, published in 2003, came about at the request of Janice's graduate students when she was a faculty member at the University at Buffalo, The State University of New York. At the time, some of those students were practicing teachers and some were striving to become teachers. All of them were enrolled in reading education courses; however, the course from which this book originally evolved was an elective. This point is meaningful primarily because, as professors and students are aware, students often choose electives that are less demanding than required courses. This elective was not easy. There were many other courses in which to enroll that would have been far easier, but these graduate students chose a more difficult route. Becoming a teacher of strategic reading processes is exceedingly difficult. It is much harder than teaching almost any other subject in education because it permeates all subjects. It is a way of thinking and a state of mind that must be engaged at every opportunity throughout the school day. Recognizing these opportunities as they occur in relation to a classroom of children with very different motivations, abilities, and interests makes teaching strategic processes a complex undertaking. The amount of reflection and self-awareness that must accompany this instruction is what makes it difficult. It is a personal journey that requires a teacher who is willing to open him- or herself up entirely for critical examination and who is willing to adapt to the ever-changing needs of his or her students. Few are willing to take on this challenge, which is why it is important to know that the graduate students whose work enlivens this book willingly undertook it. They are tremendous individuals who gave entirely of themselves—often overlooking their own personal needs to selflessly teach struggling readers.

The second edition came about at the request of several professors across the United States who used the first edition in their courses and found it beneficial. One of those was Keli Garas-York, who then was one of Janice's graduate students and is now a professor at Buffalo State College. Dr. Garas-York's lesson plans and reflective memos figured prominently in the first edition and are repeated in the second edition as excellent examples of what successful strategic-processing instruction looks like and of what reflective practitioners do. Lynn Shanahan at the University at Buffalo, The State University of New York, has also taken on the mantle of strategies instruction and has worked her magic throughout the Buffalo area by spreading the word.

Throughout the past decade, new issues in literacy education have made focusing on strategic processing more important than ever. At the time of the first edition's publication, political pressures in the United States had created a sense of urgency to teach all children how to read by grade 3. The result of those pressures was the No Child Left Behind legislation that created Reading First. Throughout the 2000s, the ensuing reforms were primarily predicated on the theoretical premise that if children can learn to decode words using their knowledge of phonics and phonemic awareness, then successful comprehension will follow. In turn, the number of children learning to read by grade 3 would increase, and the number needing intervention would diminish. This premise shifted the focus for some researchers and became the driving force within instruction. Ultimately, however, when the final reports of Reading First's impact were released, the findings indicated that these code-based interventions had no significant impact on comprehension.

The result was that comprehension and strategies instruction have re-emerged as critical issues in research and instruction. Core reading programs published in the past decade have incorporated much of the research related to comprehension strategies instruction. However, as Dewitz, Jones, and Leahy (2009) found, the five most widely used commercial core reading programs do not provide the type of explicit instruction or the gradual release of responsibility that is the foundation of comprehension strategies instruction. Further, Dewitz, Leahy, Jones, and Sullivan (2010) found these publications woefully inadequate in their attempt to provide students with the procedural and conditional knowledge associated with strategy use. What continues to be problematic since the publication of the first edition is that teachers tend to misunderstand what strategic processing involves; they focus on isolated strategy use rather than on strategic processing, and they focus on activities rather than strategies. Teachers may engage students in activities, but they do not provide the requisite instructional elements to teach *strategic processing*. Very often a teacher actually performs the strategies rather than teaching the students how to use the strategies independently. That is, a teacher may determine a purpose for reading rather than teaching the students how, when, and why they should determine their own purposes for reading. Thus, students are not actively engaged in the decision-making process regarding which strategies to use and when to use them; as a result, they do not learn to become planful, self-regulated readers who possess a repertoire of strategies to assist them as they read. That is, they lack *agency*, and instead of intentionally planning their actions and enacting strategies to achieve them on their own, they become dependent on teachers to direct the strategic process. Struggling readers, in particular, are at a disadvantage in this scenario. Thus, the goals of the second edition are to (1) focus more actively on teaching students to become agentic, (2) update content in light of current research, (3) consider strategic processing in relation to response to intervention (RTI), (4) incorporate early literacy more, and (5) promote orchestrated strategy use within daily lessons, across an entire day, and beyond.

Chapter 1 sets the groundwork for the book by explaining what is involved in strategic processing and by distinguishing between strategies and skills—a common area of misunderstanding. It also describes the characteristics of strategic and nonstrategic readers.

Chapter 2 introduces the critical elements of strategies instruction (CESI) model, which is grounded in research and clinical practice. A number of strategy instruction models are compared as a way to situate the CESI model. Then, the key components of

CESI are described using examples from the authentic teaching contexts created by our graduate students: creating a safe environment, providing explicit instruction, reducing processing demands, and creating opportunities for verbalization.

Chapter 3 aims to situate teaching strategic processing within RTI frameworks and provides an overview of responsive teaching as it pertains to strategies instruction. We define and describe responsive teachers and responsive teaching. Then we discuss the history of RTI and what a multi-tiered intervention framework looks like when it incorporates strategies instruction, and conclude with the four key elements of sound core reading instruction and seven key elements of sound intervention instruction that incorporate strategic processing.

Chapter 4 describes a multitude of methods for assessing strategic processing. The premise of the chapter is that assessment must be ongoing and integrally related to instruction. Assessment cannot be an end product because strategic processing is active and dynamic and must be assessed *while it occurs*. Thus, the assessments described are process oriented. Assessments must also be used to individualize instruction, as teachers are encouraged to generate and continually refine hypotheses about individual students' strengths and needs as strategic readers, based on the recursive cycle of ongoing assessment and instruction.

Chapter 5 describes profiles of different types of students who struggle with comprehension, followed by theoretical explanations for their difficulties. It also explains the types of cognitive strategies that will assist readers who have various comprehension difficulties, and it provides the background material for Chapter 6, in which the research supporting various comprehension strategies is reviewed. Text anticipation, maintenance, and fix-up strategies are discussed in detail, and lesson plans and instructional materials for each strategy are provided. Each shared lesson is authentic, having been created and implemented by teachers in a graduate course. The teachers' reactions to, and reflections on, the lessons give readers insight into how successful the lessons were and how children reacted to them.

Chapter 7 describes the theories underlying word recognition strategies and provides sample lessons and guidelines for instruction. It also includes lists of children's literature that are well suited for use in instruction focusing on word recognition.

Chapter 8 explores teachers' growth and development as they learned about teaching strategic processes and describes the journeys on which these extraordinary teachers embarked. Through journal entries and portfolios, it tells graduate students' poignant and, at times, painful tales of reflection and self-discovery. You might consider reading this chapter first so that you have a vision of what the journey looks like from the beginning. For those readers choosing to read this chapter first, it is imperative that you read it again, and yet again, for it is the heart and soul of the entire book. As you begin to understand these personal journeys, you will begin to understand what strategy instruction is really about. It is not about individual strategies, lesson plans, activities, or texts— it is about people learning with one another and from one another. It is about the feeling one has when one looks into the eyes of a child and truly feels his or her frustration. It is about knowing and, more important, realizing that you may have caused that frustration. It is about being driven to understand complex theories because you want to make a difference in the literate life of that frustrated child. It is about learning how to inspire. It is about creating a safe space in which to learn. It is about the feeling one has when a child with fragile self-esteem takes a risk as a reader because you have gently nurtured him or her into the world of literacy. We encourage you to take the challenge of becoming a teacher of strategic processes. It is a difficult, but most rewarding, journey.

Finally, in Chapter 9 we provide a set of tools for "putting together" the complexities of strategies instruction in your classroom. We describe how to plan and organize strategies instruction across both a day and a week. We then pinpoint 10 tips for getting started with strategies instruction based on questions that teachers frequently ask. We conclude by sharing tools to help teachers reflect on and improve their own practice as a strategies teacher.

Contents

TEACHING STRATEGIC PROCESSES IN READING

What Does It Mean to Be Strategic?

We begin this text by clarifying and defining our use of the term *strategies* and what it means to be *strategic*. Over the years the term *strategy* has taken on varied meanings within the field of literacy instruction (Dole, Nokes, & Drits, 2009) and has often been used synonymously with the term *skills* (Afflerbach, Pearson, & Paris, 2008).

We define cognitive strategies as actions an individual selects deliberately to attain a particular goal. Our definition is similar to that of Dole et al. (2009), who defined a cognitive strategy as "a mental routine or procedure for accomplishing a cognitive goal" (p. 348). Cognitive strategies, then, are any mental actions or procedures we use deliberately when we want to accomplish a particular goal. *Goals* refer to the "particular reasons, intentions, or motives that persons have for their actions" (Alexander & Jetton, 2000, p. 297). If our goal relates to reading, then we might use specific reading strategies. If our goal is related to solving mathematics problems, then we might use specific mathematics strategies. If our goal is to drive home from work safely, then we might use safe driving strategies. Thus, cognitive strategies include a broad range of mental actions.

Given that the goal of this text is to help readers become strategic, we will narrow our definition of cognitive strategies to pertain specifically to reading strategies. Afflerbach et al. (2008) defined reading strategies as "deliberate goal-directed attempts to control and modify the reader's effort to decode text, understand the words, and construct meanings of text" (p. 368). Common to both definitions of cognitive strategies and reading strategies is the notion that *strategies* are deliberate and help one attain a goal. While reading, the reader must intentionally choose to use strategies, and the intentional choice of a strategy is aimed at attaining a particular goal. For readers that goal may be, as Afflerbach et al. (2008) noted, to decode text, to understand words encountered in the text, or to construct meaning.

In contrast to *strategies*, *skills* are fluid, automated processes that are enacted without the reader's conscious awareness. Afflerbach et al. (2008) defined reading skills as "automatic actions that result in decoding and comprehension with speed, efficiency, and fluency and usually occur without awareness of the components or control involved"

1

(p. 368). Two features distinguish *strategies* from *skills*: automaticity and intentionality (Afflerbach et al., 2008; Alexander, Graham, & Harris, 1998; Alexander & Jetton, 2000). Skilled readers are able to fluidly and automatically decode text and comprehend it. Skilled readers typically do not have to stop to decode a word or to think about which strategy might help them understand the text better. Skilled reading is smooth and uninterrupted, and it is typically faster than strategic reading because it does not involve conscious decision making (Afflerbach et al., 2008). This does not mean, however, that skilled readers are never strategic. In fact, Graesser (2007) noted that even skilled adult readers have difficulty comprehending complex informational texts. Thus, it is not just emergent readers, but all readers—even skilled and successful readers—who are strategic at some point. Graesser (2007) suggested that "a successful reader implements deliberate, conscious, effortful, time-consuming strategies to repair or circumvent a reading component that is not intact" (p. 4). That is, skilled readers slow down and become strategic when they notice a problem and realize that they may not be able to accomplish their goal (Afflerbach et al., 2008). This ability to notice problems as they arise is also known as *monitoring*. Cognitive monitoring is one of the hallmarks of successful strategic reading, for if readers cannot detect problems while reading, or notice that attaining their goal is in jeopardy, then they cannot enact strategies to repair the problem. Afflerbach et al. (2008) note that readers are also strategic when they are initially learning to read. That is, as they are learning to identify letters, decode words, read orally, and comprehend, readers are more deliberate in their efforts. Thus, strategic reading processes are often more evident and more deliberate among emergent readers.

Because being strategic is effortful and time-consuming and requires intentionality, it also requires a level of motivation, interest, and a sense of agency (Alexander et al., 1998; Alexander & Jetton, 2000). It is often the case that you may know how to do something (e.g., using a strategy), but you may not feel like doing it at a particular time. Thus, readers may know very well how to use a given comprehension strategy, and they may know when and why they should use it, but if they are not motivated or interested in putting forth the time and effort to actually use the strategy, they may not do so.

Some have noted that there is often confusion between the terms *strategies*, *skills*, and *activities* (e.g., Dole et al., 2009; Shanahan et al., 2010). Dole et al. (2009) and Shanahan et al. (2010) noted that in core reading programs, comprehension often appears as a series of separate skills such as drawing conclusions and sequencing. Often these comprehension *skills* are "taught" and practiced by having students complete workbook pages. Both Dole et al. (2009) and Shanahan et al. (2010) noted that instructional activities and exercises that require students to complete worksheets to practice skills such as drawing conclusions are *not* ways of teaching readers to be strategic. They note that rarely do such activities require readers to think and make decisions about what they would do in their heads to improve their comprehension.

Likewise, graphic organizers such as K-W-L, Venn diagrams, and story maps are also considered instructional activities. If students are taught how to choose and use graphic organizers to enhance their comprehension while reading, then these tools may aid in strategic processing, but in and of themselves they are *not* strategies. Using a graphic organizer requires a *thoughtful* reader who *deliberately* elects to use it *while reading* as a means of fostering comprehension. If teachers suggest (or require) that students "fill out" or complete a graphic organizer while reading, then the organizer is being used as an instructional activity; readers are not consciously and deliberately choosing to use the graphic organizer on their own to enhance their comprehension. If teachers suggest (or require) that students complete graphic organizers *after* reading, then the organizers are being used as assessments. In either case, if the teacher (or anyone other than the reader) suggests using a graphic organizer, it is not a strategy because the reader is not consciously and deliberately electing to use the graphic organizer of his or her own volition.

Dole et al. (2009) also suggest that instructional practices or teaching activities/techniques, such as the directed reading–thinking activity, the language experience approach, or Making Words, should also not be referred to as *strategies*. They note that these instructional practices are used by teachers to attain an instructional objective. Inanimate objects such as a graphic organizer, or activities such as Making Words, are incapable of deliberately planning, selecting, evaluating, monitoring, and regulating behavior. Only *people* are capable of strategic thinking and processing. In this text, then, the term *strategy* refers to the deliberate cognitive process a person uses in selecting, enacting, and monitoring a plan to attain a goal. Thus, we distinguish between *strategies, skills*, and *instructional practices/teaching activities* in relation to the degree of intentionality, the level of automaticity, and the individual enacting the behavior.

Thus, being strategic requires the reader (1) to have a goal in mind, (2) to deliberately choose a series of strategic actions to help attain the goal, (3) to have the motivation to actually enact the strategic behaviors, (4) to have the ability to monitor the whole process to determine whether the goal is being attained or not, and (5) to have the ability to make adjustments as needed to ensure that the goal is attained successfully (Afflerbach et al., 2008; Paris, Wasik, & Turner, 1991; Pressley, Borkowski, & Schneider, 1989). This means that strategic readers are actively aware of their goals as readers; they are engaged in making conscious decisions about the reading process and which strategies they are using to attain their goals, and they are monitoring their process. To understand fully what it means to be strategic *while reading*, it is helpful to examine the many strategic behaviors we employ in our everyday lives. Consider the daily task of driving home from work. At times we accomplish this task in such an automated mode that we arrive home and wonder whether we really stopped at a particular stop sign or drove by certain landmarks. Driving a familiar route becomes a highly routinized process that requires little cognitive effort. In effect, we are operating on automatic pilot (Garner, 1987).

Now consider the same task—driving home from work—having heard, before, about a terrible traffic accident that is tying up the main artery leading home. Garner (1987) referred to these moments as "aha moments" (p. 19) in which we become metacognitively aware of a problem. These metacognitive "aha moments" alert us to the need to snap out of automatic pilot (i.e., our regular, routinized, or automatic way of accomplishing a goal). As these moments unfold, we begin to think and act strategically, processing a multitude of thoughts and plans in just a few milliseconds: "How long will that route be tied up? Should I just go forward and wait in the traffic? What alternate routes can I take? Should I just stay at work a little while until the traffic clears?" At this point each of these plans is possible, until we begin to consider the conditions in which this event occurred: "When there's an accident on that road, it can take hours before the traffic clears. I have a meeting at 7:00 P.M. for which I can't be late, and I have to stop at the store and pick up groceries for dinner." Given these conditions, we might decide not to waste any time and choose to take an alternate, less direct route around the accident. This entire process often takes less than a second. We enact thousands of these tiny strategic processing sequences throughout the course of a day. Sometimes the planning is for a much larger or complex event (e.g., a wedding) that requires much more thought and preparation. For such complex events a sequence of strategies, rather than a single strategy, is enacted (Pressley, Borkowski, et al., 1989), but for the most part we enact these strategic sequences so quickly that we hardly notice they are taking place.

WHAT IS INVOLVED IN STRATEGIC PROCESSING?

Strategic processing occurs when an individual plans, makes conscious choices, monitors progress, evaluates, and regulates his or her own behavior (Alexander et al., 1998; Alexander & Jetton, 2000; Afflerbach et al., 2008; Dole et al., 2009; Hacker, 2004; Paris, Lipson, & Wixson, 1983; Paris et al., 1991; Pressley, 2000; Pressley, Borkowski, et al., 1989). In the first driving scenario, on automatic pilot, little strategic processing occurred because it was not necessary for a routine drive home from work. However, the second scenario was quite different. Figure 1.1 depicts the strategic processing that occurred during this scenario. The process began with an attainable goal of arriving home. The moment we heard that an accident had occurred on the major highway leading home, we became aware of a problem. This "aha moment" or "metacognitive awareness" activated a planning phase. Baker and Beall (2009) note that metacognition generally consists of two parts: (1) knowledge about cognition, and (2) regulation of cognition. When we regulate our cognition, we are engaged in self-regulation and a closely related construct: executive functioning. It is the self-regulation aspect of regulating cognition that is particularly important in this example. Self-regulation within the control aspect of metacognition includes the ability to plan, monitor, and evaluate. Thus, in this example, as soon as we became aware of the problem (i.e., the accident on the main highway leading home),

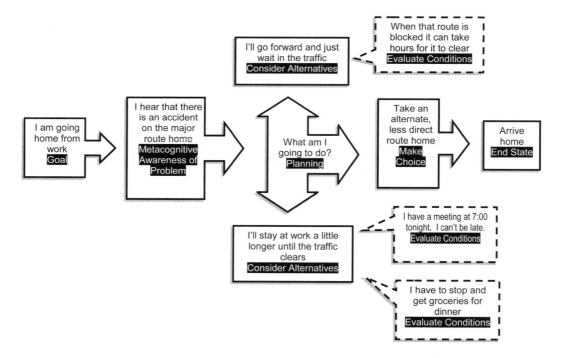

FIGURE 1.1. Diagram of strategic processing.

we began the self-regulation process, which involved planning an alternate way of getting home. Thus, a key aspect of being strategic involves planning. Planning occurs whenever we realize that something has gone wrong, when we realize we may not attain our goal, or when we realize that a change is warranted in a usual procedure. In this instance, had there been no realization of a problem, we probably would have driven home on the usual route. Without a strategic plan or intervention, we would have wound up in traffic. However, with awareness of the problem, we begin to plan different ways to attain our goal by considering various alternatives: waiting in the traffic, staying at work until the traffic clears, or taking an alternate route. With these alternatives in mind, we begin to weigh each in terms of its costs and benefits in relation to the context, or conditions, surrounding this circumstance. This ability to "weigh" the pros and cons of each possible plan is the evaluative part of self-regulation. Given the 7:00 P.M. meeting and the need to stop for groceries on the way home, there clearly is no time to wait. The decision crystallizes: *Take an alternate route home.* This evaluative thinking helped us make a decision about which plan to enact to attain our goal of arriving home. It is our intentional self-selection of a means to an end that makes our behavior *strategic.*

Goals that are attained by accident or chance do not involve strategic behavior (Paris et al., 1983). Consider a variation of the previous example in which it is our first week on the job in a new city. We do not hear about the traffic accident prior to leaving work. Not knowing the area very well, we inadvertently make a wrong turn onto a less direct, alternate route, and it steers us around the traffic accident. Unknowingly, we have avoided the congested route and attained our desired goal. In this example we are not acting strategically. Taking the alternate route was an accident involving no planful thinking, evaluation of the situation, or intentional decision making.

Likewise, obedient responses undertaken because of an external suggestion or demand are not strategic (Paris et al., 1983). For example, let's say that just prior to leaving work, the boss told us about the accident on the highway and suggested that we take an alternate route home in order to be able to arrive back at work in time for the meeting at 7:00 P.M.. We take the alternate route not because of a deliberate, well thought-out plan but because it was suggested to us as the best solution.

WHY IS STRATEGIC PROCESSING IMPORTANT?

We have known for decades that teaching the type of higher-level thinking required for strategic processing is not a regular part of the school curriculum (e.g., Durkin, 1978–1979). Dole et al. (2009) noted that two seminal studies by Duffy, Roehler, and their colleagues helped change the face of reading instruction and provided a glimpse of what true strategies instruction could look like (Duffy, Roehler, Meloth, Vavrus, Book, et al., 1986; Duffy, Roehler, Sivan, et al., 1987). These studies helped teachers and researchers see that when teachers provided explicit explanations of what strategies are, when they should be used, why they should be used, and how to perform them, students' reading achievement on standardized, nonstandardized, and maintenance measures improved.

In their examination of nine exemplary first-grade teachers, Wharton-McDonald, Pressley, and Hampston's (1998) observations found that among other factors, effective teachers provided explicit instruction, used extensive scaffolding, and encouraged self-regulation. Pressley et al. (2001) replicated these findings with a larger sample of first-grade teachers. Unfortunately, in a similar study of fourth- and fifth-grade classroom teachers, Pressley, Wharton-McDonald, Mistretta-Hampston, and Eschevarria (1998) found little to no evidence of some of the effective practices found in first-grade classrooms (as in Wharton-McDonald et al., 1998; Pressley et al., 2001). That is, there was little explicit instruction in comprehension strategies, and students were rarely encouraged to become self-regulated readers.

Thus, about every decade or so we are reminded of Durkin's (1978–1979) plea that we move beyond monitoring readers' ability to complete worksheets and begin to explicitly teach readers how to comprehend and how to be strategic as they comprehend. The research has been unequivocally clear that providing explicit instruction about strategies helps students learn to process text strategically and enhances achievement. The most recent practice guides published by the U.S. Department of Education's Institute of Education Sciences indicated that, for both primary grade readers (Shanahan et al., 2010) and adolescent readers (Kamil et al., 2008), there is strong evidence that providing explicit strategies instruction enhances reading comprehension achievement. Unfortunately, explicit strategies instruction remains a rarity. Perhaps instruction related to strategic processing is not included in schools because it is difficult to do well. Research has shown that learning to become a strategies teacher is difficult and that it takes at least 3 years to become a proficient teacher of strategic processing (Brown, 2008; Brown & Coy-Ogan, 1993; Duffy, 1993a, 1993b; Pressley, Goodchild, Fleet, Zajchowski, & Evans, 1989). Nevertheless, the value of teaching learners how to process text strategically is grounded in a wealth of sound research and theory demonstrating enhanced learning (Pressley, Goodchild, et al., 1989).

In addition to enhancing students' achievement on standardized and nonstandardized measures of reading, Paris et al. (1991) highlighted six reasons for teaching students how to become strategic readers (see Figure 1.2). First, strategies enable readers to elaborate, organize, and evaluate information contained in text. When readers can elaborate and evaluate information contained in text, it shows that they are processing text at higher levels. When readers are able to organize information contained in text, it helps them remember and recall what they have read.

Second, teaching students to read strategically can coincide with their cognitive development in other areas. That is, as children learn to become strategic readers, they become familiar with the use of strategies for enhancing attention, memory, communication, and

---

1. Strategies help readers elaborate, organize, and evaluate information in text.
2. Helps readers become familiar with using strategies to enhance attention, memory, communication, and learning.
3. Readers take control of their own learning.
4. Strategic processing requires metacognitive development and motivation. Therefore, being strategic fosters metacognition and motivation.
5. Strategic processing is valuable because it can be taught to children.
6. When students become strategic readers, growth and development are promoted across the curriculum.

FIGURE 1.2. Six reasons to teach students to become strategic readers. Based on Paris, Wasik, and Turner (1991).

learning. Many aspects of strategic processing carry over into other areas (e.g., planning, monitoring, evaluating), and when readers learn to be strategic as they process text, they are able to transfer the strategic mindset into other curricular areas more easily.

Third, because strategies are self-selected and can be used flexibly, readers take control of their own learning as they acquire a larger repertoire of strategies. When readers take control of their own reading, they become self-regulated, independent learners who can recognize and resolve decoding and comprehension problems when they encounter them.

Fourth, strategic processing requires, and therefore fosters, metacognitive development and motivation. In order to be strategic, one must be aware of the need to use strategies. This awareness involves metacognitive processes. Thus, when readers are able to recognize the need to use a strategy, they are in the process of developing metacognitive ability, which is essential for successful reading. As well, readers who recognize the need to use strategies and actually choose to use strategies to help them as they read thereby demonstrate that they are motivated.

Fifth, strategic processing is valuable simply because, as research shows, it can be taught to children. If we knew strategic processing was important, but it was too difficult for children to learn, that difficulty might suggest that it need not be taught. However, the research is quite clear that even very young children can learn to be strategic.

Sixth, teaching students to become strategic readers promotes their growth and development in all areas of the curriculum. When students learn to become strategic, they are learning to be metacognitive. As noted earlier, these metacognitive abilities include the ability to reflect on their own knowledge and the ability to regulate their own cognition. The latter ability, which includes self-regulatory functions such as planning, monitoring, and evaluating, is critical to all learning processes, not just reading.

WHAT ARE COGNITIVE STRATEGIES?

As noted earlier, there is a difference between cognitive strategies and reading strategies. The difference is primarily associated with the fact that cognitive strategies are more general and can be used in several different domains, whereas reading strategies are more specific to the domain of reading. According to Prawat (1989), strategic behaviors involve a range of techniques from heuristics to general control strategies (see Figure 1.3). Pressley, Goodchild, et al. (1989) described a similar range of strategic processes. However, they suggested that the range extended from "task-limited" strategies to "across-domain" strategies. That is, "task-limited" strategies, like Prawat's (1989) "heuristic techniques," are useful only in specific situations and in specific domains. "Across-domain" strategies, like Prawat's (1989) general control strategies, are broader and can be applied in a variety of situations and across several domains.

Located on the far left of Figure 1.3, heuristic techniques (or task-limited strategies) enable one to access relevant information during problem solving. As well, they do not require much cognitive processing and are considered to be at the lower end of the executive control continuum. Heuristics are considered "tricks of the trade" that are used in particular circumstances to aid performance. Examples of heuristics include teaching students to look at headings or introductions before reading, or teaching them a mnemonic to help them remember certain information (e.g., HOMES to help remember the

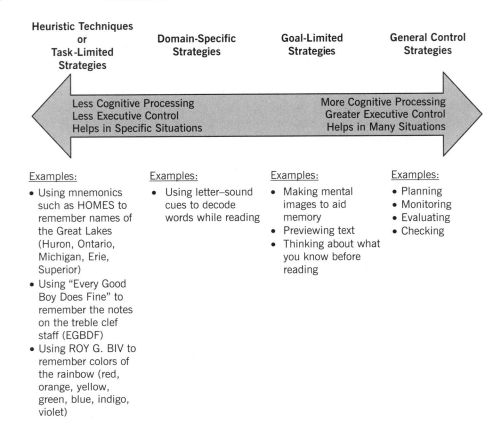

FIGURE 1.3. Range of strategic behaviors.

names of the Great Lakes in the United States, ROY G. BIV to remember colors of the rainbow, "Every Good Boy Does Fine" to remember notes on the treble clef staff). Heuristics do not necessarily transfer to new, possibly relevant situations. That is, by teaching students to use a heuristic to remember the names of the Great Lakes, this does not mean that they will suddenly become aware of many new heuristics and use them in other situations. Heuristics do not generally transfer or generalize to other domains of learning.

General control strategies involve the higher end of the executive control continuum and are more generalizable (Prawat, 1989). That is, general strategies such as planning, monitoring, evaluating, and checking retain their essential properties in any domain (e.g., reading, writing, mathematics). For example, the process of planning—of carefully considering possible alternatives prior to embarking upon a task—is essentially the same in any domain. Planning was involved in the driving scenario described earlier; it would also be used if one were planning to study for a test. No matter what domain, planning always involves considering the possible, specific actions needed to attain a goal. Such general strategies require more cognitive processing than domain-specific ones, thereby requiring greater executive control, or management, on the thinker's part.

A domain-specific strategy, such as using letter–sound cues to decode unfamiliar words, is obviously specific to reading. That is, you cannot use that strategy to help in another domain such as solving mathematics problems. Because domain-specific strategies are less generalizable and require less cognitive processing to apply, they are considered to lie at the lower end of the executive control continuum, as seen in Figure 1.3.

Goal-limited strategies, such as making mental images to enhance memory, are more generalizable in that you might use this strategy to envision story events, which will help comprehension while reading, or you might use it to help remember a list of grocery items. Goal-limited strategies are not as generalizable across domains as general control strategies because they are limited by the goal that they help one achieve (e.g., remembering, comprehending, problem solving).

As noted earlier, cognitive strategies of any form require intentionality, and intentionality means that the strategic process is available for introspection—it can be examined, discussed, and analyzed publicly or privately. In contrast, acquired *skills* are executed automatically and applied unconsciously (Afflerbach et al., 2008; Paris et al., 1991). The first driving scenario is an example of a skilled response. Arriving home and realizing that we were not aware of whether we stopped at signals or stop signs is an indication that we were using an automatic skill that had been acquired and perfected through repeated practice. Afflerbach et al. (2008) noted that, for novices, emerging skills might be used as a strategy if they are applied deliberately. Likewise, strategic processing can become automatic if practiced and repeated frequently (Afflerbach et al., 2008; Pressley, Borkowski, et al., 1989; Pressley, Woloshyn, & Associates, 1995).

WHAT ARE THE CHARACTERISTICS OF GOOD STRATEGY USERS?

To identify the characteristics that good strategy users possess, Koskinen and Blum (2002) have suggested thinking about a topic on which you consider yourself to be an expert. Think about the qualities you possess that make you an expert in that area.

Consider, as an example, that one of us (Janice) is an expert in waxing cars. She has a fair amount of knowledge about waxing cars by hand. She knows that there are many different types of waxes, most of which do generally the same job. Some give a glossier shine but do not last as long or hold up as well when exposed to various weather conditions; others do not provide as glossy a shine but hold up better. She knows the procedures for waxing a car by hand. She knows when and where it is best to wax cars—away from direct afternoon sun—and she also knows why it is important to wax a car. This information shows that, as an expert car waxer, she has an *extensive knowledge base*.

She is also *motivated* to wax cars. She enjoys the mindlessness of the task, and she enjoys the results that can be obtained in just a few hours. She is motivated because she knows that her effort pays off in the end. Thus motivation plays a key role in her becoming an expert car waxer. If she were not motivated by the task, she might not engage in it nearly as often as she does.

While waxing her car, she is also very aware of how the whole procedure is progressing. She looks critically at the way she performs the task and knows when something is going wrong. In this sense, she is *metacognitive*—she is able to monitor her performance and determine whether she should continue the task in the same manner, abandon the task, or use a more effective approach.

When she recognizes that something is not going well (e.g., she is applying the wax too thickly or it is about to rain), she is able to *analyze the task* to know how to make adjustments to her procedure. For example, if she applies the wax too thickly, she knows why it is occurring, and she knows what to do to correct the problem. Thus, she also *possesses a variety of strategies* for accomplishing the desired goal. To apply the wax more thinly, she knows she needs to moisten the applicator a bit and spread the wax over a larger portion of the car. Through her metacognitive awareness of the problem, her ability to analyze the task, and her selection of an appropriate alternate strategy from her available repertoire, she is able to solve the dilemma and attain her goal.

These five characteristics—possessing an extensive knowledge base, being motivated to use strategies, being metacognitively aware, possessing an ability to analyze the task, and possessing a variety of strategies for attaining the desired goal—comprise the qualities of experts in nearly any domain, whether it is car waxing, sewing, reading, or writing (Meichenbaum, 1977). Michael Pressley and his colleagues identified similar characteristics in their good strategy user model (e.g., Pressley, 1986; Pressley, Borkowski, et al., 1989; Pressley, Symons, Snyder, & Cariglia-Bull, 1989; Pressley, Woloshyn, et al., 1995).

These characteristics were derived from a host of expert–novice research studies conducted in the 1980s (e.g., August, Flavell, & Clift, 1984; Davey, 1988; Gambrell, Wilson, & Gantt, 1981; Garner & Kraus, 1981; Garner & Reis, 1981; Recht & Leslie, 1988). In these studies researchers examined what expert readers did as they read and compared it with what novice readers did as they read. The underlying premise of these studies was that if we could understand what expert readers do and compare it with what novice readers do, that would help us understand what we might need to teach novice readers to help them become more like the expert readers. Figure 1.4 summarizes the findings from these studies. In general these studies found that novice readers (1) focused on decoding individual words, (2) could not adjust their reading rate, (3) were not aware of alternative strategies for enhancing comprehension and memory of text, and (4) were not adept at monitoring their own comprehension.

In contrast, Paris et al. (1991) noted in their synthesis of strategy research that expert readers have (1) rapid decoding skills, (2) large vocabularies, (3) phonemic awareness, (4) knowledge of text features, (5) knowledge of a variety of strategies to enhance comprehension and memory of text, and (6) the ability to monitor their comprehension. From an instructional standpoint, our goal must include providing instruction, modeling, and guided practice so that less proficient readers begin to understand how to read and process text strategically. In terms of strategies instruction this would mean teaching novice readers and struggling readers how to use a variety of strategies in different situations, teaching them about different features of text (including text structure), and teaching them how to monitor their comprehension.

Expert Readers	Novice Readers
• Have rapid decoding skills. • Have large vocabularies. • Know a variety of strategies to enhance comprehension and memory of text. • Know about text features and text structures. • Have good phonemic awareness.	• Focus on decoding individual words. • Cannot adjust their reading rate. • Are not aware of alternate strategies for enhancing comprehension and memory of text. • Are not adept at monitoring their own comprehension.

FIGURE 1.4. Differences between expert and novice readers.

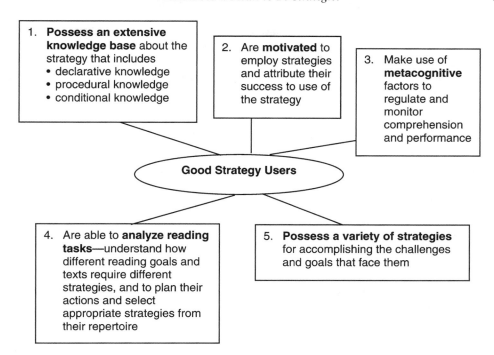

FIGURE 1.5. Good strategy user model (Pressley, 1986; Pressley, Symons, Snyder, & Cariglia-Bull, 1989).

The good strategy user model depicted in Figure 1.5 provides an overview of the five aspects that are most critical in becoming a good strategy user. Each aspect of the model is explained further as it relates to reading; however, it is important to recognize that although each component is discussed separately, the components do not work in isolation from one another. As Pressley, Woloshyn, et al. (1995) noted, each component continually interacts with the others to create a coherent process.

Possession of an Extensive Knowledge Base

One of the primary distinctions between experts and novices is the type and extent of knowledge they acquire as they become more proficient (Paris et al., 1983). Like experts, good strategy users possess a great deal of knowledge that they use to inform strategy selection and use. Cognitive and developmental psychologists have emphasized two types of knowledge: declarative and procedural. Paris et al. (1983), in their seminal work, added a third type: conditional.

Declarative Knowledge

Declarative knowledge is information about the structure of a task and the goal (Paris et al., 1983); it is sometimes referred to as "knowledge *that*." In the car-waxing example above, Janice had knowledge that some waxes provide a glossier shine but do not hold up well under various weather conditions. If her goal for the car is to have a high gloss shine, then she will use one type of wax; if her goal is to have a durable coat of wax, then she will use a different type of wax. Declarative knowledge was also involved in the opening driving scenario. Knowing that a particular blocked route would take hours to clear helped you to self-select a strategy from the three alternatives. If you had not had that declarative knowledge, you may have made a different choice and wound up in traffic.

In reading, declarative knowledge includes information about how particular reading tasks are structured. For example, expert readers know *that* stories have a particular narrative structure *that* includes setting, characters, problems or goals, attempts to solve the problem or attain the goal, and a resolution. Expert readers also know *that* they read differently when studying for a test than when reading for pleasure.

Declarative knowledge also refers to one's beliefs about the task and one's abilities (Paris et al., 1983). In the car-waxing example, a relevant belief would be, "I believe that I am a good car waxer." For readers, these beliefs would reflect the specific reading task and their perceived ability to perform it. For example: "I don't like informational books" or "Informational books are hard for me to understand."

Declarative knowledge resides in long-term memory. Derry (1990) described it "as a large, tangled network" (p. 351) that is useful only if it can be recalled when needed. The result of activating declarative knowledge is simple recall. It is important to help learners organize this level of information and establish connections that enable them to access this reservoir of declarative knowledge. For those learners who do not possess an extensive amount of declarative knowledge about reading, it is important to help them make connections between new information and their prior knowledge. New ideas and knowledge are more likely to be remembered if they are associated with prior knowledge. The role of declarative knowledge in strategic processing is that it enables such knowledge about a given strategy to be accessed quickly.

Procedural Knowledge

Whereas declarative knowledge involves information about a task's structure, procedural knowledge involves knowing how (Paris et al., 1983) to do something—how to execute or perform a given task. In contrast to declarative knowledge, the result of procedural knowledge involves transforming information into action (Derry, 1990) rather than simple recall.

Using the car-waxing task, knowing how to wax a car by hand is an example of procedural knowledge. The step-by-step procedures involved in performing the task are part of this knowledge. For car waxing those steps might include the following: (1) Start with a clean car; (2) obtain relevant materials (appropriate car wax, an applicator, and a soft dry cloth); (3) moisten the applicator lightly; (4) dip the applicator into the wax; (5) spread the wax onto the surface of the car, using smooth, circular motions; (6) apply wax to the entire surface of the car in this manner; (7) wait for the wax to dry; and (8) using a soft, dry cloth, wipe off the residue from the car's surface.

Procedural knowledge in the context of reading includes the step-by-step procedures for how to make predictions about a story outcome or how to set a purpose for reading. Without procedural knowledge, readers are unable to execute a given strategy. How often have we asked students to summarize a given passage without having taught them *how* to summarize in a step-by-step fashion? How often have we asked students to make predictions about what will happen in stories without first teaching them prediction procedures?

For those students who struggle with learning to read, it is essential to teach procedural knowledge related to reading strategies.

Conditional Knowledge

Paris et al. (1983) have aptly noted that declarative and procedural knowledge are not sufficient to enable readers to process text strategically. The ability to understand when, where, and why to use a given strategy is also essential. They termed this type of understanding "conditional knowledge."

In the car-waxing example, it does Janice no good to have the declarative knowledge about different types of car wax or the procedural knowledge about how to wax a car by hand if she does not know when she should wax a car or why she should wax a car. Conditional knowledge explains the circumstances under which a strategy should be employed, and it provides a rationale for employing the strategy. Without knowing about the utility and value of a given procedure, an individual is not likely to expend the time and effort needed to execute a strategy. Waxing a car by hand is tediously hard work. Why should I do it? If I do not see value in the activity, then I am not going to perform it. When we know that at least two coats of wax a year protect the exterior paint and prevent body rust on this valuable investment, then maybe we would be convinced to wax our car. However, if we leased a car, do not care about body rust, or do not live in a climate where body rust is a problem, then this rationale may not convince us to expend the effort to wax the car.

An example of conditional knowledge in the context of reading is knowing *when* we should make predictions and *why* it is important to make predictions while reading. For example, because we learn new information when we read expository texts, it is hard to make predictions while reading them. Thus, prediction is not a strategy that is typically used when reading informational texts. However, if we are reading a narrative text, prediction is a very useful and effective strategy. Even if a child knows how to predict (i.e., has procedural knowledge), he will not expend the effort to employ the strategy if he does not know when to do it or why it is important.

Conditional knowledge plays a critical role in strategic processing. In fact, without knowledge of when and why to use a given strategy, it is most probable that a student will not employ the strategy on her own unless she is prompted or forced to do so. In this case, the student is not independently employing the strategy; she is doing so out of compliance, which means that it is highly unlikely that she will elect to use the strategy on her own.

In time these concepts about the nature of knowledge related to strategic processing have found their way into core reading programs (Dewitz et al., 2009; Pilonieta, 2010). However, Dewitz et al.'s (2009) examination of the five most widely used commercial core reading programs found that although these published programs provided instruction related to declarative knowledge of strategies, they were woefully inadequate at providing instruction related to the procedural and conditional knowledge associated with strategy use. These findings suggest that we cannot rely on (or implement) published programs with 100% fidelity, as doing such will not provide students with the knowledge necessary to become strategic readers. Instead, it is up to schools and teachers to be sure to provide explicit instruction that teaches readers about the declarative, procedural, *and* conditional knowledge associated with strategic processing that will enable them to become planful, self-regulated readers.

Motivation

Guthrie and Wigfield's (2000) engagement model of reading development identified four primary factors that lead to engaged reading. They noted that engaged readers are able to coordinate, or orchestrate, their strategy use and their conceptual knowledge within a social setting so that they fulfill their motivations. Motivation consists of a multifaceted set of goals and beliefs that guides a reader's behavior (Guthrie & Wigfield, 1999; 2000). The behaviors that one might notice that pertain to reading include how much one persists while reading, the amount of effort one expends throughout the reading process, or the choices one makes while reading. These behaviors are guided by motivation, which includes an "individual's personal goals, values, and beliefs with regard to the topics, processes, and outcomes of reading" (Guthrie & Wigfield, 2000, p. 405).

The multifaceted nature of motivation suggests that it is not a single, unitary construct. Instead motivation consists of several components. Guthrie and Wigfield (1999, 2000) noted that motivation involves (1) goals, (2) intrinsic motivation, (3) extrinsic motivation, (4) self-efficacy, and (5) social elements. From this perspective engaged readers are intrinsically motivated, use strategies, build conceptual knowledge, and interact socially to learn from text (Guthrie et al., 2004).

Related to strategy use, intrinsic motivation and self-efficacy are particularly important aspects of motivation. Strategy instruction, Guthrie and Wigfield (2000) contend, has the potential to empower readers and build intrinsic motivation because strategy use is intentional. Readers have to make a conscious effort to be strategic; therefore, this conscious effort leads to internal changes. When students are aware of the value of strategy use (i.e., conditional knowledge), see that strategy use has benefits, and are aware that their efforts to use strategies will pay off, they are less likely to feel helpless or incompetent while reading (Schunk & Rice, 1987).

In their study of third and fifth graders engaged in concept-oriented reading instruction (CORI), Guthrie et al. (1996) found that every student whose intrinsic motivation increased also experienced increased strategy use. In fact, they found that intrinsic motivation correlated with strategy use at .8 for fifth graders and .7 for third graders. More recently, Guthrie and his colleagues found that when an instructional framework (CORI), in which motivational practices were combined with cognitive strategies instruction, was compared to strategies instruction alone and to traditional reading instruction, third graders scored higher on measures of reading comprehension, strategy use, and motivation.

Thus, students must be intrinsically motivated to employ strategies, and their personal attributions must support this usage. Miller and Faircloth (2009) noted that it is also critical that students value strategy use and see its benefits. Using strategies is hard work and requires a great deal of effort; students will expend energy only on strategies that are meaningful, worthwhile, and rewarding to them (Paris et al., 1983). The key to this goal is ensuring that students see that strategic procedures enhance their performance (Pressley, Woloshyn, et al., 1995; Schunk & Rice, 1987), and that their efforts are rewarded (Pressley, Symons, et al., 1989).

In the car-waxing example, Janice's motivation for waxing her car was twofold: She enjoys the mindless physical activity (as well as being outside), and she likes the fact that when she is done, she can see the results immediately. Although waxing a car by hand is tedious, she sees a payoff in expending that effort, and she values the end result.

Attribution theory helps explain that individuals are motivated in this manner primarily because they have a desire to understand and explain the causes of success and failure (Weiner, 1979, 1985, 1990). Four attributes are relevant to achievement-related behavior: ability (innate cognitive ability), effort (level of effort exerted), task difficulty (a general perspective on the intricacy of a particular task at a given moment), and luck (chance occurrences). Each of these four attributes has three characteristics: (1) stability, (2) locus of causality, and (3) controllability. Figure 1.6 depicts the four attributes and their characteristic features.

A *stable characteristic* is one that does not change. One's innate cognitive ability does not change, nor does the difficulty of a task at a particular moment. If the task were hard when first encountered, it would not suddenly change and become easier on its own. The task of hand-waxing a car remains the same task. Assessment of stable attributes leads to consistent expectations (Diener & Dweck, 1980). If a student attributes his success to his own ability or to the difficulty of the task, which are both stable attributes, then he will expect to succeed again with the same task (Weiner, 1985). Likewise, if a student attributes her failure on a given task to her ability, then she will expect to fail again. Effort and luck are unstable attributes; one can expend more or less effort on the same task, if one desires. Likewise luck is not an attribute that produces consistent results because it is based on chance. When outcomes such as success or failure in reading are ascribed to unstable attributes such as effort or luck, the certainty with which the same outcome can be expected in the future is diminished because with instability there is no guarantee that the same outcome will occur again (Weiner, 1985).

Locus of causality refers to where the source of the attribute lies. The source could be within you (i.e., internal), or it could be external. As Figure 1.6 shows, ability and effort are internal attributes. One's ability and the effort one exerts are within oneself. However, the difficulty of the task and luck are external attributes. One's affect (i.e., disposition or attitude) is related to locus of causality. Butkowsky and Willows (1980) found that students who attributed success to internal sources, such as ability or effort (e.g., "I'm smart" or "I tried hard"), experienced increased pride and self-esteem. When students attributed success to external factors (e.g., "I only did well because the test was easy" or "I was lucky"), lowered self-esteem occurred. If we fail at something and attribute this failure to an internal source such as ability (i.e., "I'm dumb"), we experience lower self-esteem. However, if we attribute the failure to an external source (i.e., "The test was too hard"), we preserve our sense of self-efficacy.

Controllability refers to whether or not the attribute is managed by us. The only attribute that we have conscious control over is effort. Only I can decide whether to exert

Attribution	Stability		Locus of Causality		Controllability	
	Stable	Unstable	Internal	External	Controllable	Uncontrollable
Ability	■		■			■
Effort		■	■		■	
Task Difficulty	■			■		■
Luck		■		■		■

FIGURE 1.6. Attributions for achievement-related behavior. Adapted from Weiner (1979). Copyright 1979 by the American Psychological Association. Adapted by permission.

more or less effort on a task. All other attributes are outside our range of control. We cannot control the innate ability with which we were born, we cannot control the difficulty of a task, and we cannot control luck. Unsuccessful students tend to attribute their failure to uncontrollable factors (Diener & Dweck, 1978, 1980), which means that they blame their failure on factors outside their control. Successful students tend to attribute their success to the controllable attribute—effort (Butkowsky & Willows, 1980).

How is this theory relevant for strategic readers? Expert readers attribute successful reading to deliberate, effortful execution of strategies. Strategic processing is contingent on self-selected and self-regulated behavior. The *individual* is key to successful strategy use. The only attribute that an individual has control over is effort. The internal locus of this attribute means that it has the potential to impact self-esteem. It also is an unstable attribute, meaning that how much effort is exerted on any given task varies.

Struggling readers often present motivational problems for classroom instructors. Johnston and Winograd (1985) suggested that many of these problems are related to the fact that "they are passive, helpless participants in what is fundamentally an interactive process—reading" (p. 279). Many struggling readers have low self-esteem and exhibit characteristics of "learned helplessness" (Seligman & Maier, 1967, p. 1). These characteristics are seeded in struggling readers when they begin trying to learn how to read, using the limited knowledge and strategies that they possess, and are unsuccessful. After repeated exposure to such failure, they give up and passively accept the fact that they cannot learn to read. They believe that inability, not lack of effort, is the cause of their failure—and they refuse to exert any more effort because they think it is futile to do so (Borkowski, Carr, Rellinger, & Pressley, 1990). Because they attribute their failure to an internal, stable attribute that is out of their control (i.e., ability), struggling readers tend to have low self-esteem (Hiebert, Winograd, & Danner, 1984). Simply put, they believe that they cannot learn to read because they are "dumb." Paris, Byrnes, and Paris (2009) noted that children's perceptions of their academic abilities decrease as they progress through school. They suggest that children have theories of ability and of effort that impact their perceptions of competence. Theories of ability would encompass questions such as "How good am I?", and theories of effort would encompass questions such as "How much should I try?" Because these theories of ability and effort impact perceptions of self-competence, they also influence motivation. When readers perceive themselves as competent, they will persist longer when faced with challenging literacy tasks, and they will use the strategies available to them to persevere until they have attained their goal. When readers perceive themselves as incompetent, their motivation is negatively affected, and they have difficulty maintaining focus and persisting toward the goal.

Given that effort is the only attribute that is both controllable and internal, it is the only attribute that can actually make a difference in reversing the debilitating effects of learned helplessness. Thus strategy instruction begins by focusing on teaching students that it is their *effort* that determines their success. If they put forth the effort to employ a strategy, it *will* improve their reading—on the condition that the sociocultural context of the classroom affords students the opportunity to experience firsthand how their efforts pay off in the dividend of success (Borkowski et al., 1990). Strategy instruction also must include explicit instruction about the utility of a given strategy (i.e., fostering conditional knowledge) so that students see its value, and students must be given feedback about their performance after using the strategy (Pressley, Woloshyn, et al., 1995; Van Ryzin, 2011).

Paris et al. (2009) noted that as readers develop theories of ability and effort, they also develop theories of agency and control. Bandura (1989, 2001, 2006) described agency as the intentional influence one has over how one functions and over one's life circumstances. This means that "people take responsibility for their actions and ascribe success and failure to the goals they choose, the resources they mobilize, and the effort they expend" (Paris et al., 2009, p. 267). Self-efficacy is important in relation to agency because how you perceive yourself and your ability is going to influence the goals you choose, the expectations your have, and how much effort you put forth. Paris et al. (2009) note that four factors are important in promoting positive self-efficacy and agency: (1) success, (2) feedback, (3) observational learning, and (4) social persuasion. In terms of reading and strategic processing this view means that readers will become more agentic if they are able to engage in tasks and meet with success. This does not mean that all tasks should be easy. Rather, tasks should have the proper degree of challenge to enable readers to experience success and to know that they can continue to be successful with the same task under varying conditions. Feedback plays a role in agency in that when readers are provided with positive feedback, their self-efficacy is enhanced, which enables them to set goals that are slightly more challenging. Observation fosters agency when students are able to observe others successfully accomplish tasks. Such observation enhances self-efficacy because students see that the goal is attainable. Finally, social persuasion plays a role in that when teachers or peers provide encouragement and the recognition that achievement depends on ability and effort, they foster agentic beliefs and self-competence.

Finally, Paris et al. (2009) suggested that students not only develop theories of ability, effort, and agency, but also theories of schooling and academic tasks. They suggest that classroom activities and academic tasks must be structured in a way that encourages students to engage deeply rather than superficially (Paris et al., 2009). Academic tasks that elicit intrinsic motivation and engagement should be open-ended rather than closed (Turner, 1995). Turner (1995) noted that open-ended tasks do not have right or wrong answers, which is in contrast with closed-ended tasks such as worksheets, rote drill and practice, and literal recall. Instead, open-ended tasks encourage students to engage in interpretive, critical, analytic, and evaluative thinking and might include projects and research. Paris et al. (2009) noted that open-ended tasks enhance intrinsic motivation when they encourage students to (1) *construct* personal meaning, (2) *choose* how to approach and solve a task, (3) *collaborate* with others, and (4) derive *consequences* from the task that enhance self-efficacy.

In terms of classroom instruction that will foster motivated strategy use, these points suggest that instruction should include attribution (re)training; explicit instruction related to strategic processes; positive feedback; challenging (but attainable) goals and open-ended tasks; choice in the texts that are read, the academic tasks that are assigned, and the approaches used to accomplish tasks; and collaboration rather than competition (Van Ryzin, 2011). These contextual aspects of classroom instruction will serve to enhance motivated strategy use. Figure 1.7 lists guidelines for motivating students' use of strategies. Thus, being strategic involves much more than just having knowledge of strategies. For readers to actually use and implement strategic behaviors, their knowledge of strategies must be coupled with (1) theories of ability and effort that lead to perceptions of self-competence, (2) theories of agency that enable them to take control of their own reading process and intentionally engage in strategic behaviors that lead to goal attainment, and (3) theories of schooling and tasks that suggest to them that it will be well worth their time and effort to engage in a given academic task for the intrinsic benefit it brings (Paris et al., 2009).

---

1. Teach strategies that provide appropriate challenges (not too hard, yet not too easy).
2. Strategies must be worth learning. Students must value the strategy and see its importance.
3. Students need to experience success.
4. Steady progress must be reinforced.
5. Goals should be made clear.
6. Specific, detailed constructive feedback should be given.
7. Students should be taught to self-reinforce for achieving success.

FIGURE 1.7. Motivating students' use of strategies. Based on Borkowski, Carr, Rellinger, and Pressley (1990)..

Metacognition

Metacognition, or cognition about cognition, is the key to strategic processing because it enables us to monitor our cognition and the progress we make toward achieving our goal. Flavell's (1979) model of cognitive monitoring suggested that the ability to monitor cognition occurs when four components interact with one another: (1) metacognitive knowledge, (2) metacognitive experience, (3) goals, and (4) activation of strategies. *Metacognitive knowledge* refers to our knowledge or beliefs about ourselves and others as cognitive processors, knowledge about the task and how it should be managed, and knowledge about which strategies would be effective in helping us attain our goals. *Metacognitive experiences* refer to any cognitive or affective experiences we have in relation to our thinking. For example, the feeling that you do not understand something you read or that someone said is a metacognitive experience. These experiences can help us set new goals, revise old goals, or abandon old goals. As well, these metacognitive experiences can activate strategies that help us attain either cognitive or metacognitive goals. Flavell (1979) noted that "cognitive strategies are invoked to *make* cognitive progress, metacognitive strategies to *monitor* it" (p. 909). Together these four components help readers identify which strategies to use under which circumstances to attain goals (Fox, 2009), and they help readers *monitor* their progress toward their goals and *monitor* their use of strategies.

Dinsmore, Alexander, and Loughlin (2008) noted that historically it was Baker and Brown's (1984) review of literature on metacognition that expanded Flavell's (1979) notions of it to include self-regulatory processes. These self-regulatory processes involve the control we have over our learning and thinking (Baker & Brown, 1984). Such self-regulatory control includes the ability to plan, monitor effectiveness, test, revise, and evaluate (Baker & Beall, 2009; Baker & Brown, 1984; Dinsmore et al., 2008). These processes are critical to strategic processing and to comprehension.

In the car-waxing example, Janice's metacognitive experiences enabled her to ascertain how the job was proceeding. When she noticed that she was applying the wax too thickly, she was making an evaluation or judgment about her performance on a metacognitive level. This type of awareness may be very brief, involving only that instant recognition that things are, or are not, going well. In response to that metacognitive awareness, she began to think and act strategically about what to do to resolve the problem. Hearing about the traffic accident was a moment of metacognitive awareness that prompted a consideration of various strategic actions. The metacognitive moment is an "aha" experience (Garner, 1987, p. 19), or, as Anderson (1980) described it, it is a "clunk" (p. 490) that vaults us into strategic processing in which we begin to enact cognitive strategies to resolve a problem. Without that experience we would muddle along, not realizing that a problem had even occurred.

Unfortunately, this lack of metacognition is precisely the problem that younger and less proficient readers have. Gersten, Fuchs, Williams, and Baker's (2001) review of research noted that an inability to use strategies and to be metacognitive was a leading reason that students with learning disabilities had comprehension difficulties. In particular, research has shown that younger and less proficient readers are less able to monitor and regulate their performance (Baker & Beall, 2009; Baker & Brown, 1984; Garner, 1980; Garner & Reis, 1981; Markman, 1977; Myers & Paris, 1978; Paris & Myers, 1981) than are older and more proficient readers (Baker, 1984; Baker & Anderson, 1982; Winograd & Johnston, 1982). While reading, these students would not recognize when something did not make sense or when the text was confusing. They would continue reading words, turning pages, completely unaware that their comprehension was obstructed. Therefore, fix-up strategies such as rereading, reading ahead, or talking about the materials with someone would not be used. After they finished "reading," their comprehension, recall, and memory of text was seriously impaired by their inability to monitor or detect a situation in which comprehension might be difficult. Despite rather overwhelming research evidence over several decades, incorporating instruction that is focused on facilitating metacognitive processes in routine classroom instruction has been slow, and Baker and Beall (2009) caution that instruction focused on metacognition should not become an end of itself. Instead, the goal should be to transform instruction so that the metacognitive processes that teachers and knowledgeable others model and demonstrate gradually become internalized by readers, leading to self-regulation (Baker & Beall, 2009).

Ability to Analyze the Task

Good strategy users are aware of the processes involved in successfully performing a given task or strategy (Pressley, Woloshyn, et al., 1995). Such awareness goes beyond the procedural knowledge of how to perform a strategy, and it is inherently linked to metacognition in that it involves being able to recognize, in the midst of performing a task, what to do next. If something goes wrong, a successful strategy user immediately knows how to rectify the problem and redirect efforts efficiently to attain the goal. The ultimate goal of task analysis is to assess the situation and flexibly make adjustments based on the parameters of the task (Pressley, Woloshyn, et al., 1995).

In the driving event, the metacognitive awareness about the traffic accident led to an analysis of the task involving a consideration of the conditions in relation to the goal of arriving home. In reading, specific strategies (e.g., summarizing, comprehension monitoring) have been analyzed to determine what steps are necessary to employ the strategies successfully (Garner, 1987). These task analyses are presented in Chapters 5 and 6.

Possession of a Variety of Strategies

Good strategy users possess a large repertoire of strategies (see Figure 1.8) (Pressley & Afflerbach, 1995; Pressley, Symons, et al., 1989). This repertoire can be likened to a "cognitive toolbox." When a reader has a metacognitive realization that something has gone wrong, she can reach into her cognitive toolbox to select a strategy or tool that will help resolve the difficulty. The proficient reader possesses strategies for decoding, comprehending, interpreting, and studying text. Although strategies for interpreting and studying text are essential to proficient reading, this book deals only with strategies for decoding and comprehending text. Figure 1.8 depicts the range of cognitive strategies available to readers for decoding and comprehending text. Successful readers integrate these specific strategies into higher-order sequences to accomplish the more complex goal of reading (Pressley & Afflerbach, 1995; Pressley, Symons, et al., 1989; Shanahan et al., 2010). Again, these strategies are *not* used in isolation. A good reader may begin by looking at the title and pictures for clues about the text, which trigger initial predictions, in turn, leading to a purpose for reading. As the reader begins to process the text, he monitors his comprehension and realizes that one of his predictions was accurate. He reads on and makes another prediction about what will happen next to the character. Thus, the reading process involves a multitude of strategic sequences enacted differently by individual readers. Those who possess a variety of strategies approach this complex cognitive task with an array of tools that prepares them for any difficulties they may encounter.

If an individual has a limited number of strategies available, she will struggle to make do with what she has. If her goal is to drive a nail into a wall, for example, and her toolbox contains only a screwdriver, she will employ it in a less than efficient effort to accomplish the task. It is not the best or most efficient tool, but it is the only one she has until she can acquire new, more effective tools. Comparably, in reading, a reader recognizing that the text does not make sense can stop and employ a strategy to repair her comprehension. If the only tool she possesses is to go back and reread, then she uses

FIGURE 1.8. Good strategy users possess a variety of strategies.

that strategy. If the comprehension failure occurred in the beginning of the text, for example, then this strategy will not work very well. Thus having a wide range of strategies available in one's cognitive toolbox is essential for enhancing success. Possessing the conditional knowledge associated with each strategy is an integral part of the cognitive toolbox, for it equips strategy users with the ability to determine which strategies are best suited to various textual conditions.

Interventions that teach students how to use a set of strategies in a flexible manner as they read are much more effective than teaching students to use individual strategies one at a time. Examples of interventions that not only teach students how to flexibly use a cohesive set of strategies, but also to develop a metacognitive awareness of the task and of self that fosters self-initiated and self-regulated strategy use, include the following: reciprocal teaching (Palincsar & A. Brown, 1984), informed strategies for learning (Paris, Cross, & Lipson, 1984; Paris & Jacobs, 1984; Paris & Oka, 1986a), transactional strategies instruction (TSI; Anderson, 1992; Brown, Pressley, Van Meter, & Schuder, 1996; Pressley, El-Dinary, et al., 1992), CORI (Guthrie et al., 1996), and collaborative strategic reasoning (CSR; Klingner, Vaughn, & Schumm, 1998). Research evidence has been unequivocally clear that when we teach students of various ages and abilities to use multiple strategies, reading comprehension is enhanced not only in terms of short-term comprehension of a single text, but also in terms of long-term transfer to other contexts (Almasi, Palmer, Madden, & Hart, 2011; Brown et al., 1996; Edmonds et al., 2009; Gersten et al., 2001; Van Keer, 2004; Westra & Moore, 1995). Recent research has also indicated that teaching strategies one at a time was not as effective as teaching them as a set, as in TSI (Reutzel, Smith, & Fawson, 2005).

The toolbox metaphor is useful in helping younger and less proficient readers understand and visualize the complex, abstract process of using strategies. However, the caution in using the metaphor is that teachers will become focused on teaching *the strategies* rather than teaching students to *become strategic*. Almasi and Hart (2011) argued instead that instruction should aim to be more transformational by focusing on the student rather than the content (i.e., the strategies being taught). They noted that in viewing strategies as tools, teachers and students might inadvertently gain the impression that these cognitive and metacognitive strategies are *outside* of themselves, when in fact these strategic behaviors and actions are *inside* of them. The reader is the tool. The tools/strategic behaviors are contained within; the reader actually embodies the tools. That is, the reader becomes the tools/strategies and the tools/strategies become part of the reader. It is a reciprocal and transforming process. Teachers from a transformational perspective do not tell readers when to use a strategy. Instead they focus on helping students become independent, self-regulated readers who are able to recognize when they need to become strategic, are capable of analyzing the task and the conditions to know which strategies might be the most effective for them, and are motivated to put forth the effort needed to employ the strategies.

In sum, the five characteristics of good strategy users are essential for proficient reading. Successful readers must (1) possess an extensive knowledge base about strategies, (2) be motivated to employ strategies and be agentic about their use, (3) be metacognitive, (4) analyze the reading task, and (5) possess a variety of strategies that can be used flexibly. These characteristics work in unison as a coherent whole, rather than in isolation, to produce efficient strategy use in only a matter of seconds. The challenge, however, is teaching struggling readers the value of strategy use. Once students experience the value of using strategies, they will be more inclined to use them.

WHY STUDENTS DO NOT USE STRATEGIES

When thinking about why students may not use strategies, it is helpful to do the inverse of what we did when we thought about strategic, or expert, readers. Think about something that you do *not* do well. Think about why you are not good at that particular task and how you feel when you are doing it. Although Janice is excellent at waxing cars, she is not good at many things—bowling, knitting, and dancing are but a few. When she even thinks about doing these activities, she becomes dismayed. She does not like doing these activities, she does not understand how to do them well, and she really does not care if she ever knows how to do them to any degree of proficiency. Although she knows many who are good at each of these activities, and she admires their talents greatly, ultimately she feels she has no use for those activities. She feels unsuccessful at them and when she engages in them, she feels foolish and inept. This is the same way that struggling readers feel about reading. They may know that it is an important skill to learn, but they really do not like doing it, they are not good at it, and they feel foolish and inept. They experience these feelings every day, sometimes for hours each day, while they are in school. Sometimes we even ask them to perform this task that they are so inept at, and that they dislike so much, in public, in front of their peers. Imagine if you had to perform the task or activity that you are terrible at in public and in front of your colleagues! It is a dreadful thought. Yet, poor readers face this dreaded possibility every day, sometimes for hours each day, over the course of many years.

Garner's (1990) review of strategy research analyzed the reasons why many readers do not use strategies. Five reasons, which are nearly the inverse of the good strategy user model, emerged from her synthesis: Poor readers possess (1) a meager knowledge base, (2) personal attributes that do not support strategy use, (3) poor cognitive monitoring (in our terms, poor use of metacognition), (4) primitive routines, and (5) minimal ability to transfer knowledge to new settings. In a more recent review of research Gersten et al. (2001) identified similar elements that led to comprehension difficulties for learning disabled students.

Meager Knowledge Base

Nonstrategic readers do not have a sufficient knowledge base about the reading process to support strategy use. They may lack declarative knowledge about the structure of the task, procedural knowledge about how to perform the strategy, conditional knowledge about when and why they should use a given strategy, or they may lack some combination of all three. In the example above, Janice noted that she is not good at knitting. In fact, she really knows very little about it. She knows that you need knitting needles and yarn (declarative knowledge), but she doesn't know what kind of needles. Are they all the same? She doesn't think so, but she is not sure. She has no idea at all about *how* to knit (procedural knowledge). She has heard the phrase "knit one, purl two," but she has no idea what it means or how it is pertinent. In fact, when the first edition of this book was written, Janice had so little knowledge about knitting that she didn't know how to spell *purl* correctly and it had to be corrected by the editor. She certainly does not have any conditional knowledge of when she should enact a strategy because she does not even possess a single knitting strategy. Thus, she brings no knowledge about knitting to the task.

Struggling readers are no different. They have a limited knowledge base about many reading strategies (Baker & Brown, 1984; Garner, 1987, 1990). For example, struggling readers may have some declarative knowledge about a given strategy, such as prediction. They may know *that* a prediction is a guess about what might happen in the story, but they may not know *that* good readers continually revise and update their predictions throughout their reading of the text. Thus the knowledge base is limited. They may have a general idea about *how* to predict (i.e., procedural knowledge), but they may not know *how* to make a textually relevant prediction. Their predictions may be completely "off the wall" or "out of the blue." Likewise, they may not know the conditions under which they should use prediction as a strategy. Thus, one of our instructional goals must be to provide explanations and experiences that *instantiate* (concretize) readers' knowledge base about strategies.

Personal Attributions Do Not Support Strategy Use

Strategy use is time-consuming and requires persistence. Many readers do not believe that the time and effort it takes to employ strategies will pay off; therefore, they fail to use them (Garner, 1990). Readers with high self-esteem tend to attribute their successful and unsuccessful reading experiences to their level of effort (Borkowski et al., 1990; Butkowsky & Willows, 1980), whereas readers with lower self-esteem are not as likely to initiate or persist at strategy use because they attribute their difficulties to lack of ability (Garner, 1990). These readers often have experienced years of frustration in school and rather than be embarrassed one more time, they give up. In many cases, their schools and their teachers have failed them. Rather than blaming these external sources for their failures, however, these readers tend to attribute their failures to internal, stable factors such as ability, and their successes to external factors such as luck or task difficulty (Hiebert et al., 1984).

Garner (1990) also noted that many of these students appear lazy or unmotivated, often engaging in defensive behaviors that emerge to guard the feelings of ineptitude that result from repeated exposure to failure. They often state that they "can't do it," refuse to engage in strategic actions, or become dependent on support from others to scaffold their every move. These readers lack persistence and confidence in much the same way that Janice described her own experiences with knitting, bowling, and dancing. When you are not good at something, you usually do not want to engage in it—even if someone is trying to teach you how to perform it better.

Poor Cognitive Monitoring/Metacognition

Many readers are unable to evaluate and monitor their reading process to know when something does not make sense. Instead, because they do not recognize that anything is wrong, they continue reading without stopping to employ a repair strategy. In particular, younger and less proficient readers have difficulty monitoring their reading, yet rarely do we provide instruction related to metacognition or cognitive monitoring to help them (Garner, 1990).

Sometimes the conditions of the reading task do not permit close monitoring either. Garner (1990) has noted that when memory resources are strained, it is difficult to monitor. That is, if the text is too difficult to read, or if there are interruptions, the additional load placed on memory to overcome these difficulties makes it impossible to monitor cognitive processing as well. Likewise, if readers do not see the task as important, it is unlikely that they will attend to it enough to monitor their progress with it. It is similar to my experiences with knitting or bowling: If I am spending so much energy and effort just to get the procedures down, I may not have enough cognitive resources left over to monitor my progress. I also may not care enough about my performance to expend the extra energy to monitor how well I am doing.

Routines Used Are Primitive

Garner (1990) has also noted that readers who do not use strategies often do not do so because they use a primitive routine. In effect, because these readers do not have a large repertoire of available strategies to use, or because they do not have the conditional knowledge of when and why they should use a given strategy, they rely on the strategy they know. As an example, Janice shares her own experiences when she first moved to Buffalo, New York. At first she knew only three streets: Main Street, Youngs Road, and Maple Road. Because they were the only three streets with which she was familiar, she planned all of her travels using them—even if it took longer. To drive from her home to downtown Buffalo, there are several major highways that she could have used; however, she always took Main Street (with all of its traffic lights) to travel the 15 miles downtown. Certainly this was not the easiest or most efficient route downtown, as she came to learn, but she did not care. It was the only route she knew. She felt safe using her few, carefully chosen routes. When she moved to Lexington, Kentucky, she adopted a similar strategy, relying exclusively on New Circle Road and Nicholasville Road (the busiest routes in Lexington) to navigate the new town. As a driver in a new environment, Janice clearly is not a risk taker and relies on familiar roads (that are not as efficient) rather than expending the effort to learn new, more efficient routes. She reacts in this way, in part, because she is uncomfortable with the unknown and is fearful that she may get lost.

Younger and less proficient readers often react similarly. They use and rely on the tools/strategies that are available to them even if they are an inappropriate or less effective means of accomplishing the task.

Transfer of Strategies Is Minimal

Teaching students how to transfer strategy use to new situations is one of the most difficult aspects of strategy instruction. Even if we provide the best and most thorough instruction related to strategy use, there is no guarantee that readers will use a given strategy independently when the time comes. Readers tend to learn and use strategies in the contexts in which they were originally taught. That is, they become somewhat "context bound" (Perkins & Salomon, 1989) and have a difficult time transferring this knowledge to other contexts (Garner, 1990). During reading instruction, the context includes the instructional setting (e.g., type of text, type of task, level of scaffolded support) in which the strategies were taught. When the student reads a different type of genre, engages in a different task, or engages in an activity that has a different level of instructional support (i.e., whole-class lecture, one-on-one tutoring, paired activity, group activity), the context is different, which makes it difficult to generalize the use of a strategy learned in the prior context. Chapter 5 discusses ways to facilitate transfer of strategy use to new contexts.

SUMMARY

Cognitive strategies are plans that are self-selected, evaluated, and regulated by an individual to attain a goal. Using strategies is important because they enhance learning and permit students to take control of their own learning. Good strategy users have an extensive knowledge base that includes declarative, procedural, and conditional knowledge related to strategic processes. They also recognize the value of using strategies and are motivated to use them. Good strategy users are metacognitively aware of how the process is going, are able to analyze the task to see what adjustments may be needed, and possess a variety of strategies for accomplishing the desired goal. Those who do not use strategies do not possess an extensive knowledge base about strategic processing. Furthermore, their personal attributions do not support strategy use, and they have poor cognitive monitoring, use primitive routines to accomplish the task, and are unable to use strategies in multiple contexts.

CHAPTER TWO

Critical Elements
of Strategies Instruction
Designing Effective Environments

The goal of any form of strategy instruction is to help individuals become self-regulated learners. The term *self-regulation* implies a sense of agency in regard to goals and plans as well as the learner's perceptions of ability and task demands (Paris & Winograd, 2001). Essential to the capacity for self-regulation is helping learners attain (1) knowledge about strategies for accomplishing tasks and goals, (2) metacognitive awareness of their own progress toward such goals in relation to the demands of the task, (3) real-world knowledge, (4) motivation to employ strategies independently and flexibly, and (5) a sense of personal agency (Palincsar & Brown, 1989; Palincsar, David, Winn, & Stevens, 1991; Pressley, El-Dinary, et al., 1992; Schunk & Pajares, 2005; Zimmerman, 2000). Many models of strategy instruction have been proposed in hopes of attaining these goals, and nearly all meet with some form of criticism. This chapter describes several research-based models of strategy instruction and their criticisms. A strategies instruction model, critical elements of strategies instruction, based on the extant literature base and clinical practice, is proposed and described in detail.

Some (e.g., Poplin, 1988) have criticized strategy instruction for being reductionist rather than constructivist, contending that it (1) breaks learning into parts (i.e., instruction in using isolated strategies) rather than focusing on performance of the whole reading process, (2) portrays students as passive recipients of instruction, (3) flows from the teacher to the student, (4) focuses on knowledge that can be *re*produced by the student rather than *produced* by the student, and (5) promotes school goals rather than goals important to the learner. In contrast, Pressley, Harris, and Marks (1992) contended that good strategy instruction *is* based on constructivist principles. They distinguish between three types of constructivism, based on Moshman's (1982) classification system: endogenous, exogenous, and dialectical constructivism. These distinctions are explained briefly in order to provide a theoretical grounding for the models of strategy instruction that follow.

Strategy instruction based on *endogenous* constructivism is focused on child-centered exploration and discovery of instructional principles rather than on direct teaching.

Learning occurs in a social context, and teaching and learning are inseparable from the contexts in which they occur. *Exogenous* constructivists rely more heavily on teaching than do endogenous constructivists. Modeling and explanation play a large role in this type of teaching; however, learning is not simply a matter of reproducing such knowledge but of internalizing and adapting this new knowledge to meet the particulars of a given situation. *Dialectical* constructivists believe that learning is more effective if some direct teaching occurs in the form of scaffolded assistance—hints and prompts—rather than extensive explanations. Thus, dialectical constructivism lies between endogenous and exogenous constructivism and, like endogenous constructivism, is based largely on Vygotskian principles that thought develops in social contexts (Vygotsky, 1978). In such contexts, readers gradually internalize instructional principles through guided discovery or scaffolding from more knowledgeable others and through the opportunity to interact with others as they engage in the strategic processing of text.

The notion of scaffolding is critical to strategies instruction. Analogous to the scaffolding that supports a construction site, it is a process that aids a learner "to solve a task or achieve a goal that would be beyond his unassisted efforts" (Wood, Bruner, & Ross, 1976, p. 90). There are three critical principles related to scaffolding: (1) It is provided through the interactions of more knowledgeable others and novices; (2) it is a temporary support, yet critical to particular moments of learning; and (3) it is needed only when a learner is unable to achieve the new learning on his own. In other words, scaffolding is faded or relinquished when the learner has gained the ability to accomplish the particular task or goal independently. Scaffolding is an essential element of strategy instruction, as will be seen in the models presented.

In the 1980s, strategy instruction teachers began with a focus on individual strategies but soon shifted to teaching a repertoire of strategies (Romeo, 2002). Within a number of models or approaches encouraging the development of a strategies repertoire, however, strategies were taught in a somewhat linear fashion, one at a time, so the repertoire gradually, and rather slowly, develops. More recently, multiple strategies approaches have gained attention with a goal toward teaching strategies in a more contiguous way. In the next section, several models of strategy instruction and their criticisms are reviewed to provide readers with historical grounding for such instruction.

STRATEGY INSTRUCTION FORMATS AND THEIR CRITICISMS

Table 2.1 charts the three strategy instruction formats (exogenous, endogenous, dialectical) and specific models of strategy instruction that fit within each format. The characteristics of each model of strategy instruction are also provided.

Exogenous or Step-by-Step Models

Exogenous models feature modeling, guided practice, independent student work, and a teacher who controls the instruction.

Direct Instruction

Direct instruction of strategies involves explicit step-by-step training in particular strategies (Gersten & Carnine, 1986). Individual strategies are taught by teachers who model

TABLE 2.1. Characteristics of Various Types of Strategy Instruction

Type of strategy instruction	Individual strategies taught	Explanation (declarative, procedural, conditional)	Modeling or demonstration	Guided practice	Independent student work	Metacognitive awareness	Use strategies in authentic contexts	Flexible strategy use	Motivated strategy use encouraged	Teacher in control of instruction	Student in control of instruction	Shift instruction from teacher to student	Teacher feedback is corrective	Teacher feedback is suggestive
Exogenous														
Direct instruction	■		■	■	■					■			■	
Direct explanation	■	■	■	■	■	■				■			■	■
Endogenous														
Collaborative problem solving		■				■	■	■	■		■			■
Process talk		■				■	■	■	■		■			■
Dialectical														
Explicit instruction	At times	■	■	■	■	■	■	■					■	■
Informed strategies for learning	■	■	■	■	■	■				■				■
Reciprocal teaching	At times	■	■	■	■	■	■	■				■		■
Transactional strategies instruction	At times	■	■	■	■	■	■	■	■			■		■
Guided reading	At times	■	■	■	■	■	■	■	■			■		■
Critical elements of strategy instruction model	At times	■	■	■	■	■	■	■				■		■

Note. Header span: "Characteristics of strategy instruction"

or demonstrate each strategy, provide ample guided practice and teacher feedback, and gradually diminish teacher-directed activities to foster independent student work. Student mastery of each step in the process is expected. Research has shown that this model is generally effective for teaching isolated comprehension strategies or linear progressions of multiple strategies (see Gersten et al., 2001, for a review); however, direct instruction takes on a "skills" look in that it does not provide opportunities for students to learn about the conditions under which a given strategy might be used, nor does it provide opportunities for metacognitive awareness regarding strategy use—two critical components of strategic processing. Direct instruction also presents the problem that Whitehead (as cited in Palincsar et al., 1991) referred to as "inert knowledge." This limitation is also known as a lack of transfer. That is, knowledge of a particular strategy may be recalled when explicitly questioned or told to employ it, but students may not use the strategy spontaneously. As Johnston (2004) noted:

> We hear a lot about teaching children strategies, but we often encounter classrooms in which children are being taught strategies yet are not being strategic. . . . Teaching children strategies results in them knowing strategies, but not necessarily in their acting strategically and having a sense of agency. (p. 31)

As a result of such instruction, students are not taught to employ strategies deliberately, independently, or flexibly. Teachers control the agenda for instruction, and instruction may not be tailored to the individual, personalized needs of learners (Palincsar et al., 1991; Shelton, 2010).

Direct Explanation

Similar to direct instruction models, direct explanation models (e.g., Duffy, Roehler, Sivan, et al., 1987; Duffy, 2009) include the use of modeling, guided practice, and independent practice. However, this approach differs in that it provides for teacher explanation of the declarative, procedural, and conditional knowledge associated with strategies, and it allows for a gradual shift in responsibility from teacher-directed to student self-regulated strategy use. The focus of direct explanation is on teacher verbalization, or think-alouds, of the mental processes associated with using strategies to understand text. Students taught using this approach demonstrate significantly greater awareness of the procedural and conditional knowledge of strategies, the metacognitive aspects of strategy use, and the nature of strategic reading (Duffy et al., 1987). Thus, direct explanation offers a greater awareness of elements critical to strategic processing than direct instruction. Palincsar et al. (1991) noted, however, that students do not have the opportunity to influence the learning environment during direct explanation—the teacher still retains a high profile position during instruction.

Endogenous Models

As depicted in Table 2.1, endogenous models differ from exogenous models of strategy instruction in three key ways: (1) individual strategies are not taught; (2) modeling, guided practice, and independent student work are not as evident; and (3) the student rather than the teacher is in control of the instruction.

Collaborative Problem Solving

Collaborative problem solving is an entirely student-centered approach (Palincsar et al., 1991). Students identify strategies they feel will be most useful for understanding text and for monitoring their understanding, and they evaluate the effectiveness of the selected strategies. Students are introduced to strategies via problem-solving activities that have multiple solutions to them. Each problem-solving activity features vignettes in which two fictional students trying to accomplish a reading task (i.e., studying for a test or reading to inform others) approach the task in different ways. Students discuss the strategic processing of each student in the vignettes, then combine the list of strategies they initially identified with the strategies they learned via the vignettes. Students then use the self-generated list of strategies to guide their reading of authentic texts, discussing which strategies would be most helpful for a particular text, then test the strategies out and evaluate how well the strategy worked. Any teacher instruction is given in response to the students' discussion.

Although collaborative problem solving effectively eliminates the criticism that much strategy instruction is reductionist (see Poplin, 1988), it introduces other challenges and limitations. Palincsar et al. (1991) noted that this approach is not easy for teachers to implement because they experience difficulty resisting the desire to plan the direction of the lessons, and assessment of each student is more cumbersome. Likewise, children who are unfamiliar with instructional settings that are undefined and emergent often have difficulty adapting to such contexts. In addition, students had difficulty regulating the amount of talk related to making sense of the text and talk about the strategies they used to make sense of the text.

Process Talk

Process talk is an approach predicated on the notion that strategic action gives students a sense of agency by providing them with choices and alternatives for successfully completing a given task (Ivey, Johnston, & Cronin, 1999; also see Johnston, 2004). *Agency* refers to the empowerment experienced as a product of making a choice in response to the particulars of a situation and in relation to the alternative courses of action available. People are *agents* because they are capable of making reflective decisions involving many alternatives (Rovane, 1998).

Johnston and his colleagues examined teacher and student talk about their literate processes and strategies, and about children's sense of agency in 28 classrooms across five states. They found that students in classrooms of effective teachers were more self-assured in their learning and had a greater sense of agency. The teaching in these effective classrooms was not primarily on teaching strategies, "but on arranging for strategic action to occur, and socializing children's attention to it wherever possible" (Ivey et al., 1999, p. 4). The researchers categorized these classrooms as "agency-based" and described the less effective "strategy-based" classrooms as those in which strategy instruction had a central role and learning strategies was the objective of entire lessons. However, the discourse of these classrooms was more similar to the "skills" lessons of exogenous, direct instruction models than the dialectical strategy instruction models described above. The discourse labeled as "strategy-based" did not contain any talk related to metacognition, conditional knowledge, or motivated strategy use—three critical components of authentic strategy instruction. Discussing these three components is the type of talk that creates agency. The labels that Ivey et al. (1999) attached to their classrooms do not appear to be consistent with those used in the research literature on strategy instruction. Instead, they appear to be contrasting strategy- (or agency-) based classrooms with direct instruction (or skills-) based classrooms. Regardless, the model of process talk on which their research is based is consistent with an endogenous constructivist model in which explicit instruction of strategies is secondary to student-centered discovery of strategic principles.

Dialectical Models

Table 2.1 shows that dialectical models exhibit some features of exogenous models (i.e., modeling, guided practice, independent student work) and some features of endogenous models (i.e., explanation, using strategies in authentic contexts, flexible strategy use, suggestive teacher feedback). What differentiates dialectical models, in general, is that they rely on gradually shifting responsibility for instruction from the teacher to students.

Explicit Instruction

Similar to direct explanation, explicit instruction also involves teacher modeling, explanation, and think-alouds of what, how, when, and why a strategy is used (i.e., declarative, procedural, and conditional knowledge); guided practice, in which teachers gradually release responsibility for task completion to students; and independent practice and feedback (Duke & Pearson, 2002; Fielding & Pearson, 1994; Pearson & Dole, 1987; Pearson & Gallagher, 1983). In addition, explicit instruction features application of strategies in authentic reading contexts. What distinguishes explicit instruction from previous models is that there is no assumption (as in direct instruction) that complex strategies should be broken down into separate, sequentially ordered subskills. Each time the reading task is performed during explicit instruction, the entire process is performed, not just practice with a particular strategy or skill. Another distinction is that explicit instruction promotes flexible strategy use, replicating what occurs during skilled reading (Pearson & Dole, 1987). In such contexts, learners choose and use a variety of strategies, singly or in combination, to read and problem-solve texts (Clay, 2001). Such flexibility is encouraged as readers develop their own strategic solutions to complex reading tasks. A final distinction is the use of suggestive rather than corrective feedback during explicit instruction. That is, teacher feedback to students does not "correct" errors but provides alternative suggestions, or multiple ways, of approaching the task. Teachers praise students for their efforts and for applying strategies appropriately, and they also encourage students to try alternative ways of attacking the same problem to compare various approaches.

Like direct explanation, explicit instruction provides students with a greater awareness of aspects related to strategic processing than does direct instruction. Explicit instruction takes into account the flexibility inherent in strategic processing and the need for variation in how individuals accomplish similar tasks

Informed Strategies for Learning

Informed strategies for learning (ISL) is an approach to strategy instruction that consists of 20 modules addressing four comprehension processes: planning for reading, identifying meaning, reasoning while reading, and monitoring comprehension (Paris & Oka, 1986a). The primary goal of ISL is to help students learn to be strategic as they read. Different strategies are taught in five lessons within each module. Lessons teach children about the declarative, procedural, and conditional knowledge associated with each strategy; provide metaphors that help students remember the strategy (i.e., "Be a reading detective"); and offer opportunities for guided practice to apply the strategies with social studies and science content. ISL lessons place an emphasis on teaching reading strategies and persuading readers about their usefulness. As in explicit instruction, ISL lessons feature faded teacher support, such that strategies are first modeled and explained explicitly, and then students are gradually required to generate or select strategies independently. ISL lessons also feature group discussions between teachers and students aimed at discussing students' thoughts and feelings about strategies and their usefulness.

Although ISL offers a very strong focus on metacognitive awareness and strategic processing, the sequential and somewhat scripted nature of the 20 ISL lessons means that meeting the individual needs of students is not a primary goal. Although the opportunity for student discussion and dialogue is a critical component of ISL, the teacher still remains the focal point of instruction, leaving little opportunity for students to influence instruction.

Reciprocal Teaching

Reciprocal teaching provides instruction in four strategies: generating questions from text, summarizing, clarifying portions of text, and predicting upcoming content based on content and structure of text (Palincsar & Brown, 1984, 1989). These strategies are taught as complementary sets to be used flexibly in response to the needs of the reader and the demands of the text. Instruction takes the form of dialogues between the students and the teacher, as each takes turns using the strategies to construct a meaningful interpretation of the text. The teacher may begin by taking responsibility for modeling the use of these strategies for understanding text, but students are immediately encouraged to join in the discussion by generating their own questions, summarizing, clarifying, and making additional predictions. The teacher facilitates student participation by providing feedback, explanation, and modeling. Students' use of the targeted strategies and their performance on standardized and criterion-referenced comprehension measures is significantly increased by using reciprocal teaching (Palincsar & Brown, 1984, 1989).

Although there is a much greater role for the student in reciprocal teaching, and strategies are viewed as complementary sets rather than as isolated tools, this approach is limited by the narrow range of strategies taught and the absence of motivated strategy use as a specific goal (Pressley, El-Dinary, et al., 1992). Nonetheless, reciprocal teaching forged a new path for strategies instruction through its multiple or combined strategies approach.

Transactional Strategies Instruction

Transactional strategies instruction (TSI) involves many of the same goals as previous strategy models: development of (1) a repertoire of diverse reading strategies, (2) metacognition related to the appropriate use of strategies, (3) real-world knowledge, and (4) motivation to use strategies to enhance reading (Brown, 2008; Pressley, El-Dinary, et al., 1992). Additionally TSI features teachers and students jointly constructing the meaning of text as they read; the "transaction" that occurs is one in which individual readers approach the text with individual interpretations and understandings (Pressley, El-Dinary, et al., 1992), what Brown (2008) has characterized as linking reading and thinking. However, when working collaboratively to construct meaning, their individual backgrounds, experiences, and diverse interpretations create an interpretive community in which they affect, and are affected by, one another (Rosenblatt, 1978). Brown (2008) provides an example of such interactions within a second-grade classroom:

> After this introduction, Liz [the teacher] remarked that the focal strategy for that day's lesson was visualizing, or making mental images, of the text's content. She read the first page from a text called *Mushroom in the Rain* (Ginsburg, 1991). In this story, creatures of increasing size crowd under an expanding mushroom during a storm.
> After reading a page, Liz described how she pictured a little ant seeking shelter from the rain. Without prompting, Max volunteered a text-to-text connection to *The Mitten* (Brett, 1989), another story read earlier that year: "I have a prediction, um, this

is gonna be like, um, like *The Mitten* one, like um, these um, all these insects are gonna try to come in [the mushroom]." Liz replied, "You think so? What makes you think that?" Max, alluding to a picture clue, answered, "Well I see another insect."

"You made that connection? Well, we'll see if you're right," said Liz, who took this opportunity to highlight for others how Max coordinated making connections, using picture clues, and predicting while reading. In the process, the students learned not only from their teacher but also from their deep-thinking and strategy-using peer. (p. 538)

Other students are not conversing with Max in this example, but the teacher capitalizes upon his thinking to note the connection he made while his talk provides additional strategy use, predicting and using pictures as a source of meaning making. Additionally, the teacher provided a brief focus on visualizing as she described how she pictured what was occurring in the text. Max seemed to use this support to make his prediction.

As indicative of this example, the transactional aspect of TSI implies that there is no single, "correct" interpretation of text, nor is there a single, "correct" set of strategies to attain a better or more "correct" interpretation of text. Unlike most of the other models discussed, TSI emphasizes the teaching and use of multiple, evidence-based strategies. In some cases, teachers may introduce single strategies (Brown, 2008), but *coordination* of varied strategies is the goal within the context of these collaborative conversations about text. TSI lessons feature three primary components: (1) direct explanation and instruction of word solving, comprehension, and interpretive strategies; (2) coordinated and flexible use of varied strategies; and (3) cycles of teacher–student transactions in which the group works collaboratively to make sense of the text. Much of this teacher–student discourse is focused on strategic processing (Pressley, El-Dinary, et al., 1992).

When compared with low-achieving second-grade students receiving solid but traditional reading instruction, similar students receiving TSI demonstrated greater strategy awareness and use, better comprehension of text, and superior performance on standardized tests of reading (Brown et al., 1996). TSI provided solid instruction related to strategic processing and collaborative dialogue about strategy use that enhanced students' reading ability.

In their investigation comparing multiple-strategy instruction (TSI) to single-strategy instruction (SSI), Reutzel et al. (2005) found no significant difference in the two approaches to strategy instruction on a standardized comprehension test; however, on a curriculum-based (state) reading comprehension test, there were significant differences favoring TSI. Also of interest were the qualitative analyses that indicated that single-strategy classrooms were "directed toward learning and applying the comprehension strategy rather than focusing on the use of the comprehension strategy to acquire the content found in the science information books" (p. 300). In contrast, the interwoven and transacted set of strategies that were taught within the TSI classrooms focused the teachers and children on getting, organizing, discussing, and understanding the science knowledge. The researchers noted that teachers remarked on "how much science *content* the children were learning and remembering" (p. 300). The small body of research related to TSI suggests that it has the potential to develop strategic, engaged readers. Unfortunately, as with many of the other models, practitioner-oriented information is relatively sparse. Additionally, the TSI research suggests that it takes several years for teachers to become effective.

In summary, much of the comprehension research of the 1980s and 1990s emphasized teaching single comprehension strategies within a lesson, and this model for instruction has been the focus of a number of texts for classroom teachers in the last two decades. However, approaches that focus on the orchestration of strategies simultane-ously (multiple-strategy approaches) are more representative of the strategic activity of proficient readers. Duke and Pearson (2002) referred to these strategies or processes as "comprehension routines" (p. 224) with the intent of highlighting the nature of an "inte-grated set of practices that could be applied regularly to one text after another" (p. 225), with resulting benefits of increased comprehension of text and the development of foun-dational processes that can transfer to other reading contexts. The authors suggest that TSI is one example of such routines and "borders on being a complete comprehension curriculum" (p. 225).

While acknowledging the value of the early research of "isolated strategies" (p. 4-6) the National Reading Panel (2000) referred to "multiple-strategy instruction" and work related to preparing teachers to provide such instruction as "the most important finding of the Panel's review because it moves from the laboratory to the classroom and prepares teachers to teach strategies in ways that are effective and natural" (p. 4-6). As noted previously, two examples of multiple-strategy instruction are TSI and reciprocal teaching (Palincsar & Brown, 1984; Palincsar, 2003).

Teaching for Strategic Activity within Guided Reading

Guided reading is grounded in Vygotskian theory (Vygotsky, 1978) and Clay's theory of early literacy processing (Clay, 1991, 2001) as well as constructs of assisted performance (Gallimore & Tharp, 1990) and contingent teaching (Wood & Wood, 1996). Guided read-ing (Fountas & Pinnell, 1996, 2006; Schwartz, 2005) is a small-group approach to reading instruction. At the center of guided reading is the idea of teaching for strategic activity (Clay, 1991, 2001). "Instruction . . . varies from the teacher's direct demonstration and explanation of effective reading strategies to his or her prompting, guiding, and reinforc-ing students' use of strategies as they read texts that offer opportunities to learn" (Pinnell, 2002, p. 107). As part of this focus on effective strategies and scaffolding, guided reading also includes the following components: (1) a carefully crafted introduction tailored to meet the needs of the learners within the group, (2) reading of the text (with teacher support), (3) discussion and revisiting the text, and (4) teaching for strategies. Optional activities may include extending the meaning of text and word work (Pinnell, 2002).

Through the use of appropriately selected text, careful planning, and structuring of the learning context, the teacher arranges for strategic action and draws the children's attention to it (similar to what was mentioned earlier in process talk), noting as well when there are approximations that are nearly on target. Critical to guided reading is a responsive teacher who acts and talks in response to the child's reading, with the teacher basically functioning as a scaffold (Clay & Cazden, 1990). That is, teaching for strategic activity involves in-the-moment decision making as the teacher observes and guides the strategic actions of a child and draws productive responses to his or her attention—"I like the way you worked that out for yourself. You thought about what made sense *and* looked right!" Within moments, a teacher may respond with several teaching moves that involve feedback, valuing approximations (partially correct), modeling, questioning, contingent teaching, and feed-forward responses. As the teacher guides from behind, language and prompting scaffold in a manner that supports strategy development and agency, helping readers understand that they must take control of the learning.

In the guided reading example that follows, the teacher is helping a beginning reader develop the one-to-one match (voice–print match) that is necessary for the development of the strategy of monitoring known words. A page of teacher-made text is accompanied by Hannah's drawing of her eating pizza:

"I like pizza," said Hannah.
"I like pizza too," said Susan.

CHILD: (*reading*) "I like piz-za," said Hannah. (*Her finger is under* pizza *for the first syllable of the word* pizza, *under* said *as she says the second syllable of* pizza, *and as she points under the word* Hannah *and reads* said, *she stops and looks at the teacher.*)

TEACHER: I like how you stopped. [Feedback] You almost had it when you ran out of words, didn't you? [Valuing Approximations; Feedback] Watch me. (*Reads the sentence, pointing under each word.*) [Modeling] Pizza. (*Taps the table twice while saying the word, emphasizing the parts.*) It has two parts, so we have to keep our finger under it until we finish saying it. [Modeling; Contingent Teaching] Now you try it. Make sure you keep your finger under *pizza* until you say both parts. [Feed-forward—helping the child to understand the expected response]

CHILD: (*reading*) "I like pizza," said Hannah. (*Reads and points correctly under each word as she says it.*)

TEACHER: Great! Your voice and finger went together on every word! [Feedback]

At this point in the child's development, her finger also served to scaffold, or cognitively structure, the task, but the teacher's noticing, modeling, and language serve to guide the child's behavior, putting the child on the path toward self-control. As indicated in the example, the child must take action. Tasks must be handed over to the child. Clay (1998) asserts that the child must first *act* on information before an *awareness* can be developed. This idea of acts leading to awareness may help to explain why modeling, though important, is not enough. Learners must do more than passively observe. They must *perform* the action (and receive feedback) in order to become increasingly aware of how to perform a strategic action independently. As a result, within guided reading, the issue of transfer is not as great a concern because learners are guided as they are processing "on the run," in the act of reading authentic, continuous texts—in essence, practicing the actions that readers must invoke as they are reading on their own. Over time, the teacher diminishes the level of support or guidance until the children begin to display strategic actions independently. Although gentle reminders may be needed, the children have been guided so that they understand the why, when, and how of strategy use.

As noted, highlighting or modeling of a particular strategy or strategies may occur, but the nature of the strategy instruction is conversational, similar to the dialogue described earlier in the discussion of TSI. Also, within guided reading, as in TSI, there is no hierarchy or sequencing of strategies; learners are taught to employ strategies in an integrated manner to fit the context or task at hand. Furthermore, as with TSI, this type of instruction requires training, effortful analysis of texts, and teacher–child interactions in order to develop a level of expertise. Guided reading is only one component within a more extensive literacy framework, and it is included in two comprehensive school reform models: literacy collaborative (Biancarosa, Bryk, & Dexter, 2010) and partnerships in comprehensive literacy and comprehensive intervention (Dorn & Soffos, 2012).

THE CRITICAL ELEMENTS OF STRATEGIES INSTRUCTION MODEL

As noted in previous chapters, many emergent and struggling readers share five limitations: They (1) do not possess an extensive knowledge base related to strategic processing, (2) are not metacognitively aware, (3) are not motivated to use strategies, (4) are unable to analyze the task, and (5) do not possess a repertoire of strategies. When a reader does not possess knowledge of a given strategy, it is difficult for him to "discover" it on his own, as might occur in endogenous models of strategy instruction.

Think again about those areas in which you are *not* an expert. Note Janice's earlier acknowledgment that she has basically no knowledge base related to knitting, bowling, and dancing. In fact, her understanding is so limited that she is unable to even ask questions about those areas. It would be very difficult for her to "discover" how to knit, for example, without some scaffolded support. The critical elements of strategies instruction (CESI) model proposed in this book is based on dialectical constructivist principles in which some explicit instruction (cf. Duke & Pearson, 2002; Pearson & Dole, 1987) and scaffolded support are provided for students (see Figure 2.1). Within the model, teachers may reduce processing demands to maintain students' focus on strategic processing. The model also provides opportunity for student dialogue and verbalization with one another about strategy use as meaning is constructed, as occurs in TSI (Pressley, El-Dinary, et al., 1992). These three components affect, and are affected by, one another. In Figure 2.1 circles with semipermeable borders represent each component; the broken line represents the seepage that is possible: What is contained in each component "seeps" out to help create and become the safe and risk-free environment that supports and facilitates motivated strategy use. Thus, this safe and risk-free environment is a recursive one that creates, and is created by, the other components.

FIGURE 2.1. The CESI model.

As with TSI and the assisted performance/guided participation models, the CESI model is also based on sociocultural perspectives in which learning is viewed as a "cognitive apprenticeship" that occurs "through guided participation in social activity with companions who support and stretch children's understanding of and skill in using the tools of culture" (Rogoff, 1990, p. i). In this instructional context the "tools of culture" refer to use of strategies that assist entry into the culture of literacy. As Rogoff argued, there are different values placed on different types of "literacy" within a given society. That is, "school literacy" or "written literacy" is highly valued in Western societies and requires different tools and strategies to be successful than, say, "oral literacy," which places a higher demand on memory.

Gee (1992) has contended that, in fact, there are multiple literacies, and each individual possesses many different literacies. For example, as a white, female elementary school teacher who speaks English as my native language, I am literate in traversing most Anglo-European cultures, female cultures, elementary school cultures, as well as the more traditional literacy associated with proficiency in reading and writing English texts. Gee (1992) suggested that individuals possess different "Discourses," or identity kits, that enable them to negotiate the boundaries of various literacies. Gee (1992) distinguishes between "discourse" in the common sense of dialogue or conversation and "Discourse" (with a capital *D*) that refers not only to dialogue, but to the requisite knowledge that permits us to "fit in" or be "literate" in a given culture (i.e., how to speak, how to act, how to think, how to dress).

As an example, when Janice wrote the first edition of this text, she was living in the tiny, rural, outport community of Victoria Cove, Newfoundland. At that time she was reminded daily of her "illiteracy." Although her mother is from a similar Newfoundland outport community, and over the years had taught her a great deal about the culture prior to this visit, Janice still had to be acculturated and apprenticed into the culture. Janice's mother could not possibly have prepared her for each of the day-to-day situations in which she found herself, for she did not possess the Discourse of a Newfoundlander. She was illiterate within their culture, and they knew it. She looked different, she spoke differently, and she acted differently. She was an oddity—an outsider.

Janice was the only one unable to catch even a single smelt while ice fishing. She could not distinguish between a sculpin, a caplin, and a codfish. She had no idea what the Janeway, the ACW, or VOCM was. She did not put milk or sugar in her tea, and people often wondered how she could drink such "switchel." Young Newfoundland children taught her about the habits of the moose and seals that frequented the community. They took great delight in answering her questions and were curious as to how she could have survived all of these years without such knowledge. When asked if Janice "found the days long" or if "everything's narder," she found herself unable to respond. Although the language was English, the dialect and idiomatic expressions of Newfoundlanders are entirely different, as are their customs. "Dinner" is at noon and "supper" is in the evening. There is no lunch, other than a late-night snack, referred to as "lunch" or a "mug up."

Janice's Aunt Sue, Uncle George, and Aunt Maisie, who still reside there, as well as her mother who does not, served as her initial mentors. They served as tour guides, translators, historians, and cultural brokers while educating Janice, their grateful apprentice, about the nuances of life in an outport community. Joy, who was the Postmaster and who owns the variety store and the nursery, graciously endured Janice's daily barrage of questions, and willingly shared her expertise in any topic asked about—from the nature of the moose lottery to the consequences of northeasterly versus southwesterly winds. Janice's neighbor Lynn willingly shared her expertise about Newfoundland flora and fauna and the art of gardening in a wind-swept land with an astonishingly brief growing season and more rock than soil. Each of these individuals served as a mentor who scaffolded Janice's interactions with the community and taught her how to navigate within it. When she left the community, she was able to understand the language and the culture better as a result of their mentoring, but she was still not fully literate, nor did she possess the Discourse of a Newfoundlander—a process that takes many years.

So it is with reading. As children learn the Discourse of written literacy, they learn how to speak the language of literacy, how to act literate, and how to use the tools of literacy. It is a process that takes many years to learn. It is also a process that requires a mentor who provides scaffolded assistance in the form of explicit instruction, opportunities to verbalize the strategies one is using, and reduced processing at some points to help create a safe environment for motivated strategy use. Each of these four elements is essential in becoming a strategic reader. By including them in your instruction, you will help create an environment that is strategic and a culture in which readers become mentored into the Discourse of written literacy. The four elements of the CESI model are described throughout the remainder of the chapter.

Create a Safe and Risk-Free Environment for Motivated Strategy Use

As noted in Chapter 1, motivation is critical to strategy use (Guthrie, Taboada, & Coddington, 2007; Paris et al., 1983; Pressley, Woloshyn, et al., 1995); students must be motivated to employ strategies. The activation of personal attributions that support strategy use is critical to such motivation. That is, students must view themselves as active and in control of their own processing, and they must see that their efforts pay off. However, traditional classroom cultures often do not promote or support such attributions. This lack of support in this crucial area is not usually deliberate but more of an unintentional outgrowth of Western education. We assess and test a great deal—perhaps too much. Children in such environments begin to view every interaction with their teacher as a form of assessment. As is discussed in Chapter 4, nearly every interaction with students provides an opportunity for assessment; however, how we package these opportunities makes the difference between a safe environment and an unsafe environment.

Creating a safe environment means overhauling the conventions that govern many classroom cultures. An environment must be created in which it is okay to be wrong, okay not to know how to perform tasks, okay not to understand, and okay to take time while reading. Students in typical classrooms see the purposes of assignments differently from their teachers (Duffy, Roehler, & Rackliffe, 1986; Winne & Marx, 1982). Many students see the majority of activities and lessons in school as assessment oriented. These students then become assessment-focused or performance-oriented, as Prawat (1989) described them, rather than learning-focused. They are concerned with end products and "getting done" (Anderson, Brubaker, Alleman-Brooks, & Duffy, 1985). They vie to be the first one to complete an assignment, or they neglect to read texts thoroughly for fear they may not complete a task. The ultimate goal of reading is often sacrificed at the expense of task completion. Students in such environments know that after reading a text, their teacher will want to determine how well they have understood what they read. Very often, unfortunately, teachers assess such understanding by asking a lot of questions. Prawat (1989) noted that assessment-focused students do not view errors as something useful from which to learn but as something to be avoided. Assessment-focused students who understand what they have read try to "perform" for the teacher, whereas those students who may not understand as well try to hide from the teacher. These students are often quite strategic in their efforts to "hide." They may only raise their hand to answer known-answer questions (often those that require their personal opinion). They often hope to be called on for these questions to get their "turn" over with and avoid being called on for tougher questions. These students attempt to "hide" their misunderstanding from the teacher. They feel that if the teacher finds out they do not understand the text, they will receive a poor grade. When these students do not understand the text or are confused, the goal becomes trying to "trick" the teacher into thinking they do understand, rather than trying to learn how to repair their comprehension. In these traditional, teacher-centered classrooms the focus is on end products, task completion, and assessment rather than strategic processing and understanding.

Imagine a different classroom in which students enjoy gathering with their peers to discuss their interpretations, confusions, misunderstandings, and misgivings about text (cf. Almasi, 1995, 1996; Almasi, O'Flahavan, & Arya, 2001; Fall, Webb, & Chudowsky, 2000; Johnston, 2004). These discussions include lots of opportunity to chat about confusions, why they occurred, and how to resolve them. Peers share various strategies they used to overcome the confusion or assist others who continue to struggle. Students can often be heard saying things like "I didn't understand that part of the story" or "I don't know why the author did that. It was very confusing to write it that way." In these classrooms students are not afraid to openly say they do not understand something, and they are eager to chat with their peers to resolve their difficulties. The teacher in this classroom is not making notes about who understood and who did not. Instead she is noting which strategic processes each student is using to make sense of the text. These notes permit her to chart each student's growth and development over time, and they also provide a blueprint for future instruction. The teacher also recognizes, in accord with reader response views of literacy (e.g., Bleich, 1978; Rosenblatt, 1978), that there may be multiple and conflicting interpretations. The teacher may occasionally scaffold such transactions but does not lead them by asking questions or determining the discussion agenda. There is no ready-made kit that can create a "safe" environment. The teacher and the manner in which he interacts with students and the types of learning opportunities that he arranges are key to creating such an environment.

The thinking that underlies a strategic process is often very abstract and internal. It is essential to make these thought processes as visible as possible and to assist students in learning how to become metacognitively aware of when and where strategies are used. Metacognitive awareness is the key to strategic action, but younger and less proficient readers have demonstrated difficulty with such awareness (Baker & Brown, 1984; Garner, 1987).

One way to make this concept more accessible for students is to introduce them to the notion of "clunks" (Almasi, 1991). Anderson (1980) explained that while reading, individuals engage in the "clicks of comprehension and the clunks of comprehension failure" (p. 497). Teachers can explain to students that reading clicks along like a train running smoothly on a track until you meet a "clunk." There are two types of "clunks": word clunks and meaning clunks. *Word clunks* occur when the student cannot read the word, at which point he needs to use specific strategies to overcome the problem (i.e., word recognition strategies; see Figure 1.8). He might also encounter a *meaning clunk* in which he does not understand a word, a sentence, or a larger piece of the text. To overcome a meaning clunk, he needs to use different strategies (i.e., comprehension and fix-up strategies; see Figure 1.8). Learners within a summer reading program were introduced to the clunk concept by using a cartoon character (see Figure 2.2). The clunk character represents those instances in which learners are unable to proceed with the reading

FIGURE 2.2. Clunk: A symbolic representation of something that impedes the reading process. Adapted from Almasi (1991). Copyright 1991 by the State of Maryland International Reading Association Council. Adapted by permission.

process either because they cannot identify a word or because they do not understand some aspect of the text. The cartoon character depicts that moment of becoming meta-cognitively aware that something is impeding the reading process (see Almasi, 1991, for further discussion).

One teacher, Patty DiLaura George, created a click character to accompany the clunk character (see Figure 2.3). *Click* is a cartoon depiction of those times when the reading process is "clicking" along smoothly. Many of our teachers duplicate each of these cartoon characters for their students. During read-alouds, shared readings, and guided reading lessons, they encourage students to hold up a click card when the text makes sense and to hold up a clunk card when something does not make sense. Teachers then engage students in dialogues related to those aspects of the text that made sense, those aspects that did not make sense, and why the text was confusing or not. Discussion and verbalization about clicks and clunks are essential to student growth and development as strategic readers. "Stop" and "go" signs can be used in a similar manner. The concrete manipulatives enable teachers to assess students' metacognitive awareness and their ability to monitor the reading process. The resultant discourse also enables teachers to assess

FIGURE 2.3. Click: A symbolic representation of the unimpeded reading process.

the types of comprehension and word identification difficulties students are experiencing. Such discussion facilitates assessment of the strategies students possess for repairing reading difficulties and the conditional knowledge associated with using these strategies.

The following example depicts the type of teacher–student discourse that might initially occur as students learn about clunks. The excerpt is taken from a second-grade discussion of Stephen Mooser's (1978) *The Ghost with the Halloween Hiccups.* All students were identified as struggling readers. The teacher provided scaffolded instruction on making predictions and identifying story grammar elements (e.g., setting, character, problem, solution) to prepare students for reading the book. Students read the first half of the book and then engaged in a peer discussion of that portion (see Almasi, 1996, 2002) for explanations of peer discussion). At the close of each day's discussion, the group made a chart of the questions and confusions they had about the book. On this particular day, they were concerned about the author's style of writing. The author was trying to describe one character in the book that hiccupped while he talked. So, the text appeared like this: "Happy HICCUP Halloween!" One of the students, Roger (a pseudonym), had noted the previous day that this confused him, and the teacher recorded his question on a discussion chart to remind students of the topics they wanted to discuss the following day.

1 CRAIG: Hey, it says, "Please bring me some hiccup water."

2 TEACHER: That's what Roger was confused by too. We can talk about that. Go ahead. What do you think about that?

3 CRAIG: It says he was drinking water, and he had hiccups.

4 CHARISE: Ooooh! Now I know! Now I know! Um, he was trying to say, "give me some water," but he said, "hiccup."

5 TEACHER: What do you think of that?

(overlapping talk)

6 CRAIG: M-maybe he got hiccups before he drank the water, like, "Please bring me some *(imitates hiccup sound)* water."

7 KEITH: Yeah! That's it.

8 ROGER: So, he was drinking water.

9 TEACHER: So you agree with what Craig is saying? Why did he [the author] write *hiccup* like that? What does that mean? Who thinks they might be able to start rereading this page?

10 CRAIG: "Happy *(imitates a hiccup)* Halloween!"

13 CHARISE: He has the hiccups, and every time he tries to say something, he hiccups and then he says it.

15 KEITH: Good, because she said that she thinks it sounded like a hiccup.

16 TEACHER: So, is that what happens when you hiccup?

17 KEITH: Mmmmm-hmmmm.

(a little later)

34 TEACHER: Okay, so what happened here was great! Last Friday Roger had a clunk with that. Craig, you said that you had trouble understanding that too. Did

anybody else have trouble understanding that "HICCUP" in the middle [of the sentence]?

(*Heads nod affirmatively.*)

35 TEACHER: Now, you did too, Keith? (*Keith nods head affirmatively.*) That's called a *clunk*, but it's not a *word clunk* because you could read every word there. It's called a *meaning clunk*. It means that you don't understand. Sometimes you can have a clunk where you don't understand the word because you can't read it. Sometimes you can have a clunk where you don't understand it because it doesn't make sense. It does make sense now.

36 KATHY: Yes, we figured it out.

37 TEACHER: Okay, what we did was (*points to chart listing various strategies*), we met a clunk [see Figure 2.5]. When you read it, you might have *slowed down* and *reread* it to see if you could understand it, but what we did today was we *asked each other*. We helped each other out to help us understand that clunk. We got rid of it. So, we don't really need to discuss this (*points to that question on the discussion chart*), do we?

38 ALL: Nope.

39 TEACHER: We understand that now.

40 CHARISE: What we don't understand is why did Mr. Penny get the hiccups?

(*Discussion continues on this topic.*)

The environment in this classroom is one in which the students are eager to share their misunderstandings and eager to help one another resolve them. Their focus is on constructing meaning, and they generated their own topics for discussion. These were topics that were confusing or interesting to them; hence, their motivation was high. They were able to recognize those aspects of the text that were confusing to them, and they worked collaboratively to resolve the confusion. Students are better able to recognize and resolve comprehension difficulties when engaged in peer discussions than in more traditional teacher-led discussions, in which the teacher sets the agenda for what is discussed (Almasi, 1995).

In this vignette, the teacher's talk functioned as a momentary scaffold for students (O'Flavahan, Stein, Wiencek, & Marks, 1992). She did not enter the discussion to initiate topics of discussion, to determine who may speak to whom, or to assess students' understanding. Instead she entered into the discussion to ask open-ended questions that fostered more student dialogue (see lines 2, 5, and 9). At the end of the discussion, she provided an explanation of the cognitive and strategic processes in which the students had engaged (see lines 34, 35, and 37). She noted that students were able to monitor their comprehension (i.e., identifying clunks) and were able to employ a strategy to repair the comprehension failures (i.e., asking others). Her discourse in line 35 included an explanation of the declarative knowledge associated with monitoring comprehension. That is, she wanted students to know *that* when they read, they might come to places where they do not understand the meaning of the text. This explanation was not lengthy or stilted; it was an outgrowth of the processing in which students were already engaged as they were making sense of the text they had read. She attached labels to the cognitive processing in which students were engaged. In line 37, she explained the conditional knowledge associated with monitoring comprehension. That is, she noted that *when* students realize something does not make sense, they can fix up or repair the misunderstanding by trying three different strategies: slowing down and reading ahead carefully, rereading, or asking someone. The charts she used in line 35 are reproduced in Figures 2.4 and 2.5.

The teacher also served as an academic cheerleader of sorts, particularly in line 34. Her enthusiasm was a key factor in making the environment safe for students. She celebrated their ability to identify their own clunks. In a less supportive environment, the teacher might have chastised students for not understanding the text. Instead, she encouraged students to share their misunderstanding. Thus she functioned as a more knowledgeable other who provided cognitive scaffolding that enabled these novice readers to gain insights into the Discourse of written literacy. Teacher support is critical to the creation of a safe and risk-free environment. Another critical aspect is the teacher's ability

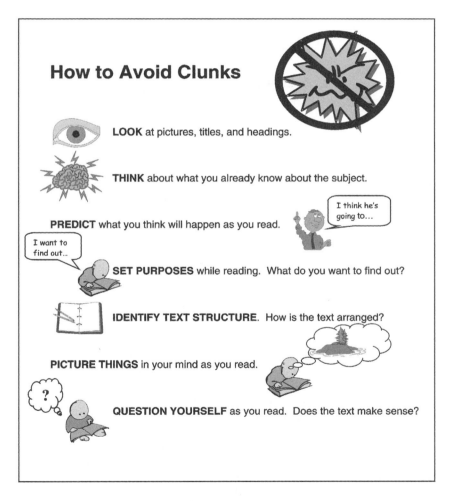

FIGURE 2.4. How to avoid clunks while reading. Adapted from Almasi (1991). Copyright 1991 by the State of Maryland International Reading Association Council. Adapted by permission.

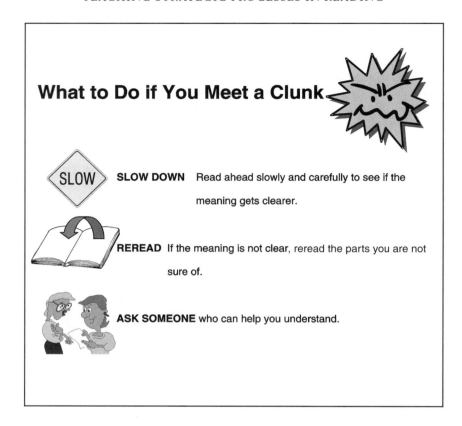

FIGURE 2.5. What to do when you meet a clunk. Adapted from Almasi (1991). Copyright 1991 by the State of Maryland International Reading Association Council. Adapted by permission.

to design instruction that is appropriate for students. The three remaining aspects of the CESI model work together to support and create this safe, risk-free environment.

Provide Explicit Instruction

Durkin's (1978–1979) now classic investigation revealed a paucity of actual comprehension instruction in elementary classrooms. As Pearson and Dole (1987) noted, Durkin's research found that a great amount of time was spent "mentioning" (i.e., mentioning the skill students were supposed to practice), "practicing" (i.e., practicing the skill), and "assessing" (i.e., giving directions to complete assignments and workbook pages), but little time was actually spent teaching students *how* to understand and comprehend text. With this lacuna in mind, much of the research of the 1980s was dedicated to examining the effect of providing comprehension instruction for students (for reviews, see Dole, Duffy, Roehler, & Pearson, 1991; Duke & Pearson, 2002; Pearson & Fielding, 1991; Pearson & Dole, 1987). That body of research revealed that explicit instruction (as defined and described above) enhances students' learning and their strategic and metacognitive awareness, particularly for struggling readers (e.g., Dole, Brown, & Trathen, 1996; Duffy, Roehler, Sivan, et al., 1987). Although research has shown that, with training, teachers can learn to be more explicit in their comprehension instruction (Duffy, Roehler, Meloth, Vavrus, Book, et al., 1986), not much has changed since Durkin's research—little comprehension instruction still occurs in elementary classrooms (Fielding & Pearson, 1994; Pearson & Dole, 1987; Pearson & Fielding, 1991; Pearson & Gallagher, 1983; Pressley, 2000).

Explicit instruction is an important component of effective strategy instruction. By itself it is not sufficient for developing strategic, self-regulated readers, but it is a necessary component of strategy instruction, particularly for struggling readers. The model of explicit instruction presented below is based on primarily on the work of Pearson and his colleagues (e.g., Duke & Pearson, 2002; Dole et al., 1991; Fielding & Pearson, 1994; Pearson & Dole, 1987; Pearson & Gallagher, 1983; Pearson & Fielding, 1991). As noted earlier, explicit instruction of strategies differs from direct instruction in several ways: (1) There is no assumption that strategies should be broken down into subskills; (2) strategies must be modeled and practiced during authentic reading tasks; and (3) there is no particular strategy or set of strategies that is "correct" in any given reading situation. Instead strategies should be applied flexibly in response to the reader, the text, and the context (Dole et al., 1991; Pearson & Dole, 1987).

Explanation

Providing a brief explanation of the declarative, procedural, and conditional knowledge associated with using a given strategy or set of strategies is essential (Paris et al., 1983). Such explanations must go beyond "mentioning" and focus on which strategy is being used, what specific knowledge is associated with the strategy, why it is being used in a given situation, why it is helpful in that situation, and how to perform the strategy. Explanation is at the heart of Duffy, Roehler, Sivan, et al.'s (1987) notion of direct explanation, during which teachers describe the mental processes that good readers use while reading text. In essence, they make the covert thought processes that normally occur during fluent reading overt and obvious. Direct explanations often occur as teachers model the cognitive processes in which good readers engage. Teachers may also engage in think-alouds in which they actually articulate the thoughts going through their head as they read text (see Block & Israel, 2004; Oster, 2001). In this way students are able to "see" the cognitive processing involved in reading. This visible demonstration is helpful for all readers but particularly for struggling readers who are often unaware of the cognitive processes involved in strategic reading and how and when to use strategies (for reviews, see Baker & Beall, 2009; Baker & Brown, 1984; Garner, 1987).

In the earlier excerpt from the second-grade discussion of *The Ghost with the Halloween Hiccups* (Mooser, 1978), the teacher provided a brief explanation of the declarative and conditional knowledge associated with the strategy of monitoring comprehension (line 35). She did not need to discuss the procedural knowledge related to *how* to monitor comprehension because the students had already shown her that they were able to monitor their comprehension in that situation.

These explanations were not lengthy, nor were they the focus of an entire lesson. Indeed, such explanations can be brief interludes that occur during read-alouds, shared reading, or as a part of guided reading. As well, teachers need not be the exclusive individuals to offer explanations. As students become more comfortable sharing the cognitive processes in which they engage as they read, they should be encouraged to share with others *which* strategy they used, *why* they used it, *when* they used it, and *how* they used it with others (see section later in this chapter on creating opportunities for student verbalization).

Explanations should also be woven into the fabric of the entire curriculum, not just during "reading class." For example, during a science lab, the teacher might model the type of thinking that occurs while reading directions to complete the lab. She might say something like, "The instructions say . . . but when I read it, I am confused. I have a clunk. I think I'm going back to reread that part to make sure that I understand. If I don't understand the instructions, I might ruin the experiment." During this brief think-aloud, the teacher communicated the declarative knowledge *that* when reading instructions to perform a science experiment, students must monitor their comprehension to make sure the text makes sense. She also communicated the declarative knowledge *that* it is possible to have a clunk when reading science text. Her think-aloud also conveyed conditional knowledge associated with *when* students need to monitor their comprehension and *why* it is important. When integrated throughout the entire curriculum, such brief explanations facilitate transfer of the strategy to new and diverse reading contexts. Without such integration, students often think that reading strategies are to be used only in "reading class," so they fail to employ them in other contexts (Garner, 1990).

Modeling

Explanation often occurs during modeling, which involves either demonstrating a strategic process or performing a think-aloud of the thoughts that occur while one reads and uses strategies. For example, during a read-aloud of *Owl Moon* by Jane Yolen, one teacher, Eileen Ludwig, explained and modeled the cognitive processes she used to the student with whom she was working:

 1 (*reading from text*) "Then we came to a clearing in the dark woods. The moon was high
 2 above us. It seemed to fit exactly over the center of the clearing, and the snow below was
 3 whiter than the milk in a bowl of cereal." I can really picture that in my mind. I see a
 4 large area that is covered by a lot of newly fallen snow. I also see some light coming off
 5 the snow from the reflection of the moon. I picture in my mind a very open area in the
 6 middle of the forest at nighttime. I picture that it is very cold outside. When the author
 7 said, "the snow below was whiter than the milk in a bowl of cereal," I thought that the
 8 snow might have just fallen or that no other people or animals were around. Because
 9 we live in an area where it snows, I know that snow does not stay white unless it is very new
10 or nothing else is around to make it dirty. I used the author's words, what I already
11 know, and my senses to help me make those pictures in my head. When I make pictures
12 in my head while I read, it really helps me understand.

—EILEEN LUDWIG

In this example, Eileen used authentic text to model the cognitive processing that occurred while she was reading. The text was highly image-laden and evoked strong sensory images. In line 3 Eileen began her think-aloud by describing the strategy she used. In lines 6–11 she explained the procedural knowledge, or *how* she actually performed the strategy, and in line 12 she explained the conditional knowledge related to *why* the strategy was helpful and important for her. Through her think-aloud, Eileen was able to show her student *when* she used a given strategy, *how* she used it, and *why* she used it when she did. It is important to note that the procedural knowledge used to perform a given strategy may vary from individual to individual. For example, not all readers may use the author's words, their background knowledge, and their senses to form images, as Eileen did. She described the process *she* used to create images. Teachers and students must be encouraged to share the variety of procedures they use to enact particular strategies, so that others can see that strategy use is a flexible process rather than one that is rigid or fixed. Eileen's think-aloud illustrates one of many possible ways to perform a given strategy.

Eileen did not communicate declarative knowledge during the think-aloud. Instead she chose to explain such information prior to reading the book: "Sometimes portions of the text help you form a picture in your mind. Some stories are better than others for making those pictures. That is because some authors use more descriptive words that help the reader draw on their background knowledge to understand the text." Here she explained the declarative knowledge *that* imagery is not a helpful strategy with all texts. She also included the conditional knowledge that imagery is a helpful strategy *when* authors use descriptive language. Eileen was enculturating her student into the Discourse of literacy by sharing the types of thinking and the language that accompanies strategic processing of text. Such talk provides information about the nature of the strategy that younger and less proficient readers may not be aware of on their own. Again, the purpose of modeling and explanation is to make visible to students the very complex and obscure nature of using strategies while reading. Pearson and Dole (1987) noted that it is sometimes difficult for teachers to become accustomed to modeling strategies and incorporating think-alouds into their daily instruction. It feels awkward at first to share one's thinking in public. However, in time and with practice, incorporating think-alouds and modeling into all aspects of the curriculum becomes second nature.

Guided Practice

Guided practice involves multiple opportunities for teachers to guide or scaffold students' strategic processing as it occurs within a wide variety of instructional circumstances. Learning to become a strategic reader is a long process that cannot be accomplished in a few lessons. Such development takes years (Pressley, 2000). Although the ultimate goal of strategy instruction is to develop independent, self-regulated readers, this is a long-term goal that is attainable through the coordinated efforts of an entire school. It is impossible for one teacher, by him- or herself, to attain this goal in one school year.

Guided practice also enables teachers to provide students with substantive feedback, *not* by evaluating the "correctness" of strategy use, but by providing opportunities for students to assess and evaluate their own strategy use. In this manner students share those strategies that work and those that do not; they discuss why particular strategies work in a given situation and why others do not. Such reflection and evaluation move learners toward self-regulation.

Pearson and Gallagher (1983) suggested a model of explicit instruction in which, during guided practice, teachers gradually "release responsibility" for the task to the students (p. 337). In this model any task can be viewed as requiring different proportions of teacher and student responsibility. Put another way, any task may require differing amounts of instructional scaffolding for a given student. In Figure 2.6, the diagonal line moves from instructional contexts requiring total teacher support (upper left) to those

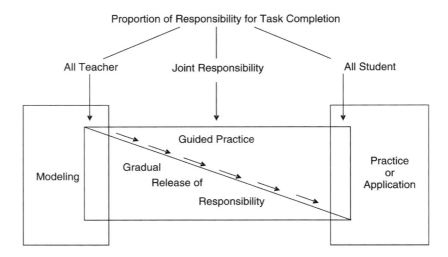

FIGURE 2.6. Pearson and Gallagher's (1983) model of explicit instruction. Reprinted from *Contemporary Educational Psychology, vol. 8*, P. D. Pearson & M. C. Gallagher, "The instruction of reading comprehension," pp. 317–334, 1983, with permission from Elsevier.

requiring no teacher scaffolding or support (i.e., independence). The ultimate goal is for students to be able to perform particular tasks (in this case, reading) on their own.

It takes a patient, willing, and "noticing" (see Clay, 2001) teacher—someone who understands the reading process and how strategies develop—to guide students as they learn how to process text strategically. Guided practice is part of this apprenticeship. During guided practice, a more knowledgeable other within the culture (i.e., either an adult or a peer) is available to provide explanation, modeling, or scaffolded assistance so that, with the other's help, learners can perform tasks that they may not be able to do independently (Vygotsky, 1978). However, such practice must be situated within authentic tasks (Brown, Collins, & Duguid, 1989; Clay, 2001; Fielding & Pearson, 1994). That is, guided practice must occur during authentic reading of whole texts so that authentic strategies can be modeled and used in the situations and contexts in which they will actually be used.

Reduce Processing Demands

The number and diversity of students in a classroom often make it difficult for a teacher to meet each learner's individual needs. Using many of the process-oriented assessments that are described in Chapter 4 helps determine students' needs, but scaffolding all students on an individual basis is difficult. Some students require more scaffolded support than others to achieve a similar reading goal. Therefore, it is important to consider various ways to scaffold students. When we are reducing processing, we are trying to break the process down a bit so that it is easier for readers to be strategic. In this sense, we are trying to make the task a little bit easier for students in terms of cognition. Thus, we are trying to reduce the amount of cognitive effort for which a reader is responsible.

Two important factors to consider when planning instruction are the amounts of cognitive activity (or responsibility) a reader must employ in (1) the social setting of the classroom (the amount of support given to students by peers and teachers either increases or decreases the amount of responsibility) and (2) the instructional task and texts that are used. In the lesson planning grid (Figure 2.7) the amount of a student's cognitive responsibility when interacting with others in the social setting of the classroom is depicted on the vertical axis and the amount of cognitive activity required from instructional tasks and texts is depicted on the horizontal axis. The amount of scaffolded support provided by each factor occurs along a continuum ranging from "more" to "less" support. The letters *A*, *B*, and *C* are used to indicate where sample lessons, described later in this chapter, fit.

The amount of social and cognitive support provided by others should be a well thought-out decision on the teacher's part. When lessons feature the teacher and the whole class engaged in any learning event, the amount of support provided to the individual from others is high if the student is actively engaged. That is, the teacher can provide explanations, think-alouds, and modeling during lessons, and the other students can provide insights regarding various ways to accomplish a given task. In this whole-class setting an individual student does not typically have a lot of cognitive responsibility. That is, because there are so many other students in the class, the cognitive responsibility throughout a given lesson is distributed across all of those students and the teacher. Of course, in this situation the teacher cannot easily monitor each student's thoughts. Thus, a limitation of using whole-class instruction is that it is difficult to evaluate and

Amount of Cognitive Activity Required by Text

	Events/ Experiences (enactive)	Movies/ Videos	Wordless Picture Books	Read-Alouds	Shared Reading	Picture Books	Texts (symbolic)
Teacher/ Whole Class	A		B				
Small Group							
Trios							
Pairs							
Individual							C

Less Cognition Concrete (semiotic) ⟵⟶ *More Cognition Abstract (linguistic)*

Amount of Student's Cognitive Responsibility (Less ↑ More ↓)

FIGURE 2.7. Lesson planning grid: Scaffolded instructional support for strategic processing.

assess individual students and the degree to which they have attained the objectives. In these circumstances it is helpful to plan to use every pupil response (EPR) techniques, in which all students communicate their understanding or their responses to the teacher. For example, each student might be given a replica of click and clunk signs with which to signal. As the teacher performs a read-aloud or uses any type of text during the instruction, students hold up the click sign to indicate that they understand the content and the clunk sign to indicate that something did not make sense. In this manner, all students are actively involved in the lesson, and the teacher can monitor them to determine whether they are able to use a particular strategy. The teacher can also use student responses to prompt discussion and dialogue about strategy use. This teacher–whole-class scenario provides the individual student with a secure environment. Students who may be struggling are not forced to perform a given strategy or set of strategies while reading on their own. Instead they receive support from others.

Small-group instruction, such as guided reading, allows the teacher to provide carefully tailored scaffolding in terms of interactions and text selections to both group and individual members, and as a result, is likely to be very supportive. In these smaller-group settings the teacher can provide more individualized scaffolding than in a whole-class setting, but the individual student's cognitive responsibility is somewhat greater than in a whole-class setting because there are fewer students among whom to distribute the cognitive activity. Small peer groups provide less support in that the teacher is not directly present throughout the entire lesson, but the presence of five or six peers can provide a great deal of support for students who may not yet be able to use strategies on their own. Trios and pairs require even greater cognitive responsibility for the individual student because less support is provided (see Van den Branden, 2000). In a trio or pair the burden for actually performing the task rests on fewer shoulders, increasing the cognitive burden for individual students, as they have to assume more of the responsibility for task completion. As shown in Figure 2.7, the individual student receives the least amount of support from others because she is completely on her own while completing a given task. This circumstance can be an anxious time for struggling readers trying to process text strategically. Although the teacher can provide one-on-one assistance in this scenario, it is obviously difficult to provide such assistance to all students in a classroom when they are working independently. Thus, the amount of cognitive responsibility for task completion is greatest when students are working independently.

The amount of support provided from the text is one that is not often discussed during instructional planning. For this discussion it is necessary to turn to a theory that has a lengthy past—that of concrete representation. Intuitively, we have heard and have attempted to mind the maxim to "proceed from the concrete to abstract," particularly in elementary instruction. However, we have not really heeded this advice in strategy instruction, and as Dewey cautioned as far back as 1910, this notion is often misunderstood.

Dewey (1910/1991) defined "concrete" as meaning that is readily apprehended by itself. What actually is concrete, however, is relative and differs from individual to individual. To fluent readers, the notions of *prediction*, *summarization*, and *comprehension monitoring* are fairly concrete because they use these strategies constantly without involving any thought or overt manipulation. However, to novice readers, understanding these terms and enacting them pose significant problems. These readers might need to relate these new, abstract concepts to things that are already known or familiar to them.

In general what is familiar is mentally concrete. Beginning with the concrete means that we should emphasize *doing* at the outset, especially in areas that are not routine or automatic. Given that strategy use, by definition, is deliberate and planful, much of strategy instruction should initially be concrete. Concrete representations in the form of actual experiences, analogies, and metaphors crystallize concepts and procedures (Prawat, 1989). The goal is to explicitly connect or make comparisons between previous concepts in one's knowledge base and the new strategy or process. Verbalization and a reflective attitude help foster these connections (Prawat, 1989). Instructional activities should be arranged so that interest in them and their outcome creates a desire to attend to that which is more *indirect and remote*—the abstract.

"The abstract" refers to that which is theoretical and is not closely associated with practical concerns. The entire act of reading is an abstract process—from the marks on the pages to the meaning that is constructed. We use lines and shapes to represent letters, which represent sounds, which when strung together, represent words—which represent ideas to which meaning is attached. The entire process is abstract and intangible. In Figure 2.7 "text" is situated at the far right or abstract end of the continuum. Text, in this sense, is linguistic text, or text that uses written language to communicate. Hartman and Hartman (1993) suggested that texts can be characterized as ranging from linguistic to semiotic. Linguistic texts include any written material—books, essays, newspapers, plays, and poems. Semiotic texts include nonwritten material—movies, videos, music, photography, paintings, even facial expressions and gestures. Semiotic texts, just like linguistic texts, can be "read" and interpreted. However, the "reading" is easier because it involves images and sounds that are concrete representations rather than symbolic abstractions. It is easier for struggling readers to understand the movie version of a book than to read the text because the act of reading, per se, is removed while watching a movie. That is, without the demands of decoding the words, readers (or viewers) can focus their attention on thinking about, and using, strategies for comprehending the text—the storyline.

This is *not* a recommendation to read all texts aloud to struggling readers. It *is* a recommendation to reduce the processing demands while students are initially learning about strategies by using semiotic as well as linguistic texts. Strategy use, by itself, is a very abstract and complex process. When coupled with the very abstract process of reading linguistic texts, the task becomes an enormous cognitive burden to novice learners. Thus, instruction can be scaffolded for students so that they learn about strategies and how to use them with "texts" that may not initially require as much cognitive energy.

Bruner's (1966) theory of cognitive development helps explain how concrete representations of material influence learning. He posited that children develop modes of representing information: enactive, iconic, and symbolic. *Enactive* forms use actions, events, or experiences to represent information. Such knowledge does not require the use of words or imagery. The teachers in the example that follows use the *enactive* mode to provide their students with a concrete experience that represented the targeted strategy (comprehension monitoring). *Iconic* forms use visualization to represent information and are governed by principles of perceptual organization. In the lesson planning grid (Figure 2.7), semiotic texts such as movies, videos, and wordless picture books fall within the *iconic* mode. *Symbolic* forms use language or symbols to represent information, as occurs in instruction using linguistic texts.

The horizontal axis of the lesson planning grid (Figure 2.7) arrays the range of texts that offer more and less scaffolded support. An event or experience (i.e., an enactive form) would provide the most concrete type of "text" for students to learn about strategy use. For example, during a university summer reading program, one pair of teachers, Liz Graffeo and Summer Sciandra, wanted to help their group of fifth-grade boys become more metacognitively aware while they read. They had noticed that each of the students was passive and cognitively aloof while reading. They had hoped to teach the students what it felt like to experience a clunk while reading. They designed an "event" to foster an actual metacognitive experience in the students. The lesson they developed would be located at Point A in the figure, because it was a lesson in which the teachers and the entire group provided scaffolded support for one another during a concrete event.

The boys had shown interest in reading texts about spiders. To heighten their interest, Liz and Summer created a very large, stuffed "spider" and attached it to the ceiling for several weeks. The day of the "event" the spider was removed from the ceiling and hidden. As the boys entered the classroom, they immediately noticed the missing spider and became alarmed. They began asking questions and tried to determine what had happened. The teachers encouraged the students to jot down their questions and develop a strategic plan for locating the missing spider. The strategic plan they developed engaged them in a search for clues around the classroom and the school. Clues were derived from physical evidence as well as interviews with the principal and the custodial staff. The boys were completely engrossed in this event and read and wrote more than they ever had previously.

This elaborate event represented a concrete experience in which the boys were metacognitively aware, suddenly, that the spider was missing. They came in and noticed "something was wrong." This feeling was likened to the same feeling one has when one experiences a "clunk" while reading. The teachers engaged the boys in a concrete experience that would help them understand the same feeling when they were reading. They drew from the initial concrete experience to help the boys understand how to monitor their comprehension while reading linguistic text. The remainder of the initial experience required the boys to develop and enact a strategic plan to locate the missing spider. This experience is similar to what proficient readers do when they notice their comprehension failures. They strategically plan ways to fix or resolve the problem. Again the teachers drew on this initial concrete experience to make connections to the use of reading strategies to repair comprehension difficulties. In this example the goal of reduced processing is strikingly evident: to *temporarily* eliminate the processing demands of reading linguistic texts so that students can learn and *use* strategies. Focusing all their cognitive effort on strategic processing during a concrete event establishes new cognitive pathways that are then available to students during reading events.

Located at Point A of the lesson planning grid in Figure 2.7, the lesson described above offers students a high level of scaffolded support both from others (i.e., teacher and whole class) and from concrete texts (i.e., semiotic). Point C, reading linguistic texts independently, offers the least amount of support. There is no opportunity for others to provide support, and the text to be read is abstract. Independent, self-regulated strategy use would need to occur at this point.

The scaffolded instruction depicted in the lesson planning grid in Figure 2.7 is not intended to move in a linear fashion from concrete to abstract. Instead, as Bruner (1966) suggested, instruction should be recursive, moving back and forth between the *enactive* (i.e., concrete actions, events, experiences), *iconic* (i.e., semiotic texts, movies, videos, wordless picture books), and *symbolic* modes (i.e., abstract or linguistic texts) modes, until the child is able to use strategic processes under all conditions (see Figure 2.8). Teaching strategic processing in this model would progress from the level of active manipulation and direct experience with the strategy to symbolic representation of the

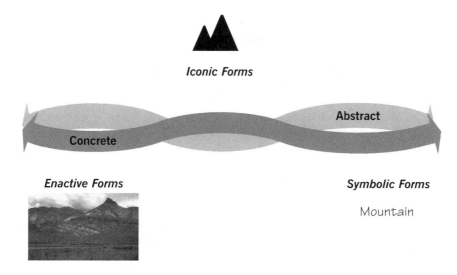

FIGURE 2.8. A recursive model of strategy instruction that reduces processing demands.

strategy while reading independently from linguistic texts. When instruction begins with formal symbolic representations that do not permit the learner to develop enactive or iconic representation, superficial, rote learning occurs rather than deep understanding of the processes involved (Bruner, 1966). Planning instruction to accommodate these different modes helps students transfer the learning from one context to another. Transfer is perhaps the most difficult aspect of learning to become a strategic reader. Thus, reducing processing in this manner is vital not only in helping students learn about strategic processing, but also in helping them use it independently in varied contexts. Similar to Vygotsky's (1978) notions, Bruner (1966) suggested that language is the tool that leads to internalization of these concepts. Thus, we turn our attention to the final component of the CESI model: verbalization.

Create Opportunities for Students to Verbalize about Strategy Use

Vygotsky (1978) suggested that, as a symbolic activity, speech has an *organizing* function that penetrates the process of tool use and produces new forms of behavior. Engaging in think-aloud types of discourse while performing a task plays a specific role in being able to carry out that task. During this process the child engages in the type of planful discourse that characterizes strategic processing. Verbalization enhances awareness by bringing subconscious (i.e., covert) thought processes to consciousness (Prawat, 1989), so that one's thoughts and processes become an object for reflection and evaluation. Such egocentric speech is the basis for inner speech, which, in its external and public form, is embedded in communicative speech. Movement from interaction with the social environment (i.e., dialogue with teachers and peers) and real objects (i.e., enactive forms and semiotic texts) to noninteractive forms of written language (i.e., reading symbolic forms of language or linguistic texts) facilitates internalization of cognitive processes. Thus language mediates experiences and helps transform them into higher-order mental operations that eventually become internalized (Vygotsky, 1978).

In its earliest stages, speech *accompanies* a child's actions and reflects the nature of the task in a disrupted and chaotic form. In later stages, speech becomes more of a planning device that *precedes* action—as in strategic processing. Once children learn to use this planning function of speech, their psychological realm is radically altered: A view of the future has become essential to the way they approach their environment and learning tasks. For teachers planning strategy instruction, this developmental step means that we must model such discourse and encourage our students to engage in it in order for them to eventually internalize such higher-order thinking.

A great deal of research and practice has emphasized the importance of verbalizing the covert thought processes that occur while reading (e.g., Bereiter & Bird, 1985; Davey, 1983; Dole et al., 1996; Duffy, Roehler, Sivan, et al., 1987; Paris et al., 1983; Pearson & Fielding, 1991; Pressley, El-Dinary, et al., 1992). Kucan and Beck (1997) noted that think-alouds of the strategic processes used while reading can come in the form of teacher modeling during instruction and guided practice, or as students think aloud and verbalize their own cognitive processing. Research has clearly indicated that when students are taught to verbalize and think aloud, their comprehension and achievement are significantly greater than students who do not receive these opportunities.

When such discourse is generated in social contexts (e.g., whole-class, small-group, or peer discussions) students have the opportunity to hear multiple and varied ways in which teachers and peers use strategies to process text. These collaborative discussions provide students with the opportunity to assume authority and responsibility for their own thinking (Greene & Ackerman, 1995; Li et al., 2007; Van den Branden, 2000) and to observe the higher-level thought processes of others before trying to accomplish similar tasks on their own (Almasi, 1995; Goatley, Brock, & Raphael, 1995; Wilkinson, Soter, & Murphy, 2010). Learning in these social environments can occur incidentally, as learners observe the cognitive processes of the group, or more directly, when teachers or peers scaffold the interaction so that learners become capable of engaging in more strategic processing than they would have independently (Rogoff, 1990; Vygotsky, 1978). Additionally, "when students participate in discourse environments and engage in dialogue or communication, their learning is not confined to knowledge constructed as a product in such a context, but also includes a developing understanding of and ability to use the processes by which such knowledge is constructed" (Kucan & Beck, 1997, p. 290).

We will examine a transcript of a lesson to see how a teacher scaffolds and provides opportunities for students to verbalize their cognitive processes. Patty DiLaura George, a clinician in one of our summer reading programs, conducted the lesson with a group of six struggling first-grade readers. The children had all completed first grade the previous year; however, most would repeat first grade in the fall. Patty was teaching the children how to monitor their comprehension by using "stop" and "go" signs as concrete representations of the clunks of comprehension failure and the clicks of successful comprehension. In this whole-group lesson, she used the wordless picture book *Good Dog Carl* by Alexandra Day (1985). The lesson represents a fairly high degree of instructional scaffolding and would fall at Point B in the lesson planning grid (Figure 2.7).

Patty introduced the children to the concept of monitoring their comprehension in an earlier lesson when she introduced the "stop" and "go" tags. In this lesson, since *Good Dog Carl* was a wordless picture book, she encouraged the children to organize or gather up a storyline in their heads as they studied the pictures. She also encouraged them to think about whether the pictures made sense. The children were told to turn their tags to the "stop" side if the story did not make sense, or to the "go" side if it did make sense. In the book, the mother leaves Carl (the dog) to look after the baby. In this excerpt, Patty turned to the page in which Carl and the baby are playing with mother's jewelry (note that all children's names are pseudonyms):

52 CALEB: They're playing with the jewelry.

53 TEACHER: Oh, my goodness.

54 CHERI: (*giggling*) Look at the dog.

55 TEACHER: Oh, I see lots of stops, and I see some go's. That's okay, it just depends how it makes sense to you or maybe it doesn't. Stephen, why doesn't that make sense to you?

56 STEPHEN: Because, um, how could both of 'em get dressed up?

57 TEACHER: How could they get dressed up in those things? Hmmm, that's a good question.

58 CALEB: The baby could climb on the dog's head, get up there and done that thing.

59 TEACHER: Well, Caleb, that might be a good idea. Maybe that's how it happened. And I see lots of go's, too, so that tells me that you do understand what's happening in the story. I like how you're thinking about that and paying attention [to the pictures]. (*Turns page to reveal picture of baby at the edge of a laundry chute.*) Uh-oh.

60 CALEB: Oh, no, the laundry slot!

61 TEACHER: How did you know that was the laundry slot, Caleb?

62 CALEB: Because it says *laundry* on the top, and there was a laundry bag down there.

63 TEACHER: Good for you.

64 STEPHEN: Uh-oh, he's gonna fall.

65 TEACHER: You're a good thinker. I see Caleb has the go sign facing me because he understands what's going on now. That baby is getting ready to go down that chute. (*Looks at Patrick.*) Oops. How come your tag is not on? Can you put your tag on for me, and Stephen, are you showing me stop or go?

66 CURTIS: I don't think it makes sense.

67 TEACHER: Why doesn't it make sense?

68 CURTIS: Because how can a dog open a laundry thing?

Several aspects of the CESI model are operating in this excerpt. First, using the stop and go tags and the wordless picture book reduced the processing demands for the children, which made the environment a safer one in which to try using the new strategy. In line 55, the teacher facilitated the safe and risk-free environment further when she noted that she saw tags turned to both stop and go. She made it clear in this example (and throughout the lesson) that it was okay if the children turned their tags to either side— "it just depends how it makes sense to you." Throughout the lesson, the children did not seem encumbered by this process, displaying their understanding, or lack of it, without hesitation. Patty continually used phrases to foster a safe environment, such as when she noted, "I like how you're thinking about that and paying attention [to the pictures]" (line

59), "Good for you" (line 63), and "You're a good thinker" (line 65). In this manner, she created a safe environment by selecting safe texts and safe ways to display the strategies used, and she acted as an "academic cheerleader" by encouraging the children to take risks and by supporting their efforts.

Patty also provided frequent opportunities for students to verbalize their thoughts. Usually she accomplished this by asking an open-ended question such as, "Why doesn't this make sense to you?" or "Why does this make sense to you?" In line 55, Patty encouraged Stephen to explain why that page did not make sense to him. As in this example, the children were always anxious to share their thoughts, and the others often added explanations to help the individual understand that part of the text, such as Caleb did (line 58). Patty also encouraged Caleb to verbalize how he knew the picture was a laundry chute (line 61). In this manner, she fostered a sociocultural environment in which students shared the strategies they used to construct meaning from text. Caleb's explanation may have provided another child, who did not know how to use that strategy, with a new tool for constructing meaning.

Finally, we see the students beginning to use the language of literacy (in line 66). Throughout the lesson, Patty used the phrases "that does make sense" and "that doesn't make sense." In this manner she modeled the type of discourse that literate individuals use. She also modeled literate actions later in the lesson when she turned to a page that showed the baby getting into the aquarium: "Uh-oh! Looks like trouble! Think about that card. Does that make sense to you in the story? I see what's going on. I can understand when I look at it. So if I had my tag up, I would show the go side because I can see that a lot of trouble is going on there, and I can understand how that can happen. So I have the go sign showing." In effect, as Gee (1992) noted, she was mentoring the students in the Discourse of written literacy. As she taught them how to talk and how to act during literacy events her classroom was a site in which "children are *becoming* literate" (Johnston, 2004, p. 22). Here (line 66) we also see that Curtis appropriated this language quickly and easily.

Patty also found opportunities to incorporate direct explanation into this lesson. When appropriate, she slipped in information about the declarative, procedural, and conditional knowledge associated with monitoring one's comprehension while reading:

122 TEACHER: Get ready to turn that card. Take a look at the pictures, think about whether it makes sense or not, and then turn your card. (*Turns page to reveal picture of dog eating food taken from refrigerator.*)

123 CALEB: How can a dog eat baby food?

124 TEACHER: So, you're asking me that question, so what side should you have [your tag showing], Caleb?

125 CALEB: Stop.

126 TEACHER: Right, because you don't understand how that dog could be eating that baby food or the food that the people eat, right?

127 CALEB: Oh! I got it! It's on "go" for me now. (*Turns tag from stop to go.*)

128 TEACHER: Oh, wow! (*Smiles broadly.*)

129 CALEB: Because I got the idea figured out!

130 CHERI: Me too!

131 TEACHER: Good for you, Caleb. Caleb, when you looked at the pictures a little more closely, did it help you understand?

132 CALEB: Yeah, it's just that when the dog . . .

133 CURTIS: (*Interrupts.*)

134 TEACHER: Curtis, one minute. Let's listen to what Caleb is saying. Can you say that again, Caleb?

135 CALEB: Um, the dog must have been on the top and put a hole in the can, and then he started to turn his head, and it started to come out in the cup.

136 TEACHER: You know what, Caleb? Sometimes that happens when you're reading. You don't understand something (*turns tag to stop*), and then you figure it out and you do understand it (*turns tag to go*). That's okay. Good.

Patty reiterated the procedural knowledge associated with *how* to monitor comprehension (line 122). She noted that students should read the text (in this case, look at the pictures) and think about whether it made sense. Because the lesson was fairly concrete and conducted as a whole group, she also added in the step of physically manipulating the tags. When Caleb displayed his ability not just to monitor his comprehension but also to repair it (line 127), Patty celebrated with him and then quickly explained what had occurred. Her explanation (line 136) identified the declarative knowledge associated with comprehension monitoring. She noted *that* sometimes you might not understand something while reading, but it can clear up. This declarative knowledge is something of which struggling readers are often unaware. At other points in the lesson, she also communicated conditional knowledge. Whenever a learning situation presented itself, Patty took advantage of the opportunity.

These examples depict the recursive relationship of the CESI model. Patty began by creating a fertile environment for motivated strategy use through her text selection and the concrete nature of her lesson. As the lesson unfolded we saw explicit instruction, reduced processing, and verbalization working in unison to nurture the safe environment. In this way the safe environment creates, and is created by, the other three components, as depicted in Figure 2.1.

SUMMARY

The CESI model is based on dialectical constructivist notions, in which explicit instruction and scaffolding are provided. These notions are also rooted in sociocultural theories of learning, in which learning the Discourse of written literacy is viewed as a "cognitive apprenticeship" that occurs in a social milieu. The key aspect of the CESI model is the creation of a safe and risk-free environment. Such an environment creates, and is created by, the recursive actions of explicit instruction, reducing processing demands, and providing opportunities for students to verbalize cognitive processes. These elements work together to create an environment for motivated strategy use.

CHAPTER THREE

Responsive Teaching Frameworks within Response to Intervention

I n this chapter we provide an overview of what is involved in responsive teaching, particularly as it pertains to strategies instruction. As well, we situate such responsive instruction in relation to the response-to-intervention (RTI) frameworks currently being used and implemented.

WHAT IS RESPONSIVE TEACHING?

Responsive teaching and assessing begins with responsive teachers who are attuned to their students. This means that teachers are tuned in to every aspect of their students, including their interests, attitudes, emotional dispositions, culture, linguistic capabilities, strengths as a literacy learner, and those aspects of literacy learning that challenge them. In short, responsive teachers know their students very well. These teachers observe their students very carefully and monitor their learning very closely as the students engage in the process of reading and writing in authentic contexts. Specifically, responsive teachers watch their students as they read real texts and as they write texts for real purposes, observing carefully and monitoring progress closely so that they can make instructional adjustments and modifications, as needed, for students in all aspects of their learning and in all contexts.

A number of studies have considered exemplary teachers and their impact on student learning and engagement. Michael Pressley and his colleagues began a series of studies in the late 1990s that examined characteristics of effective literacy instruction in primary and elementary classrooms. Wharton-McDonald et al.'s (1998) observations of nine first-grade classrooms found that among other factors, effective teachers provide explicit instruction (both preplanned and impromptu), use extensive scaffolding, and encourage self-regulation. In other words, effective teachers are, first and foremost, *responsive*. These findings were replicated with a larger sample of first-grade teachers in Pressley et al. (2001). More specifically, effective teachers were able to match texts and tasks to each student's degree of competence. They provided texts that were just a bit challenging for students so that they would remain engaged and push the boundaries of their learning, but not so challenging as to become frustrating. Effective teachers also monitored students' reading and writing closely so that they were aware of the optimal time when students might need assistance. That is, those teachers who were most effective at enhancing student achievement were able to respond to their students' needs by providing just the right amount and type of support at just the right time.

In a sense these exemplary teachers adhered to the "Goldilocks Principle" (Gee, 2000). They did not provide too much assistance that would make students dependent on them, and they did not provide too little assistance that would make students frustrated. Instead, through their very careful observations of students as they read and write, and their ability to monitor students during those processes, they knew just the right amount of assistance and what type of scaffolding would help a particular student at a particular time. Gee's (2000) premise suggests that the responsive teacher draws on past experiences of that student's (and other students') reading and writing to determine just the right amount of scaffolded support to provide in a particular situation. Our past experiences combine with present experiences to help us take action, or make decisions, about which experiences are relevant and which are irrelevant in this particular moment. Through the process of sorting through past experiences, we eliminate ways to scaffold that are perhaps too general (e.g., this reader has a comprehension problem) or too specific (e.g., this reader has problems with gap-filling inferences) so that we can provide the appropriate amount and type of scaffolding. The danger with too much scaffolding is that the reader can become dependent on it and fail to develop into an independent, self-regulated reader. In addition, too much scaffolding may interrupt the flow of the lesson such that students are unable to maintain a coherent perception of the goals of the lesson (Wharton-McDonald et al., 1998). The danger with too little scaffolding is that the reader becomes overwhelmed by the task's difficulty, which leads to frustration.

Responsive teaching occurs throughout the instructional process. That is, responsive teachers make instructional decisions based on students' needs before the lesson as they plan for instruction (e.g., selecting texts at students' appropriate levels, identifying objectives), during the lesson as warranted by students' progress (e.g., explicit explanation of strategy, elaborated explanation of benefits of strategy use, model/think-aloud of strategy), and after the lesson as they reflect on student performance and the effectiveness of the instruction (Brown, 2008; Fullerton, 2001; Maloch, 2002, 2004; Rodgers, 2004; Smith, 2011).

Brown's (2008) study comparing the instruction of transactional strategies instruction (TSI) teachers to non-TSI teachers showed that TSI teachers used different types of scaffolding than non-TSI teachers. TSI teachers consistently mentioned a larger variety of comprehension strategies than non-TSI teachers, who tended to focus only on making connections to prior knowledge and predicting. In contrast, TSI teachers tended to refer to the entire repertoire of comprehension strategies (e.g., predicting, making connections to prior knowledge, summarizing, visualizing, and clarifying confusions). The type of scaffolding that TSI teachers provided during instruction also involved a great deal of explicit explanation of the nature of strategic processing (e.g., what it is, how to use it, where to use it, when to use it, and why it is helpful while reading), whereas non-TSI teachers tended to focus more on stating information without explaining the processing underlying it or the purpose. TSI teachers also verbalized their thinking via modeling and think-alouds more than non-TSI teachers, who never engaged in this form of scaffolding. Finally, TSI teachers encouraged students to verbalize their own thinking aloud and to elaborate on and clarify their thoughts about the text, and the way they were processing text, whereas non-TSI teachers tended to scaffold by asking readers text-based questions. In short, strategies-instruction teachers sought to scaffold and respond to the *process* of reading and constructing meaning (i.e., how readers are reading), whereas non-TSI teachers sought to scaffold the *products* or *outcomes* of reading and constructing meaning (i.e., what readers read).

Responsive instruction is action-oriented. That is, it occurs in the moment, during the process of reading. Thus, the type of scaffolding or instructional decisions teachers make during responsive teaching must cohere and be well aligned with the nature of responsive instruction. In other words, teacher scaffolding in responsive instruction must also be oriented toward the actions that occur while one reads, which means that scaffolding must be focused on the strategic or cognitive activity of the learner while reading authentic, continuous text. This approach stands in contrast to scaffolding that is focused on the products of reading, such as what the text means, or the type of scaffolding that might occur while reading words in isolation or contrived texts.

Responsive teachers seek out teachable moments as students engage in the process of reading; these teachers exploit those moments as opportunities to extend students' understanding of how strategies are used (and how they are useful) while in the process of authentic reading experiences. This is at the heart of responsive teaching: being planful before the lesson and reflective after the lesson, but most important, being responsive *during* the lesson to interject the right type of comment or question at the right time to help students become independent, self-regulated, and strategic readers (Smith, 2011).

Unfortunately, in their study of literacy instruction in upper elementary classrooms Pressley, Wharton-McDonald, Mistretta-Hampston, and Eschevarria (1998) found that fourth- and fifth-grade classroom teachers exhibited little to no evidence of some of the effective practices found in first-grade classrooms (as in Wharton-McDonald et al., 1998; Pressley et al., 2001) and in TSI classrooms (as in Brown, 2008) that reflect responsive teaching. Their study found that there was little explicit instruction in comprehension strategies and rarely were students encouraged to become self-regulated readers.

In order for readers to become strategic, responsive teaching must occur at all grade levels and with all students—not just in first grade and not just with struggling readers and writers. Given these characteristics and contexts of responsive teaching, getting it "just right" is not easy. It takes a self-regulated teacher who examines and reflects constantly on teaching and learning. Such reflection must occur not only about the students' learning, but also about her own learning

Research on teacher expertise has suggested that experts allocate more time to understanding learning *problems*, whereas novice teachers tend to allocate more time seeking different *solutions* (Sternberg & Horvath, 1995). For example, expert literacy specialists would use informal assessments such as running records and observations of student performance during instruction to help them understand and evaluate the problems a struggling reader has, whereas a less-experienced, or non-expert, literacy specialist would expend a great deal of energy seeking solutions to the reading problem without having a thorough understanding of it. Expert teachers (or literacy specialists) may be able to allocate more time to understanding a reader's problems possibly because their experience and extensive knowledge base frees them from tasks that are more procedural or "resource-consuming" (Sternberg & Horvath, 1995, p. 13). These expert teachers are able to conserve cognitive resources because their vast experiences enable them to see patterns in students' learning problems. For example, they may have worked with many students in the past who have had comprehension monitoring problems. The expert teacher draws upon those experiences, culls them into patterns, and sorts out relevant characteristics to guide decision making related to their observations and reflections about a current student. Expert teachers are able to distill thousands of observations and reflections into patterns to understand a student's learning problem. As a result, these reflections continually rachet up their knowledge and competence (Berliner, 1988; Sternberg & Horvath, 1995).

As such expert, responsive teachers observe learners, they are able to separate the wheat from the chaff, discarding unimportant behaviors and responses while discerning features and patterns of response that indicate each learner's current processing. For example, in their study of reading instruction expertise, Gallant and Schwartz (2010) found that novice teachers viewed errors as simply something that needed to be fixed in order to improve accuracy, whereas experienced intervention teachers connected these observations of student responses to the next steps needed for student learning and teacher instruction. These experts organized learner responses into meaningful data, finding and organizing patterns of responding. Specifically, "intervention teachers interpreted their observations in terms of concepts and strategies that link through meaningful patterns to future goals" (Gallant & Schwartz, 2010, p. 15). The examples of teacher reflections that follow may help to clarify how teachers get from Point A, observations, to Point B, linking of concepts and strategies, to Point C, the development of next steps or future goals.

In an investigation of teachers' collaborative teaching and reflections (Fullerton & Dunston, 2010) two teachers, Patty Grant and Rebecca King, collaborated in their tutoring of a child and reflected on the experience in a written log as well as in their discussions after daily lessons. Patty and Rebecca were concerned that their student, William (a pseudonym), had a tendency to get too bogged down with the details of the story and illustrations, and as a result, he had difficulty comprehending or formulating the meaning of the entire story (the "gist"). The teachers' initial attempt at scaffolding focused on his observed problem, recounting too many details to recall the story and not developing an understanding of the main idea. They zeroed in on teaching him to discern the main idea, but together, they quickly realized that their intended scaffolding had "leapfrogged" beyond William's current understandings. Their collaborative reflections led them to realize that they needed to use William's responses as the guide to next steps. In addition, they used the idea of "connecting the dots," along with a visual representation, to better help him conceptualize the task. As these excerpts from their reflection logs suggest, sometimes the design of the lesson and the appropriate level of scaffolding takes time to get "just right."

> Before reading, William was able to very clearly express several details he remembered from the story. However, when I asked him to bring those details into one main idea statement, he had a difficult time. . . . He continuously relied on recalling details instead of synthesizing what he knew to make a main idea statement. We will need to continue scaffolding this process in the following week.
>
> —REBECCA'S log

Patty, Rebecca's co-teacher, responded after a lesson she had taught:

> For chapter two William successfully pulled the important details for the two sections he read, whereas in previous lessons he wanted to name every detail. Thinking

> back to a statement you [Susan] made before about William needing to preview an entire new text to establish meaning for himself, I feel it to be truer than ever.
>
> —PATTY'S log

These reflections and their discussions led the teachers to recognize some connections, what William could do independently, and how they might use his understandings to scaffold and move him further toward what he needed to learn:

> Patty had already started a similar procedure on Monday and Tuesday, where she would stop William at various points in his new book and have him give her two to three details from the pages. After he had given details, she would then guide him . . . to create a title for the chapter in the book. . . . To take this process a step further, I wanted William to become broader in his details, so I created a dot-to-dot sheet for him to complete. On this sheet were three dots, labeled "Important Detail #1, Important Detail #2, Important Detail #3." William's job was to generate three important details from the story (one from the beginning, middle, and end) to connect those dots to show that the details were all linked, and then create a main idea statement from those details to write in the center of the triangle made [by connecting the dots]. For the modeled "Main Idea Dot-to-Dot," I first explained the format of the sheet, and then we took turns providing important details. I asked him to give me the first important detail, but he ended up giving me one from the middle of the story. Nevertheless, it was a good detail statement. We completed the rest of the sheet together as I continued to explain the process of linking details to make a main idea statement.
>
> —REBECCA'S log

Despite considerable analysis and reflection along with links to the child's ways of responding and understandings, initial teaching led to some scaffolding mishaps and approximations before Rebecca and Patty problem-solved, initiated a trial solution, and ultimately determined how best to provide clear and explicit instruction to William. Ultimately, they chose methods that made the task clear to William, helping him to "connect the dots," to arrive at the main idea. Each of these characteristics—being attuned to the child's feelings, knowledge, and current response patterns and ensuring that the child takes action and that each teacher move, as the scaffold is built, is tailored to bolster the responses and knowledge the child brings to the task—are integral to responsive teaching. Furthermore, when such reflections, whether written or verbal, are shared by teachers, the observations, analyses, and hypotheses about learners they contain develop as chains of reasoning (Lyons, 1994) that move understanding forward, furthering the expertise of teachers and increasing their capacity to assist learners. The collaboration and construction of knowledge discussed here have important implications for the professional development of teachers and for interventions within the overall design of RTI.

How Do Responsive Teaching and Strategies Instruction Relate to RTI?

Being responsive is at the heart of the premise underlying RTI, which arose in conjunction with the reauthorization of the Individuals with Disabilities Education Act (Public Law

108-446; IDEA, 2004) as a means of providing effective, evidence-based intervention for at-risk students, specifically targeting those with early reading problems (e.g., Johnston, 2010b; McMaster, Fuchs, Fuchs, & Compton, 2005; O'Connor, 2000; Vaughn, Linan-Thompson, & Hickman, 2003; Vellutino et al., 1996). As well, it has become an alternate means of identifying struggling learners. RTI is typically implemented as a multi-tiered approach to providing struggling learners with assistance. Often RTI features two to four tiers of instruction with the nature of instruction changing at each tier (Fuchs & Fuchs, 2006). Fuchs and Fuchs (2006) have also noted that the nature of instruction is typically varied on the basis of intensity of the intervention, its duration, the size of the group in which it is delivered, or the degree of expertise the instructors have.

RTI differs from previous frameworks for helping struggling readers in that it is intended to provide assistance *early*, when it is first noticed that the learner is not successful in typical classroom literacy instruction. RTI is in contrast with what Allington (2008) referred to as the "wait-to-fail" model or "discrepancy" views (McEneaney, Lose, & Schwartz, 2006) that existed previously. With the "wait-to-fail" model learners often struggled for years without receiving the support needed to be successful academically. This widespread oversight did not happen purposefully but by default because of the manner in which learners were identified as being eligible or qualified for additional support. Classroom teachers referred struggling learners to a school team, which then assessed their achievement level and their IQ. If a gap existed between the level at which the learner was achieving and his or her IQ, then the learner qualified for intervention services. However, if the gap between the learner's achievement and IQ was not large, then learners did not qualify for intervention services. Thus, struggling learners often remained in classrooms, sometimes for years, without receiving the instructional support that would have helped them be successful. As well, because the assessments used to measure achievement and IQ were typically standardized tests, they did not provide classroom teachers with specific information about learners' strengths and needs. That is, the results of these measures did not inform instruction, nor did they provide information about whether instruction was meeting learners' needs. Another inadvertent outcome was that linguistically and culturally diverse children were overidentified as needing intervention services (Klingner & Edwards, 2006), and many were misidentified (Fletcher et al., 2002).

With the emphasis on early intervention and alternate forms of assessment, RTI was intended to eliminate these distressing problems. The process for identifying struggling learners and providing appropriate interventions was deliberately vague so that schools would have the opportunity to use assessments and interventions that were appropriate for their particular students. In practice, readers or writers exhibiting signs that they are not adequately progressing in regular classroom or core instruction are referred to a problem-solving school personnel team that meets to recommend targeted interventions to support each student's needs in the classroom (Fuchs & Fuchs, 2006; Gersten et al., 2008). This team often consists of classroom teachers, special education teachers, coaches/interventionists, speech pathologists, administrators, instructional aides, and/or school psychologists. Ideally, the team identifies interventions that might help the struggling learner become successful, and those learners receive the help they need *right away* rather than having to wait.

RTI is intended to provide excellent classroom instruction that is more responsive to students' needs; however, early surveys indicated that instead of RTI being driven by classroom teachers and classroom instruction, special education professionals were being asked to oversee how it was implemented (Spectrum K12/Council of Administrators of Special Education, 2008). Three years later implementation has changed somewhat. In April 2011 Spectrum K12 School Solutions (2011) and several education organizations conducted an online survey of K–12 administrators to determine the degree to which RTI was being implemented in districts. In that survey 57% of all districts reported that the RTI process was a unified effort among general education and special education. Thus, after three years it seems RTI is more of a joint effort within districts than it was early on.

In its early stages of implementation, over 50% of all school districts in the nation did not have a defined RTI process in place and less than 25% of district staff had been trained in RTI (Spectrum K12/Council of Administrators of Special Education, 2008). More recently 68% of all districts reported that they were either fully implementing RTI or in the process of implementing RTI, 26% were either piloting RTI in a limited number of schools or planning to do so, and 6% were either investigating or not implementing RTI (Spectrum K12 School Solutions, 2011). However, although school districts have begun implementing RTI, initially they had difficulty developing the RTI process, which led to a number of frustrations.

In their descriptive study of four school districts implementing RTI models, Almasi, Edwards, and Hart (2011) found that the transition from a "wait to fail" or discrepancy model of intervention to the RTI model that relied on early intervention to meet the needs of struggling readers meant that school personnel had to move from a familiar, comfortable model to an unfamiliar one. This transition meant that as school districts were attempting to define and articulate their RTI process, they also had to implement it (i.e., building the plane while flying it). This left many districts scrambling to find adequate resources and materials. One quick way districts found to implement RTI was to rely on commercially published programs as their interventions. That is, in order to quickly operationalize the RTI process and implement interventions at varied tiers, districts defaulted to using interventions that were already developed. Thus, particular tiers were associated with particular interventions (i.e., particular programs) regardless of whether the intervention met an individual student's need. In other words, the districts used what Wanzek and Vaughn (2007) referred to as "standardized interventions" that are already developed and ready to use. These interventions have determined, in advance, which reading elements and skills will be taught, the order in which they will be taught, and often feature scripted lessons to ensure fidelity to the program. As well, they are typically of a fixed duration (i.e., a fixed number of weeks). Fuchs and Fuchs (2006) referred to these types of interventions as "standard treatment protocols" and described them as being affiliated more with research than practice. When standardized interventions are used in practice, a group of learners all receive the same intervention regardless of their individual needs. An understanding of instructional interventions that expects all students in a particular tier to learn at the same pace, at the same time, and use the same strategies in the same way removes context, variability, and diversity from the definition (Klingner & Edwards, 2006).

By defining the RTI process as one that relies on standardized interventions, the school districts in the Almasi, Edwards, and Hart (2011) study found that, over time, many students' needs were not met. They also found that districts were strapped in terms of available resources. Schools found that they needed more interventions (i.e., programs) to meet students' individual needs because the interventions they were selecting were standardized. These decisions led to strains on personnel and to scheduling nightmares.

Many schools found themselves using instructional aides or pulling any available teacher, regardless of area of certification, to implement these standardized interventions, which meant that the students with the greatest needs were being taught by those least prepared to help them. For decades research has been unequivocally clear that struggling readers are best helped by those with extensive training, expertise, and a vast understanding of literacy (Allington, 2008; Almasi, Palmer, et al., 2011; Gersten & Dimino, 2006; Johnston, 2010b; Mathes, Howard, Allen, & Fuchs, 1998; McCarthy, Newby, & Recht, 1995; Miller, 2003; Pinnell, Lyons, DeFord, Bryk, & Seltzer, 1994; Santa & Høien, 1999; Speece, Mills, Ritchey, & Hillman, 2003; Wasik & Slavin, 1993; Vaughn et al., 2003). Struggling readers are not served well when they are taught by anyone other than those with advanced training and certification in literacy education—even when a standardized intervention is used.

Standardized interventions are in contrast with what Wanzek and Vaughn (2007) referred to as a more "individualized approach" or what Fuchs and Fuchs (2006) referred to as a "problem-solving approach," in which interventions are tailored to capitalize on each learners' strengths and meet their individual needs. These interventions differ from child to child and cannot be implemented by using a prepackaged program. In other words, they are responsive. Strategies instruction fits within this approach in that it is responsive to each learner's individual strengths and needs. The International Reading Association (IRA) has been a proponent of the latter perspective, emphasizing that RTI is not a specific program or model; instead it involves responsive teaching and differentiation (IRA, 2010).

OVERVIEW OF DYNAMIC INTERVENTIONS IN A MULTI-TIERED FRAMEWORK

Typically, RTI features two to four tiers of instruction with the type, intensity, frequency, and duration of instruction, as well as the number of children in the group, varying within each tier (Fuchs & Fuchs, 2006). Those who view RTI as primarily serving prevention advocate for the importance of more tiers, whereas those who see RTI as a mechanism for identification and classification prefer fewer tiers (Fuchs & Fuchs, 2006). Along similar lines, some suggest that Tiers 2 and 3 should be designed to gradually increase the level of intensity as students continue to have difficulty; in contrast, those whose stance is prevention advocate for intervening early with intensity and frequency. In a three-tier model, Tier 1 is core reading instruction, Tier 2 is supplementary intervention, and Tier 3 is placement in special education. In contrast to this three-tiered model that often works in stepwise fashion, others have advocated for interventions that work together simultaneously within a four-tiered model (Dorn & Henderson, 2010; Dorn & Schubert, 2008; Dorn & Soffos, 2012), with the intention of intervening early but also providing more long-term interventions for those who need them. Within this section, we discuss RTI as a network that employs synergistic frameworks of instruction and intervention. Expressly, classrooms and interventions provide early, consistent, collaborative, complementary, and layered instruction to support struggling readers.

In spite of the high-quality instruction that may be present in particular classrooms, such instruction is not enough for some students. In those situations, progress monitoring indicates that classroom environments are unable to meet the needs of these specific students, and the school must respond with an intervention to change the trajectory of progress. Dorn and her colleagues (Dorn & Henderson, 2010; Dorn & Schubert, 2008; Dorn & Soffos, 2012) posit that problem-solving approaches must provide two waves of literacy defense—one focused on prevention by intervening early in grades K–3, the second in grades 4–12—for learners who continue to struggle and are likely to need longer-term interventions as they have become increasingly confused and unmotivated.

Underpinning these two waves of defense is a four-tiered framework that coordinates and integrates classroom instruction, interventions, and special education. Tiers 2 and 3 involve an early and fluid response to intervention rather than the three-tiered, stepwise models. Dorn and Henderson (2010) characterize this layered approach as grounded in Clay's (2001, 2006) theory of acceleration—"assess, intervene, adjust the teaching if the student is not learning" (p. 95)—rather than a tiered model grounded in remediation— "try this and if it does not work, do the same with more intensity" (p. 95). Instead, in a four-tiered model, there are several guiding principles:

- Intervene early!—before the learner's confusions become habits and the learner becomes frustrated or passive.
- Provide intensive instruction, possibly one-to-one or at least small-group, differentiated and tailored to meet the needs of individuals and that shores up processing with attention given to strategic activity or problem-solving strategies.
- Observe and assess systematically so that data-driven decisions can be made about the necessary characteristics of the current intervention and the need for follow-up (Dorn & Henderson, 2010).

These guiding principles serve as the foundation of two comprehensive schoolwide literacy improvement models, the comprehensive intervention model (Dorn & Soffos, 2012) and literacy collaborative (Biancarosa et al., 2010). These models emphasize differentiation of instruction and comprehension, with multiple layers of intervention made available for those not reading on grade level (along with intensive professional development and coaching for teachers). For example, classroom instruction (Tier 1) involves a comprehensive framework of differentiated instruction involving whole-group activities focused on scaffolded and strategies-based literacy development. Reading and writing are taught as reciprocal processes. Likewise, small-group lessons provide responsive teaching and differentiated instruction, guided reading and guided writing, as well as literature discussion. One-to-one time involves reading and writing conferences and interventions that support students who are struggling in one or more areas of literacy development.

In later grades, classroom literacy instruction builds in more literacy independence through approaches such as reading and writing workshop activities as well as literature discussion; increased attention is given to content areas, with strategies instruction woven throughout all subject areas. Moreover, the teacher provides additional assistance to those having difficulty. As an example, a student may receive more intensive one-to-one time in word study and in problem-solving strategies to use with unknown words, perhaps for a brief period after a small-group-guided reading lesson. The teacher may also increase the frequency of sessions with particular groups—for example, in guided reading groups, comprised of those who are struggling. Instead, or in addition, the teacher may meet with two or three students together, rather than a group of six, in order to maximize the attention given to these at-risk students.

In models that are synergistic, students receiving Tier 1 with differentiated instruction in the classroom are also receiving a small-group intervention (Tier 2) or a one-to-one intervention (Tier 3) with a reading teacher/specialist. Again, the purpose is to intervene early, with intensity, and to design interventions that meet the needs of individuals—" a child, not a group, learns to read" (Lose, 2007, p. 277). If a child does not make satisfactory progress after quality instruction in the classroom, and layered interventions (Tier 2 and 3) have been provided, a referral and special education placement are completed (Dorn & Soffos, 2012).

Again, more intensive instruction may be provided by the classroom teacher in Tier 1, and depending on the type of intervention in Tiers 1–4, instruction may be provided in the classroom or in a pull-out context. It is critical that a school and all stakeholders—teachers, students, parents, and administrators—share a common vision for core classroom instruction and interventions. Otherwise, there may be lots going on in classrooms and a number of interventions, but cohesion and integration may be lacking. As members of the school community move forward with RTI, ongoing communication, collaboration, and integration of instruction are critical. In the next section, we focus in more detail on sound classroom (core) instruction and how effective strategies instruction can be employed.

RESPONSIVE TEACHING IS FOUNDATIONAL TO RTI: WHAT SOUND CORE INSTRUCTION THAT INCORPORATES STRATEGIES INSTRUCTION LOOKS LIKE (TIER 1)

As mentioned previously, IDEA (2004) legislation identified two goals for RTI: (1) providing an alternate means of identifying struggling learners, and (2) providing responsive instruction early to students who may be struggling. Johnston (2010b) has noted that in some ways these two goals are at odds with one another because those who focus more on one than the other approach them in different ways. He noted that for those who focus on the first goal, the aim is "*identifying* students with LD [learning disabilities]" (p. 602). For these individuals RTI has a measurement focus and the goal is to standardize measurements given to students in terms of the nature and frequency of those assessments. In short, Johnston (2010b) noted that when RTI is focused on identifying students with LD, it is focused on "the qualities of the *student*" (p. 602) and measuring those qualities.

For those who focus on the second goal, RTI is seen as "a strategy for *preventing* LD" (Johnston, 2010b, p. 602), and rather than focusing on measuring students' qualities, the focus is on the quality of instruction provided to students. Johnston (2010b) further noted that an instructional focus emphasizes responsive teaching and assessments that inform instruction, which means that the assessments used within classrooms in a given school might not be uniform because different types of instruction require different types of assessments to determine the progress students are making.

In its position statement on RTI the IRA suggested that "RTI is first and foremost intended to prevent language and literacy problems by optimizing instruction" (IRA, 2010, p. 2). They further note that a successful RTI program "begins with the highest quality classroom core instruction" that is responsive to individual students. They also explicitly note that core instruction may not meet students' needs, which may mean making modifications to core instruction to meet the needs of particular students and to take advantage of their abilities.

Similar recommendations are offered by the IRA and the National Council of Teachers of English (NCTE) in their Joint Task Force on Assessment publication, *Standards for the Assessment of Reading and Writing* (IRA & NCTE, 2010). Standard 3 is particularly relevant: "The primary purpose of assessment is to improve teaching and learning." This tenet affirms that assessment must inform instruction to be considered valid. Thus, IRA and NCTE have recommended that RTI's primary goal is to prevent learning disabilities by providing optimal core instruction.

The notion of providing the best possible core instruction as a means of preventing students from struggling and of reducing the number of students with LD can often be in conflict with the perspective that views the primary purpose of RTI as identifying students with LD. This is, as Johnston (2010b) aptly noted, primarily because of differing views of assessment. Often in RTI frameworks assessments are viewed in terms of their purpose. Assessments tend to be used as (1) universal screening instruments, or (2) measures for monitoring ongoing progress. Universal screening instruments are seen as quick assessments that can be given to the whole class as a means of predicting which students might be struggling or at risk. The instruments that experts often recommend for universal screening tend to be those that are quickly administered, quickly scored, and quickly interpreted, which means that they are very brief (often taking only minutes to administer). These screening instruments can be administered to a group or to individuals, depending on the assessment. These instruments also tend to have high predictive validity, which means that the scores on the universal screening assessment (e.g., a 1-minute maze task of reading comprehension) can be used to predict how students might achieve on another criterion measure of achievement such as a standardized achievement test of reading comprehension. The intent is to provide teachers with a cursory glance of the class as a whole to gain insight as to which students might struggle academically in the future.

In 2010 the National Center on Response to Intervention's Technical Review Committee identified and rated several screening measures in terms of the degree to which they were reliable, valid, generalizable, and efficient (National Center on Response to Intervention, 2011). For reading, 12 screening measures were reviewed. These measures ranged from 2-minute brief screenings of oral reading fluency and word recognition that are administered individually (e.g., AIMSweb's oral reading subscale, Dynamic Indicators of Basic Early Literacy Skills [DIBELS] letter naming fluency, nonsense word fluency, oral reading fluency, and phonemic segmentation fluency subscales) to longer group-administered assessments of nearly 1 hour that included both word recognition and comprehension subscales (e.g., Gates–MacGinitie Reading Test [GMRT], Iowa Test of Basic Skills [ITBS] reading subscale). Each measure identified by the National Center on Response to Intervention is product-oriented. That is, each tends to measure the outcomes of reading (e.g., oral reading accuracy, oral reading fluency rate, comprehension) rather than measuring the processes of reading (e.g., strategies used while reading; metacognitive ability). Thus, these measures are not designed to inform instruction; they do not provide information that will help teachers design lessons to fit particular needs, nor do they enable a teacher to differentiate instruction to make it more responsive to a particular student. Instead, these measures are designed to adhere to psychometric principles (i.e., reliability, validity, generalizability) that ensure that they are administered and implemented with fidelity. This is the conundrum that educators face with RTI and how it is implemented. The methods that are valued in terms of the first purpose of RTI (identifying students with LD) require fidelity and adherence to strict psychometric properties. The measures that meet these criteria do not provide the kind of information that facilitates and informs the type of responsive instruction that is necessary to attain the second purpose of RTI (reducing the number of students with LD by enhancing the quality of core instruction).

In a classroom focused on teaching students to be strategic and on providing optimal core instruction that is responsive to students' strengths and needs, ideally such screening measures would be used to help teachers locate those students who might need more in-depth classroom assessment (e.g., observations, running records, informal reading inventories, think-aloud protocols) so they would know where instruction should begin. In-depth assessment enables teachers to gain insight into each student's strengths and challenges as a reader so that they can design, alter, and revise instruction to meet each student's particular needs. Process-oriented follow-up assessments such as running records can provide an abundance of information about which strategic processes the reader uses, when he or she uses them, and how he or she uses them. Such information cannot be obtained from measures used for universal screening because, again, those measures primarily focus on the products of reading (i.e., oral reading accuracy, fluency, comprehension) and provide broad-based information about how successful a reader is compared to other readers, rather than helping teachers understand the specific processes a particular reader uses while reading.

Instead, many schools use the screening measures as predictors of who might not make progress in the core program. Teachers then implement the core program and monitor students' progress over time. Those children who do not make adequate progress, according to the progress monitoring measures, are often targeted for Tier 2 interventions.

The National Center on Response to Intervention (2011) also evaluated progress monitoring measures. Several of the same developers (e.g., AIMSweb, DIBELS, STAR Reading Enterprise Assessments) that offered universal screening measures also developed progress monitoring measures. The key difference is that the progress monitoring measures enable teachers to track student progress over time to determine whether students are improving and making progress with a given intervention. As with the universal screening measures, the progress monitoring measures were primarily concerned with measuring the products of reading (i.e., oral reading fluency, letter naming, nonsense word fluency, phonemic segmentation), and very few attempted to even measure comprehension. Those that did relied on maze tasks as the primary means of measuring comprehension. That is, comprehension was measured by having students read a passage in which every seventh word was deleted. In place of the deleted words students were given a choice of three words and asked to select that which would best fit in the sentence. Students are given about 2 minutes to complete the task. As with the universal screening measures, these measures provide no indication of the strategies students use while reading and no specific information about students' progress that would enable a classroom teacher to revise or alter instruction in a meaningful manner.

The universal screening and progress monitoring measures that have come into widespread use for RTI are focused on fidelity of implementation and administration rather than on providing information that informs instructional decisions. This suggests that, for many schools, the focus is on identifying students with LD rather than providing optimal core instruction to *prevent* students from struggling. These schools typically use the same assessments or measures for all students. That is, they may choose to use the same screening measures and progress monitoring measures for all students—regardless of each student's strengths and needs as a reader. This would be similar to physicians using the same medical tests for every person regardless of his or her symptoms, or using medical tests that lack specificity (e.g., determines that a patient is not healthy vs. that he or she has high cholesterol). Schools that have adopted procedures similar to these are approaching instruction in RTI as a standardized intervention (Fuchs & Fuchs, 2006; Wanzek & Vaughn, 2007).

For those who approach instruction in RTI as a set of standardized interventions, selecting and using a core program means following it to a tee. That is, it is regarded as imperative to maintain fidelity to the program. During the Reading First era in the U.S. program, fidelity became a staple of reading instruction. The rationale behind adhering closely to a published program is that if the program is considered to be "research-based," then in order to attain the same achievement results as researchers, teachers must duplicate the instruction in the published program exactly without making modifications of any kind, including any changes based on students' linguistic, cultural, or ethnic background or their academic strengths and needs. Unfortunately, the practical aspects of implementing research-based instruction in real classrooms are often not considered. School personnel often don't read the original research on which the program was based to consider whether the students in the original research were similar in age, cognitive ability, linguistic ability, culture, or ethnicity to their own students in the school. As well, they often are unaware of whether the published program is actually similar to the intervention that was used in the original research.

In their content analysis of the five most widely used commercial core reading program in the United States, Dewitz et al. (2009) found that these programs do not provide the type of explicit instruction or the gradual release of responsibility that is foundational to comprehension strategies instruction (as is discussed in later chapters). Further, Dewitz et al. (2010) found these publications woefully inadequate in their attempt to provide students with the procedural and conditional knowledge associated with strategy use. These research findings are astonishing. They suggest that, even if classrooms followed these core programs with 100% fidelity, they would *never* attain the same results as were obtained in the original studies on which they were supposedly based because they simply do not provide the same type of instruction as was provided in the original research studies. Thus, adhering blindly to these core programs (as would be the case if one used the core program as a standard intervention) without altering or revising them in response to students' strength and needs would not lead to research-based results anyway.

For those of us who are concerned primarily with providing optimal instruction, we typically focus our attention on designing the best instruction possible and then adjusting and revising it to meet the unique needs of individual students. Thus, providing solid core instruction is at the heart of being able to provide responsive instruction to struggling learners. The key elements of solid core instruction are provided in Figure 3.1.

Classroom Teachers with Expertise in Literacy

The first and most critical element necessary for optimal core instruction is not a particular program. Instead, the key element in optimal core instruction is a knowledgeable teacher who has expertise in literacy (IRA, 2010; Johnston, 2010b). In fact, Johnston (2010b) noted that the Federal Register's (2006) final regulations concerning the IDEA of 2004 clearly stated that students who struggle must be taught by teachers with the requisite content expertise—both before and after the students are classified as disabled. This means that students, even during instruction in their core reading programs in Tier

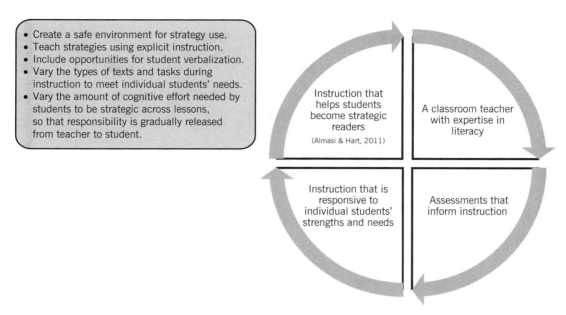

- Create a safe environment for strategy use.
- Teach strategies using explicit instruction.
- Include opportunities for student verbalization.
- Vary the types of texts and tasks during instruction to meet individual students' needs.
- Vary the amount of cognitive effort needed by students to be strategic across lessons, so that responsibility is gradually released from teacher to student.

Instruction that helps students become strategic readers
(Almasi & Hart, 2011)

A classroom teacher with expertise in literacy

Instruction that is responsive to individual students' strengths and needs

Assessments that inform instruction

FIGURE 3.1. Key elements of sound core instruction that incorporate strategies instruction.

1, should be taught not only by certified teachers, but also by teachers with expertise in literacy. Expertise in literacy goes beyond simply taking an additional class or providing one-shot professional development sessions in literacy. Expertise in literacy requires that teachers take extensive graduate-level coursework that is focused on making links between theory, research, and practice so that teachers are able to construct research-based understandings about how literacy develops and how to help those who struggle with literacy. Ideally, classroom teachers delivering core instruction (and interventions at Tiers 2 and 3) should have a level of understanding equivalent to a master's degree in literacy education. This level of expertise is needed to ensure that teachers are capable and knowledgeable decision makers. If we expect that teachers will be able to provide responsive instruction that meets students' individual needs, they must have an extensive knowledge of theory, research, and pedagogy related to literacy education.

Fuchs and Fuchs (2006) noted that, when RTI takes an individualized or problem-solving approach (rather than a standardized intervention approach), it requires a high level of teacher knowledge and expertise. When classroom teachers have extensive expertise in literacy, they are better able to provide core instruction that *prevents* language and literacy problems, which is at the heart of solid core instruction. Such expertise is particularly important when adjustments need to be made to core instruction to meet the needs of learners with diverse strengths and needs. As well, when schools rely on core reading programs—such as one of the five most frequently used programs in the United States, which Dewitz et al.'s (2009) study found to be woefully inadequate in terms of providing true research-based strategies instruction—then it is also essential that teachers have extensive expertise. Such expertise enables teachers to understand the flaws that Dewitz et al. (2009) noted and make adjustments to the core program to fill in the missing pedagogical pieces.

Assessments That Inform Instruction

The second element that is important for solid core instruction is to select assessments that provide information about *how* children read so that teachers can design, alter, or revise instruction based on students' strengths and needs. Although screening measures can be used to identify those students who might need additional (and deeper) diagnostic assessment and also to provide aggregate data about the whole class in a timely fashion (IRA, 2010; IRA & NCTE, 2010), they cannot provide information that informs instruction. Thus, the type of assessment that is critical to solid core instruction is that which will help teachers learn more about what their students do *while* they are reading. The assessments described in Chapter 4 are all appropriate for this purpose (e.g., observations, running records, informal reading inventories, think-aloud protocols). These assessments provide information that can help a knowledgeable teacher understand the strategic processes a reader uses (and does not use) to make sense of text. Once teachers have such an understanding, then they can begin to generate hypotheses (by using the STAIR method described in Chapter 4) about the type of instruction that will help the reader become more strategic. These hypotheses can be tested and evaluated by designing and implementing initial lessons. After the lessons are completed, teachers should reflect deeply on the effectiveness of those lessons for a particular child and make needed revisions or alterations to the hypotheses and future lessons. In this way assessment is an integral part of the instructional process in that it informs and gives guidance to the teacher so that the resulting instruction is responsive to the student—and therefore effective.

Instruction That Is Responsive

Solid core instruction must be responsive to each child's individual strengths and needs. When instruction is prepackaged or standardized to the extent that all children are receiving identical instruction, it is impossible to differentiate instruction to meet individual students' needs. Tier 1 instruction is not intended to be an initial "cut" at helping struggling students. That is, we should *not* approach core instruction as if we were "taking a stab" at helping as many kids as possible by aiming for the middle—knowing that some children will not be served well by a generic set of lessons provided to all students. In this scenario, those students who don't "get it" after a certain amount of time in Tier 1 core instruction will be "helped" when they move on to Tier 2. Instead, solid core instruction should aim to be responsive to *every* student, which means that the instruction must be differentiated and responsive. This means different texts, different tasks, different objectives, and different lessons, each uniquely designed to meet individual students' strengths and needs. Solid core instruction is hard; it *should* be difficult to implement, and it *should* be where schools spend the most amount of time ensuring that staff are well prepared to implement it, because it is the first place where we begin to prevent learners from struggling. To attain this goal, responsive instruction is critical to good, solid core instruction.

Instruction That Helps Students Become Strategic Readers

The final element of solid core instruction involves designing instruction that helps students become strategic readers. Teachers tend to misunderstand what strategic processing involves, and they therefore may not have an in-depth knowledge of how to help students become strategic. Instead, they focus instruction on teaching students isolated strategies (e.g., predicting, making connections, setting purposes) rather than teaching students to become strategic. As well, they focus on activities rather than strategies. Teachers may engage students in an activity, but they do not provide the requisite instructional elements to teach the *strategic processing underlying the activity* (discussed in later chapters). Very often the teacher actually performs the strategy rather than teaching students how to use the strategy independently. For example, a teacher may set a purpose for reading rather than teaching students how, when, and why they should set their own purposes while reading. Thus, students are not actively engaged in the decision-making process regarding which strategies to use and when to use them. As a result they do not learn to become planful, self-regulated readers who possess a repertoire of strategies to assist them as they read.

Studies have shown that teachers tend to do a lot of telling during their instruction, rather than modeling or scaffolding in ways that require students to actively participate in the thinking process (Taylor, Pearson, Peterson, & Rodriguez, 2003, 2004; Taylor, Peterson, Pearson, & Rodriguez, 2002). Taylor et al.'s studies (2002, 2003, 2004) also found that instruction that was more teacher-focused and that involved more telling than helping students learn how to take responsibility for learning was associated with lower reading achievement. Thus, struggling readers, in particular, are at a disadvantage in this scenario.

Chapter 2 provided an overview of designing such instruction so that (1) a safe environment is created to foster strategic processing, (2) strategies are taught using explicit instruction, (3) opportunities are included for student verbalization in instruction, (4) the types of texts and tasks are varied during instruction to an meet individual student's need, and (5) the amount of cognitive effort needed by students in order to release responsibility for strategic processing from teacher to student is varied in lessons in response to students' needs.

READERS WHO NEED SUPPORT INSIDE AND OUTSIDE THE CLASSROOM: SOUND INTERVENTION INSTRUCTION THAT INCORPORATES STRATEGIES INSTRUCTION

We have already pointed out varying perspectives related to RTI, but perhaps the viewpoint that has the best potential for bringing about what is most advantageous for learners is Wixson's (2011) definition: "RTI is best thought of as a comprehensive, systemic approach to teaching and learning designed to address learning problems for all students through increasingly differentiated and intensified assessment and instruction" (p. 504). In what follows, we use this definition as the lens through which to examine necessary elements of interventions within RTI. Whether intervening instruction is provided inside or outside the classroom, decisions that teachers make and approaches they select should be based on systematic observations of learners (Clay, 2005) and assessments that are authentic and ongoing. No matter which tier, assessments that tell something about *how* children read are needed in order to inform instruction (see Figure 3.1). Only through such process-oriented mechanisms of assessment and analysis can teachers ascertain students' current processing in reading and writing and the critical next steps that will move them forward in their literacy development. The key elements of sound intervention instruction are presented in Figure 3.2. Of course, some of these elements are characteristic of sound core instruction as well, but they are important to address in relation to interventions.

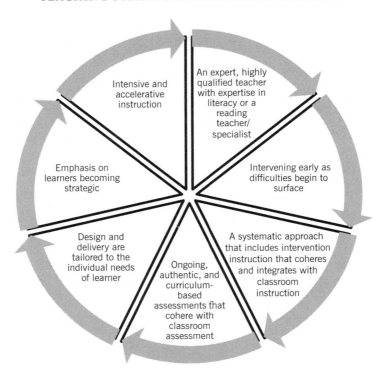

FIGURE 3.2. Key elements of sound intervention instruction that incorporate strategies instruction.

Interventions Provided by an Expert

Reading improvement is dependent upon expert, exemplary teachers (e.g., Allington & Johnston, 2002; Lipson, Mosenthal, Mekkelsen, & Russ, 2004; Pressley et al., 2001; Taylor, Pearson, Clark, & Walpole, 2000; Taylor et al., 2003). This is imperative whether we are talking about classroom or intervention instruction. Interventions must not be delegated to paraprofessionals or volunteer tutors (Allington, 2008) no matter how interested or dedicated. Additionally, just as with classroom teachers, expert intervention teachers must be supported within environments that promote ongoing professional development, collaboration, inquiry, and coaching (Fullerton & Quinn, 2002; Lyons & Pinnell, 2001; Rodgers, Fullerton, & DeFord, 2002; Rosemary, Roskos, & Landreth, 2007; Scanlon, Gelzheiser, Vellutino, & Schatschneider, & Sweeney, 2008; Vogt & Shearer, 2011). Without these supports, it is difficult to maintain excellence in intervention delivery.

Interventions Provided Early as Difficulties Begin to Surface

Earlier in this chapter, we referred to one of RTI's most important premises: assistance is provided early, an approach that greatly differs from the "wait to fail" (Allington, 2008) or discrepancy approach (McEneaney et al., 2006). We know that children who struggle in the early grades typically struggle throughout the grades (Juel, 1988; Stanovich, 1986). Intervening early has the potential to halt such cycles of failure.

According to Scanlon and Sweeney (2008), the research that helped to conceptualize RTI can be traced to Marie Clay's (1987) article, "Learning to Be Learning Disabled." Clay asserted that the learning disability (LD) classification may result because early instruction was not responsive to the learner's instructional needs. She cautioned that classification as LD must wait until instructional efforts have intensified in order to help the learner overcome learning difficulties. It was this view that served as one of the foundational principles of Reading Recovery, Clay's one-to-one intervention for struggling first-grade readers (Clay, 1985, 2005), later research related to Reading Recovery (Clay, 1982, 1993; D'Agostino & Murphy, 2004; Pinnell, 1989; Pinnell, et al., 1994; Schwartz, 2005), as well as other intervention research (Mathes et al., 2005; Scanlon, Vellutino, Small, Fanuele, & Sweeney, 2005; Vellutino & Scanlon, 2002; Vellutino, Scanlon, Small, & Fanuele, 2006).

A Systemic Approach Including Instruction That Coheres and Integrates with Classroom Instruction

Past criticisms of pull-out programs have highlighted the lack of congruence and integration of what was being taught in classrooms versus in supplementary or Title I/Chapter 1 programs (Allington & McGill-Franzen, 1988; Allington, Steutzel, Shake, & Lamarche, 1986; Bean, Cooley, Eichelberger, Lazar, & Zigmond, 1991; Johnston, Allington, & Afflerbach, 1985). Over time, what has become clearer is that this issue arises from more systemic concerns regarding the lack of communication and collaboration on common visions of what is most important in a school and for a child (Costello, Lipson, Marinak, & Zolman, 2010; Wixson, Lipson, & Johnston, 2010; Vogt & Shearer, 2011). Yet, "it is common for children needing the most careful and focused instruction to travel among several teachers and specialists, each with their own instructional predilections" (Johnston, 2011, p. 529). Such concerns continue despite decades of recognition that these practices are fraught with inefficiency and ineffectiveness (see Allington & McGill-Franzen, 1988; Johnston et al., 1985). Cohesive and integrated instruction in classrooms and interventions must incorporate a *systemic* approach wherein responsible and responsive professionals (teachers and administrators) collaborate and communicate to assess, plan, implement, and monitor quality instruction across classrooms and interventions (Dorn & Henderson, 2010; Dorn & Soffos, 2012; Lyons & Pinnell, 2001; McNaughton & Lai, 2008; Scanlon & Sweeney, 2008; Vogt & Shearer, 2011; Wixson, 2011).

Ongoing, Authentic, and Curriculum-Based Assessments That Cohere with Classroom Assessment

Just as there is the need for a systemic approach to instruction, there is a related need for coherence in assessment (Dorn & Henderson, 2010; Lyons & Pinnell, 2001; Vogt & Shearer, 2011). This does not imply a one-size-fits-all approach to assessment; rather, it involves a comprehensive, schoolwide endeavor that considers the assessment and diagnosis of individuals through a problem-solving approach within the broader context of the school (Dorn & Henderson, 2010). Within a systemic approach to assessment, administrators, teachers, and literacy professionals collaborate and communicate as they make decisions about assessment as well as the planning and implementation of instruction, particularly for those who are most at risk or struggling. School leadership and literacy teams (Dorn & Soffos, 2012; Vogt & Shearer, 2011), intervention teams (Dorn &

Soffos, 2012), and schoolwide or RTI assessment walls (Dorn & Soffos, 2012; Meyer & Reindl, 2010) support systemic approaches as well as schoolwide accountability. Assessment walls have been suggested as an essential component of data gathering and accountability. Individual students' reading and writing assessment data (gathered at designated points across the year) are placed on a card, and during specified grade-level meetings, teachers move students' cards to reflect the proficiencies of below, approaching, meeting, or exceeding that serve as headings on the wall. While accountability is one aspect of this process, this visual display's primary intent is to promote discussion and problem solving at grade-level and schoolwide literacy meetings. Assessment walls are placed in locations where faculty meet and work collaboratively (see Dorn & Soffos, 2012; Meyer & Reindl, 2010, for more details).

Both before and after interventions, assessments are administered to identify students who need assistance (initial or further), and, most important, the assessments guide the design and/or selection of the intervention so that it provides the best fit for the individual student (Dorn & Soffos, 2012). In addition, ongoing assessments are needed to continue to determine the student's changing strengths and needs and to provide feedback as to how the intervention is working; in other words, to determine the student's *response to intervention*. As we've noted here, as well as in Chapter 4, such assessment must be process-oriented and authentic so that those collaborating to support the child in the classroom and in intervention contexts may gain insights into instruction—ways to scaffold learning and design lessons that meet curricular *and* individual learner needs.

Design and Delivery That Are Tailored to the Individual Needs of Learners

The element of design and delivery of instruction directly hinges upon assessment that is authentic and process-oriented. The expert teacher knows what the learner knows. Without information that clarifies how a learner responds to various texts, tasks, and contexts, it is difficult to design and deliver an intervention that matches the learner's needs. When assessments are used that enable teachers to identify strengths as well as needs, they become a foundation for teaching that is focused on learners' strengths rather than on their deficits.

In order to use what is known about each learner as the foundation for teaching and learning, our assessments, observations, and diagnostic teaching must constantly inform us of what is an emerging understanding within the learner's knowledge store and repertoire of strategies as well as what is solidly understood or fossilized (Gallimore & Tharp, 1990). Expert teaching always builds upon what is known; the known provides the teacher with an entry point to teach what is new (Clay, 1993; Pearson, 1996). Thus, the learner's understandings become the foundation for the scaffolding that the expert teacher uses to assist and guide, moving the learner toward self-regulation and independence. This view of instruction is transforming for the learner, but also for the teacher. As the expert teacher searches for contexts and tools that take advantage of the learner's knowledge and success, further success is promoted, and a risk-free environment is created. As a result, it is likely that the teacher sees the child differently, as more capable. Attunement between teacher and learner is built from the scaffolding and supportive interactions, and the learner, as a result, is more likely to take an active stance toward learning and independence. In turn, the learner's theories of self are positive and efficacious (Dweck, 2000). What this description represents for classrooms and interventions is not a model built upon deficits; rather, it is a world of possibilities built upon strengths.

Emphasis on Learners Becoming Strategic

In the environment just described, the learning context promotes the likelihood that students will become increasingly strategic. As discussed in the section on core instruction, quality strategy instruction is explicit and scaffolded as teachers work toward gradually transferring responsibility for strategic activity to the learner while observing and responding to the learner's needs. The same is required of all tiers of intervention, but perhaps more so—the child must view the intervention context as safe, positive, interesting, and motivating. In the past, interventions have been characterized as focused on skill and drill. Such a concern speaks in further support of ensuring that those who are most at risk or struggling receive instruction from those who are most capable. A teacher who has become, or is learning to become, a strategies teacher is more likely to be concerned with figuring out questions related to what constitutes strategies and skills. Like many of the teachers who share their teaching in this book, they will explore the best ways to provide strategies instruction and work toward teaching learners to become strategic, understanding that it is not about teaching a strategy, but teaching the learner to become increasingly strategic in flexible and integrated ways. Such teachers will reflect upon what it means to be independent and self-regulating. Most important, in order for students to become independent and self-regulated strategy users, all elements of sound core and intervention instruction must be in place.

Interventions Must Be Intensive and Accelerative

What was once termed *remedial* instruction was not accelerative. Instruction was characteristically repetitious and rote, often delivered in a piecemeal, slowed-down pace. In contrast, the notion of acceleration is foundational to Clay's (1979) conceptualization of the intervention, Reading Recovery. "Acceleration depends upon the teacher's selection of the clearest, easiest, most memorable examples with which to establish a new response, skill, principle, or procedure" (p. 53). Specifically, when responsive teaching is coupled with carefully sequenced lessons tailored to the child's needs and responses, there is greater likelihood that the child will be able to improve more rapidly, in most cases, at rates that will allow him or her to catch up with grade-level peers. (Clay, 2005). Accelerative contexts are generally short-term, so there is an underlying urgency to the design of the instruction and the teacher's decisions. The teacher is cognizant that instruction must be constantly strong, goal-oriented, well planned, and well delivered because there is a limited time to assist the learner in getting on track, and the highly capable teacher is always mindful in this regard. The notion of acceleration coupled with short-term intervention support is in stark contrast to interventions or educational placements that span years if not learners' entire school careers.

As a starting point for identifying effective interventions, school personnel may want to explore the What Works Clearinghouse website (*http://ies.ed.gov/ncee/wwc*). Established by the Department of Education and its Institute of Education Sciences (IES), the resources at this site are frequently updated and offer educators information about intervention effectiveness. Exploring the site and using the information and guidelines within this chapter should assist teachers in an evaluation of interventions. Throughout this chapter, the goal of a comprehensive, systemic plan for RTI has been linked to the goal of strategic development in all learners, particularly those who are at-risk or struggle. In order to achieve this goal, we recommend that teachers and administrators develop schoolwide long-range plans for comprehensive change and growth, mapping out how the school currently functions, creating a needs assessment, and working toward instructional and professional development plans. (See Vogt & Shearer, 2011, for suggestions and examples.) Such self-study will identify the necessary steps to take toward incorporating the key elements of sound core and intervention instruction presented here.

SUMMARY

This chapter provided an overview of what is involved in responsive teaching, particularly as it pertains to strategies instruction. We defined responsive teachers as those who are attuned to every aspect of their students. Responsive teachers observe their students very carefully and monitor their learning very closely. As well, responsive teaching occurs throughout the instructional process—while planning instruction, while teaching, while assessing, and after the lesson during reflection. Teacher scaffolding in responsive instruction must also be oriented toward the actions that occur while learners read, which means scaffolding must focus on the strategic or cognitive activity of learners, rather than on the products of their reading.

The chapter then described connections between responsive teaching and RTI frameworks. In describing the history of RTI, we noted that it differs from previous frameworks for helping struggling readers in that it is intended to provide assistance early instead of waiting until struggling readers actually fail. We also provided an overview of what a multi-tiered intervention framework would look like. We noted that RTI frameworks tend to be based on either a standardized treatment perspective, in which all struggling students receive a similar intervention, or a problem-solving perspective, in which instruction and intervention are differentiated to meet individual students' needs. The problem-solving perspective is aligned with responsive instruction and strategies insruction.

We then described four key elements of sound core reading instruction that incorporates strategies instruction: (1) a classroom teacher with expertise in literacy, (2) assessments that tell something about *how* children read and thereby inform instruction, (3) instruction that is responsive to individual students' strengths and needs and provides appropriate scaffolding, and (4) instruction that helps readers become strategic. As well, we described seven key elements of sound intervention instruction that incorporates strategies instruction: (1) a highly qualified teacher with expertise in literacy or a reading teacher/specialist; (2) intervening early as difficulties begin to surface; (3) a systematic approach that includes intervention instruction that coheres and integrates with classroom instruction; (4) ongoing, authentic, and curriculum-based assessments that cohere with classroom assessment; (5) design and delivery tailored to the individual needs of learners; (6) emphasis on learners becoming strategic; and (7) intensive and accelerative instruction.

CHAPTER FOUR

Assessing Strategic Processing

O ne of the greatest difficulties of assessment is determining the validity of the assessment process itself. That is, how can we be sure that we are really assessing what we think we are assessing? When assessing strategic processing, the goal is to determine how proficiently the reader is using strategies as he processes text. But strategic processing occurs internally, mentally, and is not available for public observation. Thus it is difficult to determine which strategies readers are using, when they are using them, and how they are using them. The goal of this chapter is to introduce several forms of informal assessment that can be used collaboratively to provide an overall picture of how a reader processes text strategically.

WHAT IS IMPORTANT TO ASSESS IN STRATEGIC PROCESSING?

Consider the following scenario. Two fifth graders, Dylan and Sam, are given the same reading assignment by their language arts teacher:

> Read *Sarah, Plain and Tall* by Patricia MacLachlan. Prepare an essay on the following topic related to your reading of this story. Select one of the main characters (e.g., Sarah, Pa, Caleb) and describe that character's development from the beginning of the novel to the end. Be sure to explain how the character's traits evolved over time, why you think the character evolved in this manner, and, using support from the text, show that the character's appearance, dialogue, actions, or thoughts revealed that the character possessed a given trait.

Dylan is unhappy with the essay assignment. He would much rather take a multiple-choice test about the book. As he is reading the book, he remembers that when he takes a multiple-choice test about books, it always helps him to read for details. While he is reading, he decides to use a story map to take notes on the basic story elements: setting, character, problem, attempts to solve the problem, and the resolution. He reads the book in its entirety and then begins the essay assignment. He selects Sarah as the character to write about in his essay and uses his notes to help him as he writes.

Sam is also unhappy with the essay assignment because he too prefers multiple-choice tests. He decides that he will prepare for the assignment as he reads. He also decides that he will focus his essay on Sarah, since she is the main character. As he reads, he decides to use three character maps to help record information related to Sarah's appearance, how she talks, her actions, and her thoughts. He will use one character map to track her traits at the beginning of the story, one for the middle, and one for the end. He marks the page numbers where he located his supporting evidence on his character map, and he thinks about what type of trait Sarah is exhibiting, based on that evidence. When he finishes reading the book, he compares the three character maps to see how Sarah's traits evolved over the course of the book. He uses those notes to help him as he writes his essay.

Both students were given the same task but used different strategies for accomplishing the same goal. Which student approached the task more strategically? To consider this question more formally, recall each of the five characteristics of a good strategy user introduced in Chapter 1 and think about which of those characteristics Dylan and Sam exhibited in the descriptions above (see Figure 4.1). In each cell describe how Dylan and Sam exhibited strategic characteristics and use the figure to compare.

What kind of declarative knowledge about the task might these boys need to be able to perform it successfully? They would need to know *that* essays require a different type of preparation than other assessments. They would need to know *that* it helps to organize

Characteristic	Dylan	Sam
Possesses Knowledge Base: Declarative Knowledge (knowing that . . .)		
Procedural Knowledge (knowing how to . . .)		
Conditional Knowledge (knowing when and why . . .)		
Motivated		
Metacognitive		
Able to Analyze the Task		
Possesses a Variety of Strategies		

FIGURE 4.1. Comparison of Dylan's and Sam's strategic processing.

their thoughts before writing the essay, *that* all directions in the assignment must be attended to, and *that* essays require them to think across the entire text and use evidence from the text to support their claims. In this example, Dylan knew *that* the essay required some form of organization before writing it, but he chose to organize his ideas by thinking about all story elements rather than focusing exclusively on character development, as directed in the assignment. Sam also knew *that* he needed to organize his thoughts, but he chose to do his organization while he read because he knew that he needed to see how the character developed over the course of the entire book. He also elected to organize his ideas by using a character map, in which he could take notes about the character's dialogue, actions, and thoughts. Both boys were aware *that* they needed to do something to help them organize their thoughts about the reading, and each chose to organize their thoughts in different ways.

The two boys also differed in the procedures they used to accomplish the task. Dylan elected to read for details, take notes on story elements, select a character, and then use his notes to organize his thoughts before writing. Sam decided which character he would write about before he started and took notes while he was reading. He then used his notes to help him see how the character developed over time. Although the boys used different procedures, they were both able to accomplish the task—with different degrees of success, most assuredly.

Conditional knowledge informs us about *when* and *why* to use a given strategy. In this example, Dylan knows that he must take some notes to help organize his ideas before writing, but he fails to think about the conditions. He prepares for an essay in the same manner that he would prepare for a multiple-choice quiz. We do not know *why* he chooses to prepare in the same manner as for a multiple-choice quiz. Alternatively, Sam recognizes that *when* preparing for an essay, he must think in a particular style. He must gather evidence and then think across that evidence to see development in the character's behavior.

In terms of motivation, both boys note they do not enjoy essay assignments, but they both put forth effort to accomplish the task—though Dylan does not appear to put forth the same degree of effort as Sam. Had they been totally unmotivated, they would not have attempted to complete the task.

Metacognitive awareness would indicate that the boys were able to monitor their progress as they attempted to achieve their goal. It seems that Dylan may not be quite as metacognitively aware as Sam, in that he was unable to recognize that extensive note taking was a prerequisite to writing. Sam seemed to show that he was aware of his process and was able to monitor it by taking notes throughout the reading of the text.

Dylan's inability to analyze the task is his greatest weakness. He was completely unaware that writing an essay about character development would require more elaborative thinking. He did nothing to attend to the essay's requirement that he use evidence from the character's appearance, dialogue, actions, and thoughts to support his writing. Instead, he applied the strategy he used in another context—multiple-choice tests. Sam, on the other hand, showed that he was keenly aware of the requirements of the task and used appropriate strategies to help him achieve the goal.

We are unsure what other types of strategies the boys possess. We do not know whether Dylan chose to take notes on story elements because he did not know any other strategies, or whether he knew of other strategies but chose not to use them because they were too time-consuming (which would be a motivation problem). The problem could also be that Dylan knows about the appropriate strategy but is not able to analyze the task and does not know the conditions under which he should employ the strategy. This confusion would indicate that he is having trouble transferring strategy use to different contexts. While Sam used a successful strategy, we do not know whether he possesses a variety of strategies or only the one that was right for this assignment.

When we assess students' strategic processing, it is essential to frame the assessment in terms of the five characteristics of good strategy users so that we gain insight into them as self-regulated, independent strategy users. Using this gauge as an assessment tool enables us to examine the complete context in which strategic processing occurs. The next section describes a variety of informal assessments described in terms of which aspect of the good strategy user model each informs. Unfortunately, no single assessment tool provides all this information. We must use an assortment of authentic assessment tools and continuously collect information to gain insight through an interactive approach to the whole process (Lipson, 1996; Lipson & Wixson, 2008).

INDIVIDUAL INFORMAL ASSESSMENTS OF STRATEGIC PROCESSING

Assessment consists of two tiers: "internal assessment" designed for instruction (i.e., informal assessment) and "external assessment" designed for accountability (i.e., formal assessment) (Calfee & Hiebert, 1991; Valencia, 2007). Furthermore, both societal and political forces influence reading assessment, and awareness of these influences is important as we make decisions about the tools we use as well as how and when we assess (Afflerbach, 2007; Afflerbach & Cho, 2011; Valencia, 2007). Assessments designed for external accountability use a single index of student achievement that often stands apart from curriculum and instruction. These assessments are objective, standardized measures that provide comparison of an individual student's score to a normed sample (e.g., California Achievement Test, Terra Nova, Woodcock–Johnson Reading Mastery test). Such tests typically utilize a multiple-choice format and include subtests related to word attack, comprehension, and vocabulary. Formal assessments of reading are primarily concerned with the products of reading—that is, with how well a student performs in relation to others of the same age.

Unfortunately, the high-stakes environment associated with external assessment has permeated classroom assessment as a result of progress monitoring mandates. Theoretically, systematically tracking student progress is a sound endeavor, but all too often, mandated assessments have produced unintended consequences (Black, Harrison, Lee, Marshall, & Wiliam, 2004; Black & Wiliam, 1998; Valencia, 2007). Perhaps the most important is that these assessments do not necessarily promote student learning (Black et al., 2004). One consequence is that teachers become confused about the underlying purposes and goals of assessment and instruction. Black and colleagues (2004) identify this confusion as "formative use of summative tests" (p. 15). Adams (2011) shares a poignant example of such usage by well-intended teachers. In her account, she noted that a team of teachers asking for her advice did many things right to support an 8-year-old Haitian boy's English language and literacy development: They supported the child's language growth, they emphasized reading and discussing literature, and they attended to word recognition and comprehension. Yet, the teachers found that his language development was progressing, but his reading was not. In efforts to support the learner, they worked with him after school 4 days each week on decoding the nonsense words from DIBELS.

Ultimately, they brought their concerns about the boy's lack of progress to Adams. "Where they went awry was in using a test to teach," states Adams (p. 19). Unfortunately, such examples are increasingly common in schools. Given the emphasis on certain types of assessment within schools, teachers' confusions are understandable; clarification and knowledge of the uses and differences in assessments are crucial in helping teachers select appropriate and authentic assessments that will maximize learning.

Moreover, progress monitoring instruments frequently lack the specificity, flexibility, explicit and timely feedback, and engagement that are hallmarks of inquiry-based classroom assessments (Valencia, 2007). Such assessments are designed for instruction, often developed by classroom teachers, and are strongly linked to curriculum and instruction. These tools can be readily used by teachers to inform what they will teach and when. These assessments include performance-based, authentic assessments of literacy via observations, interviews, informal reading inventories, running records, miscue analyses, and discussion. They are used in conjunction with instruction so that assessment and instruction inform one another. Rather than comparing students' scores, the goal of informal assessments—assessment of learning—is to inform instruction so that students attain higher levels of literacy (Black et al., 2004; Calfee & Hiebert, 1991). We agree with Black and his colleagues' (2004) view of assessment:

> Assessment for learning is any assessment for which the first priority in its design and practice is to serve the purpose of promoting students' learning. It thus differs from assessment designed primarily to serve the purposes of accountability, or of ranking, or of certifying competence. An assessment activity can help learning if it provides information that teachers and their students can use as feedback in assessing themselves and one another and in modifying the teaching and learning activities in which they are engaged. Such assessment becomes "formative assessment" when the evidence is actually used to adapt the teaching work to meet learning needs. (p. 10)

Although formative, or informal, assessments can be used to evaluate the products of students' thinking (e.g., responses to comprehension questions), in this chapter we are concerned with those tools that inform teachers about the *processes* students engage in while they read. By using these assessments, we are able to gain insight into those covert thought processes that occur while students read, thereby identifying the types of strategic processing students do, or do not, employ.

As just noted, assessment of this nature must be a discursive practice that is intimately connected to instruction. Klenk and Almasi (1997) developed a model of ongoing assessment based on the work of Gillett and Temple (1994). A simplified version of this model is depicted in Figure 4.2. The three primary components are observing and assessing students, planning and implementing instruction with students, and generating hypotheses about students. The process can begin at any point in the cycle. Information gained from an assessment helps the teacher (1) generate an initial hypothesis about the student's strengths and weaknesses as a reader, and (2) plan and implement instruction to further support that student. Assessing the results of instruction can also generate hypotheses about the student. Thus the model depicts a recursive process in which all components are integral to one another. The remainder of this chapter describes informal assessments of strategic processing, as depicted in Figure 4.2, and describes the process of generating hypotheses about students' strategic processing.

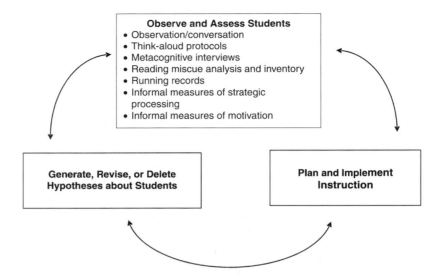

FIGURE 4.2. Model of ongoing assessment and instruction. Adapted from Klenk and Almasi (1997). Copyright 1997 by the New York State Reading Association. Adapted by permission.

Observation and Conversation

Lipson (1996) noted that teachers rarely use classroom conversations to gain insight into students' reading performance. Obviously, it is easier and more efficient to administer a test to the entire class than to take time out to chat with each individual student. However, the type of information that one gains from talking with students helps us understand *why* they are reading as they do. Think about the information provided in the example with Dylan and Sam. How did the teacher gather this information? It is possible that the teacher asked the students to explain in writing how they went about preparing for the essay—an excellent means of gathering information about strategic processing from a large group. However, the same information may have been gathered by simply chatting with each boy and jotting down a few quick notes (i.e., anecdotal records). Knowing how each boy prepared for the essay provides insight that helps the teacher understand the resulting product—the essay itself. It is likely that Dylan's essay would not be as well organized or address all of the required points that Sam's essay did. Sam's performance would earn him a higher grade on the essay than Dylan. However, without the knowledge about strategic processing, the teacher does not know why Dylan performed as he did and cannot adjust her instruction to meet his needs adequately. Responsive teaching requires teachers to identify the specific needs of individual students as well as the contexts surrounding their performance (Gay, 2002; Lose, 2007; Pressley & Afflerbach, 1995; Pressley, Brown, El-Dinary, & Afflerbach, 1995).

As we engage in our daily instruction, it is essential that we make time to record anecdotal notes based on our observations and informal conversations with our students. One method that some teachers find helpful is to carry a clipboard with 3″ × 5″ index cards, arrayed for her students, taped to it (see Figure 4.3). As an observation is made about a child, the teacher flips to that child's card and jots the note directly on it. Another method, perhaps easier, is to clip a sheet of white mailing labels to the clipboard and jot down observational notes for each student on an individual label. At the end of the day, the labels are peeled off and placed in each child's folder. Team teaching with other grade-level teachers, reading specialists, or special education teachers provides an ideal opportunity for one of the teachers to observe and make anecdotal notes about the students while the other teacher provides instruction (Klenk & Almasi, 1997). For example, one of our graduate students, Angela, was observing a student select a book to read for pleasure in reading clinic; she made the following anecdotal note:

> [The student] fumbles through pile [of texts] not looking at back cover or opening them [the texts] up to see text, but just glancing at the covers of a few, then grabs *Teen* magazine. [I then asked the student why she selected that particular text. She replied,] "'Cause I like reading about famous people."

Such informal observations, chats, and notes take on diagnostic value (Lipson, 1996; Lipson & Wixson, 2008). When reflecting on observations and conversations, it is important to consider which aspect of strategic processing is being revealed. That is, which of the five characteristics from the good strategy user model does this behavior inform? From Angela's observation, she was able to learn a bit more about her student's motivation for reading and her procedural knowledge about selecting texts to read for pleasure. She knows that her student enjoys reading biographical information and news about famous people of interest to teenagers. She also knows that the student does not appear to have a strategy for choosing texts, since she did not look at anything other

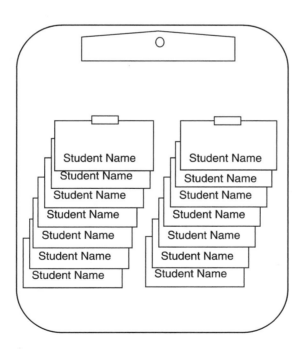

FIGURE 4.3. Using a clipboard to take anecdotal notes of student performance.

than the front cover before selecting one. Although these hypotheses are based on a very limited amount of information, they do provide a beginning foundation for ongoing assessment. Angela can now test her hypotheses under a variety of conditions to see if they legitimately depict her student's motivation and procedural knowledge for selecting texts. Without such information, she does not know how her student is selecting texts or why she is selecting them. She only knows which text has been selected.

Observation and informal conversation are potentially illuminating sources of information about the ways our students process text. As noted in Table 4.1, observation and conversation can inform every aspect of the good strategy user model. In addition to this methodology, Table 4.1 displays other types of assessments and how each is useful in relation to the good strategy user model. These assessment approaches are explained further in the remaining portion of the chapter.

Verbal Report Data

Another way of gathering similar information about a reader's strategic processing is to develop a more planned conversation. Such information is often referred to as "verbal report" or "self-report" data. Think-alouds, metacognitive interviews, and text interviews are primary ways of attaining such information. First the benefits and limitations of verbal report data are presented, followed by detailed explanation and examples of each type of data.

TABLE 4.1. Using Classroom-Based Assessments to Evaluate Students' Strategic Processing

	Strategic processing constructs (good strategy user model)						
	Extent of Knowledge Base			Motivation	Metacognition	Ability to analyze task	Variety of strategies
Type of assessment	Declarative knowledge	Procedural knowledge	Conditional knowledge				
Observation/ conversation	■	■	■	■	■	■	■
Think-aloud protocol	■	■	■	■	■	■	■
Metacognitive interview/text interview	■	■	■	■	■	■	■
Miscue analysis and Reading Miscue Inventory		■	■		■		■
Running records		■	■		■		■
Index of reading awareness	■		■		■		
Metacomprehension Strategy Index	■		■		■		
Motivation to Read Profile				■			

Benefits of Verbal Report Data

The benefits of using think-alouds and interview data are numerous. First, verbal reports focus more on process than product (Afflerbach & Johnston, 1984; Garner, 1987). Strategy use is a process, not a product, so this method serves as a primary means of obtaining information about how (or if) students strategize. The higher-level cognitive processes that are usually unavailable for inspection become accessible as the user describes them (Afflerbach & Johnston, 1984; Meichenbaum, Burland, Gruson, & Cameron, 1985).

Limitations of Verbal Report Data

The outcome of think-alouds and interviews depends on readers' capacity to talk about their abilities (Lipson, 1996). Garner (1987) noted several limitations of verbal report data. First, it is difficult to observe the workings of the mind with accuracy. As a strategic process becomes automatic, only the final products are left in memory to be reported. Hence, individuals either draw inferences about what they actually did, use their prior knowledge about what ideal readers would do, or provide incomplete reports (Garner, 1987). No individual has complete accessibility to, or is consciously aware of, all ongoing cognitive and metacognitive processes.

In addition, memory failure may play a role in verbal reporting (Garner, 1987). The accuracy of a verbal report is affected by the distance between the time the processing occurred and the time it is reported. This is not a problem for think-alouds, but it is relevant to interviews, which should be conducted as close as possible to an actual reading event.

Another crimp in the accuracy of interviews occurs when students describe useful strategies but, in reality, do not employ them as they read (Garner, 1987). These students typically have declarative and procedural knowledge about the strategy but are not motivated to use either. For these reasons it is important to use verbal report in conjunction with performance data to validate any emerging hypotheses regarding a student's strategic processing.

We must also be aware of the possibility that students often respond in a manner they think will please adults, so that what they say may not actually reflect what they do. In addition, it is important to note that our questions or probes may be leading, inadvertently cueing a student about more appropriate behaviors (e.g., "So, do you go back and reread when something doesn't make sense?") (Garner, 1987). When designing interview protocols, it is important to use open-ended questions and to minimize the number of probes (e.g., "What do you do when something doesn't make sense while you are reading?").

Finally, it is important to note that some young children have limited language skills and may not be able to respond adequately to questions or to communicate the strategies they are using to process text (Clay, 1998, 2005; Garner, 1987). In this case, rather than relying solely on open-ended responses, we must reduce the verbal demands by using pictures or letting them choose multiple-choice options.

These limitations should not deter teachers from using verbal report data. They are discussed to help us avoid the pitfalls that can occur without proper planning. The benefits far outweigh these limitations. As indicated in Table 4.1, the information gained from think-alouds and interviews, if done well, can shed light on every aspect of strategic processing. These benefits are further discussed as each type of verbal report data is explained in more detail.

Think-Alouds

Think-alouds are one type of verbal report in which an individual expresses everything that he or she is thinking while performing a given task. Think-alouds have been used as a method of inquiry in research, a method of instruction, and as a means of examining the cognitive processing that occurs during social interaction (Kucan & Beck, 1997). As a method of inquiry, think-aloud protocols are an effective means of assessing learning that go beyond traditional methods of assessing the products of reading comprehension (e.g., responses to comprehension questions, retellings, summaries). These protocols provide a glimpse of the way in which readers process text while they are reading (Kucan & Beck, 1997). Think-alouds enable teachers to "see" those strategies a reader employs, when she employs them, where she employs them, and how she employs them. Conversely, the protocols also reveal a student's failure to learn specific strategies (Bereiter & Bird, 1985).

The criticisms of think-aloud procedures are well known. The amount of cognitive processing that must occur while engaged in a think-aloud is extensive and can interfere with the cognitive processing it takes to read a text. Asking an individual to read the text *and* verbalize every thought that occurs to him while reading adds to his cognitive processing load. This cognitive load may disrupt or slow down the reading process (Bereiter & Bird, 1985). To reduce these limitations, Bereiter and Bird (1985) suggested that teachers model think-alouds for students in their everyday instruction and provide opportunities to practice think-alouds. Garner (1987) suggested that another way to reduce the processing load is to engage students in stimulated recalls, in which a portion of an audio- or videotape is played back so that students can then explain the cognitive processes in which they were engaged.

Think-alouds are relatively simple to employ; however, they are rarely used in classroom instruction or assessment. Any text can be used to elicit a think-aloud, although the selected text should probably not be at a child's frustration level. Garner (1987) suggested that think-alouds begin with general instructions such as, "Tell me what you are thinking as you complete this task" (p. 69). Initial directions can be followed with prompts and probes such as, "Don't forget to tell me what you are thinking about" or "Can you tell me more?" (Wade, 1990, p. 444). As the individual reads the text aloud, he verbalizes the thoughts that occur to him. These thoughts can be recorded on video- or audiotape, or the teacher can write them on a copy of the text as the student reads. After the student is finished reading, the teacher categorizes the data. A good beginning is to consider the data in terms of the five characteristics of good strategy users to see whether any clues are given relative to declarative/procedural/conditional knowledge, motivation, metacognition, ability to analyze the task, and the variety of strategies possessed.

Think-alouds provide valuable information about how a student reads text. Reading and writing conferences serve as a logical time to talk with students and collect such data. Teachers are able to see how a student processes text while he is actually engaged in the task. This procedure eliminates the problems related to self-report data, because the student is sharing exactly what he is doing while he is reading. There is no opportunity for memory failure or for misreporting.

One challenge that teachers often face, however, is eliciting this kind of response from the quiet or less verbal student. Some teachers have found it helpful to practice doing think-alouds with less verbal students by using puzzles and mazes before asking them to perform a think-aloud while reading. A graduate student, Eileen Ludwig, was working with a very quiet student, Maria. She explains her student's progress in this area as well as her own progress as a teacher of strategic processing:

> In the beginning of our sessions, Maria had an extremely hard time verbalizing. As time progressed, she became much more verbal. My goal was to get her to talk more about what she was thinking and doing as she read. Although [by the end of eight lessons] she still could not do this [successfully while reading], she was able to verbalize and tell me what she was thinking and doing as she completed puzzle mazes. I feel that using this concrete experience in the beginning of each lesson really made her open up and become more relaxed during the lessons. Since she was able to complete these puzzles, I also feel that this built her self-esteem and motivation. In addition, throughout lessons I modeled by thinking aloud what I do as I read. I could also see my own growth with using this procedure. In the beginning of instruction, I had a difficult time modeling what I would do by thinking aloud. As time went on, engaging in think-alouds became much more natural and comfortable for me [to use as an instructional tool].
>
> —EILEEN LUDWIG, reflective memo

Think-alouds are a powerful tool for assessment and, as Eileen has noted above, for modeling the cognitive processes that students can use during reading instruction. Think-alouds are difficult to use initially, but they quickly become an essential assessment and instructional tool. From the previous discussion, it should be clear that we value the use of think-alouds in classrooms, but we also think it is important to offer a final caveat: Teachers need to be cautious in regard to usage with *beginning* readers, bearing in mind the child, the context, and the frequency of use. Gaining insights into what learners are thinking and doing is critical, but as teachers, we must be clear in our understanding of knowledge *about* cognition as opposed to the regulatory processes that operate *on* cognition (Clay, 1998). For example, asking beginning readers to attempt to talk *about* reading *while* reading is likely to interfere with the cognitive processes that operate *on* reading. In other words, asking a beginning reader or a child who has extreme difficulties with reading to call up processes may actually interfere with fluency and the employment of strategic activity (Clay, 1998). In the case of beginning readers who are struggling, Clay (1998, 2005) has suggested that it may be more helpful to provide feedback or talk with the child just after a strategic action, drawing the child's attention to the helpful response or, at times, asking the child how he figured it out. Essentially, with effective acts comes awareness; thus the strategic actions of a child have the potential of becoming self-tutorial.

Metacognitive Interviews

Metacognitive interviews can be constructed to examine all five constructs related to strategic processing (see Figure 4.4). They can also be used to gain insight into student perceptions, print conventions, text handling, and purposes for reading. It is important that these interviews be just that—interviews rather than paper-and-pencil surveys. Many children are unaware of their cognitive processes and need to have all of their resources available to think about how they read. If they are expected to write about how they read, they might be inhibited by their inability to spell a word, or they may not be motivated

1. When you are reading, what do you do when you come to something you don't know?

   a. What do you do when you read something that doesn't make sense?

   b. What do you do when you come to a word you don't know?

2. Which do you like best, reading out loud or to yourself? Why?

3. Which do you think takes longer, reading out loud or reading silently? Why?

4. What types of things does your teacher have you do during reading time?

5. Do you like to read? Why or why not?

6. Do you read at home? How often?

   a. Where do you read?

   b. Do you read to yourself or to someone else?

   c. What types of things do you like to read?

7. Let's say the kindergarten teacher has asked you to help her during reading time. How would you teach a kindergarten child how to read?

8. Do you think it's important to know how to read? Why or why not?

9. What is a good reader? How could you be a better reader?

10. Do you ever read anything easy in school? If so, what?

FIGURE 4.4. Sample metacognitive interview, blank version. Developed by Beth Davey, University of Maryland.

to write all of the strategic processing that they really use. It is easier for children to talk about these processes than to write about them.

An example of a typical metacognitive interview is provided in Figure 4.4 (this one was developed by Beth Davey). The questions in this interview are intended to determine the strategies a reader uses during comprehension and decoding. In addition, answers to the questions also lend insight into a student's motivation, attitudes, and attributions related to reading.

A great deal of information can be gathered just by asking these simple questions. Take the case of Jason, a struggling second-grade reader who is 8 years old. Jason's responses to the questions on the metacognitive interview are shown in Figure 4.5. These responses provide information about how he views the reading process and the manner in which he processes text. While reading his responses, think about the strategic behaviors he uses. From the outset, it is evident that Jason may not be a risk taker or may have low self-esteem. He noted on two occasions (e.g., questions 1 and 1b) that he would seek help from an adult rather than attempting to decode unknown words on his own. He also noted in question 4 that he felt nervous when reading out loud. We know that Jason seems to value reading (question 8) and enjoys it (question 5), but he does not seem comfortable with the act of reading. This information tells us about his attributions and motivations.

We also learn about the types of strategies he possesses, his knowledge base, and his metacognitive awareness in questions 1, 1a, 1b, 7, and 9. In terms of comprehension, it seems as if Jason is not able to monitor his comprehension (question 1a). This is not an uncommon response for struggling readers. Sometimes when asked what they do when something doesn't make sense, they state, "Nothing, I just keep reading." Such responses indicate that the reader is unaware that text *should* make sense, which can also be an indicator that a student is too print-focused. This premise is supported by Jason's responses to several questions in which he focuses on sounding and blending (questions 1, 1b, 7). He also notes that the books in school are too difficult for him to read because the words are too big (question 10). This answer reveals Jason's frustration with the reading materials in school. If a text were at a frustration level, then it would make sense that attention would be focused on print and decoding rather than on comprehension. All cognitive resources would be needed to decode the words.

From Jason's comments we get a picture of a classroom in which this child is often reading out loud from texts that are too difficult for him. Certainly this scenario would be damaging to one's self-esteem. Jason does note that he makes images in his head while reading (question 5). Mental imagery (visualization) is a good comprehension strategy, and it would be worthwhile to see whether Jason truly uses this strategy when reading authentic text. Conducting an interview that is performance-related would be an important next step. Text interviews provide a framework for incorporating the insights gained from the metacognitive interview with performance data.

Text Interviews

Text interviews give students the opportunity to interact with texts as they think about how they read. To prepare for a text interview, select a variety of texts that represent diverse interests, genres, and ability levels—at least 15 different types of texts (narrative books, expository books, magazines, newspapers, etc.). Display the texts in an attractive manner on a table and then begin the interview process. Figure 4.6 displays a text interview developed and used by students in a master's level course. Several of the students

1. When you are reading, what do you do when you come to something you don't know?

   "I ask my mom or I raise my hand to ask the teacher to sound and blend. I make the sounds of the letter it makes pretty good."

   a. What do you do when you read something that doesn't make sense?

      "I never did that before. I don't know. Everything makes sense pretty much."

   b. What do you do when you come to a word you don't know?

      "Ask a grown-up what the word is. I sound and blend."

2. Which do you like best, reading out loud or to yourself? Why?

   "To myself because it doesn't interrupt people or disturb people. I like it to be quiet."

3. Which do you think takes longer, reading out loud or reading silently? Why?

   "Reading out loud. It disturbs me."

4. What types of things does your teacher have you do during reading time?

   "I have to read out loud one at a time. Then we read it again. Then we make a word. I feel nervous when I read out loud."

5. Do you like to read? Why or why not?

   "Yes, because if it doesn't have pictures I can make the pictures in my head."

6. Do you read at home? How often?

   "Fifteen minutes a day by myself."

   a. What types of things do you like to read?

      "Dr. Seuss."

7. Let's say the kindergarten teacher has asked you to help her during reading time. How would you teach a kindergarten child how to read?

   "Help him sound out the words. Start with easy words and go to harder words."

8. Do you think it's important to know how to read? Why or why not?

   "Yes, because then you couldn't read the newspaper and wouldn't know what was going on in the world."

9. What is a good reader? How could you be a better reader?

   "I have no idea. They write books or read a lot. I don't know."

10. Do you ever read anything easy in school? If so, what?

    "No. Never. They have bigger words than usual."

FIGURE 4.5. Jason's responses to the metacognitive interview.

Provide a selection of varied texts that represent diverse interests, genres, and ability levels.

INTEREST

1. What types of texts do you like to read?
2. Take a look at these texts. Have you ever read any of them before? If so, which ones? What did you think of them?
3. Do you see anything here that you would like to read? Why or why not?
4. Who are your favorite authors? What do you like about their books?

READING LEVEL

Frustration Level (Read Aloud)

5. Which text, or what type of text, would you like someone to read to you?
6. What types of text does your family read to you?
7. Which of these texts would be really hard for you to read? What makes it hard?
8. What do you do when you don't understand what you read?
9. What do you do when you come to a word you don't know?

Instructional Level

10. Which of these texts would you like to read, but think you might need a little help to read it on your own?

Independent Level

11. Which of these texts would be easy for you to read on your own? What makes it easy?
12. Which of these texts would you choose to read on your own for fun? Why?
13. Which of these texts would you like to read to a younger child? Why?
14. Which of these texts would you feel comfortable reading in front of your class? Why?

TEXT HANDLING/STRATEGIC AWARENESS

15. How would you go about reading this text?
16. What kinds of things do you do before you start to read?
17. What kinds of things do you do while you are reading to help you read the text?
18. What kinds of things do you do while you are reading to help you understand the text?
19. What kinds of things do you do after you read to help you understand or remember the text?

PURPOSE OF READING

20. Which of these texts would you use to find facts about _____? How would you go about reading this text?
21. [Select two texts of different genres] What is different about these texts? Which type of text do you prefer? Why?

CHARACTERISTICS OF STRATEGIC READERS

22. Do you know someone who is a good reader? If so, what makes him or her a good reader?
23. How do you feel about reading? Why?
24. Is it important to learn to read? Why or why not?

FIGURE 4.6. Example of a text interview. Developed by Angela Bies, Anita Brocker, Erin David, Renee Danielewicz, Sheila Ewing, AnnaMaria Figliomeni, Chastity Flynn, Keli Garas, Renee Guzak, Jill Hatfield, Bob Hirsch, Jennifer Izzo, Krista Jaekle, Eileen Ludwig, Jaime Quackenbush, Mike Rock, Kathy Sadowski, Donna Von Hendy, and Kristin Zahn (Spring 2000).

had the children bring in favorite books from home and texts used in school to supplement their collection. Students can also talk about the books they brought from home and why they enjoy them so much, as well as talk about their classroom texts. These procedures may provide tentative evidence of emerging strategic processes and can be further corroborated when used in conjunction with a variety of systematic observation (Clay, 2006) tools, such as running records and miscue analysis, which are discussed in the next section.

Systematic Observation Tools

When children are beginning to read, or when they are struggling to learn and must exert much cognitive energy for the tasks at hand, the strategic demands may be too great to allow explanations of processing *while* reading. Through the early work of Kenneth Goodman (1965) and Marie Clay (1966), tools are available that provide "windows on the reading process" (Goodman, 1973, 2009). Such real-time or "online" representations of a student's reading allow inferences to be made about his or her strategic processing through analysis of miscues (Goodman, 1965; Walker, 2012) and self-corrections (Clay, 1991, 2001; Forbes, Poparad, & McBride, 2004) made while reading aloud.

Miscue Analysis and the Reading Miscue Inventory

Miscue analysis is an uncommon example of a tool, initially conceived for research (Goodman, 2009), which became an important inquiry-based assessment and instructional tool with which to study the reading process. Goodman (2009) credits his wife Yetta, who completed one of the early investigations, a longitudinal study of six beginning readers (Goodman, 1971, as cited in Goodman, 2009). Subsequently, the protocol for research transitioned into a classroom assessment, the Reading Miscue Inventory (RMI), coauthored with colleagues Watson and Burke (Goodman & Burke, 1972; Goodman, Watson, & Burke, 1987, 2005). Their work in miscue analysis has influenced numerous other assessments, particularly informal reading inventories (e.g., Qualitative Reading Inventory) that are used to determine instructional levels and strategic processing. Although the RMI has been used extensively in research settings (see Brown, Goodman, & Marek, 1996), and its theoretical base has been quite influential, it has not gained as much widespread classroom usage because of its complexity (Reutzel & Cooter, 2011).

Miscue analysis is a means by which teachers can evaluate and interpret the significance of a reader's miscues in relation to the context of the passage being read orally. The underlying theoretical assumption is that readers' miscues are not random but are cued by sources of information (meaning/semantic, language structure/syntactic, visual/graphophonic) that readers use to process text. To conduct a miscue analysis, an actual text or portion of text is photocopied or typed. As a student reads orally, codes are annotated directly on the text, serving as a reading record that is then analyzed. Such reading records and analyses are often included in a variety of commercial assessment programs, but are only part of what was originally conceptualized as the RMI.

In the RMI, a reading passage or text is selected that is of appropriate length and difficulty to provide at least 25 miscues. The reader reads orally while the reading is tape-recorded. After reading, the learner is also required to provide a retelling. All miscues are marked and subsequently, substitution miscues are coded and then analyzed based on semantic/meaning, syntactic/language structure, and visual/graphophonic similarities.

Patterns of miscues are interpreted in order to guide instruction. Errors that are semantically the same, or meaning-based, are "better" errors than those that change the meaning. The student's retelling is also scored and analyzed.

Lipson and Wixson (2008) have noted problems with the RMI. First, it privileges meaning-changing errors, and as a result, the assessment may not provide enough attention to word analysis difficulties that are concerns for younger, beginning readers or those who are struggling. Furthermore, materials that are advocated in the procedures of the RMI may be beyond the instructional level of text and may result in reading efforts that are at the frustration level. Finally, Lipson and Wixson identify similar concerns noted by Reutzel and Cooter (2011), that the administration and scoring are complex and time-consuming. Given the constraints of this assessment, Reutzel and Cooter suggest that running records may be more practical for classroom use.

Running Records

Running records provide a record of what young readers do and say while reading continuous texts. Once the record is taken, the teacher can review the child's oral reading and make on-the-spot teaching decisions as well as using it as a guide to plan future lessons (Clay, 2006). In order to take a running record, all that is needed is a text, paper, and a pencil, although teachers may choose to use Clay's running record sheet in *An Observation Survey* (2006, pp. 80–81) to record responses. To assist with record keeping, some teachers insert each regularly documented running record assessment in notebooks tabbed with children's names to facilitate analysis of changes in strategic processing over time.

Running records may serve two functions: (1) They may assess text difficulty—whether a text that the learner is reading is at an appropriate level of difficulty (easy, instructional, or hard). In other words, the running record may facilitate selection of an appropriate text. (2) They may be used as a guide to monitor a learner's progress, including his or her problem-solving and strategic activity while reading. To determine the strategies a reader is using while reading, within a guided reading or strategy lesson for example, the teacher will most likely choose to assess after a text is read once by the reader, often the day after the text was introduced and the child completed the first reading with teacher support. It may be particularly helpful to compare two or more running records taken across a few days or within a few weeks to analyze a student's changes in processing.

Often teachers may use running records as a means of determining a student's reading level at designated times of the year. Some schools or districts adopt published "benchmark" systems that incorporate running records to determine the reading levels of students. These commercially produced kits include text passages or little books to assess students at a wide range of levels. In some, a reading record (modified running record that is coded on a printed copy of the text) is followed by comprehension questions and/or retellings. In some classrooms, teachers use leveled texts to take running records of children's reading, usually followed by questions and a retelling. All texts are unseen texts, also referred to as "cold" reads, with students having had no previous exposure to the reading material. A limited introduction should be provided, however. Typically the text or text portion is fairly brief, no more than 150–200 words (perhaps as little as 100 words for a beginning reader).

What is often missing from commercial kits is continuous, ongoing assessment. In the original conceptualization of running records, they were seen as providing regular, ongoing, systematic assessment of learners' strategic processing. Assessing only at the beginning, middle, and end of the year offers limited information to guide daily instruction.

CODING AND SCORING RUNNING RECORDS

Although the conventions for coding a running record versus a miscue analysis are somewhat different, both use similar terms for oral reading responses. Figure 4.7 presents reading behaviors, conventions (notations) for coding a running record, and the description of each behavior. *Omissions* occur when the reader skips a word, several words, parts of words, a sentence, or an entire page. *Insertions* occur when an extra word (or words) is inserted in the text. Usually these errors are not significant. Good readers will often insert a word here or there to make the text more fluent or more meaningful. However, a reader who inserts words consistently may be overrelying on background knowledge to read rather than attending to the print. *Substitutions* occur when an incorrect word is substituted for the word in the text (e.g., substituting *house* for *home*). Substitutions provide evidence of the types of information or cues that the reader is using. When substitutions result in nonwords (e.g., pronouncing *corner* as *karmra*), such errors suggest that the reader is neglecting to gather meaning and language to aid in the processing of the text and instead is searching for information primarily at the word level using only letter–sound correspondences. *Repetitions* (rereading) of a word or phrase often occur as a part of monitoring, searching/gathering information, and problem solving. For example, a reader may monitor her reading, recognizing that she has incorrectly read a word, and she may return to the beginning of a sentence or previous phrase to gather meaning or syntactic information to assist in problem solving. In other words, she cross-checks contextual information (meaning and/or structure) with print/visual information, potentially resulting in a self-correction. In some instances, repetition occurs when the reading is dysfluent, and the reader rereads to maintain fluency and meaning. Repetitions may also occur, sometimes frequently, when the process "stalls," and the reader has recognized that he does not know how to proceed. This is the first step toward improvement, because the reader has at least recognized that he does not know a word, signaling monitoring in its most basic form, and the teacher then has opportunities to teach the child how to problem-solve unknown words. In essence, repetitions signal important evidence of particular reading behaviors of the learner as well as implications for the teacher's responses and decision making.

Once a running record is coded, the teacher scores it to determine an accuracy rate (also see Clay, 2006). The formula below is used to calculate accuracy. The number of errors made by the reader is indicated by *E*, and the number of running words read from the text is indicated by *RW* (Clay, 2006).

$$100 - \frac{E}{RW} \times \frac{100}{1}$$

Using running records to determine easy, instructional, and hard levels of text provides teachers with a clear summary of strengths and weaknesses through an analysis of the number and type of word recognition and comprehension errors that occur across a range of texts. Figure 4.8 summarizes the three levels of reading based on text difficulty. Note that these levels represent how the text was read by a particular child rather than the level of the text itself. Texts that are used for instruction should be within the learner's

Reading Behavior	Coding Convention	Description of Behavior
Accurate reading	✓	The word is read correctly.
Substitution (incorrect response)	<u>bone</u> reader's response ball text	The reader's incorrect response is on the top. The word in the text is on the bottom. In this example, the reader said the word *bone* instead of *ball*.
Omission	$\frac{-}{\text{the}}$	The reader omitted the word *the* in the text.
Insertion	$\frac{\underline{the}}{-}$	The reader inserted the word *the*, which was not in the text.
Repetition	R ✓✓ <u>bone</u> R ball	The line indicates where the repetition (rereading) started. In some cases, only one word is repeated, indicated with the R. Repetitions are noted, but are not errors. In the example, there is also a substitution.
Appeal You try it Told Appeal/You try it/Told	A Y T — | A | |— | There | | Y| | T	The reader does not attempt a word and may indicate to the teacher that he or she does not know the word or will not proceed (indicated by *A* for *appeal*). The teacher's initial response is "You try it" (indicated by *Y*), but if the reader is unable to proceed or responds incorrectly, the teacher provides a "told" (indicated by a *T*). Note that learner responses are recorded on the top and that teacher responses or what is represented in the text is on the bottom, below the line.
Self-correction	SC <u>bone</u> | SC ball |	The reader initially read/stated *bone* for the word *ball* in the text, but immediately self-corrected by reading the word in the text, *ball*.
Teacher's Scoring and Analysis (The teacher first scores errors and self-corrections, then analyzes them.)	**Scoring and Analysis Convention**	**Explanation**
Error	E	The reader's response was incorrect and scored as an error (unless subsequently self-corrected).
Self-correction	SC	The reader initially misread but then self-corrected. A self-correction is not coded as an error.

(cont.)

FIGURE 4.7. Reading behaviors, scoring, coding, and analysis conventions for running records.

Meaning	M	The meaning of the text (up to the error) influenced the reader's response.
Structure/Syntax	S	The syntax (up to the error) influenced the reader's response.
Visual/Print Information (letters or word)	V	The visual/print information influenced the reader's response.

FIGURE 4.7. *(cont.)*

instructional range; in other words, the instructional range indicates that this particular child can learn with instructional support at this level. Because the running record contains errors, it indicates evidence of problem solving (Clay, 2006). When a running record shows a child is reading a text within the easy range, the reading suggests that this is a level of text that the child can process (problem-solve) easily and independently without instructional support. When the reading is hard, or too difficult, it is at the frustrational level, and it is unlikely that productive problem solving can occur, and the reading process will not come together for the learner.

Figure 4.9 is an example of a running record. The number of running words—in this case, the entire text of *Along Comes Jake* (Cowley, 1996)—is 86 words. (Note that in beginning texts, the number of words in the entire text may be fewer than 100 words.) The number of errors that William, a first-grade reader, made while reading is 7. These numbers are placed into the formula.

$$100 - \frac{7}{86} \times \frac{100}{1} = 91\%$$

William read *Along Comes Jake* at 91% accuracy, making 7 errors in 86 words. Although the text is within an instructional range (above 90%), it does not indicate a high level of monitoring during reading. In fact, there was only one self-correction during the reading. The self-correction ratio is determined by the following formula:

$$\frac{SC}{E + SC}$$

Easy (Independent)	95–100% accuracy	The reader can learn and process text independently at this level.
Instructional	90–94% accuracy	The reader can learn and process text with instructional support at this level.
Hard (Frustration)	Below 90% accuracy	The reader is unlikely to learn and process text, even with support, at this level.

FIGURE 4.8. Levels of reading based on text difficulty.

Given the example of the child's reading in Figure 4.9, the numbers placed within the formula would be

$$\frac{1}{7 + 1} = 1:8$$

To determine whether the self-correction ratio is within an effective level of processing, it is helpful to consider that the closer the ratio is to one, the better. Therefore, a ratio of 1:8 again suggests that William is not monitoring his reading. A closer analysis of his running record may help to explain what is occurring as he reads. (For additional information about scoring running records, see Clay, 2006.)

ANALYSIS OF RUNNING RECORDS

As indicated in the example in Figure 4.9, William read the first two pages of text accurately. On page 4, he substituted *paint* for *painting*. When analyzing his processing, the teacher circled M (meaning), S (structure), and V (visual/graphophonic) in the error analysis column, indicating that his substitution was a close approximation of the word—he substituted a word that closely corresponded to the meaning, structure, and visual/print information of the word in the text. When William's teacher analyzed the sources of information used for the other substitutions, she found that he was consistent in using meaning and structure in his attempts, but that with the exception of the self-correction, he neglected the visual or print information. In other words, in almost all cases, he did not monitor or notice that the print information did not correspond to what he'd said. After analyzing the errors and self-corrections, William's teacher wrote a brief summary of his strengths, needs, and next steps:

> William is consistently using the illustrations and meaning along with the language to help him process text. He neglects the visual or print information indicating that he does not notice when there is a mismatch between the print and what he is saying. His self-correction on page 11 confirms what was noted in the last running record—he is able to notice or monitor with known words such as *Mom* for *Dad*. However, his errors indicate that he is not monitoring and checking the meaning and language that he uses against the visual/print information. I need to help him notice that his attempt does not look right!

If this were a text at the earliest reading levels, his teacher might be satisfied with the substitutions that William is making since he is using meaning, but at this point in his learning, his teacher knows that without closer attention to the print, he cannot make sufficient progress in building a proficient processing system. In fact, after William finished reading, the teacher went back to the substitution on page 8, praised him for thinking about the story and what made sense, while also reminding him, "There are other ways to check. A word needs to makes sense *and* look right." She then guided him in an examination of *cleaning/bathroom* and offered an opportunity for William to apply what she had just discussed by returning to page 11: "Now, just like you did on that other page, read this sentence and make sure everything makes sense *and* looks right" (referring to the substitution of *bricks* for *wood*).

Child: William

Date:

Teacher: Susan

Text: *Along Comes Jake   86 running words   Fountas & Pinnell level C/Reading Recovery level 6*
Publisher: Sunshine series, Wright Group/McGraw Hill

Page	Text	Coding	Scoring		Analysis	
			E	SC	E MSV	SC MSV
2	Ben helps Anne with the laundry.	✓✓✓ ✓✓✓				
3	Anne helps Dad with the garden.	✓✓✓ ✓✓✓				
4	Ben helps Mom with the painting.	✓✓✓ ✓✓ paint⁄painting	1		(M) (S) V	
5	And then along comes Jake!	✓ R —⁄then | ✓✓✓⁄T	1			
6	Mom helps Dad with the car.	✓✓✓ ✓✓✓				
7	Dad helps Ben with the washing.	✓✓✓ ✓✓✓				
8	Anne helps Mom with the bathroom.	✓✓✓ ✓✓ cleaning⁄bathroom	1		(M) (S) V	

#	Text	Record	E	SC
9	And then along comes Jake!	✓ — ✓✓R✓ <u>then</u>	1	
10	Ben helps Dad with the windows.	✓✓✓ ✓✓✓		
11	Dad helps Mom with the wood.	Mom | SC ✓✓✓ Dad | ✓✓ <u>bricks</u> / wood	1	Ⓜ Ⓢ v Ⓜ Ⓢ v
12	Mom helps Ben with the bike.	✓✓✓ ✓✓✓		
13	And then along comes Jake!	✓ — ✓✓✓ <u>then</u>	1	
14	Dad helps Anne with the shopping.	✓✓✓ ✓✓ <u>groceries</u> / shopping	1	Ⓜ Ⓢ v
15	Mom helps Ben with the cooking.	✓✓✓ ✓✓✓		
16	And then along comes Jake!	✓ — ✓✓✓ <u>then</u>	1	M S Ⓥ

FIGURE 4.9. Example of William's running record of *Along Comes Jake* with scoring and analysis.

After the running record, the teacher's attention was focused on teaching for strategies. Another less productive option would have been to return to his omission of the word *then*, but such a decision would have focused on word-level accuracy rather than strategic activity. Closer scrutiny of William's reading suggests that on page 9, he may have used his recall of the repetitious language to say, "And along comes Jake." His reading on this page maintained the meaning and the syntax, but he also noticed near the end that something wasn't right, perhaps in relation to one-to-one matching. However, when he reread, perhaps in an attempt to correct, he omits the word again. His response, as well as the subsequent omissions of the same word, suggests that William had monitored the first time around, recognizing that he did not know the word when he reread. As a result, rather than sit and passively wait for the teacher to tell him the word, he made the strategic decision to use meaning and structure to maintain fluency and keep his reading going. Such a response from the learner suggests a sense of agency, engagement, and independence as well as the likelihood of future strategy use.

At some other point, after recording that the word is unknown, the teacher will likely incorporate it into a word work activity and/or in a future book selection and introduction. As the teacher continues to work with William during small-group instruction, she will keep track of progress in regard to monitoring and select appropriate texts that ensure opportunities for William and the other children in his group to practice the strategic behavior of cross-checking cues, one against another, eventually leading to integration of information and more efficient processing. Thus, running records offer instructional opportunities immediately after their completion, through the teacher's carefully selected teaching points matched to the student's current problem solving (as illustrated by William's teacher); running records also serve as a powerful tool to determine whether texts and teaching (e.g., book introductions, scaffolding, and prompts) are resulting in learning. (For more information about teaching points and prompting, see Fountas & Pinnell, 1996, 2006; Johnson & Keier, 2010).

Informal Reading Inventory

Another assessment option is the use of an informal reading inventory (IRI). Much like running records, an IRI is used to determine the student's independent, instructional, and frustrational reading level for oral and silent reading. An IRI consists of a series of graded reading passages that range in difficulty from emergent reading (preprimer) to eighth grade. Students read word lists to determine at which level oral reading should begin. Then they are asked to read a passage at that level orally. During the oral reading, the teacher records the student's miscues. Following oral reading, the student is told to retell the passage and then asked several comprehension questions to determine the comprehension level. Based on the student's performance, the teacher administers other passages of either higher or lower levels to determine the student's independent (i.e., level at which the student can read fluently with good comprehension), instructional (i.e., level at which the student experiences a bit of stress while reading), and frustrational (i.e., level at which the student is unsuccessful with decoding and comprehension) reading levels. Examples of commercially prepared IRIs include the Basic Reading Inventory (Johns, 1993) and the Qualitative Reading Inventory (Leslie & Caldwell, 2011). Additional information is gained by conducting a miscue analysis to determine the learner's use of cues and strategies.

Beginning-of-the-year and end-of-the-year assessments to determine students' level of reading have become much more commonplace in classrooms. Yet, we would point out that assessing and determining grade-level information is merely a starting point. Both miscue analysis and running records are intended to be analytic tools, and when used, for example, as part of a beginning of the year assessment, they also provide a baseline of the sources of information or cues (meaning, structure, and visual information) that a reader uses, and even more important, a baseline of the learner's strategic activity. (IRIs can also be used for this purpose.) However, if teachers intend to monitor each learner's ongoing processing and strategic activity, it is essential to assess at least monthly to determine growth and next steps in order to design instruction that is at the cutting edge of students' learning.

The type of information gained from a running record or miscue analysis gives an indication of the cues and word identification strategies as well as some comprehension strategies (e.g., monitoring). As with any type of assessment, they do not provide a complete picture of all strategic processing used while reading. They are also unlikely to provide insights into a reader's motivations or the degree of declarative knowledge possessed (see Table 4.1).

GROUP-ADMINISTERED INFORMAL ASSESSMENTS RELATED TO STRATEGIC PROCESSING

Several tools have been developed to assess strategic awareness and motivation: the Index of Reading Awareness, the Metacognitive Awareness of Reading Strategies Inventory, the Metacomprehension Strategy Index, and the Motivation to Read Profile. Each of these tools provides teachers with a means of quickly assessing children's awareness and use of strategic behavior and their motivations for using strategies (see Table 4.1). Group-administered assessments provide a rapid means of assessing the entire class. All of the assessments reviewed here have exhibited high reliability and validity. However, the multiple-choice format taps only students' self-reports of strategic behavior, not their actual performance in authentic contexts. For this reason, caution when interpreting data from these measures is advised. It is possible that a student may report using a given strategy or strategic behavior but may not actually use it while reading. Additionally, the closed-ended nature of multiple-choice questions means that the child is limited to the response options only. This limitation may invite guessing or random selection of responses that is not indicative of a reader's true processing style. Gambrell, Palmer, Codling, and Mazzoni (1996) have alleviated this problem slightly in their Motivation to Read Profile by providing an additional conversational interview format to afford a more in-depth look at students' motivations.

Strategy use is flexible, varies from individual to individual, and varies depending on the context. Multiple-choice formats are scored in a manner that assumes that one response is "better" or "more correct" than others. This assumption does not take into account the flexibility of strategy use or the possibility that a particular context may warrant multiple plans. These measures provide only a quick index of strategic awareness and motivation. As with any assessment, they should be used in conjunction with other assessments and performance data to provide a more complete picture of students' strategic processing.

General Strategy Use

Researchers have developed several assessments to measure students' awareness of strategy use. These are self-report measures that can be administered to a whole class, which makes them useful particularly at the beginning of the year because students can complete them within a short period of time. They are best used to gain a general sense of students' self-perceptions of their strategy use. Because they are self-report measures, they do not provide direct evidence that students *actually* use these strategies when they read. They reflect students' perceptions of the strategies they think they use when they read. As well, it is possible that students may report using strategies because they think that is what the teacher would like them to do. Thus, there is a possibility that students may respond in a socially desirable way to gain teacher acceptance. Nevertheless, these measure provide a quick overview of the class to give insight into where instruction might begin at the start of a school year.

Index of Reading Awareness

Several researchers have developed instruments designed to assess readers' strategic awareness. Paris and Jacobs (1984) initially developed a metacognitive interview designed to assess how students evaluate reading tasks and their own abilities, how they plan to reach a specified goal, and how they use monitoring strategies. The interview data from that investigation was used to develop a 22-item multiple-choice assessment, known as the Index of Reading Awareness (Paris & Oka, 1986a), which assesses knowledge of task goals, planful use of strategies, and evaluation of comprehension (see Table 4.1). For example, the question " 'What do you do if you don't know what a whole sentence means?' " (p. 35) is followed by three multiple-choice responses, each awarded a point value of 0, 1, or 2. Scores on the index range from a low of 0 to a high of 44.

Metacognitive Awareness of Reading Strategies Inventory

The Metacognitive Awareness of Reading Strategies Inventory (MARSI) is also a self-report measure that is designed to assess middle and high school students' perceived use of reading strategies while reading (Mokhtari & Reichard, 2002). The MARSI includes items related to three types of strategies: (1) global reading strategies (i.e., strategies oriented toward a global analysis of text, such as critical evaluation, prediction, and making connections to prior knowledge); (2) problem solving (i.e., strategies such as visualizing for solving problems when the text becomes difficult to read; and (3) support reading strategies (i.e., use of outside reference materials, taking notes, and other functional or support strategies such as summarizing and paraphrasing). The survey items are presented on a scale from 1 to 5 where 1 = "I never or almost never do this" and 5 = "I always or almost always do this." This measure has been reported to have high reliability. Mokhtari and Reichard reported a Cronbach's alpha coefficient of .93 for the entire scale.

Metacomprehension Strategy Index

Schmitt (1990) developed an assessment of strategic reading processes known as the Meta-comprehension Strategy Index (MSI). The MSI assesses students' awareness of strategies used before, during, and after reading narrative text. The strategies assessed include (1) predicting and verifying, (2) previewing, (3) purpose setting, (4) self-questioning, (5) drawing on background knowledge, and (6) summarizing and using fix-up strategies (see Table 4.1). The 25-item multiple-choice assessment includes four response options that are coded as either correct (1 point) or incorrect (0 points). Scores on the MSI range from a low of 0 to a high of 25.

Assessments must reliably measure the construct (in this case, strategic awareness). Reliability means that the measure consistently scores a given trait accurately. Schmitt (1990) reported a reliability of .87 (Kuder–Richardson Formula 20) for the MSI, which indicates a high degree of reliability. An assessment must also demonstrate that it is valid—that is, that it measures what it purports to measure (in this case, strategic aware- ness). Schmitt has reported the MSI to be a valid measure of strategy awareness that offers teachers a quick assessment of students' abilities. For this reason, teachers might find it most beneficial to use at the beginning of the year, administering it to the entire class to gain quick insight into each student's awareness of strategies and how to use them. However, Schmitt cautioned that the MSI provides just one measure of students' reading abilities and should be used in conjunction with multiple sources of informa- tion.

Motivational Assessments

Motivation to Read Profile

Gambrell et al.'s (1996) Motivation to Read Profile (MRP) is an instrument designed to assess a reader's self-concept and the value of reading. These two elements are essential to motivated strategy use (Paris & Oka, 1986b). The MRP contains a Reading Survey and a Conversational Interview. The Reading Survey is a group-administered 20-item multiple-choice questionnaire with a 4-point response scale. The 10 items related to self- concept are intended to provide information about students' perceived competence and performance in reading. The other 10 items on value provide information about the value students place on various reading tasks.

The Conversational Interview is administered individually to students and consists of 14 open-ended questions that elicit information about motivation as it relates to read- ing narrative text, informational text, and reading in general. This interview provides information about students' motivation during authentic reading experiences that supple- ments the information gleaned from the Reading Survey. The Reading Survey has a mod- erately high reliability ($\alpha = .75$ for self-concept subtest; $\alpha = .82$ for value of reading), and the MRP as a whole has proven to be a valid measure of student motivation (Gambrell et al., 1996). The authors cautioned that the MRP is a self-report instrument and therefore subject to the same limitations as any verbal report data (i.e., metacognitive interviews). Again, teachers might consider administering the MRP to the entire class at the begin- ning of the school year to gain insight into each student's self-concept as a reader and the value he or she places on reading. Those students who exhibit low self-concept or are struggling readers may be selected for the Conversational Interview portion of the MRP to find out more about their motivation for reading. Like the MSI, the authors of the MRP suggest that it be accompanied by close classroom observation to verify or reject any emerging hypotheses about student motivation.

Motivation for Reading Questionnaire

The Motivation for Reading Questionnaire (MRQ), developed by Wigfield and Guthrie (1997), uses 11 subscales to measure specific aspects of motivation for reading: (1) Reading Efficacy (3 items), (2) Reading Challenge (5 items), (3) Reading Curiosity (6 items), (4) Reading Involvement (6 items), (5) Importance of Reading (2 items), (6) Reading Work Avoidance (4 items), (7) Competition in Reading (6 items), (8) Recognition for Reading (5 items), (9) Reading for Grades (4 items), (10) Social Reasons for Reading (7 items), and (11) Compliance (5 items).

The MRQ was developed for use with students in grades 3–6. It consists of 53 items and uses a 4-point Likert response scale. Responses range from 1 = "very different from me" to 4 = "a lot like me." Reliabilities for each of the motivation constructs ranges from a low of .43 (extrinsic motivation/reading grades) to a high of .81 (extrinsic motivation/competition), which suggests that the subscales have modest to high reliability. A shorter version (18 items) of the MRQ was also developed for use as a pre- and post- assessment (Guthrie et al., 2004; Wigfield, Guthrie, Tonks, & Perencevich, 2004).

GENERATING HYPOTHESES ABOUT STUDENTS' STRATEGY USE

Ongoing assessment and instruction are integral to the model described in Figure 4.2. Assessment and student response to instruction provide critical information that enables us to hypothesize particular strengths and needs of students as they pertain to strategic processing. Teachers continually engage in this recursive process of generating, revising, and altering hypotheses about students. However, this is usually a very informal process. Afflerbach (1993) developed a system that formalizes this process to permit close scrutiny of the reader, textual task, and contextual factors that contribute to hypothesis formation. The STAIR system (System for Teaching and Assessing Interactively and Reflectively) consists of compiling and maintaining information based on observations, informal assessments, and instruction to plan for students' individual development. It consists of three components: (1) observing and assessing students; (2) generating, revising, and deleting hypotheses about students' needs; and (3) planning and implementing instruction to meet students' needs. Figure 4.10 depicts a sample recording sheet used to describe original hypotheses. The teacher, Eileen, began her ongoing assessment and instruction by drawing on information gleaned from a metacognitive interview, a text interview, and an instructional lesson related to activating background knowledge. She then used the information from her observations and interviews to generate an initial hypothesis about the student's needs and instructional plans. The recursiveness in the assessment/instruction process is apparent: Eileen was able to gather information from informal assessments and observations made during instruction to help her plan. Each component of the ongoing assessment model depicted in Figure 4.2 informs, and is informed by, the other (Klenk & Almasi, 1997).

Although initial hypotheses are generated, it is important to realize that these hypotheses are based on limited information in one particular context. As instruction and assessment proceed, the original hypothesis may be altered, revised, or dropped altogether, based on more information.

Figure 4.11 depicts the next phase of the STAIR system—ongoing assessment, instruction, and reflection on hypotheses. In Eileen's reflection on the previous lesson,

System for Teaching and Assessing Interactively and Reflectively (STAIR)
Original Hypothesis

Teacher: Eileen Ludwig   Date: _____

Student: Maria

Context: Metacognitive/text interview and initial lesson related to activating background knowledge.

Text: 13 different narrative and expository texts available for text interview. One was self-selected for use in lesson on previewing text and activating background knowledge.

Task: Maria was taught how to make predictions while reading a story. She was also taught how to use textual evidence to make predictions and why making predictions is important.

Original Hypothesis and Source(s)

Hypothesis # _1_ :

Maria does not seem to use any comprehension strategies before, during, or after reading to help her make sense of text.

Original source/evidence supporting hypothesis:

During the metacognitive interview Maria was asked, "What do you do while you are reading to help you understand what you are reading?" Maria responded, "Nothing, I just keep reading." When asked, "What do you do after you read to help you understand and remember what you read?" Maria responded, "I don't do anything." She was also asked, "What about if you are studying for a test, do you do anything to help you remember?" Maria responded, "No, nothing." When Maria was asked if she did anything before she read something new, she said, "I just look at the words inside the book to see if they are too big or hard." Maria's Individualized Education Plan (IEP) also indicated weak comprehension when reading silently and orally. Based on discussions with Maria's classroom teacher and the resource director, it seems as if Maria does not use any comprehension strategies to help her understand text. Observations during the first instructional lesson also support this hypothesis.

Instruction to address hypothesis:

An overall plan is to introduce Maria to a variety of comprehension strategies that she can use flexibly before, during, and after reading. Instruction will need to teach Maria the declarative, procedural, and conditional knowledge associated with strategy use so that she sees the value and benefit of using strategies. Think-alouds will be used to assess her emerging use and awareness of comprehension strategies while reading.

FIGURE 4.10. Example of a completed STAIR original hypothesis sheet. Blank STAIR form adapted from Afflerbach (1993). STAIR: A system for recording and using what we know about our students. *The Reading Teacher, 47*(3), 260–263. Copyright 1993, International Reading Association. This material is reproduced with permission of John Wiley & Sons, Inc.

System for Teaching and Assessing Interactively and Reflectively (STAIR)
Ongoing Assessment, Instruction, and Reflection on Hypothesis

Teacher: Eileen Ludwig _____   Date: _____

Student: Maria _____

Context: Instructional lesson on making predictions

Text: *Ira Sleeps Over*, by Bernard Waber

Task: Maria will learn how to make predictions while reading. She will
         learn how to use textual evidence to help her make predictions,
         and she will learn why making predictions is important for
         comprehension.

Hypothesis #1:

Maria does not seem to use any comprehension strategies before, during,
or after reading to help her make sense of text. It is important that she
begin to verbalize more about what she is thinking and doing as she reads
to help her comprehend.

Hypothesis _____ **maintained** _X_ **revised** _____ **dropped**

Source of information:

Based on previous lessons, I believe that Maria will use some
comprehension strategies with explicit instruction. The previous lesson
involved activating prior knowledge and previewing text in order to read
and understand expository text. Maria did use her background knowledge
and experiences to help her understand what she was reading for this
lesson. However, a great deal of time was needed to help Maria activate
her background knowledge before she could use this strategy. I have also
noticed that Maria will make predictions before and while reading if
she is asked to do so. However, I am not sure that she will use these
comprehension strategies on her own. Based on my observations, she still
needs a great deal of modeling and guided practice. In addition, I have not
observed Maria using many other comprehension strategies before, during,
or after reading on her own. Although Maria will sometimes use the author's
pictures to help her, I do not think Maria makes her own mental images as
she reads.

Detailed reflection and explanation:

After doing the lesson on making predictions and indicating what evidence
was used in order to make predictions before and during reading, I
realized that Maria can use this strategy if she is provided with a great
deal of modeling and guided practice. I do feel that she may not use this
strategy on her own, unless it is continually reinforced. I also realized
that many times she seemed to be able to make predictions but would have
trouble verbalizing why she made them. In addition, through questioning I
found that Maria had a difficult time understanding the parts and structure
of a story. I feel that if she could understand and organize the parts and

(cont.)

FIGURE 4.11. Example of a completed ongoing STAIR hypothesis maintenance sheet. Blank
STAIR form adapted from Afflerbach (1993). STAIR: A system for recording and using what we
know about our students. *The Reading Teacher, 47*(3), 260–263. Copyright 1993, International
Reading Association. This material is reproduced with permission of John Wiley & Sons, Inc.

structure of a story, she could better understand what is going on in the story. While reading *Ira Sleeps Over*, Maria was able to draw from some of her own experiences and relate it to the story. Activating background knowledge and drawing on her own experiences are skills that we worked on in our first lesson together. This is a strategy that will continually be reinforced throughout future lessons. I feel that if Maria has plenty of guided practice and feedback with this strategy in various contexts, it can become a strength for her.

Instruction to address hypothesis:

I will continue to model how to make predictions and give Maria several opportunities for guided practice. I will provide her with a lot of positive feedback in order to make her more self-confident. Furthermore, I will always tell Maria why we are learning certain strategies and why they are important. Maria will also be given opportunities to verbalize about the strategies she is using. We will start off with more concrete experiences, which can help reduce the processing demands and help her to become more confident as a reader. While reading texts, I will give her opportunities to verbalize what she is thinking and doing as she reads. I hope that by organizing the elements through a story chart, Maria will better understand the elements and, therefore, better understand the story.

FIGURE 4.11. *(cont.)*

she realized that it was important for Maria to be able to verbalize more completely what she was thinking and doing as she read. Therefore, Eileen revised her original hypothesis slightly to reflect her new insights based on observation, assessment, and reflection. The continual refinement that comes with disciplined reflection and examination of data from assessments and instruction provides teachers with an effective tool for tracking students' progress and meeting their individual needs more effectively. Eileen later reflected on her own learning as a teacher of strategic processing, noting:

> As a teacher and learner of reading strategies, I feel that completing these STAIR hypotheses was extremely helpful to me. Hypothesizing about my student's needs and determining the most essential instruction to address those needs really helped me to stay focused. The hypotheses allowed me to think about what I need to do as a teacher in order for instruction to be beneficial for my student.
>
> —EILEEN LUDWIG, process portfolio

SUMMARY

It is difficult to assess the covert mental operations that occur during strategic processing. Teachers must be able to assess whether students (1) possess the declarative, procedural, and conditional knowledge associated with strategy use; (2) are motivated to use strategies; (3) are metacognitive; (4) are able to analyze the task; and (5) possess a variety of strategies. Formal standardized assessment tools are unable to measure such processes.

Informal classroom-based assessments, such as think-aloud protocols, metacognitive interviews, text interviews, running records, reading miscue inventories, and informal reading inventories are useful means of assessing this type of strategic processing. Questionnaires such as the Index of Reading Awareness, MARSI, the MSI, and the MRP also provide insights related to strategic processing. Assessment of strategic processing must be a discursive process that is intimately connected to instruction and hypothesis generation. Each element informs, and is informed by, the other to meet students' needs.

CHAPTER FIVE

Why Students Struggle with Comprehension

This chapter has several goals. First, it provides a research-based overview of comprehension from the perspective of reading researchers, cognitive psychologists, educational psychologists, and literary theorists. It then provides different profiles of students who struggle to understand and explanations of the sources of their comprehension difficulty. These explanations are organized according to two types of comprehension dilemmas: semantic issues and higher-order processes (i.e., inferencing, comprehension monitoring, and knowledge). Each dilemma is explained in relation to authentic classroom examples, and suggestions for how to alleviate each dilemma are also provided.

Because Paris and Hamilton (2009) noted that there are many definitions of comprehension and little consensus, we begin this chapter by discussing definitions of comprehension in order to arrive at a common understanding of how we are using the term. After defining comprehension, we then consider profiles of students who exhibit comprehension difficulty. This background information provides the groundwork for Chapter 6 in which we share hands-on tools and resources related to comprehension strategies instruction.

DEFINING COMPREHENSION

In 1999 the U.S. Department of Education, Office of Educational Research and Improvement, convened the RAND Reading Study Group (RRSG; RAND, 2006). The RRSG comprised esteemed reading researchers whose goal was to propose a national reading research agenda in the area of reading comprehension (Snow & Sweet, 2003). The group began its work by examining current research and theory to define reading comprehension as "the process of simultaneously *extracting* and *constructing* meaning through interaction and involvement with written language" (Snow & Sweet, 2003, p. 10). By defining comprehension in this manner, the group recognized that comprehension involves simultaneous processes in which readers must be able to decode and identify words to understand the literal meaning of a text. They also recognized that the decoding process,

111

by itself, is insufficient for comprehension (Pressley, 2000). Fittingly, the RRSG definition noted that comprehension also includes the processes involved in constructing meaning. That is, it involves using one's prior knowledge to make connections to the text, drawing inferences, and using higher-level thinking to critically evaluate the text. However, we have problems with using the term *extract* because we believe that the entire reading comprehension process is *constructive* in nature. That is, we believe that meaning does not reside *in* the text, as something to be extracted. Instead, like Duke and Carlisle (2011), we believe that meaning is actively constructed.

These notions are derived from Kintsch's (1998) construction–integration (CI) model of comprehension, which proposes that readers derive a mental model of text, or construct meaning, simultaneously from two sources. The first source is a set of propositions derived from the text at the sentence-by-sentence level (i.e., local coherence or the microstructure of the text) and propositions derived from the way the text is organized as a whole (i.e., global coherence or macrostructure). Together this set of text-derived propositions constitutes what Kintsch (1998) called the *textbase* (p. 49). Along with the propositions derived from the text, the second source used simultaneously by readers includes propositions from long-term memory, which consist of relevant information contained in prior knowledge and experience (i.e., schemata) that help readers understand and make connections to the text and thereby arrive at personal interpretations of the text. The mental model that is simultaneously constructed from the propositions in the text (i.e., the textbase) and the connections between it and relevant prior knowledge from long-term memory form what Kintsch (1998) called the *situation model* (p. 49). Constructing a situation model requires that readers "integrate the textbase and relevant aspects of the comprehender's knowledge" (Kintsch, 1998, p. 107). Graesser (2007) noted that while strategy use exists in the CI model of comprehension, a strategy is "simply a piece of knowledge that is stored in long-term memory that is periodically activated and recruited during the integration process" (p. 11). Thus, the prior knowledge readers access would include knowledge not just of topics and content, but also knowledge related to strategies. The declarative, procedural, and conditional knowledge related to strategies is part of the knowledge base that readers draw upon as they integrate the textbase with their prior knowledge to construct meaning. The integration process requires readers to make inferences and connections between the textbase and prior knowledge to be able to construct a coherent representation of the text—to make sense of it. Paris and Hamilton (2009) noted that the CI model is both a "bottom-up model because it begins with decoding the literal text, and it is a top-down model because the situation model depends on prior knowledge, vocabulary, and the activation of relevant schemata" (p. 35).

Using variations of the term *construction* in the definition of comprehension is critical because the word implies that readers are actively engaged in the process of making meaning. They are thinking and making strategic decisions in an attempt to make sense of the text. Thus, our definition of reading comprehension to this point values the notion that reading comprehension is a process of constructing meaning.

However, the RRSG definition of comprehension also noted the importance of social interaction to the comprehension process. Readers are engaged in an ongoing dialogue with themselves, others, and the author as they are making sense of the text. We value this aspect of the RRSG definition; however, we prefer the term *transaction* rather than *interaction*.

Reader response theorists such as Rosenblatt (1978) used the term *transaction* rather than *interaction* to describe reading as an organic and dialogical process. Rosenblatt often used the analogy of billiard balls striking one another to describe one aspect of the differences between a transaction and an interaction. In a game of pool the balls strike and bounce off one another. Although the direction the billiard ball moves can be altered, the billiard ball itself remains unchanged as a result of this *interaction*. In contrast, during a *transaction*, one must envision the billiard balls being made of clay. When one ball strikes another, not only will the direction the ball moves be altered, but the ball itself is also altered permanently as a result of the experience. So, too, during reading transactions, the individuals who read the text, the text, and the context are altered by the experience.

From a transactional perspective, meaning is contingent not only on the text but also on the reader, the reader's background experiences (i.e., schemata), and the context in which the text is read. Changes to any of these factors will alter the meaning that is constructed. Thus, the transactional perspective maintains that it is possible to have multiple and even conflicting yet valid interpretations of a given text. If we accept the notion that each individual's prior knowledge or schemata influence the manner in which he or she reads and comprehends text, then we must also accept the reader response notion that multiple and conflicting meanings can coexist validly. Thus, in our definition of comprehension we include aspects derived from the CI model, in which comprehension is seen as a constructive process that involves constructing a textbase and integrating it with prior knowledge to create a situation model, but we also acknowledge that comprehension occurs in a social setting. The meaning that is constructed is located in the actual reading event, not the text. Thus, we define reading comprehension as the *process of constructing meaning while transacting with text*. The notion of what influences this process is the final aspect that is important to consider in defining reading comprehension.

Kintsch (1998) noted that whether a reader is actually able (or willing) to put forth the effort to transform a textbase into a situation model depends on "numerous influences" (p. 104), including noncognitive elements such as emotions, body states, and motivation. According to the RRSG definition, comprehension is a complex process that "entails three elements: (1) the *reader* who is doing the comprehending, (2) the *text* that is to be comprehended, and (3) the *activity* in which comprehension is a part" (Sweet & Snow, 2003, p. 2). Literary theory helps us understand these varied influences on comprehension in terms of reader, text, and activity/context factors a bit better.

Some literary theorists (e.g., the New Critics—I. A. Richards, 1929) believe that comprehension and meaning can or should be acquired from the text alone. That is, they believe text has a single, correct meaning "within" it that is independent of the reader. From this perspective a reader's job is to attempt to find the "correct" meaning in the text. When comprehension difficulties occur, they are attributed to a deficit in an individual's reading skills. From this perspective all readers would need to have identical prior knowledge, or schemata, in order to "accurately" understand a given text. This perspective stands in contrast to that of the RRSG, presented above, and that of reader response theorists such as Rosenblatt.

Reader response theorists have maintained that meaning is not contained in the *text* but is the result of a transaction between the reader, the text, and context (cf. Beach & Hynds, 1991; Bleich, 1978; Marshall, 2000; Rosenblatt, 1978). Thus, from a reader response perspective, meaning resides in the reading *event* and emerges as the reader, the text, and the context transact. Figure 5.1 depicts the manner in which reader, textual, and contextual factors work as readers construct meaning from text.

Reader factors include those aspects of an individual that make him or her unique (e.g., age, beliefs, gender, emotional state, ethnicity, intelligence, motivation, personality,

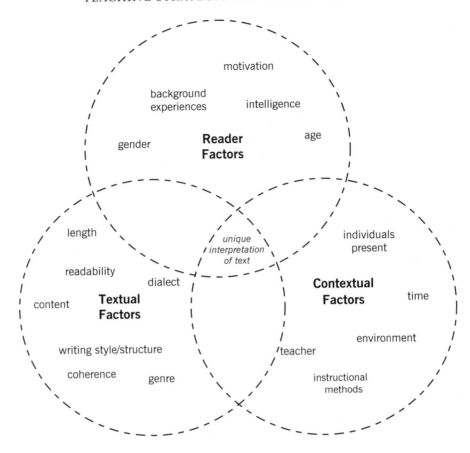

FIGURE 5.1. Impact of reader, text, and context on a reader's understanding.

values). Each reader factor has an impact on how an individual responds to, and inter-
prets, text (Beach & Hynds, 1991; Marshall, 2000). For example, the influence of an
individual's background knowledge and experiences on comprehension has been thoroughly articulated in the reading research (see Anderson & Pearson, 1984, for a review).
Each of these factors alone can influence the manner in which one makes sense of text,
but when all of the factors are operating concurrently, it means that the comprehension
process (and whether a reader will or will not put forth effort to construct meaning) is
infinitely complex.

   A reader's stance, or orientation, toward the text is also an important reader factor
that influences comprehension. Rosenblatt (1978) described two primary stances: aesthetic and efferent. When a reader adopts a primarily *aesthetic* stance, he is focused on
the reading experience; that is, he is primarily interested in the enjoyment of the reading experience. When a primarily *efferent* stance is adopted, the reader is focused more
on what information can be gleaned or taken away from the text. Rosenblatt (1991)
explained that readers never assume a completely aesthetic or efferent stance. As Figure
5.2 illustrates, even a reader with a predominately aesthetic stance (Point D) adopts an
efferent stance at some point during the reading. Likewise a reader at Point A, although

reading primarily to take information away from the text, adopts an aesthetic stance at some point. However, a reader with a primarily aesthetic stance would not read and understand a text in the same manner as he would if he adopted a primarily efferent stance. This reader may be more interested in the literary experience and enjoying that experience than in the literal details of the text. Thus, the purpose one has for reading influences the stance one takes while reading and ultimately the meaning one constructs.

Textual factors also influence the manner in which a reader understands text (Beach & Hynds, 1991; Marshall, 2000). Duke and Carlisle (2011) broadened the RRSG definition of comprehension to include not only written text but also oral text. In that same vein, we believe that comprehension occurs not only with written and oral text, but also with any "text." That is, we use a broad definition of text as anything that communicates or stands for something. This definition encompasses linguistic text (i.e., printed or oral texts that communicate) such as books, journals, poems, letters, and blogs, and it moves beyond language-based text to include semiotic texts (i.e., signs or symbols that communicate) such as pictures, gestures, events, music, dance, art, or film/video. Our contention is that we use strategic processes to make sense of, or bring meaning to, any text. Defining text broadly is essential to the fourth element (i.e., reducing processing demands) of our CESI model.

In terms of conventional printed text, factors such as the length of the text, its readability, the author's style of writing, the text's genre, and the content of the text affect the way a reader reads and understands it. Younger and less proficient readers often have difficulty reading longer texts, and all readers tend to have greater difficulty reading informational (i.e., expository) text than narrative text. The manner in which the author writes is also critical. A text lacking cohesion or organization will severely impact the manner in which a reader understands it. Each of these conventional text factors, however, presupposes that we are preparing learners to become "users, more or less competently, of an existing, stable, static system of elements and rules" (Kress, 2000, p. 154).

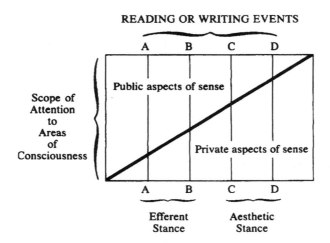

FIGURE 5.2. The efferent/aesthetic continuum. Reprinted from Rosenblatt, L. M. (1991). Literature—S.O.S! *Language Arts, 68*(6), 444–448. Copyright 1991 by the National Council of Teachers of English. Reprinted by permission.

Kress (2000) argued that instead of viewing individuals as *users* of language, they should be viewed as *remakers* or *transformers*:

> From the outside, semiotic systems, language included, are seen as sets of resources available in a given culture, which are given their regularities by larger cultural values and social contingencies. They are deployed according to cultural histories and individual interest in particular social interaction with their distributions of power. (pp. 156–157

That is, as when we participate in language and communication, we use various tools that are available in a given culture and that are valued by that culture to use language and to communicate. When we read, these tools might be strategies such as making connections to prior knowledge or making predictions. As teachers we typically teach students to *use* these tools to become better readers. However, Kress's (2000) perspective reminds us that society and culture are in a constant state of flux that necessitates the ability to make adjustments, changes, and adaptations. This notion of the learner living in a dynamic, ever-changing society suggests that we have to replace the notion of preparing *users* to that of preparing *transformers* who are capable of making decisions and constantly transforming the resources, or tools (or strategies), available to them to meet their ever-changing needs in an ever-changing society. For example, digital immigrants (those born prior to the arrival and dissemination of digital technology) have had to transform and adapt the way they process text, and they may process text and use different strategies than digital natives (i.e., those born since the arrival and widespread dissemination of digital technology) (Leu et al., 2008; Prensky, 2001). Prensky (2001) contended that digital natives prefer to receive information quickly, engage in multiple tasks simultaneously, view graphics before text, and have access to network capabilities. Many digital immigrants may also now have similar preferences, but this shift has meant that they have transformed themselves and the resources and strategies they use when processing text as society has been transformed.

This view of text as a more dynamic (rather than a static) system of communication relies on teaching learners to become agents of change who are *transformers* rather than strategy *users* (Almasi & Hart, 2011). That is, they adapt and make changes to the strategies and the way they are used depending on the text and context. This perspective is more aligned with Rosenblatt's notions of literacy as a transactional process in which the reader, the text, and the context are changed by the meaning-making event—in essence, each is *transformed* by the process (Almasi & Hart, 2011).

Context also plays an important role in determining how an individual comprehends text (Beach & Hynds, 1991; Marshall, 2000). The instructional decisions a teacher makes in the classroom provide the context for young readers. Whether a text is read in school or out of school, alone or with a partner, silently or aloud, with preparation or without preparation—each factor has the potential to alter crucially the reading experience. For struggling readers who have low self-esteem, the emotional burden of having to read aloud in front of peers in school can be a traumatic experience. Even proficient readers' comprehension is often negatively impacted when reading in this context. Teaching students strategies such as tapping background knowledge, setting purposes for reading, or making predictions prior to, and during, the reading process enhances comprehension. Conversely, when such instruction is not provided and students are merely told, for example, to "read Chapter 2" without any preparation or instruction, comprehension is profoundly impacted, particularly for younger and less proficient readers. Thus, the instructional activities and decisions that teachers make influence the context in which learners find themselves and ultimately the meaning that can be constructed during a literary event.

These three elements (reader, text, and activity/context) all occur within a sociocultural context that "both shapes and is shaped by the reader" (Snow & Sweet, 2003, p. 2). That is, the sociocultural context in which the reader finds herself will influence the meaning she constructs, and the reader also influences and shapes the sociocultural context, which includes anything within the social or cultural context that might shape or influence learning. Sociocultural perspectives on learning (e.g., Vygostky, 1978; Rogoff, 1990) suggest that learning occurs in a social context and is a form of "cognitive apprenticeship" in which learners interact with others who might guide or stretch their thinking in some way to help them acquire the "tools of culture" (Rogoff, 1990, p. i) that they will need to be successful. The New London Group (2000) has argued that if our goal is to help students achieve a degree of mastery in practice, then we must immerse them in a community in which they engage and participate in authentic versions of, and experiences with, the practice so that they can learn to recognize contextual and sociocultural patterns. In order to move beyond simply situating or placing students in a learning environment and hoping that they will absorb knowledge indirectly, we must provide overt (or explicit) instruction that helps scaffold their efforts so that they become aware of what they are learning and begin to exert some control over it. The New London Group further noted that overt instruction must also be coupled with critical framing in which students are taught to step back from the learning situation and critically evaluate and constructively critique it in relation to the context. This process enables learners to understand the settings and circumstances under which particular strategies are more and less helpful, and thereby leads learners to actually revise their strategic behaviors and in the process *reauthor* themselves as learners. In essence, transformed practice is the outcome.

In a classroom context focused on comprehension and learning to become literate, this approach means that students learn how to be strategic and how to alter their strategic processing so that they are able to be flexibly adapt to varying conditions and contexts. The tools needed to be strategic vary from one context to another. The "tools of culture" that influence and shape one's learning are found at various levels from the most immediate local context (e.g., the home, the classroom) to larger contexts (e.g., the family, school, the community, the region, the state, the nation). Imagine these tools as a set of ever-widening concentric circles where the perimeter of each circle is noted by a dotted line to reflect that each context influences, and is influenced by, the other, as shown in Figure 5.3. However, in theory these circles move beyond what is depicted in Figure 5.3. Each circle is defined by varied social, political, economic, cultural, ethnic, linguistic, and gendered ways of viewing the world. The varied values, beliefs, and ideals within each circle influence and shape the other circles.

Each of these contexts plays some role in shaping which tools of culture influence literacy learning. For example, in the local context the teacher might be concerned about her students' comprehension and might begin teaching students to be strategic. However, other teachers in the same grade level might not value strategic processing or may not want to put forth the effort to learn how to teach students to be strategic. The school itself may be under pressure to increase reading achievement test scores. The district's solution for such schools might be to require teachers to use prepackaged programs that focus on skills rather than strategic processing. The push to use prepackaged programs

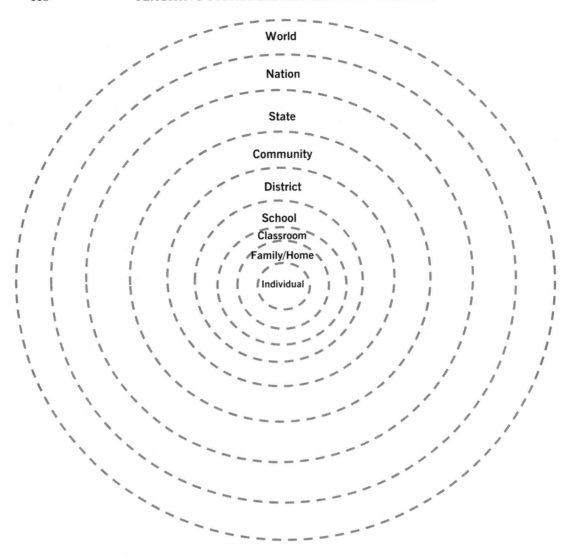

FIGURE 5.3. The sociocultural context of learning.

might come from particular ideological and theoretical views of learning that suggest that all children, regardless of their individual differences, can benefit from a particular method of teaching. The push to use prepackaged programs may also stem from a sense of urgency in administrators or legislators to do something—*anything*—quickly to fix the problem. Or, such pushes may come from clever marketing within the publishing industry aimed at selling products. Regardless, the instructional decisions that teachers make in terms of which cultural tools to share with students are shaped by larger sociocultural influences. Conversely, the instructional decisions teachers make also shape those larger sociocultural influences. Thus, reading comprehension is a recursive process in which all sociocultural elements influence and shape one another.

These notions underscore that reading comprehension is *not* simply a text-based event in which the goal is to decode the words and derive a literal understanding of those words that anyone reading the same text might also derive. Instead, reading comprehension is context-dependent. That is, the meaning that one constructs varies depending on the context and each of the elements in that context. As well, the tools needed to be strategic in one context differ from those needed in another (Almasi & Hart, 2011). For example, readers may use or value different strategic processes when reading and comprehending in online environments than when reading traditional print materials (Coiro & Dobler, 2007; Leu et al., 2008). This would be considered a textual factor that influences the strategic tools needed. Likewise, readers may use different strategic processes under different conditions depending on their motivation, interest, and ability (e.g., reader factors). When we consider that reader, textual, and contextual factors shape and are shaped by the larger sociocultural context, we gain a picture of the complexity of reading comprehension. Figure 5.4 depicts this relationship. At the center is an individual's unique interpretation of text that has been constructed during the transaction of reader, text, and context within the sociocultural context.

We have considered many factors in our effort to construct a definition of reading comprehension. Based on these factors, we define reading comprehension as *the process of constructing meaning in which readers, texts, and contexts transact within in a sociocultural context.* With this definition in place we turn our attention to describing various types of comprehension difficulties and the nature of those difficulties as manifested by readers.

STUDENTS WHO STRUGGLE WITH COMPREHENSION

In contrast with the complex perspectives of reading comprehension described above, some have argued that reading comprehension is more simplistic. When the first edition of this text was published, instructional practices in literacy in the United States were being shaped by the No Child Left Behind legislation that created Reading First. Pressure was being exerted to teach all children how to read by grade 3. Riddle Buly and Valencia (2002) noted that the assumptions underlying these notions seemed to be that students who struggle in later grades lack fundamental reading skills that should have been attained prior to grade 3. These educational reforms were predicated in large part on the theoretical premise that skilled reading and comprehension rely primarily on the ability to decode words fluently. That is, if readers can decode the words, then they will be able to comprehend the text. This notion has its roots in automaticity theory (LaBerge & Samuels, 1974; Samuels, 2004) and is known as the *bottleneck hypothesis* (Fleisher, Jenkins, & Pany, 1979). Hoover and Gough's (1990) "simple view" of reading follows a similar line of reasoning, arguing that skilled reading consists simply of decoding and linguistic comprehension, which are viewed as inseparable parts. As well, reading comprehension, according to the "simple view," relies on "graphic-based information arriving through the eye" (p. 131).

Reading First programs at that time in the United States were intended to provide explicit instruction in phonics, phonemic awareness, fluency, vocabulary, *and* comprehension. However, instructional practice focused largely on phonics, phonemic awareness, and fluency. Thus, instructional practice during that time was guided largely by automaticity theory and the simple view of reading. At the same time as these theoretical

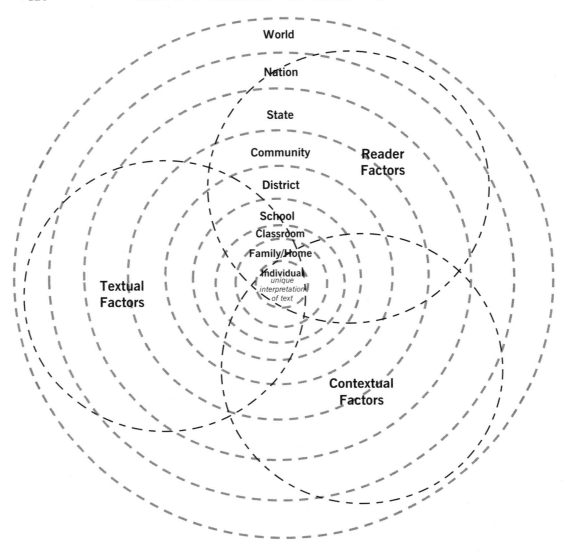

FIGURE 5.4. Reader, textual, and contextual factors in transaction within a sociocultural context.

notions were influencing policy and literacy practice in the United States, a great deal of research was being conducted in the United Kingdom that was aimed at studying poor comprehenders (i.e., readers who have good decoding skills but poor comprehension). These studies dispelled the notion that comprehension problems arise from poor decoding skills because they focused on identifying readers who, despite adequate decoding skills, were poor comprehenders (e.g., Cain & Oakhill, 2006; Cain, Oakhill, & Bryant, 2000; Nation & Snowling, 1999; Yuill & Oakhill, 1988, 1991).

Ultimately, the final report of the Reading First program indicated that the code-based interventions that focused on phonics, phonemic awareness, and fluency had no significant impact on comprehension for children in grades 1, 2, or 3 (Gamse, Jacob, Horst, Boulay, & Unlu, 2008). These findings are similar to that of many other studies. Almasi et al. (2011) reviewed research on interventions that foster narrative comprehension for struggling readers and found similar results. Those interventions that focused solely on decoding and/or fluency were not as successful at enhancing comprehension as interventions that included both decoding and comprehension instruction. Further, interventions that focused exclusively on comprehension were consistently successful at enhancing comprehension. Similarly, a meta-analysis conducted by Edmonds et al. (2009) found that interventions that focused on fluency and word study to improve comprehension had no impact, whereas comprehension interventions were superior to all other forms of intervention.

Although decoding is obviously critical for reading, these recent research findings should put to rest the notion that an instructional emphasis on decoding (i.e., phonics, phonemic awareness), by itself or even in large part, leads to significant improvement in comprehension—it does not. When students struggle with comprehension, they must receive instruction that assists *that domain*, and the nature of comprehension problems varies considerably across students.

Valencia's (2011) review of research depicted vast differences among individual students' reading difficulties. Her review suggested that students' reading difficulties are multifaceted and that "reader profiles change with development and instruction" (p. 33). In particular, she noted that understanding the complex nature of students' reading difficulties is critical in RTI in order to provide instruction targeted to help each student's weaknesses. However, she cautioned that instruction should not be so narrow or limited that it does not support other areas of instruction. That is, if students have difficulty with word identification, instruction should not be focused exclusively on word identification at the expense of developing comprehension. Some interventions may produce desired results in word identification at the expense of comprehension and fluency.

Several studies have attempted to determine the nature of struggling readers' difficulties. Leach, Scarborough, and Rescorla (2003) examined students in the United States with "late-emerging comprehension problems" and found that nearly half of the fourth graders in their sample (*n* = 31 of 66, or 47%) had late-emerging comprehension problems. Of those with such problems, the nature of them varied. Specifically, nearly one-third of these students had comprehension deficits but no word-level deficits, another third had word-level deficits but no comprehension deficits, and another third had both comprehension and word-level deficits. These findings—that a full one-third of these students had adequate decoding skills but poor comprehension—like those of the studies from the United Kingdom, add further evidence to dispel the theoretical premises underlying automaticity theory and the simple view of reading. As well, the fact that nearly half of the students had late-emerging comprehension problems suggests that even if we were somehow able to help all students become competent readers by grade three, these students' comprehension problems would exist regardless.

Riddle Buly and Valencia (2002) were interested in describing the profiles of students who had failing scores on state reading assessments. Their contention was that representing students' literacy achievement with one score on a state assessment oversimplifies and masks information about the nature of students' strengths and weaknesses. They administered several different assessments focused on word identification (of real words and pseudowords in and out of context), comprehension (reading comprehension and vocabulary), and fluency (rate and expression) to fourth graders who scored below benchmarks on a statewide standards-based comprehension test. Six different reader profiles were identified. Table 5.1 summarizes the reader profiles, the percentage of students in each category, and their performance on word identification texts, comprehension tests, and fluency tests. Automatic word callers comprised 18% of students in their sample. These students could read words quickly and accurately but lacked comprehension. Struggling word callers, who made up 15% of the sample, were able to read quickly and fluently; however, their reading accuracy and comprehension were weak. Word stumblers (18%) were those students who had adequate comprehension but struggled with word identification and fluency. Most of these students were native English speakers. Slow comprehenders comprised 24% of the sample. These students, like the word stumblers, came primarily from homes where English was spoken. Their comprehension was very strong and their ability to read words accurately was adequate; however, their fluency was weak. Students identified as slow word callers (17%) were similar to the automatic word callers in that they were able to read words accurately but had weak comprehension and lacked fluency. These students read slowly but accurately and lacked comprehension of what they read. The final group, disabled readers, comprised 9% of all students. These students were weak in all three areas: word identification, comprehension, and fluency.

In this chapter we focus primarily on those students with difficulties in comprehension—that is, those students who are word callers (whether automatic, struggling, or slow word callers) or disabled readers who are weak in all areas. Those interested in providing assistance to word stumblers and slow comprehenders will want to refer to Chapter 6, which deals with strategies that enhance word recognition.

Paris and Hamilton (2009) noted that if a reader does not have adequate background knowledge, the text predominates as the reader attempts to integrate the textbase with insufficient background knowledge. They noted that this leads to difficulty making inferences and connections because the details derived from the text are disconnected. In contrast, readers who are not using much of the information derived from the text rely on their background knowledge and experience to derive comprehension.

TABLE 5.1. Profiles of Struggling Readers

Reader profile (percent of students)	Word identification	Comprehension	Fluency	Percent English learners
Automatic word callers (18%)	Above average	Below average	Above average	63%
Struggling word callers (15%)	Below average	Below average	Above average	56%
Word stumblers (17%)	Below average	Average	Below average	16%
Slow comprehenders (24%)	Average	Above average	Below average	19%
Slow word callers (17%)	Average	Below average	Below average	56%
Disabled readers (9%)	Substantially below average	Substantially below average	Substantially below average	20%

Note. Adapted from Valencia (2011). Reader profiles and reading disabilities. In A. McGill-Franzen & R. L. Allington (Eds.), *Handbook of reading disability research* (Table 3.2, pp. 25–35). New York: Routledge. Copyright 2011 by Routledge. Reprinted by permission.

SOURCES OF COMPREHENSION DIFFICULTIES

Although Riddle Buly and Valencia's (2002) research provides a more refined understanding of the nature of reading difficulties, those students who are poor comprehenders struggle for different reasons. That is, the source of their comprehension difficulty varies individually. Nation's (2005) review of research described the sources and causes of poor comprehension, particularly among those who have adequate word identification—those whom Riddle Buly and Valencia (2002) and Cartwright (2010) refer to as *word callers*. From the perspective of the construction–integration model (CI) of reading, these readers are able to read accurately and develop a textbase, but they have difficulty making the connections needed between their prior knowledge and the textbase to develop a situation model.

Nation (2005) identified several factors that contribute to poor comprehension. We discuss those most related to strategy instruction: (1) semantic and memory-related issues, (2) faulty higher-order discourse processes (inference making, comprehension monitoring), and (3) insufficient knowledge. We examine each of these issues in brief.

Semantic and Memory-Related Issues

Nation (2005) noted that some poor comprehenders tend to have difficulty with nonphonological but meaning-related aspects of oral language. That is, they have difficulty bringing meaning to text when some semantic issues are present rather than having difficulty with accurately decoding the text. These issues should not be misconstrued as general difficulty with all aspects of oral language. Instead, they pertain to issues of recalling and retrieving meanings, understandings, and knowledge-related information. Nation and Snowling (1999) found that poor comprehenders tend to have difficulty recalling abstract words and concepts (e.g., *humble*) more than concrete words and concepts (e.g., *hand*), and they tend to have greater difficulty making categorical associations between words (e.g., cat/dog are types of pets; crayon/pencil are writing instruments) than functional associations between words (e.g., hair/brush; leaves/rake). They suggested that many poor comprehenders may not have developed a semantic memory that is categorical. These types of problems manifest during reading as difficulties related to constructing meaning. They might include weaknesses in (1) understanding the meanings of words, (2) understanding figurative language, or (3) making connections between concepts to make inferences or to recognize patterns. These semantic difficulties may be attributable to deficiencies in what is known as *gist memory*.

Reyna and Brainerd's (2011) research suggested that we have two separate systems for memory (i.e., verbatim memory, gist memory) that affect what and how we remember. Verbatim memory captures the exact, literal nature of an event. A verbatim representation of text would reflect a precise duplication of the text. Unfortunately, verbatim memory is very short-lived. As readers, we use traces of verbatim memory and fill in the gaps using what is known as gist memory, which enables us to develop a general sense of the text. When we read, it is hard to remember every word we read. Instead, we construct a "gist" representation that consists of distilling the exact words that were read into the general meaning or idea. For example, consider this portion of text:

Sophie sped to Kroger to pick up some lettuce, tomatoes, a flat iron steak, fresh bread, and a cheesecake for dessert, and paid for it with her debit card.

A reader might simply recall that "the character went to the grocery store." The reader has used gist memory to use a few traces of the verbatim text (or textbase) to distill and condense the literal details down by putting aside specifics that might not be as relevant to the entire text (e.g., lettuce, tomatoes, flat iron steak, fresh bread, cheesecake) and recall the primary aspect of the text (e.g., went to the grocery store) to form a gist representation.

Reyna and Brainerd (2011) note that gist representations are vaguer and more subjective than verbatim representations: "The gist of a problem or situation is its subjective interpretation based on emotion, education, culture, experience, worldview, that is, anything that affects essential *meaning*" (p. 182). In terms of reading comprehension this means that gist memory enables us to recall a general sense of the text, but what we recall and how we recall are affected by many other factors. Any of the reader, textual, or contextual factors described above and noted in Figure 5.2 would influence gist memory.

Applying these principles to reading comprehension, gist memory enables us to filter information derived from the textbase (and from verbatim memory), sort it, and organize it so we can access it more easily later. This means that some aspects of what we read verbatim are tossed aside or forgotten and others are retained as we attempt to reconstruct or build a gist memory that is smaller. Gist memory looks for patterns and relationships to condense and categorize information into smaller units. These smaller units are then connected and combined to create an interpretation of the event (or the text). Because gist memory relies on the brain's ability to organize, categorize, store, and retrieve information, this is one area where reading comprehension problems begin. In order to construct a gist, readers need to be able to retrieve the meanings of words, the relations between them, and the patterns in the text and make connections between and across them. If a reader has difficulty organizing, categorizing, storing, or retrieving information using gist memory, then his or her comprehension is going to be affected.

The poor comprehenders in a study by Weekes, Hamilton, Oakhill, and Holliday (2008) had difficulty recalling word pairs that were semantically associated, but had no difficulty recalling word pairs that were phonologically associated. As well, they had fewer false recollections of word pairs. Reyna and Brainerd's (2011) research has shown that false recollection is attributed to gist memory. Thus, Weekes and his colleagues (2008) suggested that the poor comprehenders in their study had difficulty recalling semantically associated words and had fewer false recollections because of reduced gist memory.

In terms of Riddle Buly and Valencia's (2002) reader profiles (see Table 5.1), a large proportion of the students (over 50% and in some categories nearly 66%) who were automatic word callers, struggling word callers, and slow word callers were also English learners. For those students it is likely that semantic issues led to their difficulty with comprehension. Riddle Buly and Valencia described these students in more detail noting that their knowledge of word meanings was limited, and although they understood English at a surface level, they had difficulty with the complexities of English as a second language. These difficulties would include semantic issues related to understanding multiple meanings of words and figurative language. A small proportion of the other students in their sample of automatic, struggling, and slow word callers who were not English learners had great difficulty with receptive vocabulary. For these students semantic issues related to word meanings, words with multiple meanings, and figurative language would also be problematic in terms of comprehension. These findings suggest that when we are attempting to help students who struggle with comprehension, we have to examine multiple sources of information so that we are prepared to help them learn strategic behaviors that might be of the most use for them. For those students who struggle with comprehension (and not word identification), we must also consider their facility with receptive and expressive language to see if semantic issues might be impeding comprehension.

What do these findings about semantics suggest in terms of teaching poor comprehenders to become strategic? The primary link between strategic processing and semantics is that if readers are having difficulty organizing, categorizing, storing, and retrieving semantic information, then our instruction must focus on teaching them how to recognize when they struggle and to help them learn to be strategic in the way they organize, categorize, store, and retrieve information (or schemata) from text while they are reading. Strategies that help students prepare for reading, anticipate what the text will be about, and organize their thoughts while reading facilitate schemata storage and retrieval. We refer to these strategies as *text anticipation strategies*. They include previewing the text, activating prior knowledge, setting purposes, making predictions, and identifying text structures. Each of these strategies is described more fully in Chapter 6.

Higher-Order Processes

Nation (2005) also noted that many poor comprehenders often struggle with higher-order processes such as inferencing and monitoring comprehension. These readers may have adequate receptive vocabulary and sufficient understanding of word meanings, but for some reason they simply cannot maintain focus or attention on comprehending text while reading.

There are several possible reasons for this problem. First, as Riddle Buly and Valencia (2002) suggested, some of the students in their sample who were very fluent readers (the automatic word callers and struggling word callers) may have been reading too quickly to attend to comprehension. These students may focus on the speed and pace of their reading at the expense of comprehension. This is one of the worries of focusing a great deal of attention on fluency assessments. Some readers will simply focus on reading quickly and will not consider the prosodic features of fluency (intonation, pitch, stress) that actually bring meaning to text. As well, they may be reading so quickly that their focus is only on fluency (e.g., struggling word callers) and not on understanding what they are reading.

In other cases the text itself might contribute to the problem. A text that is lengthy, too difficult, or poorly organized may place readers in a situation in which maintaining focus and attention on comprehension just becomes too difficult.

Contextual circumstances help explain other causes of comprehension problems related to higher-order processing. A reader's attention or motivation may wane while reading because the text is not interesting to the reader or because the reader is not motivated to read that particular text. Alternatively, the reader himself may have other problems (e.g., social, physiological, familial) that cause him to be distracted or unmotivated while reading. The result is a passive reader who does not monitor comprehension while reading and who often processes text in a piecemeal fashion. That is, as each new segment of text is encountered, a new schema or new idea is generated. Wade (1990) referred to these readers as "non-integrators" (p. 447). Such readers never develop a connected, integrated understanding of the text; that is, they don't develop a coherent situation model of the text. To gain a better understanding of how these readers experience text, consider the following passage taken from Rumelhart (1980) and the subsequent analysis:

Business had been slow since the oil crisis. Nobody seemed to want anything really elegant anymore. Suddenly the door opened and a well-dressed man entered the show-room floor. John put on his friendliest and most sincere expression and walked toward the man. (p. 43)

Generally, as people read this text, they begin by making a hypothesis (or in the language of strategies, *predictions*) about the text's topic. After reading the first sentence, people often activate schemata related to gas stations, oil businesses, or other businesses that depend on the oil industry. They may also become confused because the text is dated and many readers may not have a historical understanding of the "oil crisis" that emerged after the Organization of Petroleum Exporting Countries (OPEC) imposed an oil embargo in 1973 that lasted until March of 1974. As the second sentence is read, they refine and alter the schemata they have selected and their prediction to include the notion of *elegant*. Often, good comprehenders think of businesses that rely on the oil industry but that also have something to do with elegance. Readers consider schemata related to large cars or even the fur industry at this point. As they read on, they continue to modify and refine their hypotheses based on the new information contained in the text. After reading the entire passage, readers generally agree that John sells some type of large, luxury car, and that his business has been affected by the oil crisis. The process of activating schemata, generating hypotheses, determining if the incoming data "fit" with the selected schemata, and refining or altering schemata based on the incoming data are ongoing and cumulative processes. However, readers with comprehension problems who struggle to create a coherent situation model may generate new notions about the text's meaning with each bit of new information instead of attempting to integrate and connect all of the pieces of information together to create a coherent understanding. For example, after reading the first sentence, they may activate their schema for gas stations. After reading the second sentence, they may activate their schema for mink coats. After reading the third sentence, they may activate their schema for buying furniture. While reading each sentence, no attempt is made to link it to preceding and succeeding sentences. Instead, new schemata are activated with the introduction of each piece of new information, leaving the reader with a very disjointed interpretation of the text. The problems described in this example involve difficulties with making inferences and monitoring comprehension.

Inferencing

Inferencing is a critical component of comprehension because it enables readers to construct coherent representations of text. McKoon and Ratcliff (1992) defined inferences as "any piece of information that is not explicitly stated in the text" (p. 440).

Younger readers generate fewer inferences than older readers (Oakhill et al., 2003), and less proficient readers generate fewer inferences than more proficient readers (Cain, Oakhill, Barnes, & Bryant, 2001). As well, Nation (2005) noted that poor comprehenders (e.g., word callers) have difficulty making inferences when they are reading or listening. Thus, poor comprehenders tend to have substantial difficulty making inferences. Cain and Oakhill (1999) found that these difficulties are not related to poor working memory as these poor comprehenders continue to struggle to make inferences even when they are permitted to look back at the text to help them. They found that when poor comprehenders are provided with scaffolding and instruction to help them learn to search the text to find the information on which to base inferences, they are successful. Cain and Oakhill (1999) concluded that the poor comprehenders in their study failed in their first attempts at making inferences because their initial reading goal was oral reading accuracy and not comprehension. They noted that questioning revealed that these poor comprehenders had the requisite prior knowledge to make the inference. Thus, their poor comprehension was not related to insufficient prior knowledge, working memory, or an inability to search and locate information in the text. Instead they concluded that "strategy differences may be the source of this finding: The less skilled comprehenders may be poorer at knowing when and how to relate general knowledge to the text in order to supply missing details" (Cain & Oakhill, 1999, p. 501). These readers needed to learn the procedural knowledge of *how* to make inferences and the conditional knowledge of *where* and *when* to make inferences in order to be successful.

Cain and Oakhill (1999) further concluded that the inability to make text-connecting inferences is more likely a *cause* of comprehension failure than a result of comprehension failure. Their research suggested that teaching students how to process text strategically by providing explicit instruction related to how, when, and where to make inferences would be beneficial. Although some researchers such as Dewitz, Carr, and Patberg (1987) found that inference training was beneficial, other researchers such as Sipe and Brightman (2009) found that simply providing young children with the opportunity to think about what might have happened during the page turns in a picturebook (or "page breaks," as they are called) with little direction from teachers enabled second graders to make seven different types of responses involving inference. Sipe and Brightman (2009) noted that the latter is a more naturalistic approach that can be incorporated into storybook read-alouds and that it incorporates the type of naturalistic integration of strategies instruction into lessons that Pressley, El-Dinary, et al. (1992) envisioned during transactional strategies instruction.

Kintsch (1998) noted "how much time and resources the reader has strongly determine the amount of inferencing that occurs" (p. 194). Thus, if a reader is rushing through the text (as automatic and struggling word callers would be), or if a reader is focused more on word reading accuracy (as automatic and slow word callers would be), then he or she is more likely to make fewer inferences. McKoon and Ratcliff (1992) would refer to these readers as "minimalists" who make only the inferences they absolutely must.

Part of what makes inferencing difficult is that there are many types of inferences. Younger and poorer comprehenders tend to make the fewest amount of inferences needed (McKoon & Ratcliff, 1992). In describing his construction–integration (CI) model, Kintsch (1998) noted: "Text comprehension depends as much on the reader and the pragmatic situation as on the text itself. What readers bring to the text, their goals and prior experience, has been studied under the label of inferencing in text comprehension" (p. 189). He noted that true inferencing really is concerned with the ability to use logic, particularly deductive reasoning, to draw reasonable conclusions.

Kintsch (1998) classified four different types of inferences (see Table 5.2). The first type, logical inference, uses similar thought processes as syllogisms. An example of a syllogism is: if *A* and *B* are true, then *C* is true. The logical inference (or syllogism) is valid if all three parts are true. Here is an example of a valid logical inference:

Example 1: Logical Inference

Major Premise (*A*) All mammals give birth to live babies and nourish them with milk.
                    (True)

Minor Premise (*B*)   Cats give birth to live babies and nourish them with milk. (True)

Conclusion (*C*)   Cats are mammals. (True)

This type of thinking, logical inferencing, requires a great deal of deep processing and problem solving that requires readers to actually derive and produce new information. In the example above, the conclusion (*C*) at which the reader arrives is new information derived from piecing together each of the two true propositions, *A* and *B*. That is, the information in text *A* defines behaviors that mammals exhibit, and the information in text *B* identifies cats as an example of an animal that exhibits the same behaviors. If the reader accepts the information in text *A* and text *B* as true, then she can make the logical inference that *cats are mammals*. Kintsch (1998) noted that logical inferences are generative. That is, they require the reader to use the information contained in the text to produce new information. Making an inference produces the new information. The new information is not available to the reader by any other means. This type of logical inference requires deliberate, strategic processing. Table 5.2 depicts each type of inference.

Kintsch (1998) also noted, however, that some types of inferencing are automatic (i.e., transitive inferences). Here is an example of a transitive inference:

TABLE 5.2. Kintsch's Classification System for Inferences

	Generation (produces new information that is derived from the text by inference)		Retrieval (adds preexisting information from prior knowledge to the text)	
Controlled process	#1		#3	
	Type of inference:	Logical	Type of inference:	Bridging or text-connecting
	Text:	All mammals give birth to live babies and nourish them with milk. Cats give birth to live babies and nourish them with milk.	Text:	Maria wanted to buy a new home. She worked two jobs.
	Inference:	Cats are mammals.	Inference:	Maria worked two jobs to earn enough money to buy a new home.
Automatic process	#2		#4	
	Type of inference:	Transitive	Type of inference:	Elaborative or gap-filling
	Text:	Two cats sat on a fence. A rabbit hopped underneath them.	Text:	Mark dug a hole to plant the tree.
	Inference:	The cats are above the rabbit.	Inference:	Mark used a shovel to dig the hole.

Note. Adapted from Kintsch (1998). *Comprehension: A paradigm for cognition* (Table 6.1, p. 189). New York: Cambridge University Press. Copyright 1998 by Cambridge University Press. Reprinted by permission.

Example 2: Transitive Inference

Major Premise (*A*)	Two cats sat on a fence.
Minor Premise (*B*)	A rabbit hopped underneath them.
Conclusion (*C*)	The cats are above the rabbit.

In this example the reader does not have to put forth quite as much effort as in the previous example to make the inference (C) that the cats are above the rabbit. This information is not directly stated in the text and requires the reader to take information from text *A* and text *B* and combine that information with information from prior knowledge of spatial relations (*fence*, *underneath*) to generate the inference that the cats must be above the rabbit. Although this type of inference, like the logical inference in the first example, still requires generative thought to produce new information, transitive inferences are more automatic for readers. Kintsch explained that for many transitive inferences readers often make use of visual imagery to make the process more automatic.

Kintsch's (1998) definition of inference would technically not include any inferences other than those that require logical inferences, as in the first example above. However, he acknowledged that most people do not define inference in such narrow terms, and rarely in educational settings do we even engage learners in the type of deductive thinking required by logical inference. Instead we tend to define *inferences* as the ability to make connections between our prior knowledge and the information in the text. Kintsch argued that these types of inferences require the reader to retrieve information rather than generate new information. Thus, Kintsch has suggested that, "although the term *inference* is suitable for information generation processes, it is a misnomer for retrieval processes" (1998, p. 189). Given that most people define and think of *inference* as the ability to make connections between prior knowledge and the text, we include both understandings of inference in our definition. Kintsch noted that some bridging inferences are controlled. That is, they require deliberate, strategic processing in order to make connections across sentences and link that information to prior knowledge to make an inference. He referred to these inferences as *searches for bridging knowledge* or *bridging inferences*. Baker and Stein (1981) labeled these types of inferences *text-connecting inferences*. Thus, inferences that require the reader to make connections across sentences are known as either bridging or text-connecting inferences (see #3 in Table 5.2). Because Baker and Stein's term is more familiar, we use it here. Here is an example of a text-connecting inference:

Example 3: Bridging Inferences/Text-Connecting Inference

Major Premise (*A*)	Maria wanted to buy a new home.
Minor Premise (*B*)	She worked two jobs.
Conclusion (*C*)	Maria worked two jobs so that she would be able to earn enough money to buy a new home.

In Example 3 the reader has to take the information from the first sentence (that Maria wanted to buy a new home), combine it with information from the second sentence (that Maria worked two jobs), and then search for bridging information from prior knowledge (you earn extra money when you work two jobs) to connect the two sentences and make the inference that she probably worked two jobs to earn money to buy a new home.

In contrast with text-connecting inferences, which are controlled and involve retrieval processes, some inferences that require retrieval are automatic. When making these inferences, readers must supply the missing information (or implied information) by filling in the gaps in the text using prior knowledge. These inferences, which require the reader to add information from prior knowledge, are known as *elaborative inferences* (see #4 in Table 5.2). Baker and Stein (1981) referred to them as *gap-filling inferences*. Again, because the term *gap-filling inference* is more familiar, we use that term. Here is an example of a gap-filling inference:

Example 4: Elaborative Inference/Gap-Filling Inference
Mark dug a hole to plant the tree. (Mark used a shovel.)

The text does not directly state how Mark dug the hole, so the reader must make an inference as to how this task would be accomplished. In essence, the reader must "fill in the gap" or supply the missing information that is implicitly cued by the phrase *dug a hole*. In this case the inference the reader might automatically make is that Mark used a shovel to dig the hole. The inference is quickly and automatically made because it is common for people to use a shovel to dig a hole. This common information makes it easy to access the information from prior knowledge.

Sipe and Brightman's (2009) study about the responses second graders made during page breaks is an example in which readers make gap-filling inferences to fill in missing information between the pages. Key to the success of the study was using texts in which the page breaks elicited gap-filling inferences. As an example, they used Mo Willems's (2003) *Don't Let the Pigeon Drive the Bus*, in which the bus driver explains to the reader that he has to leave and asks the reader to watch his unattended bus for him while he's gone. He reminds readers to make certain that Pigeon does not drive the bus. The rest of the book proceeds with Pigeon making varied attempts to persuade the reader to let him drive the bus:

1 Pigeon: I thought he'd never leave.
2 [page break]
3 Pigeon: Hey, can I drive the bus?
4 [page break]
5 Pigeon: Please? I'll be careful.
6 [page break]
7 Pigeon: I tell you what: I'll just steer. My cousin Herb drives a bus almost every day.
8 [page break]
9 Pigeon: True story.

At each page break the teacher in Sipe and Brightman's (2009) study simply asked children, "What do you think happened between here (*pointing to one double-page spread such as #1 above*) and here (*pointing to the next double-page spread as in #3 above*)?" They did not ask any specific questions because they wanted to see the types of responses and inferences children naturally made without teacher guidance. This simple question asked at each page break yielded a plethora of responses and inferences from the children in their study.

Kintsch and Kintsch (2005) have noted that there are lots of gaps to be filled while reading, and readers make inferences as they construct a textbase and while they construct situation models. Some of the gaps that need to be filled occur locally (i.e., across sentences) and others occur more globally (i.e., across the whole text). An example of a global inference would be the ability to infer the theme of a story. Both gap-filling and text-connecting inferences are used, but the process requires the reader to make an inference from the entire text. Research conducted with undergraduates has shown that more proficient readers were more concerned with making global inferences to generate a coherent sense of the text as a whole, whereas less proficient readers were more concerned with making inferences to establish local coherence (Magliano & Millis, 2003; Millis, Magliano, & Tadaro, 2006).

Local inferences are more diverse and rely on the reader's ability to understand different coherence relations within the text in order to make both gap-filling and text-connecting inferences. Graesser, McNamara, and Louwerse (2003) noted that ideas in a text ideally "hang together in a meaningful and organized manner" (p. 83). Coherence relations help "organize text content" (Graesser et al., 2003, p. 83) and are constructed in the reader's mind using inferencing. Halliday and Hasan (1976) identified a complex taxonomy of various cohesive relations that link one word, phrase, sentence, or item in text to another. In terms of comprehension and inferencing, the following types of cohesive relations seem most relevant: coreference and conjunctions.

Coreference refers to any two words (or phrases) that refer to the same thing in a sentence or across sentences (Graesser et al., 2003; Halliday & Hasan, 1976). Pronouns (or anaphora) are examples of coreference in that they are reliant on words or phrases in a prior sentence (i.e., an antecedent) to make sense, but their meaning is the same. That is, the pronoun and its antecedent phrase refer to the same thing. Pronouns such as *he, she, him, her, my, mine, it, this, that, what,* and *who* are examples of pronouns we use to refer to previously introduced people, places, or things (i.e., the antecedent). Graesser et al. (2003) noted that when pronoun use is vague or ambiguous, comprehension becomes especially difficult. We use an example from Michael Buckley's (2007) *The Fairytale Detectives*, which is the first book in the Sisters Grimm series, to illustrate how pronouns are used as coreference:

1 **I'm** going to die of boredom here, Sabrina Grimm thought as **she** looked out the
2 train window at Ferryport Landing, New York. The little town in the distance
3 seemed to be mostly hills and trees next to the cold, gray Hudson River. A few
4 two- and three-story brownstone buildings huddled around what appeared to be
5 the town's only street. Beyond **it** were endless acres of evergreen forest.
6 Sabrina could see no movie theaters, malls, or museums, and felt using the word
7 *town* to describe Ferryport Landing was a bit of a stretch. (p. 1)

In line 1 of the example the author uses the personal pronouns *I'm* and *she* to refer to one of the main characters, Sabrina Grimm (highlighted in gray in the example). Beginning the narrative with a personal pronoun means that the reader must make a local inference immediately in order to understand to whom "I'm" refers. As well, the author uses the adverb *here* in the first line to refer to Ferryport Landing, New York, which is introduced later in the first sentence. Thus, the author makes it difficult for readers to identify the main character and the location from the onset of the book. In line 5 the author uses the pronoun *it*, but it is unclear whether the pronoun is referring to the town of Ferryport Landing, which is in line 2. If so, the sentence would be interpreted as, "Beyond the town of Ferryport Landing were endless acres of evergreen forest." Or, could "it" refer to "the town's only street," which is also in line 5? In the latter case, the sentence would be interpreted as, "Beyond the town's only street were endless acres of evergreen forest." The meaning is unclear because of the pronoun referent and the need to make a local inference across sentences. Certainly the gist of the paragraph is that the town is small and is surrounded by forest, but we are unsure of the precise meaning of that one particular sentence.

Conjunctions are used to connect adjacent clauses or sentences (Graesser et al., 2003). They help readers bring meaning to the text by providing clues as to how clauses relate to one another and how the text as a whole is organized. Halliday and Hasan (1976) identified several subcategories of conjunctions, which are identified in Table 5.3. In helping poor comprehenders, it is not so important that they learn types of pronouns and conjunctions. Instead, it is important that they learn how texts are structured and that authors sometimes provide "clue words" in the text that can help with comprehension. Thus, the examples in Table 5.3 include conjunctions and other parts of speech. Some clue words help us understand how text is connected because they indicate causality (i.e., causality conjunctions) or contrast (i.e., adversative conjunctions) or time (i.e., temporal conjunctions). Others (i.e., additive conjunctions) add information to extend what is already in a sentence. The following example, also taken from Michael Buckley's (2007) *The Fairytale Detectives*, provides illustrations of several types of conjunctions (as well as multiple pronoun referents) as they are used in narrative text:

1   "They locked us in their house for two weeks so they could go on a cruise
2   to Bora-Bora," Sabrina said.
3   "I think it was the Bahamas," Daphne said.
4   "It was Bermuda, **and** at least they brought you back some nice T-shirts from
5   their trip," said Mrs. Smirt. "**Anyway**, it is all water under the bridge now. We

TABLE 5.3. Types of Conjunctions

Type of Conjunction	Function	Examples
Additive	To add more information to what is already in the sentence	*and, also, furthermore, in addition, besides, that is, in other words, moreover*
		To indicate comparison: *likewise, similarly, in the same way*
		To indicate dissimilarity: *on the other hand, in contrast, alternatively*
Adversative	To indicate contrast between information in each clause	*but, however, although, yet, though, only, nevertheless, despite this, on the other hand, instead, on the contrary, anyhow, at any rate*
Causal	To indicate causality	*so, then, hence, therefore, consequently, because, for this reason, it follows, on this basis, to this end*
Temporal	To indicate time	*then, next, before, after, during, when, at the same time, previously, finally, at last, soon, next day, an hour later, meanwhile, at this moment, first, second, third, in conclusion, up to now*

Note. Based on Halliday and Hasan (1976).

6 found a *real* relative who is actually eager to take you into their home. **But** to
7 be honest, girls, even if she was an imposter I would hand you over to her. We
8 have run out of families who want you." (p. 4)

In line 4 the additive conjunction *and* is used to add information about the trip to Bermuda. The additive conjunction indicates that the information in the second clause ("at least they brought you back nice T-shirts from their trip") supplies additional detail that is linked to the first clause ("It was Bermuda"). Using conjunctions typically assists readers with comprehension because they make the connection clearer. Unfortunately, there are several pronouns used in the same segment that might make it problematic for struggling comprehenders to understand to whom *they* refers because the referent occurs in prior paragraphs. In line 5 the adversative conjunction *anyway* is used, which indicates that the information that follows is in contrast with the information it precedes. The inference that would need to be made is that the girls (Sabrina and Daphne) have been complaining about previous foster homes, and Mrs. Smirt is contrasting their complaints with the notion that they do not need to worry about unfit foster parents anymore. Unfortunately, using an idiomatic expression like "it is all water under the bridge" might make it difficult for those students who struggle with semantic issues. As discussed in the previous section, some children might not have an understanding of this idiomatic expression to grasp its meaning that something from the past can be forgotten now. Thus, it might be difficult for some readers to understand what the author was contrasting.

Finally, in line 6 the author uses the adversative conjunction *but* to indicate contrast with the previous sentence (that they would be handed over to a "real relative," which is later revealed to be their grandmother). The contrasting notion is that the girls would be handed over to this individual regardless of whether she were an actual relative or not. These examples help provide an understanding of how local coherence can impact comprehension while reading narrative text. Expository text structures, in particular, use similar signaling devices to help reveal the organization and purpose of the text. We discuss these issues later in Chapter 6 when sample lessons related to "identifying text structure" are shared.

Comprehension Monitoring

Comprehension monitoring involves the ability to evaluate or assess the progress made in attaining one's goal. In the case of reading this means evaluating and assessing progress made toward constructing a meaningful understanding of text. If the reader notices that satisfactory progress has not been made, then repair (fix-up) strategies are used in an attempt to get back on track. As noted in Chapter 1, metacognition and comprehension monitoring are essential to becoming a good strategy user, and an inability to monitor comprehension is often a reason why readers are unable to be strategic.

Because comprehension monitoring is a process that is difficult to observe overtly, some researchers have devised tasks (e.g., error-detection tasks) or altered texts so that they contain anomalous information (Baker & Beall, 2009). In these error-detection tasks, errors (or anomalous information) are intentionally placed in the text, and readers are rated on the degree to which they are able to identify the errors. Some error-detection tasks contain errors related to external consistency, as in the following example: *My car had a flat tortilla.* In this example the reader should notice that the sentence does not make sense because a car might have a flat tire but it would not have a flat tortilla—even though tortillas are flat. These studies found that younger and less proficient readers have difficulty recognizing inconsistencies or anomalies in text (August et al., 1984; Garner, 1980, 1987; Markman, 1977; Myers & Paris, 1978; Paris & Myers, 1981; Yuill & Oakhill, 1991). The problem with these tasks, as Baker and Beall (2009) and Yuill and Oakhill (1991) noted, is that sometimes students are reluctant to find "errors" in text because they believe text is infallible and that it should make sense. However, even when students were explicitly told that the text contained nonsense words and inconsistencies, poor comprehenders were less likely to identify them than students in control conditions. These findings suggest that poor comprehenders (i.e., automatic, struggling, and slow word callers) have great difficulty noticing when their comprehension is failing, which makes it unlikely that they will employ fix-up strategies to repair comprehension (Baker & Beall, 2009; Nation, 2005). In Chapter 6 we share teaching ideas, sample lessons, and transcripts from lessons in which these struggling readers are taught how to monitor their comprehension.

Knowledge

Nation (2005) and Wharton-McDonald and Swiger (2009) noted that knowledge of words and their meanings and prior knowledge of textual content are important for comprehension. It is also well known that vocabulary knowledge correlates highly with comprehension. However, Nation (2005) noted that, even in studies in which instruction was careful to either include familiar vocabulary in the text or to teach readers the requisite prior knowledge they would need to understand the text, poor comprehenders still had difficulty understanding the text (Cain et al., 2001). Thus, Nation (2005) concluded that although prior knowledge has an important role in comprehension, many poor comprehenders have difficulty understanding text because they often have difficulty accessing prior knowledge and semantic information quickly. Thus, our instruction may need to focus on ways to help these struggling comprehenders access prior knowledge more efficiently. As well, we may need to be concerned with readers who are able to access prior knowledge—but it is inaccurate prior knowledge that could lead to incongruity between it and the information in the text.

Schema theory provides one explanation of how prior knowledge about a topic, whether accurate or inaccurate, can influence comprehension (e.g., Anderson & Pearson, 1984). Schema theory posits that all knowledge is packaged into units known as *schemata* (Rumelhart, 1980). Schemata can be likened to a series of "mental file folders" (Tompkins & McGee, 1993) in which information is stored. As we attempt to comprehend incoming information from text, we search our mind for schemata that will enable us to make sense of this new information. When we find an appropriate schema (even if it contains inaccurate information), it is activated and linkages are made between the new information contained in the text and the old information contained in the schemata. As a result of these linkages, schemata are continually updated and changed during a process known as *instantiation* (Rumelhart & Ortony, 1977).

A lack of prior knowledge or an inability to access it becomes a dilemma for readers who may not have an appropriate schema in their conceptual framework that would enable them to make sense of the text. As an example, read the following text from *Curse of the Red Cross Ring* by Earl Pilgrim (2000) and think about how well you understand it.

"Listen, men," said Az, "you'd better start dipping the fish in right away, and make sure the cuts are wrapped tightly around the pins. Don't let the boat get too far away from the doorways. Hey," he yelled from the top of the engine house, "tie up that span line and don't let her go out any further. Hold everything fast; I'll watch the swells" (pp. 172–173)

In this example a reader may have very little background knowledge or only partially instantiated schemata for the topic under consideration. If one knows little about fishing—in particular, cod fishing off the coast of Newfoundland in the early 1900s—then this paragraph might prove difficult to understand. Comprehension may be partially impaired, and the text may require a great deal of effort to understand as a result. Gee (1992) would explain the dilemma in terms of the reader not possessing the appropriate Discourse that would enable her to understand the text. Even though Janice was immersed in the culture while learning the Discourse of a Newfoundlander during her 6-month stay in Newfoundland, as she read Earl Pilgrim's *Curse of the Red Cross Ring* she found this paragraph to be particularly difficult to understand. In fact, her Uncle George spent nearly an hour drawing a diagram and explaining the requisite terminology related to cod traps, punts, and fishing to help her understand it.

In school these problems may become obvious from students' written and oral responses to text. In the following example a fourth-grade student was reading *The Patchwork Quilt* by Valerie Flournoy (1985). After reading the book he wrote the following in his response journal:

I dont [don't] like this story Because I don't have eny [any] quilts at home and I dont [don't] now [know] what they look like so I would now [know] what one looks like so I would understand it better.

Although the child is clearly having difficulty with written expression, he is monitoring his comprehension and is aware that his comprehension was hindered because he did not have the appropriate schemata available to understand the story. After reading this student's journal entry, the teacher is now aware that she must teach this child strategies to repair comprehension when he realizes that he does not have sufficient background knowledge to understand the text. Additionally, the teacher might consider providing a bit more of an introduction prior to reading the text that would provide more background knowledge about quilts and quilting. Drawing on the notion of making learning as concrete as possible, the teacher might have provided students with realistic, hands-on experiences to instantiate their schemata for quilts before reading. The point at which the student read and reacted to Valerie Flournoy's (1985) *The Patchwork Quilt* would be an ideal time to use hands-on experiences. The teacher and students might bring in quilts from home, especially those that are family heirlooms. With actual quilts available to touch, examine, and study, students can engage in a discussion of what quilts are used for, how they are made, why people might attach sentimental value to a quilt, or why a person would make one by hand rather than simply purchasing one. As the discussion progresses, the ideas can be captured on a semantic web. Had the teacher provided such hands-on experience with authentic quilts prior to reading the story, the student, by his own account, may have understood the story better. This process is similar to that used in the language experience approach (Stauffer, 1970), in which students first engage in an authentic experience (e.g., a field trip, an observation, a tour, a science experiment), after which they generate verbal descriptions of the experience that is recorded on paper (usually by the teacher or other adult). The recorded language is often in the form of connected prose that tells a story or describes the event, but it may also be recorded in the form of a web. The student-generated text is then used for instruction that focuses on word recognition, comprehension, and fluency.

Some might argue that it is the teacher's responsibility to *make sure* students have the appropriate prior knowledge before reading a text. We would argue, however, that it is impossible to be able to forecast which students possess particular prior knowledge for every text. Likewise it is difficult to forecast all of the prior knowledge that will be needed to make connections to text. Instead, if we are truly trying to prepare readers to be independent, self-regulated learners, then our job is to provide instruction that teaches them how to recognize when they are struggling to understand text (i.e., how to monitor their comprehension) and how to repair their comprehension using appropriate strategic actions. As in the example above in which the child struggled to understand *The Patchwork Quilt* because he did not have prior knowledge of quilts, the reader was able to monitor his comprehension and knew that he was having trouble understanding the text because he was not really sure what a quilt was. However, he did not know what to do to help himself after that point. He was able to recognize that he had a problem (which is excellent), but he did not know how to use repair strategies to help himself. Our goal, then, is to provide readers with instruction that helps them learn how to be successful in that situation.

McNamara (2001) examined the effect of prior knowledge and coherence on comprehension. She found that readers with high prior knowledge benefited more from reading texts that had low coherence first. McNamara theorized that this was because the readers would be more likely to generate the inferences needed to understand the text, given that it lacked coherence, and they needed to enact strategic processes to organize and bring meaning to it. On the other hand, readers with low prior knowledge (like the child above who lacked knowledge of quilts) benefited more from reading text that had high coherence. It seems that when readers lack sufficient prior knowledge, or have difficulty accessing prior knowledge, it helps when the text is highly organized and its structure is apparent. Thus, when we know readers may lack prior knowledge of a topic, particularly when they are reading informational text in a content area (e.g., science or social studies) in which they are learning new content information, it is important to try to provide text that is well structured and highly organized. If that is not possible, then students will need to be well equipped with strategies related to building prior knowledge and recognizing implicit text structures. Each of these strategies is discussed in Chapter 6.

In another example of prior knowledge difficulties, a group of fourth graders had just read the story *Soup's New Shoes* by Robert Newton Peck (1986). In the story a young boy (Soup) purchased a new pair of shoes for three dollars and then took advantage of a warm March day to try them out on his walk to school. The setting of this realistic fiction story (i.e., March, in Vermont, in the 1930s) was particularly troublesome for these students living in the 1990s in a part of the United States that does not typically see snow or cold temperatures in March. After reading the story the group engaged in a peer discussion of the text that revealed their struggle to understand the setting. Although the students clearly have schemata available for "March," they had none for the notion of "snow in March," as this transcript demonstrates (all names are pseudonyms):

1 BRIAN: I think they wore a lot of clothes for March because it said (*reading from text*), "Soup unbuttoned his coat and took off his hat, the one with the red earlappers, then slowly unbuckled his left shoe." He's got lots of stuff on. It's in March.

2 HENNA: It was snowing out.

3 DEREK: It's usually just cold in March.

4 BRIAN: I know, it's not *that* cold in March, is it? But they said on page . . .

5 HENNA: I don't think it's cold in March.

6 BRIAN: (*Reading from text*) "A warm March day took away most of the snow." (Almasi, 1993, pp. 223–227)

The students also had difficulty understanding the manner in which shoes were fitted and sold in the 1930s when X-ray machines were used to determine the appropriate size shoe to purchase:

1 TRACY: I wonder why, um, um, Soup said that in the shoe store the guy had an X-ray machine?

2 BRIAN: I don't know why, because why would the shoe man buy, a shoe salesman buy that kind of equipment just to sell shoes?

3 DEREK: They usually have just the shoe, the foot measuring thing. You take off your shoe and stick your foot on there.

4 HENNA: Not a machine, they don't have them back .. .

5 AARON: An X-ray machine—he's probably like a doctor and a shoe salesman in one.

6 ALL: Yeah.

7 TRACY: That's what I thought.

8 DEREK: Did they have X-ray machines back then?

9 BRIAN: They said it was 1930.

10 TRACY: What he said, he said it was for to see if the foot fit in the shoe.

11 HENNA: Like how big your bones were and how much you had to grow.

12 AARON: Pretty clever.

13 DEREK: But your skin is over your bones. You can't see your skin in an X-ray.

14 BRIAN: If you want to see your skin in an X-ray machine, what's an X-ray machine for?

15 HENNA: That's true. You can see your skin outside the X-ray machine.

16 JARED: That's why they call it an X-ray machine.

17 DEREK: 'Cause just to see if the foot could fit in the shoe then why'd they do that for? 'Cause your skin's gonna be over the bone when it goes into the shoe.

18 AARON: You could probably see right through the shoe.

19 BRIAN: Well actually, the X-ray machine is just so you can see how big your foot really is.

20 HENNA: And how much you'll grow.

21 BRIAN: . . . and the skin will just cover it up, the foot, not really a big part of it.

22 AARON: He's probably like a doctor and like . . . I don't know what you call, but it's a doctor, but they check your feet just in case you, like broke it or something.

23 TRACY: If he only wants it for feet, why don't he make a little small one for feet?

24 ALL: Probably is.

25 BRIAN: 'Cause how could a shoe salesman afford that big thing?

26 AARON: But why would they want an X-ray machine unless so somebody would help see what happens?

27 DEREK: He don't buy it, the store has it.

28 BRIAN: They don't sell 'em in stores do they?

29 DEREK: No! No! The store can get one. He don't have to buy it—the store guy.

30 JIGUAO: I want to know why the shoe salesman just buy a X-ray machine just for the feet?

31 BRIAN: Well that's a question we've been on for a pretty long time. Probably just to be fancy.

(Almasi, 1993, pp. 223–227)

In both of these events students are engaged in a peer discussion of the text. That is, the teacher is not present in the discussion to ask questions or guide interpretation. Instead, students have come to the discussion prepared to construct meaning dialogically with one another. As they read, they made note of any questions or concerns they had (either in a response journal or on sticky notes). They bring those questions and concerns to the peer discussion and are encouraged by the teacher to help one another collaboratively construct meaning. In the two examples from *Soup's New Shoes* we see the impact of prior knowledge (or the lack of prior knowledge or the presence of inaccurate prior knowledge) on students' comprehension. In lines 1 and 2 of the second excerpt Tracy and Brian struggle to understand why an X-ray machine would be in a shoe store. Derek drew on his available schema for buying shoes in line 3 to explain the type of equipment that he has seen in a shoe store. In line 5 Aaron attempted to make a link between his schema for buying shoes and X-ray machines. His schema for X-ray machines suggested that only doctors used such equipment. In making the connection he thought about what kind of doctor might be associated with feet. Although he does not use the term *podiatrist*, he was aware of some type of doctor that specializes in foot care. Therefore, he suggested that perhaps the shoe salesman is also a podiatrist. This is a fascinating attempt at integrating information across text to make sense of it. It shows Aaron's ability to engage in critical thinking, and it also shows that he is focused on making sense of the text. In line 10 Tracy directed the group back to the information in the text by noting the purpose of using an X-ray machine to sell shoes. The ensuing discourse (lines 11–21) displays the students' collaborative effort to understand how an X-ray machine might be used to measure feet, despite the fact that their available schema for buying shoes did not include such information.

Many teachers who have watched this video excerpt and are familiar with the story have suggested that the students' focus on setting was trivial. The theme of the story centered on friendship, and the setting was not critical to this theme at all. These teachers believe that the students' discussion would be at a higher cognitive level if they examined the theme. However, for these students the theme of friendship was very obvious, and their schema for friendship was well instantiated. They understood the theme and gave it very little attention in their discussion because they understood it so well. They needed to spend time during their discussion working collaboratively on those aspects of the text that were confusing to them. Thus, they focused much of their attention on examining the setting and were able to use a repair strategy (i.e., "asking one another") to help them understand the text better.

Wade (1990) suggested that some students have difficulty activating prior knowledge and using it to make predictions from relevant textual cues. These readers generally are "non-risk takers" (Wade, 1990, p. 446). That is, they view reading primarily as a task in which they decode the words on the page and are so focused on decoding that meaning is secondary. Earlier in this chapter we referred to these readers as "word callers." These readers, in particular, benefit from learning how to use previewing strategies such as looking at the titles, pictures, and headings and thinking about what they already know concerning the topic, to help them learn how to anticipate the types of words that might appear in a given text. For example, by activating prior knowledge about "buying shoes" (their schema) before reading *Soup's New Shoes*, readers might call to mind several words that will appear later in the text. By activating such background knowledge prior to reading, readers facilitate later word recognition. Readers who do not use previewing strategies approach each word in the text "cold." They read without any expectations or any form of active processing. They simply "call out" the words, as if the words were unconnected to one another. Comprehension is usually negatively impacted by this type of reading.

In the examples above, students could have activated their schema for "buying shoes" by glancing at the title, *Soup's New Shoes*. However, the pictures in the story do not provide any clues indicating that the setting is that much different from the present day. In this situation there is little that the students, on their own, could do to prepare them for the setting-related difficulties they encountered. The teacher could have provided background information about buying shoes in the 1930s and about Vermont in the spring, which would have alleviated the schema availability problems. However, in this instance the teacher did not anticipate the possible confusion over the time period and the setting. It is impossible to anticipate every comprehension clunk that students may encounter and provide background knowledge to instantiate every schema. Thus it is important to teach students to monitor their own comprehension and enact repair strategies when clunks of this nature are encountered. The type of peer discussion featured in the above examples, in which students bring their own questions to the discussion about which they truly are confused (rather than focusing on teacher-posed questions), fosters the ability to recognize and resolve comprehension problems and leads to higher-level thinking (Almasi, 1995). These examples illustrate that even when schema availability problems are not anticipated, students can still learn how to resolve comprehension problems if the instructional context fosters independence and strategic processing.

Recent research has been concerned with readers who have inaccurate prior knowledge similar to the examples above related to *Soup's New Shoes*. These studies are concerned with what happens when readers have misconceptions about a topic and attempt to integrate that inaccurate prior knowledge with text. How are learning and comprehension affected by inaccurate prior knowledge? When prior knowledge and text are incongruent, readers may simply ignore the discrepant information in the text. Another possibility is that the high degree of effort it would take to reconcile the disparate information may limit the amount of effort readers are willing to expend to make connections. Some have argued that using "refutation" texts, or texts that contain information that deliberately and explicitly refutes the prior knowledge-based misconceptions readers are likely to have, are useful in altering these misconceptions.

Diakidoy, Mouskounti, and Ioannides (2011) examined the impact of reading refutation text on learning and comprehension, compared to reading typical expository text. They suggested that refutation text might not influence the amount of content recalled or retained as much as help create coherence within the information that is retained. Their study found that reading refutation text increased learning and increased the number of valid inferences generated (both text-connecting and gap-filling inferences). However, the gains for learning, recall, and inference generation were greater for students with low and inaccurate prior knowledge when they read the refutation text.

In contrast with the previous study, which examined comprehension after reading, Kendeou and van den Broek (2007) investigated the effect of prior knowledge and text structure on undergraduate students' comprehension *while* reading. They found that the reading process is influenced by misconceptions and text structure. In particular, readers with misconceptions (such as misconceptions about Newton's first law of motion that every object persists in its state of rest or uniform motion in a straight line unless an external force acts on it) read nonrefutation text at the same rate and activated prior knowledge and integrated it with the text as often as readers without misconceptions, but the content of their inferences contained more incorrect information, which resulted in fewer valid inferences. While reading refutation texts that contradicted their prior knowledge, however, readers with misconceptions read more slowly and used different strategies. These findings suggest that when reading refutation texts, readers with misconceptions are able to make connections between their prior knowledge and the text. This enables them to detect the inconsistency between their prior knowledge and the text. The ability to recognize the inconsistency enables them to activate strategies that help them attain a coherent understanding of the text.

Unfortunately these studies of inaccurate prior knowledge were conducted with undergraduate students in an isolated lab-like setting, which means that we are not sure whether the findings would be similar for elementary-age students in real classrooms. From these studies we might conclude that we need to provide students with refutation text so they are more apt to recognize and resolve incongruities with their prior knowledge. However, as noted earlier it would be very burdensome and unrealistic in a classroom to (1) measure students' prior knowledge before every reading, and (2) have refutation text available that directly refutes each student's inaccurate prior knowledge. Instead, we have to take the findings and build on them. The key point is that readers with inaccurate prior knowledge or little prior knowledge must be confronted with the conflicts between their prior knowledge and the text. Vygotsky's (1978) notion that learning occurs first in a social setting is important here, in that if students can interact with others who might help (politely) point out inconsistencies between ideas in the text and their prior "knowledge" and help resolve the inconsistencies by collaboratively connstructing a coherent interpretation, then in time students would internalize the ability to recognize incongruities and resolve them.

My (Janice's) work with fourth graders examined this precise issue (Almasi, 1995). My findings suggested that when average and below-average readers were involved in peer discussions of text after reading, they were better able to recognize and resolve inconsistencies in the text, in their prior knowledge, and in their interactions with their peers. These findings suggest that providing learning contexts in which children are able to dialogically construct meaning with their peers (as in the above example of the fourth graders' discussion of *Soup's New Shoes*), they eventually internalize the ability to monitor their comprehension (i.e., recognize inconsistencies) and enact strategic processes to resolve the conflict.

SUMMARY

Reading comprehension is the process of constructing meaning in which readers, texts, and contexts transact within a sociocultural context. At times, however, meaning construction is inhibited or impaired. Because there are so many variables involved in constructing a meaningful interpretation of text, many readers struggle with comprehension. Some are able to read words accurately and many read with fluency, yet they struggle to comprehend. The focus of these automatic, struggling, and slow word callers is on decoding, and they do not view reading as a meaning-construction process. Many of these struggling comprehenders have difficulty with semantic issues that inhibits their ability to understand the meanings of words and the way text is organized. Others have difficulty with higher-order processes such as making inferences and monitoring comprehension. Still others have difficulty accessing and retrieving prior knowledge. For those readers who do not have appropriate prior knowledge or who are unable to access prior knowledge to make connections to the new information in the text, teaching them how to preview text and correct or access their prior knowledge helps reduce these problems.

Some readers have the opposite problem and tend to overrely on their prior knowledge to understand text. These readers have difficulty recognizing when the text does not support the schema they have selected to help understand it. Teaching these students to (1) set purposes; (2) generate, confirm, and revise predictions; and (3) identify text structure helps focus their attention so that they can anticipate, organize, and categorize textual information. For those readers who have difficulty focusing their attention throughout the entire reading process, strategies that will help them focus attention, such as visualization, monitoring comprehension, and identifying text structure, can assist them in overcoming this difficulty. We examine these strategies in more detail in Chapter 6.

CHAPTER SIX

Strategy Instruction
That Enhances Comprehension

As noted in Chapter 2, the CESI model is a recursive one in which a safe environment for motivated strategy use creates, and is created by, opportunities for students to verbalize about strategic processing, opportunities for teachers to provide explicit instruction, and opportunities for teachers to reduce processing to foster awareness and understanding of strategic processes. This model provides the instructional framework for the ideas contained in Chapters 6 and 7. The purpose of this chapter is to provide teachers with hands-on tools and resources (i.e., sample lessons, texts, and teaching ideas) that will make beginning strategy instruction less cumbersome.

IMPLICIT INSTRUCTION OF COMPREHENSION STRATEGIES

Implicit, or endogenous, strategy instruction provides an instructional context in which readers gradually internalize instructional principles through guided discovery and scaffolding from more knowledgeable others (Vygotsky, 1978). Two models of such instruction (e.g., collaborative problem solving and process talk) were described in Chapter 2. Ideally such strategy instruction should occur seamlessly. As children read and discuss texts, the reading event itself (i.e., the reader, the text, the context) provides the materials of instruction. During implicit strategy instruction, students have the opportunity to interact with others as they strategically process text. The teacher plans the learning event by carefully selecting texts that require readers to use specific strategies. For example, some texts have an obvious structure that facilitates comprehension; others are written with image-laden language that fosters use of visualization as a comprehension strategy. As students read these texts, they may automatically use these strategies to understand the meaning, without consciously understanding the principles underlying their use (Walker, 2012). Following the reading, students might engage in a peer discussion of the text in which they initiate the topics of discussion and work collaboratively to construct an understanding of the material, as we saw in the examples in Chapter 5 of fourth graders' peer discussions of *Soup's New Shoes* (Almasi, 1993, 1995, 2002; Almasi et al., 2001; Gambrell & Almasi, 1996). During these discussions, students used a variety of strategies as they made sense of the text.

As an example of this type of instruction, read the following text (Bartlett, 1932, p. 65) and think about the strategies you use to process, or make sense of, the excerpts. In other words, engage yourself in a think-aloud of sorts, in which, as you read, you identify and label the strategic processes you use to make sense of the text.

The War of the Ghosts

1 One night two young men from Egulac went down to the river to hunt seals, and
2 while they were there it became foggy and calm. Then they heard war-cries, and
3 they thought: "Maybe this is a war party." They escaped to the shore and hid
4 behind a log. Now canoes came up, and they heard the noise of the paddles, and
5 saw one canoe coming up to them. There were five men in the canoe, and they said:
6 "What do you think? We wish to take you along. We are going up the river to
7 make war on the people."
8 One of the young men said, "I have no arrows."
9 "Arrows are in the canoe," they said.
10 "I will not go along. I might be killed. My relatives do not know where I have
11 gone. But you," he said, turning to the other, "may go with them."
12 So one of the young men went, but the other returned home.
13 And the warriors went on up the river to a town on the other side of Kalama.
14 The people came down to the water, and they began to fight, and many were killed.
15 But presently the young man heard one of the warriors say: "Quick let us go home:
16 that Indian has been hit." Now he thought: "Oh, they are ghosts." He did not feel
17 sick, but they said he had been shot.
18 So the canoes went back to Egulac, and the young man went ashore to his house,
19 and made a fire. And he told everybody and said: "Behold I accompanied the
20 ghosts, and we went to fight. Many of our fellows were killed, and many of those
21 who attacked us were killed. They said I was hit, and I did not feel sick."
22 He told it all, and then he became quiet. When the sun rose he fell down.
23 Something black came out of his mouth. His face became contorted. The people
24 jumped up and cried.
25 He was dead.

For most people of Anglo-European backgrounds, this text is somewhat difficult to understand. There is no "correct" way to read this passage. That is, there is no single set of strategies, or pattern of strategy use, that will produce a "better" interpretation. Each individual approaches the text differently and uses different strategies to process it. After reading it for the first time, many students in our graduate courses often break into spontaneous conversation with one another as they try to make sense of the text. These conversations are lively and focused. Often the discourse includes discussion of the *way* in which they arrived at their different interpretations. I (Jannice) often hear questions such as, "What made you think that?" Sometimes people share places in the text in which they had vivid images, such as in lines 2–5 or 22–24. Sometimes they share places in which they recognized that their comprehension was suffering, "I thought I understood it until he said, 'Oh, they are ghosts' " (line 16). The entire focus of the discussion is an effort to construct meaning collaboratively. This type of reading event is an example of implicit instruction that is based on endogenous constructivist principles (as discussed in Chapter 2), in which learning occurs in a social context that gradually permits learners to internalize instructional principles through guided discovery and interaction with more knowledgeable others, rather than through explicit instruction (Pressley, Harris, et al., 1992). In these reading events, students who may not be familiar with a particular strategy (e.g., imagery) hear the others discussing the vivid images in lines 2–5 and 22–24, and, although they may not have known about using imagery previously, they incidentally learn some *declarative* knowledge about its existence, and from the discussion they learn *conditional* knowledge about how others used it. Over time readers accumulate knowledge about a strategy such as imagery, and they may try using it in the future while reading independently. This is the type of learning environment that is depicted in Chapter 5 in the fourth-graders' discussion of the setting in *Soup's New Shoes* by Robert Newton Peck.

Strategy instruction that is based on dialectical constructivist principles, in which the teacher takes a more active role in the discussion by providing hints and prompts to facilitate student scaffolding and learning (Pressley, Harris, et al., 1992), is exemplified in Chapter 2's sample discussion of Stephen Mooser's (1978) *The Ghost with the Halloween Hiccups*. This type of discourse occurs during transactional strategies instruction (TSI; Pressley, El-Dinary, et al., 1992). The teacher serves as a more knowledgeable other who scaffolds the instruction by providing labels and explanations for the strategic processing, as it occurs. Teachers might also initiate discourse about strategic processing by prompting students with open-ended probes such as, "How did you figure that out?" or "Why do you think that?"

Such discussions might also focus on the manner in which students processed the text to arrive at a particular interpretation. During this type of "strategy talk," students learn how others were able to make sense of the text. Over time, with accumulated experiences of such incidental learning, students gradually internalize the requisite declarative, procedural, and conditional knowledge associated with proficient strategy use. However, communicating such information is never the explicit goal of an implicit instructional lesson.

Kucan and Beck (1997) suggested that these implicit learning environments may be sufficient to help students learn about the process of constructing meaning. One concern, however, is the fact that the efficacy of implicit instruction is contingent upon readers who are able to engage actively in the process—a problem for struggling readers who are passive and unaware of, and unable to use, strategic processes. Can we provide the boundless amounts of time that might be required for all readers to discover and internalize these principles? Another concern is more global: readers who may be completely unaware of particular features of strategic processing that would help them. For example, there is a wealth of research indicating that readers of varying abilities have difficulty comprehending expository text structures. How can readers who have no schema available for expository text structure include it in their discussion?

Instructional practice need not be an either–or situation. It is possible to provide *all* readers, proficient and less proficient, with both implicit and explicit strategy instruction so that they reap the benefits of both environments. Suppose, as students engaged in a peer discussion similar to that described in the commentary following the "War of the Ghosts," the teacher took anecdotal notes. These notes would describe the strategies that were used to construct meaning, the manner in which students used strategies (i.e., where, when, and how), which students used particular strategies, and how successful their strategic actions were for constructing meaning. From these notes the teacher would formulate hypotheses about the type of explicit instruction needed to help her students develop even more facility for comprehending similar text in the future. These hypotheses might pertain to any aspect of the good strategy user model described in Chapters 1 and 2. The teacher would then plan an explicit instruction lesson, or series of lessons, designed to introduce new strategic knowledge and to refine or expand existing knowledge. During these lessons the teacher would provide explanation and modeling of the new ideas and then ample opportunity for students to engage in guided practice in a variety of authentic reading contexts. Ideally, these guided practice events would take on the character of implicit instruction so that responsibility for selecting and using strategies is ceded back to the students. The teacher would then continue to involve all students in implicit instructional contexts to see how and whether they were using the new information taught via explicit instruction. This is the nature of reflective practice and ongoing assessment and instruction of strategic processes that is described in Chapters 3 and 4. It is a dynamic and recursive process, but the instructional aspect of it need not, and should not, solely reflect one ideological perspective.

EXPLICIT INSTRUCTION OF COMPREHENSION STRATEGIES

As described in Chapter 2, explicit instruction in dialectical models of strategy instruction provides an opportunity for more teacher influence over the learning environment and the nature of the instruction. The teacher identifies the objectives and goals for the lesson and provides explanation, modeling, and guided practice to help students attain them. Over time the teacher gradually releases responsibility for directing the instruction to the students, until they are capable of engaging in the process entirely on their own. As Pearson and Dole (1987) noted, it is essential that explicit instruction be provided using authentic texts in which the reading process is performed. That is, explicit instruction of strategies should not occur in isolation, without connected text, or as a distinct and separate activity. It must be embedded within, and linked to, authentic reading events. During explicit instruction, teachers must be attuned to the learning environment so that they are able to identify opportune moments in which to insert strategy-related language and provide opportunities for students to engage in similar practice. These opportunities for student verbalization and dialogue about strategy use enable them to "try out," or appropriate, strategy language for their own use.

With this overview in mind, the remainder of the chapter focuses on the background research and teaching tools related to those research-based comprehension strategies that are used most often by good readers. It should be noted that although each strategy is presented in isolation and the sample lessons focus on teaching only one strategy at a time, strategies should *not* be taught in a series of step-like lessons. Strategy use is a dynamic, fluid process that varies from individual to individual and from context to context. Strategy instruction should reflect this fluidity. Ideally, the ideas presented here can be used by teachers as an initial guide, to be adapted and altered to fit the needs of particular students in particular contexts. Brown (2008) and Shanahan et al. (2010) have suggested that for teachers new to strategies instruction, it may be easier to begin by teaching one strategy at a time and gradually work their way toward fluidly integrating all strategies into instruction. The ideas that follow are presented in a linear fashion because they are bounded by the limitations of publishing them in a two-dimensional format. This linear presentation might make the uninformed reader think that each strategy is mutually exclusive and could be taught apart from other strategies. Many of the "single" strategies presented below, in a sequence, overlap and are essential components of other strategies; the strategies are mutually dependent on, and continually inform, one another. However, for the sake of clarity, they are divided into three categories: (1) text anticipation strategies, (2) text maintenance strategies, and (3) fix-up strategies.

Text Anticipation Strategies

Text anticipation strategies are a family of strategies that include (1) previewing the text by looking at the title, pictures, and headings; (2) activating prior knowledge; (3) setting purposes; (4) generating, verifying, and updating predictions; and (5) identifying text structure. Table 6.1 identifies all comprehension strategies and provides teachers with an overview of the declarative, procedural, and conditional knowledge that might be associated with each strategy so that such knowledge is more easily infused into explicit instruction. As well, Table 6.1 provides a description of teaching methods and activities that might be used during instruction to help foster strategic processing.

Readers use these strategies flexibly and in combination with one another as they read. These strategies help readers avert difficulties accessing prior knowledge and semantic issues. The key element of each of these strategies is prior knowledge, which includes general world knowledge, specific knowledge related to the content of text, and knowledge about the way a specific text is organized (Dole et al., 1991)

Readers use previewing strategies to sample aspects of the text. The cues gathered during this sampling process can be derived from (1) any semiotic or linguistic feature of the text (i.e., title, pictures, headings, or the text itself) as well as (2) the manner in which the author has organized the text (i.e., text structure). These cues help readers activate and make links to relevant background knowledge (i.e., schemata). These same cues, coupled with the activated background knowledge, enable readers to make predictions about what might happen (Afflerbach, 1990; Anderson & Pearson, 1984). These predictions often become a reason (i.e., a purpose) for continued reading and help readers anticipate the meaning of the text. Readers are motivated to continue reading to determine whether their prediction is accurate. Predictions are monitored and checked against textual information as more text is read (Collins, Brown, & Larkin, 1980) and are verified, rejected, or altered as a result. This process means that new purposes for continued reading also are set. This entire process is a cyclical and recursive one that is repeated over and over while one reads, and at any given point a reader may have multiple predictions and purposes for reading (Shanahan et al., 2010).

Previewing Text and Activating Prior Knowledge

Previewing the text by glancing at the pictures, titles, and headings, and by activating relevant prior knowledge enables the reader to anticipate the content. Based on their reviews of the research, Shanahan et al. (2010) and Pressley, Johnson, Symons, McGoldrick, and

Kurita (1989) identified prior knowledge activation as an effective research-based strategy to teach children. They contended that prior knowledge affects comprehension by creating expectations that direct attention to relevant aspects of text, permitting inferential elaboration of text, facilitating recall of text, and affecting interpretation. Research has shown that the knowledge readers possess affects the manner in which they see the world and the manner in which they understand text (Anderson & Pearson, 1984). Prior knowledge affects what is recalled from text (Anderson, Pichert, & Shirey, 1983; Bransford & Johnson, 1972; Pearson, Hansen, & Gordon, 1979; Recht & Leslie, 1988; Taft & Leslie, 1985) and one's interpretation of text (Anderson, Reynolds, Schallert, & Goetz, 1977). The results of these findings suggest that strategic readers activate their background knowledge in all three domains (general world knowledge, textual content, and text structure) before and during reading (Pearson & Fielding, 1991; Pressley, Johnson, et al., 1989).

As noted earlier, prior knowledge may interfere with reading comprehension if existing knowledge conflicts with textual information or is inaccurate. Lipson (1983) found that when children in grades 4, 5, and 6 read passages that were congruent with their religious backgrounds, their ability to recall and make inferences was greater and included fewer distortions than when they read passages that were incongruent with their religious background. Similarly, Alvermann, Smith, and Readence (1985) found that sixth-grade students were wary of believing a science text when it conflicted with their previous knowledge. Because readers often ignore or dismiss incongruent information on their own, it is essential for them to participate in social environments that provide the opportunity to share their thoughts with others as meaning is constructed: Peers do not permit incongruities to be ignored or dismissed as readily as occurs during independent reading. The group holds readers accountable for their interpretations and facilitates meaning construction. Janice's research (Almasi, 1995) found that fourth graders were better able to recognize and resolve such incongruities when in peer discussion than in teacher-led discussion environments. Thus social environments such as peer discussion are essential for alleviating the comprehension difficulties associated with prior knowledge that conflicts with textual information.

When teaching students how to activate their prior knowledge, it is important to remember that the goal is to teach them how to use the strategy on their own. Helping students learn to use strategies independently means that lessons should communicate the declarative, procedural, and conditional knowledge associated with activating prior knowledge (see Table 6.1), and they should enable students to perform the strategy on their own while scaffolded by the teacher. As noted in column 4 of Table 6.1, activating prior knowledge is a strategy that should be used when reading all texts. Hence, selecting texts for such lessons should pose no problem in the classroom. Figure 6.1 displays a sample lesson plan adapted from Angela Bies's work with a struggling fourth grader. The lesson contains marginal glosses to indicate where each element of the CESI model occurs. (All sample lessons are presented to facilitate insight into how explicit strategy instruction is enacted in the preparatory stage. Teachers must modify and make adjustments while teaching to meet the needs of individual students.)

The sample lesson has only two goals: to teach students how to activate prior knowledge and to teach them how to organize activated prior knowledge when new information is encountered while reading. Explicit strategy instruction should not be overwhelming.

(text resumes on page 155)

TABLE 6.1. Declarative, Procedural, and Conditional Knowledge Associated with Comprehension Strategies

Comprehension strategy	Associated declarative knowledge[a]	Associated procedural knowledge[a]	Associated conditional knowledge[a]	Teaching methods
Previewing text	Readers need to know *that*: • Before reading any text, it is helpful to preview it. • Previewing involves looking at the title, pictures, table of contents, headings, chapter titles, subheadings, or any other textual feature to gain an idea of what the text will be about.	*How* to preview text: • Look at the cover of the text. • Study the title and the pictures. • Think about what clues are given to see what the text might be about. • Open the text and look at the table of contents, chapter titles, and headings to gain more clues about what the text will be about. • Flip through the book and glance at the pictures, charts, or graphs to gain more clues about what the text might be about. • Read the back cover or introductory statements to gain more clues about what the text might be about.	*Where* is it helpful to preview text? • As you read all types of text. *When* is it helpful to preview text? • Previewing is helpful *before* you read. • Previewing is often helpful *while* setting purposes. • Previewing is often helpful *while* making predictions. *Why* is it helpful to preview text? • Previewing helps prepare you for reading (reduces schema availability problems). • Previewing helps you anticipate what the text will be about so that you can activate relevant prior knowledge, set purposes, and make predictions as you read.	• Picture walks. • Rich discussion.
Activating prior knowledge	Readers need to know *that*: • Activating prior knowledge means thinking about what you know about the topic of the text. • What you already know about the world can help you understand what you read. • As you read, you should continually try to make connections between what you know and the new ideas in the text.	*How* to activate prior knowledge: • Look at the title, pictures, headings, or chapter titles in the text to gain an idea of what it is about. • Think about what you already know about the topic. • Sometimes it helps to write down what you already know about the topic. • As you read, try to make connections between what you know about the topic and the new ideas in the text.	*Where* is it helpful to activate prior knowledge? • As you read all types of text. *When* is it helpful to activate prior knowledge? • If done *before* you read, it will help you anticipate what the text will be about. • Anticipating what the text is about will help you set purposes for reading and make predictions. • If done *while* you read, it will help you update and revise your predictions, and it will help you set new purposes. • If done *after* reading, it will help you evaluate and monitor how well you understood the text.	• Semantic webs and semantic maps to organize ideas. • The "K" portion of K-W-L procedure (see Figure 6.3). • Vocabulary language prediction activities.

148

(cont.)

	Readers need to know *that*:	*How* to...	Where/When/Why	Activities
			Why is it helpful to activate prior knowledge? • It helps you prepare for reading (reduces schema availability problems). • It helps you to focus your attention while reading (reduces schema selection and retrievability problems).	
Setting purposes	• We can read for different purposes. • Purposes are plans we make that tell what we want to find out as we read text. • When we set purposes, it guides the reading process. • When we set purposes, it helps focus attention while reading. • We read differently when we have different purposes in mind. • We can set purposes to learn new information, confirm predictions, identify text structure, or perform a task.	*How* to set purposes: • Look at the title, pictures, headings, or chapter titles in the text to gain an idea of what it is about. • Think about what you already know about the topic. • Think about what you would like to find out about the topic or about the story. • Sometimes it helps to write down your purposes. • As you read, think about whether the information in the text answers your purpose. • Revise your purpose or generate new purposes based on the information in the text.	*Where* is it helpful to set purposes? • As you read all types of texts. *When* is it helpful to set purposes? • Setting purposes *before* reading helps focus your thinking while you read. • Setting purposes *while* reading helps guide your reading. *Why* is it helpful to set purposes? • It helps you prepare for reading (reduces schema availability problems). • It helps you to focus your attention while reading (reduces schema selection and retrievability problems).	• Directed reading–thinking activities. • The "W" portion of K-W-L procedures (see Figure 6.3). • Maintain journal/log while reading (see Figure 6.5). • Complete story maps while reading (see Figures 6.8 and 6.9). • Complete graphic organizers that indicate expository text structure while reading (see Figures 6.13, 6.14, 6.15, 6.16, 6.17, 6.18, and 6.19).
Generating, verifying, and updating predictions	• Predictions are guesses or hypotheses about what we think will happen in the text. • Predictions are good guesses based on your prior knowledge and clues from the text. • Making predictions helps focus our attention and guides our reading.	*How* to predict: • Look at the title, pictures, headings, chapter titles, or any other clues in the text to gain an idea of what it is about. • Think about what you already know about the topic. • Think about the clues in the text and try to make links between those clues and what you already know about the topic. • Based on these clues and what you already know, make a guess about what you think is going to happen in the text.	*Where* is it helpful to predict? • As you read all types of texts. *When* is it helpful to predict? • Predicting *before* reading helps focus your thinking while you read. • Predicting *while* reading helps guide your reading. *Why* is it helpful to set purposes? • It helps you prepare for reading (reduces schema availability problems). • It helps you focus your attention while reading (reduces schema selection and retrievability problems).	• Directed reading–thinking activities. • Maintain journal/log while reading (see Figure 6.5). • Vocabulary language prediction and story map activities.

149

TABLE 6.1. *(cont.)*

Comprehension strategy	Associated declarative knowledge[a]	Associated procedural knowledge[a]	Associated conditional knowledge[a]	Teaching methods
Generating, verifying, and updating predictions *(cont.)*		• As you read, look for information in the text that tells you whether your prediction was on target, slightly off, or completely off. • As you read, you may make adjustments to your predictions and make new predictions as you gather information from the text. Making predictions sometimes helps you determine your purposes for reading.		
Identifying text structure	Readers need to know *that*: • Authors organize writing in different ways. • There are two types of text: narrative and expository. • Narrative text contains story grammar elements: setting, characters, problem, goal, attempts to solve problem, resolution. • There are five types of expository text structures: description–definition, sequential, comparison, cause–effect, problem–solution. • Authors use cue words to signal text structures. • Some texts are poorly organized or do not use cue words, making them difficult to understand.	*How* to identify text structure: • Look at the title, pictures, headings, chapter titles, or any other clues in the text to gain an idea of how it is organized. • Skim through the text. • Look for cue words. • Decide on type of text.	*Where* is it helpful to identify text structure? • As you read all types of texts. *When* is it helpful to identify text structure? • Identifying text structure *before* you read gives you an idea of how the text is organized so you can anticipate what types of information will be forthcoming. • Identifying text structure *while* you read helps focus your attention and enhance comprehension and recall of text. *Why* is it helpful to identify text structure? • It helps you prepare for reading (reduces schema availability problems). • It helps you focus your attention while reading (reduces schema selection and retrievability problems).	• Story map activities (see Figures 6.8 and 6.9). • Expository text graphic organizers (see Figures 6.13, 6.14, 6.15, 6.16, 6.17, 6.18, and 6.19).

150

	Readers need to know *that*:	How to	Where/When/Why	Activities
			It helps you maintain your attention while reading (reduces schema maintenance problems).	
Imagery/ visualization	Readers need to know *that*: • Authors use very descriptive language when they write. • If you make a picture of the text in your mind as you read, this will help your comprehension.	*How* to make mental images: • As you read, think about the author's words. • Think about what you already know about the topic. • Use your five senses to draw a picture of those words in your mind. • Change your picture as the text changes.	*Where* is it helpful to image? • As you read all types of texts, but especially image-laden text and text that is not ambiguous. *When* is it helpful to image? • Making mental images is helpful to do while you are reading. *Why* is it helpful to image? • It helps you understand and remember what you read better. • It helps you maintain your attention while reading (reduces schema maintenance problems).	• "Sketch and share" activities
Comprehension monitoring	Readers need to know *that*: • Sometimes text does not make sense as you read it. • You should stop regularly and check to make sure that you understand what you are reading.	*How* to monitor comprehension: • While reading, stop periodically. • Ask yourself whether you understand what you are reading. • If you do understand, keep reading. • If you do not understand, use a fix-up strategy (reread, read ahead, ask someone) to help you understand the text better.	*Where* is it helpful to monitor comprehension? • As you read all types of text. *When* is it helpful to monitor comprehension? • Continually as you read. *Why* is it helpful to monitor comprehension? • It helps you maintain your attention while reading (reduces schema maintenance problems). • It helps you know when you need to use strategies to enhance your understanding.	• "Stop and go" or "click and clunk" activities

151

---

[a]Note that the declarative, procedural, and conditional knowledge associated with each strategy is not comprehensive and most certainly varies from individual to individual. These features should not be taught in a lock-step manner as if they were static.

Teacher: Adapted from a lesson by Angela Bies

Title: Pack Your Bags!

Topic: Identifying and organizing prior knowledge using semantic maps

Grade Level: 2–4

STAIR Hypothesis Being Addressed:
              Students are unmotivated to read informational texts and fail to apply comprehension strategies when the text is not of interest.

Goals of Lesson:

Students will learn to:
- Identify and organize prior knowledge using a graphic organizer
- Organize new information from text using a graphic organizer

Materials:

- *Cats* by Gail Gibbons
- Paper for making semantic maps
- At least two different colored markers
- Student self-assessment forms

Introduction

Create a safe environment

Reduce processing demands

Explanation: conditional knowledge

The lesson will begin by trying to relate the process and purposes of activating prior knowledge to other tasks in everyday life. Engage students in a conversation about what we might do if we were preparing to go on a trip. Students will share various things they do to prepare for trips. This information might include packing, purchasing some means of transportation, buying maps, etc. After students share, relate this process to reading by noting, "Before we go on a trip we have to do lots of things to get ready. We have to do similar things before we read. We have to get our minds ready to take a trip to another place. In a sense we have to get our minds ready by 'packing' information that we might need for the journey. What kinds of things do you do to get ready to read?" Students share various strategies they use before they read. As students share strategies, record them on a chart and note that the purpose of this lesson is to teach students a strategy that will help them prepare for reading—thinking about what they know about the text.

Verbalization about strategy use

Explanation: declarative knowledge

Description of Instructional Experience

Verbalization
Explanation: procedural knowledge

Explain that good readers think about what they already know about the subject before they start reading to help them better understand. Ask students to think about *how* they might do this. Try to elicit the procedural knowledge about how various students activate their prior knowledge. If students have difficulty verbalizing, display a variety of texts about cats, including *Cats* by Gail Gibbons.

Modeling that communicates Procedural knowledge

Using a think-aloud procedure, model how you would go about activating your prior knowledge before reading any of these texts. "Before I start to read, I usually look carefully at the book. I read the title and look at the pictures. As I look at the cover of this book, I notice that the title is *Cats*. Hmmm, I know a lot about cats because I have a cat. I guess this book is going to tell me about cats. As I look at the cover and the pictures, I notice lots of pictures of cats too.

(cont.)

FIGURE 6.1. Sample lesson teaching students how to activate prior knowledge.

I'm pretty sure this book is going to be about cats. I'm going to stop and think for a moment about what I already know about cats. Sometimes it helps me prepare for my reading if I write down what I already know about the topic. So I'm going to take a few minutes to do that."

Explanation: conditional knowledge

At this point explain that by organizing what we know about the topic on paper it helps us organize what we know in our heads. This helps make learning the new information in the text easier to understand because we can link it to what we already know.

Modeling

Model how to use a graphic organizer to record thoughts about what you know about cats. Think aloud as you record the information. "A web is one way to organize what we know about the topic of cats. We draw a circle and in the middle put the topic of the text. Since we are reading about cats I'm going to put *cat* in the middle of our circle. Now, I'm going to think about what I know about cats." Record the information and ask students to share information they know about cats as well. At this point you might ask pairs of students (depending on how much scaffolding you want) to work together to create a web of information they know about cats.

Guided practice

After recording this information, you may model how to group or categorize similar information. For example, you might group all information about characteristics, habits, or habitat together and model how to provide a superordinate label for this information. Pairs of students might try doing this with the information they recorded on their webs.

Explanation: declarative knowledge

Explain that once you have thought about and reviewed what you know about the topic, you might think about things you would like to find out about the topic—this is called setting a purpose. Model and demonstrate how you might quickly look at the pictures and the text of *Cats* and compare it to what you have recorded on your web to generate a purpose. "I know a lot about cats, but when I look at the pictures in this book, they make me wonder about how cats can jump so high. I also wonder why they sleep so much." As you model how to set purposes, record them on spokes of the web and explain to students that "as we read we might find information that matches what we already know, we might find information that is different than what we already know, and we might find new information. Our purposes serve as a guide for our reading so we know what we would like to find out." Have students think about what they might like to find out about cats, add spokes onto their webs, and record their purposes.

Think-aloud

Modeling

Explanation: declarative knowledge

After preparing the web by noting known information about cats and things that you would like to find out about cats, model the thought processes that occur as you begin to read the text. You might use language like, "Hmmm, this says that cats _____. I already knew that. See, I have it on my web. I'm going to place a check beside that information on my web to show that what I already knew matched what the book says." As you read information that is consistent with the known information on the web, place a check mark beside it to note congruence between prior knowledge and textual information. You might choose to use a different color marker once reading begins so students can see the difference between information that was generated prior to reading and information that was generated as a result of reading. As you read information

Modeling

(cont.)

FIGURE 6.1. *(cont.)*

153

that is new or that answers one of your purposes, add that information onto the web using the different colored marker. "Wow, the book says that cats _____. I didn't know that. That's something new that I learned. I'm going to add that onto my web." If information in the text conflicts with known information, then you can place a question mark beside that information on the web and put a page number to indicate where the conflicting information was found. "Oh my, the book says _____. That is different than what I thought. I thought that cats _____. I'd better check on that information."

Guided practice

After modeling reading several pages in this manner, begin to relinquish some of the responsibility to students. You might have pairs of students read the text together, and using a different colored marker, display how the textual information compares to the information contained on their webs. If students need more scaffolding, then you might read the text aloud one page at a time and ask them to look at their webs and update them based on the new information contained on each page. The goal, however, is to enable students to do this on their own without such guided support.

Conclusion

Verbalization

Have students complete a self-assessment form and then, after reading the entire text, engage students in a discussion in which they talk about how activating prior knowledge as they read helped them. Students can share information about how they used the strategies of previewing text, activating prior knowledge, and setting purposes while they read.

Assessment

- You will know whether students can identify and organize prior knowledge using a graphic organizer if they are able to add their prior knowledge onto the web initially, by their responses to questions 1–3 on the self-assessment, and by their concluding discussion.
- You will know whether students are able to organize new information from text using a graphic organizer if they are able to update their webs while reading, by their responses to question 4 on the self-assessment, and by their concluding discussion.

STUDENT SELF-ASSESSMENT OF STRATEGY USE

1. Thinking about what I already knew about cats was:

    very easy   easy   a little hard   very hard

2. Setting purposes before reading was:

    very easy   easy   a little hard   very hard

3. Putting my thoughts on a web was:

    very easy   easy   a little hard   very hard

4. Adding onto my web while I read was:

    very easy   easy   a little hard   very hard

5. Thinking about what I already know before reading

    _____
    _____
    _____

FIGURE 6.1. *(cont.)*

154

The lessons should be clearly focused so that students can easily grasp the concept. In this sample lesson activating prior knowledge was compared to taking a trip. This analogy was intended to make the strategy more concrete for students, so that they could liken it to something they have already done. Processing is slightly reduced in this manner but the lesson as a whole is fairly abstract because it requires students to use linguistic text. Figure 2.7 is reproduced in Figure 6.2 to illustrate the types of scaffolded support offered in each lesson. In this sample lesson the portions in which the teacher was modeling occur at Point 4 in Figure 6.2. That is, the teacher was reading the text aloud to the students and engaging in a think-aloud of the strategic processes she was using. During the guided practice portion of the lesson, the students were paired to read the text (i.e., shared reading) as they used the strategy. The guided practice portion of the lesson is located at Point 26 in the table. The distance between Points 4 and 26 represents a fairly large "jump" in terms of the level of scaffolded support provided between instruction and guided practice. Some students may need more scaffolded support during guided practice. Careful analysis of each student's assessments (i.e., completed graphic organizers, completed self-

		Amount of Cognitive Activity Required by Text						
		Less Cognition Concrete (semiotic) ←————————————→ More Cognition Abstract (linguistic)						
		Events/ Experiences (enactive)	Movies/ Videos	Wordless Picture Books	Read-Alouds	Shared Reading	Picture Books	Texts (symbolic)
Amount of Student's Cognitive Responsibility (Less → More)	Teacher/ Whole Class	1	2	3	4	5	6	7
	Small Group	8	9	10	11	12	13	14
	Trios	15	16	17	18	19	20	21
	Pairs	22	23	24	25	26	27	28
	Individual	29	30	31	32	33	34	35

FIGURE 6.2. Lesson planning grid: Planning for transfer and the gradual release of responsibility across lessons.

assessments, and responses during discussion) will determine whether students require more or less scaffolding during future instruction.

Angela introduced her student to a semantic web as a means of organizing this information. The K-W-L organizer depicted in Figure 6.3 is another tool that many teachers and students find useful. The key is to teach students how to use and enact the strategy. The type of graphic organizer used is unimportant. Students should be encouraged to use whatever means best suit them. Some students find that simply making a list is sufficient and prefer not to use graphic organizers at all. Many students find completing such organizers burdensome, even though they enhance comprehension. As Angela reflected on her lesson, she noted:

> When I explained to her [the student] that it might be helpful if she sketched her own organizer each and every time she began reading a new text until she was used to organizing knowledge mentally, she gave me a shocked look and said, "EVERY TIME???" I explained that she didn't *have* to do it every time, but that practicing it with fun reading like *Cats* or her books at home would help her know how to do it when it will be especially useful, such as when she needs to read for science or social studies.
>
> —ANGELA BIES, reflective memo

When other teachers taught similar lessons, they found that their students also benefited considerably. Eileen Ludwig taught her student how to activate prior knowledge, set purposes, and use the K-W-L chart as an organizer. She noted:

> In previous lessons, I had a hard time knowing whether [the student] was using her own prior knowledge in order to help her understand. After showing [the student] pictures of animals, talking about different animals, and previewing the text, [the student] seemed to be able to talk a lot more about what she already knew about animals. She even talked about some of her own experiences that related to animals. . . . Since [the student] rarely talks about her own experiences, I was thrilled when she started telling me everything she already knew about animals and how that knowledge related to her own life. After our classroom discussion I thought of several more ways in which I could have helped [the student] activate her prior knowledge. If I had more time, I would have also used a video, a computer program, or other visual aids dealing with animals. Since [the student] seems to be a very visual person, I think that this would have helped her understand the text even more. . . . I feel that [the student] definitely benefited from using the K-W-L chart. I feel that writing down everything she knew allowed her to see how much she did actually know. When I asked her about everything she knew, she responded, "I don't really know that much." In reality she did know quite a bit about polar bears—the animal she chose to read about. She was actually able to see this by looking at the chart.
>
> —EILEEN LUDWIG, reflective memo

As Eileen found in her lesson, the K-W-L procedure (Ogle, 1986) is helpful for facilitating an active processing of expository (i.e., informational) text. However, many teachers tend to use this wonderful organizer as if *it* by itself were the strategy. Remember that *only people are strategic.* Thus, it is critical when using the K-W-L organizer to make

K—What we know	W—What we want to find out	L—What we learned and still need to learn

Categories of information we expect to use:

A.   E.

B.   F.

C.   G.

D.   H.

FIGURE 6.3. K-W-L chart. Adapted from Ogle (1986). K-W-L: A teaching model that develops active reading of expository text. *The Reading Teacher, 39*(6), 564–570. Copyright 1986 by the International Reading Association. This material is reproduced with permission of John Wiley & Sons, Inc.

sure, as Eileen did, that it is accompanied by explicit instruction within the CESI framework that teaches students how to be strategic as they activate their prior knowledge.

The K-W-L procedure involves three steps: (1) accessing what students *know*, (2) identifying what students *want* to learn, and (3) noting what students *learned* after reading the text (see Figure 6.3). The first step, accessing what students know, is relevant to strategic processing in that it reminds students to activate prior knowledge and experiences. However, without the teacher's explicit instruction, the *K* portion of the organizer will not help students learn what accessing prior knowledge means, or how to access prior knowledge, or when/where they should use the strategy. Ogle described two aspects of the process of accessing prior knowledge. The first step is simply to brainstorm information to see what students know about the topic. For example, if students were about to read the text *All About Deer* by Jim Arnosky (1999), the brainstorming session might focus on accessing information that students have about *deer*. As students share information about the topic, record it in the *K* column of the K-W-L chart (see Figure 6.3).

Ogle (1986) noted that the second part of accessing background knowledge is to think about general categories of information that might be encountered on the topic when reading. Using the information recorded in the *K* column, see whether there are clusters or groups of information that form more general categories. For example, some of the information shared by students about deer might involve physical characteristics, descriptions of habitat, eating habits, or survival skills. Each set of related ideas could be grouped together and given a superordinate label. Ogle noted that students often find it difficult at first to group information they have brainstormed and identify a superordinate label. This step might require teacher modeling and guidance initially; it is a crucial step because it involves the type of active and deep processing that Beck and McKeown (1991) recommended. Brainstorming information is helpful for accessing relevant schemata; the process of grouping such information together helps students learn how to make connections and comparisons between types of information.

Again, the key is to provide explicit instruction that helps students understand the declarative, procedural, and conditional knowledge associated with activating prior knowledge and gradually transfer the responsibility for making decisions about where and when to use the strategy from teacher to student. If the teacher takes the initiative for using organizers such as K-W-L, then it is the teacher who is being strategic, *not* the student. Strategy instruction as a whole is contingent upon teaching students to deliberately enact strategies *on their own*. If the teacher continually taps background knowledge for students and guides activities, such as those just described, without fostering their independent use of the underlying cognitive strategies, then students will not transfer strategy use to independent reading. Many teachers engage in the good practice of introducing new stories by tapping students' background knowledge, but if this practice is not accompanied by explicit instruction aimed at teaching students how, when, where, and why they should tap their own background knowledge *independently*, they will remain reliant on the teacher's assistance.

Setting Purposes

Good readers are aware of their purposes for reading and use them while reading to guide, monitor, and evaluate their progress (Blanton, Wood, & Moorman, 1990; Garner & Reis, 1981). The purpose or plan readers have for reading focuses their attention while reading and guides the selection of textual information to retain in memory. As readers process text, their purposes for reading (1) determine what they will recall, (2) influence their interpretation of text, and (3) provide readers with a plan for reading and a sense of security as to where they are going (Anderson et al., 1983; Blanton et al., 1990).

In their seminal study, Anderson and colleagues (1983) asked high school sophomores and juniors to take the perspective of either a home buyer or a burglar while reading a passage about what two boys did at one of the boy's homes while skipping school. Their findings suggested that the perspective taken selectively influenced the type of information recalled from the text. The implication for instruction is that teaching students how to set sound purposes while reading will enhance their recall and retrieval of textual information.

Rowe and Rayford (1987) found that (1) purposes serve as cues for activating relevant background knowledge to make predictions about passage content, and (2) purposes that focus on familiar topics elicit more elaborated schemata. Without solid purposes in mind, students may have difficulty activating and selecting appropriate schemata.

Setting purposes is a strategy that is often misunderstood. Classroom teachers often either set purposes for their students or assign reading without encouraging students to set their own purposes. Blanton and colleagues (1990) suggested that teacher-directed purposes are often superficial and aimed at having students locate and recall literal information. Poorly defined purposes can misdirect students by leading them away from information that would help them develop a deep understanding of the text. Purposes also can be either too narrow or too broad in scope. Overly narrow purposes are too specific (e.g., "Read to find out what the main character did after breakfast"). Overly broad purposes do not pique or sustain interest throughout the duration of the reading event (e.g., "Read to find out what the story is about"). Although these teacher-designated purposes facilitate student comprehension, they do not promote students' independent strategy use. The goal of independent strategy use is to teach the students *how*, *when*, and *why* they should set their own purposes for reading. When the teacher formulates and enacts the strategies, rather than teaching the students how to use the strategy independently, students are removed from the decision-making process regarding which strategies to use and when to use them. As a result, they do not become planful, self-regulated readers who possess a repertoire of strategies to assist them as they read. Struggling readers, in particular, are at a disadvantage in this scenario.

Generally readers set purposes that serve to update or enhance their knowledge about a topic, to confirm or disconfirm predictions, to learn about the structure of the text, or to perform a task (Blanton et al., 1990). As we read, we are engaged continually in the process of setting purposes, seeking information that satisfies those purposes, and setting new purposes. Students must be given the opportunity to participate fully in this recursive process so that it meets *their* goals and purposes for reading rather than those of the teacher. Learning how to generate meaningful purposes will make reading more motivating for students. This instruction also must include explanation of the declarative, procedural, and conditional knowledge associated with setting purposes (see Table 6.1).

Figure 6.4 displays a sample lesson in which students learn how to set purposes. The explicit instruction portions of the lesson are located at Point 2 of Figure 6.2: In terms of the amount of scaffolded support provided, the instruction occurs with the teacher and whole class as they watch a video. Guided practice occurring with pairs of students as they watch the video is located at Point 23.

Teacher: Adapted from a lesson by Eileen Ludwig.

Title: Grocery Shopping

Topic: Activating prior knowledge and setting purposes for reading.

Grade level: Can be adapted to any grade

STAIR hypothesis being addressed:
                Students use background knowledge at times to help them
                understand text, but they require a great deal of modeling, guided
                practice, and reinforcement. Students are unable to set purposes
                for reading to enhance comprehension.

Goal of Lesson

Students will learn to:
- Preview text in order to help activate prior knowledge
- Set purposes for reading

Materials

- Informational video related to a topic being studied in social studies or science
- Multiple informational texts related to similar social studies or science topic
- K-W-L chart (see Figure 6.3)
- Student self-assessment sheets

Introduction

Reduce processing demands by relating strategy to concrete task

Begin by having students share reasons for going grocery shopping. Draw a web on the board to record students' ideas. Explain that grocery stores are full of all kinds of items and that when people go to grocery stores, they go for many different reasons. Use the list the students generated to reiterate some of the different items people might buy at a grocery store. Explain that when we go grocery shopping, we have a "purpose" or a reason for going. We might have to buy meat products or dairy products or snacks. Each person that enters the store will have different things to purchase. Explain that it is often helpful when we go grocery shopping to make a list of the items we would like to purchase so we do not forget anything.

Explanation: declarative knowledge

Explain that reading is similar to going shopping in that when we read, we should have a reason, or purpose, for reading. Just like when we shop, our purpose may be different from someone else's purpose. Explain that we might read to learn new information or to learn how to do something. Explain that just as it is helpful to make a list for shopping, it is also helpful to jot down purposes for reading so we do not forget why we are reading. Setting purposes helps guide our reading so we do not get "lost" amid all of the information in the text. Explain that in this lesson, we are going to learn how to set purposes while we read.

(cont.)

FIGURE 6.4. Sample lesson teaching students how to set purposes for reading.

Reduce processing demands by using semiotic text (video)

Model/think-aloud

Explanation: declarative knowledge

Description of Instructional Experience

Explain that we are going to learn how to set purposes first by watching a video, and afterward we will use the same process while we read.

Explain that before we read or watch a television program, we usually have a reason for doing so. We select what we watch or read based on what interests us. Explain that we are going to watch a video about _____ (whatever science or social studies topic is being studied). Model and demonstrate how to preview the video before watching it. You might engage in a think-aloud of the thought processes that occur to you as you glance at the title and the pictures on the front of the case and as you read the text on the back of the case. During the think-aloud note that when previewing the text, it is important to preview the video (or book) before watching it because it will give you an idea of what it is about. Explain that when previewing, it is helpful to look for clues that might give an indication of what the video (or book) is about. "As I look at the front I notice the title. This gives me an idea that it might be about _____. I also see pictures of _____. The title and pictures make me think that this video is going to be about _____. Does anyone notice anything else about the front cover that might give us ideas of what it might be about?" Have students share what they notice and what they think the video will be about.

Model/think-aloud

Remind students that in addition to previewing text before reading (or viewing), it is also important to think about what you already know about the subject to get your mind ready. "Remember that before we read or watch anything, it is always a good idea to think about what we already know about the subject. I'm going to use the *K* column of a K-W-L chart to record everything I know about _____. First I'm going to think about what I know and then I'm going to list it in the *K* column." Engage in a think-aloud as you share information that you know about the topic.

Guided practice

After modeling, students can then pair with one another to share other information they know about the topic and record that information on a K-W-L chart. For increased scaffolding students can jointly record their information in *K* column of one chart rather than each having to complete his or her own.

Explanation: declarative and conditional knowledge

Explain that, just like when we go shopping, when we read or view a video we should also have reasons for reading/viewing. This helps guide our reading/ viewing and helps us remember the information. Explain that this is called "setting a purpose" for reading or viewing.

Modeling
Explanation: procedural knowledge

Explain how to set a purpose by modeling. "*Purposes* are our reasons for reading or watching a video. When I set purposes, I start by looking at the title and pictures, as I already did. This gives me an idea of what the book or the video will be about. So, after looking at the cover of this video I think this video is going to be about _____. As I looked at the cover I then thought about what I already know about the subject and recorded it on my K-W-L chart. This will help me make connections as I watch the video. Now that I have made some guesses about what the video will be about and have thought about what I already know about the subject, I can begin to think about what

Explanation: conditional knowledge

I would like to learn or find out as I watch the video. This will help me think about and remember the new information as I watch." Then begin to generate

(cont.)

FIGURE 6.4. *(cont.)*

some questions about the subject or issues that you are wondering about. Demonstrate how to record your purposes in the *W* column of the K-W-L chart. Explain that the *W* column is kind of like a "shopping list." Just like in a grocery store a shopping list helps us remember what to buy, the *W* column of the K-W-L chart helps us remember what to look for as we read or watch a video.

Guided practice

Verbalization

With their partners have students think about what they might like to find out as they watch the video and record that information in the *W* columns of their charts. After recording this information, have students share the procedures they used to set purposes. This provides students with the opportunity to see how others accomplished the same task but perhaps used a different procedure.

Model/think-aloud

Explain that you are now ready to begin viewing the video and that it is important to keep your purposes in mind as you watch. Begin watching the video. As you come to places in which your background knowledge was affirmed, stop the video and model your thought processes. "Wow, I'm going to stop the video here for a moment because I just realized that they are talking about the same thing that I wrote in the *K* column of my chart. I really do understand that information. I'm going to place a check beside that information just so I can tell that what I knew was similar to what the video said." Continue watching the video and stopping at various places in which your prior knowledge was affirmed, purposes were answered, or new information was learned. Each time stop briefly, engage in a think-aloud, and then jot the relevant information on the K-W-L chart. When purposes are answered, record the relevant information beside the purpose in the *W* column. There may also be times when you think of new purposes to add to the *W* column. Be sure to model how to generate and add new purposes as they occur to you. New information that is learned but is not related to a purpose can be recorded in the *L* column.

Guided practice

Encourage students to record similar information on their charts. It might be helpful to ask them to raise their hands to stop the video as they notice information that either affirms prior knowledge, answers a purpose, or is new information. Although this process is time-consuming, it will provide students with a supportive environment in which to learn the strategy.

Verbalization

After viewing portions of the video, the whole class, or small groups of peers, can engage in a discussion in which they discuss how the information in the video compared to the prior knowledge recorded in the *K* column, whether the purposes recorded in the *W* column were answered, and if any new information was learned and recorded in the *L* column.

Conclusion

Verbalization

Have students complete a student self-assessment form and then use that information to engage them in a discussion of their experiences with setting purposes in this lesson. Be sure to have students explain what purposes are, how to set them, and why it is important to set purposes.

(cont.)

FIGURE 6.4. *(cont.)*

Transfer to new contexts

Explain that the same process of setting purposes that was used to watch a video is also helpful to do as we read books. Display the other books on the topic being studied and explain that sometimes some of our purposes are not answered by one source of information. It is the same as going to a grocery store for a particular item and finding out that the store does not have it. You have to go to another store to find it. It is the same with reading. Sometimes we can't get all the information we'd like to get from one video or one book. We have to look at other sources. Explain that in the next lesson we will use these other sources to help us find information to answer those purposes that were not answered by the video we watched today.

Assessment

- You will know that students can preview text in order to help activate prior knowledge by looking at the *K* column of their K-W-L charts, their self-assessments, and their comments during discussion.
- You will know that students can set purposes for reading by looking at the *W* column of their K-W-L charts, their self-assessments, and their discussion.

STUDENT SELF-ASSESSMENT

1. Thinking about what I know before watching the video _____

_____

2. Setting purposes before watching the video _____

_____

FIGURE 6.4. *(cont.)*

Note that the lesson began by using an analogy to connect the process of setting purposes while reading to something with which students would be familiar—grocery shopping. Such analogies help reduce processing and create a safe environment by linking an unfamiliar process to a more familiar one. This analogy works because it shows that, just as different people have different reasons for going to a store, different readers have different reasons for reading. Likewise the link to shopping is helpful in that, just as shoppers often make lists to help them remember their reasons for going to the store, so can readers make a "list" of reasons, or purposes, that describe what they would like to find out.

Eileen Ludwig, the student who designed the lesson on which this sample is based, found that her student had difficulty noticing whether her purposes were answered:

> When comparing what she learned to questions that she wanted to learn, [the student] did seem to have difficulty. For instance, some of her questions were answered, but she said that they weren't answered. When we looked at our chart again, I had to help her realize that she did answer some of the questions.
> —EILEEN LUDWIG, reflective memo

During Eileen's initial lesson, she waited for a postreading discussion to identify and record the information that was learned. For this reason the sample lesson was altered from the original to include the component in which the teacher modeled how to stop the video and place checks beside information from prior knowledge that was affirmed while watching the video, how to record answers to purposes as the information was learned, and how to add new information to the *L* column *as* it was being learned rather than waiting until afterward. Although this procedure inevitably lengthens the lesson, the discourse and thought processes that are shared are invaluable. Such discourse enables students to see that setting purposes is an ongoing process in which initial purposes are set, information is encountered that answers those purposes, and then new purposes are set.

Often the strategic processes related to setting purposes occur simultaneously with making predictions. That is, as we think about our goals for reading and what we want to find out, we often (particularly when reading narrative text) make predictions at the same time. Figure 6.5 provides a sample organizer that students can use to record purposes and predictions.

Generating, Verifying, and Updating Predictions

Like setting purposes, prediction is a recursive process that occurs throughout reading. We might begin reading by glancing at information from the title, pictures, headings, and the back of the book. This initial information enables an active reader to tap into available schemata and begin to generate predictions about the text. These predictions serve a similar function as setting purposes for reading: They become an impetus to continue reading. We want to read on to determine whether our prediction is affirmed or refuted by the text. New predictions then emerge, based on the incoming information as we continue reading. Setting purposes while reading and making predictions facilitate the ability to activate and retrieve prior knowledge and relevant schemata because they compel readers to actively monitor comprehension. This active processing focuses a reader's attention so that relevant schemata are selected and retrieved. Without a purpose readers may struggle. As an example, read the following text about a christening taken from Anderson and Pearson (1984):

> Queen Elizabeth participated in a long-delayed christening ceremony in Clydebank, Scotland yesterday. While there is still bitterness here following the protracted strike, on this occasion a crowd of shipyard workers numbering in the hundreds joined dignitaries in cheering as the HMS *Pinafore* slipped into the water.

In this instance you may have the schema available for "christening," as it is used in this text, but you may have difficulty *selecting* the appropriate schema. You may have been expecting to read about a baby's baptism after activating your schema for "christening." Based on your prior knowledge, you were predicting, or anticipating, seeing information in the text to confirm this hypothesis. When reading the ensuing passage about a ship's christening, good comprehenders are able to monitor their comprehension and note the conflict between their hypothesis and the information in the text (e.g., presence of Queen Elizabeth, presence of shipyard workers, presence of a ship). In noting the conflicting information, good comprehenders search their schemata for an alternate schema that incorporates the textual information. In this case, the original prediction would be rejected and a new one selected to reflect the incoming information. Once the prediction is altered or rejected, the reader can make new predictions and set new purposes based on this revision.

Title of Text: _____

Purpose (What do I want to find out?)	What I Found Out	Where I Found It (page number)
Prediction (What I think will happen)	Did It Happen?	Where Did I Find It? (page number)

FIGURE 6.5. Sample journal for recording purposes and predictions.

For poor comprehenders, however, the process of monitoring and recognizing that an inappropriate schema has been selected or retrieved is difficult. This problem may be caused by semantic issues such as we discussed earlier, an inability to monitor comprehension, or a combination of both. Often these readers become wedded to the schema they selected initially and have difficulty adjusting to new ideas. Wade (1990) described these readers as "schema imposers" (p. 448). These readers often make the text "fit" the schema they initially selected, regardless of the incoming textual data. In the example above, these readers would continue to believe that the text was about a baptism. They might justify their understanding in the following manner. After reading the first sentence, they might think, "Wow, Queen Elizabeth attended this child's baptism. Maybe the child is of royal lineage." After reading the second sentence, they would probably disregard the information about the strike and hold onto the information about the shipyard workers, thinking, "Okay, the queen attended this event and so did all of these shipyard workers. Maybe one of the child's parents is royalty, and the other parent is the captain of a ship, and all of the shipyard workers were invited to the baptism." The last segment of the second sentence, about the HMS *Pinafore* slipping into the water, might be pondered, "I guess the child's initials were HMS, or maybe the last name was Pinafore. Anyway, all of the people cheered as the baby was dipped into the water."

In this example the reader held onto the activated schema after it no longer fit, forcing the incoming information from the text to fit it. Schema imposers often ignore information that refutes, conflicts, or challenges the meaning they have constructed. These readers overrely on prior knowledge at the expense of textual information. They have difficulty updating and revising predictions because they are not monitoring their comprehension.

Good readers are able to generate predictions on their own and monitor those predictions for accuracy as they read (Brown, 1980; Collins, Brown, & Larkin, 1980; Palincsar & Brown, 1984; Shanahan et al., 2010). They use prior knowledge of the text content, the structure of the text, and the textual cues to generate predictions and construct meaning (Afflerbach, 1990; Shanahan et al., 2010). Prior knowledge enables them to select relevant cues from the text, which, in combination, helps them generate textually appropriate predictions.

As noted in Table 6.1, readers make predictions when reading any type of text, and they do so continually while reading. Predicting helps focus our attention while reading and gives us a purpose for reading. Thus prediction is intimately linked to each of the other text anticipation strategies. Our procedural knowledge about the process of prediction directs us to sample, or preview, the text to gain cues. As we sample the text, our background knowledge is activated and, ideally, we make linkages between that background knowledge and the cues in the text to generate textually appropriate predictions.

Younger and less proficient readers are often unable to generate textually appropriate predictions. At times their predictions seem to be "off the wall" or have nothing to do with the text. One teacher, Chastity Flynn, noticed this problem with one of her first graders:

> I had difficulty in the beginning because some of her predictions were off the wall. When I began probing to find out how she was thinking, it suddenly hit me that she did not fully understand the process of predicting. [The student] seemed to think that you could say whatever you wanted because there would be no penalty. So I

explained that she was right, but we still want to make sure we look for clues from the title and illustrations.

—CHASTITY FLYNN, reflective memo

Irrelevant or off-the-wall predictions usually occur when readers do not use the cues in the text to guide the prediction process but rely solely on their background knowledge to generate predictions. This might occur when readers overrely on prior knowledge and are less focused on text. As with any other strategy, explicit instruction focused on prediction must communicate the associated declarative, procedural, and conditional knowledge. However, additional challenges occur in that competent prediction requires all of the text anticipation strategies and clues from the text. Thus instruction must be aimed at teaching students how to recognize and use cues from text to generate, verify, and revise their predictions.

As simple as generating predictions may seem, many readers of all ages and abilities are surprisingly unfamiliar with the process. One teacher, Jill Hatfield, noted this problem after teaching a lesson on prediction to a struggling fifth-grade reader. Although her lesson was on prediction, it was geared at a less concrete level (Point 7 in Figure 6.2). Jill thought that because the student was in fifth grade, she would already be somewhat familiar with prediction:

> One problem that I ran into in this lesson was assuming that [the student] had a lot of the background knowledge about what a prediction is. . . . I assumed that she knew or had some prior experience with predictions. Apparently this is not the case. When I asked her what a prediction was, she said, "I don't know." I asked her what she thought it might be, and she remained quiet. I then gave her an example, and we talked about it. This lesson taught me to be more prepared when dealing with my student. I assumed that she had more background information [about predicting] than she did. Because of this I had to adjust my lesson by adding support for her so that she could understand and take part in what we were going to do.
>
> —JILL HATFIELD, reflective memo

After this lesson Jill adjusted her future plans by making the concept of prediction more concrete. She used games (such as Clue) and jigsaw puzzles to explain and model the prediction process used while reading. She transferred these notions to linguistic text later in the same lesson. These lessons were much more successful in that they taught her student the process of how to predict without the processing demands (and frustration) that often accompany reading:

> For most of my lessons on prediction I have been trying to explain to [the student] that prediction is like making a guess by using the clues that you see or read about in the story. When I told her that we were going to be playing a game for today's lesson, she laughed and seemed to visually relax. She loves to play games, and as we played I had her talk about what she was thinking as she guessed who she thought did it. When I was trying to think of what "common things" I could use in my lessons with [the student to make prediction less abstract], it never occurred to me to think outside the idea of books. I felt like if I just found the right book to use with her, that she would "get" prediction. Instead it was a simple board game that

made her understand the idea of gathering clues and thinking about what might happen.

—JILL HATFIELD, reflective memo

The key to Jill's lesson was her ability to transfer the concrete process of predicting while playing Clue or building a puzzle to the reading process. Simply playing games and building puzzles without all of the metacognitive verbalization and thinking aloud that she included would not have yielded the same successful results. Her lessons were tailored in the same way as any other explicit instruction lesson, except that her "text" was not a book but a board game. Such lessons provide the most amount of scaffolded support and are located at Point 1 of Figure 6.2. An example of a similarly concrete lesson is displayed in Figure 6.6.

In this lesson Eileen used an overnight bag as her "text" to introduce the concept of prediction. In this manner she was able to teach her students the declarative, procedural, and conditional knowledge associated with prediction, free of the cognitive burden of having to make predictions while decoding the text. She then transferred the same process to authentic text; however, she continued to provide a highly scaffolded environment in which she read the text to the students so that they could focus their cognitive efforts on using the pictures and words to make textually appropriate predictions and monitor their prediction process. The degree of movement related to scaffolded support was very slight in her lesson. She began the lesson at Point 1 in Figure 6.2, with the overnight bag as text, and moved to Point 4 when she read *Ira Sleeps Over* (Waber, 1975) to the students. This highly scaffolded environment enabled students to experience success in a safe environment.

Other teachers have found that using videos, movies, or sitcoms as "text" (Point 2 in Figure 6.2) and wordless picture books, such as Tomie dePaola's *Pancakes for Breakfast* (1978) (Point 3 in Figure 6.2), provide an equally safe and risk-free environment in which students more easily practice generating and monitoring their predictions. Eileen also used a prediction chart to help students record their predictions and monitor them as they read, which helps focus their attention while reading.

Figure 6.7 depicts an alternate prediction guide that can be used in similar lessons to help readers focus on the procedural steps involved in prediction: (1) looking for clues in the text or pictures, (2) thinking about what you know from prior knowledge, and (3) connecting the clues you observed and your prior knowledge to make a prediction.

Learning how to generate predictions is clearly important; however, without the ability to monitor whether one's predictions are confirmed or disconfirmed, students are left without the tools to become active readers. This aspect of prediction is really more of a comprehension monitoring strategy (i.e., a text maintenance strategy that facilitates schema maintenance). However, it is included in this section because it is inherently linked to the generation of predictions. One way to help students learn how to monitor their predictions in a concrete manner is to engage them in an activity that integrates elements inherent to vocabulary–language prediction activities (VLP; Wood & Robinson, 1983) and story grammar instruction (i.e., setting, character, problem, solution) (Whaley, 1984). By combining these two activities, students not only prelearn vocabulary and predict story events, but they also use the organizational scheme of a story map (see Figures 6.8 and 6.9) to guide, structure, and monitor their predictions (King, 1990). The process is similar to that used in directed reading–thinking activities (DR-TA; Stauffer, 1969). Students are encouraged to use the clues from the text to generate predictions prior to reading and then read to confirm or revise those predictions. The distinction is

Teacher: Eileen Ludwig

Title: What's in the Bag?

Topic: Generating predictions while reading

Grade level: 2–4

STAIR hypothesis being addressed:
Students are unaware of strategies that can facilitate their comprehension and recall of text.

Goal of Lesson

Students will learn to:
- Make appropriate predictions while reading
- Indicate the evidence used to make predictions
- Monitor their predictions as they read

Materials

- *Ira Sleeps Over* by Bernard Waber
- Overnight bag filled with various items needed for a sleepover (e.g., toothbrush, pajamas, blanket, teddy bear)
- Chart with three columns (What I Predict, Clues I Used to Make Predictions, What Happened)
- Writing supplies
- Response journal

Introduction

Explanation: declarative knowledge

Begin lesson by telling students that there are certain things that readers can do to help them understand a story. One of these things is making predictions. Predictions are guesses about what you think will happen in the story. Explain that today you will be learning how to make predictions while reading.

Procedural knowledge

Explain that you can use the evidence, or clues, in the story and your background knowledge to help make predictions.

Conditional knowledge

Explain that people make predictions before reading and while reading a story. Making predictions can help you understand text because it gives you a reason to keep reading. You read on to find out if your prediction is correct or incorrect. You can also change your predictions as you begin to read and gather more clues.

Reduce processing demands by using concrete "text"

Verbalization

Display the overnight bag filled with items that someone might take to a sleepover. Keep the bag shut and ask students to carefully observe the bag and, using their prior knowledge, think about what this type of bag might be used for. As students share their predictions, record them in the "What I Predict" column of the prediction chart. Be sure to have students share the clues and background knowledge they used to generate each prediction. These clues should be recorded in the "Clues I Used to Make Predictions" column of the chart.

(cont.)

FIGURE 6.6. Sample lesson teaching students how to predict using a concrete event.

Verbalization

After making predictions with the bag shut reach in and pull out one item. Have students carefully observe this "clue" and think about whether the clue supports any of their predictions. Have students share their thinking aloud, either with a partner or with the whole class, about how they arrived at their prediction so that everyone can hear the strategic processing being used to observe the clue, link it to relevant background knowledge, and decide whether it supports or refutes predictions. Ask students whether they would like to change their

Declarative knowledge

predictions based on this first clue. Be sure to explain that it is always okay to change your predictions based on the evidence. This is a sign of a good reader. Continue taking out one item at a time and engaging students in a discussion in which they observe the clue, link it to relevant background knowledge, and decide whether their prediction is supported or refuted.

Procedural knowledge

At the conclusion of the activity reiterate the process used to make predictions: Observe clues, think about what you know about such evidence, make a link between the clues and your background knowledge, and make a prediction.

Declarative knowledge

Also be sure to emphasize that when you are predicting, there are no right or wrong answers. Predictions are good guesses based on the evidence and information you already know about.

Description of Instructional Experience

Explain that you are going to use this prediction process as you read the book *Ira Sleeps Over* by Bernard Waber. Introduce the book by showing the cover and reading the title. Explain to students that, just like making predictions with the overnight bag, when you read books you look for "clues." The clues in a book are available by looking at the title, the pictures, and the words.

Explanation: declarative/ procedural knowledge

Model/think-aloud

Model how to make predictions by looking at the cover and the title. You might say something like, "When I read the title, it makes me think this story may be about someone who sleeps over somewhere. I don't know anyone named Ira, but maybe that is the name of the boy in the picture on the cover. It looks like he really likes that green blanket." After predicting, explain how you came to those predictions. "I think it is about a boy named Ira who sleeps over somewhere based on the clues I gathered from the title. I thought he probably liked that green blanket because in the picture he is wrapped in it." Write your prediction in the "What I Predict" column of your chart and write the clues that helped you make that prediction in the "Clues I Used to Make Predictions" column.

Verbalization

Have students observe the title and pictures more closely and generate ideas about what they think will happen. Be sure to elicit language in which students have the opportunity to share how they arrived at the predictions they made. Depending on the level of scaffolded support required, you may either record students' predictions and clues on a class chart, or students may work in pairs to share their predictions and clues with one another and record them on a chart.

Explanation: procedural knowledge

Explain that we will be able to check to see how accurate our predictions are as we read the story. Emphasize that there are several ways to gather clues to make predictions: what we read, the pictures, and what we already know about

(cont.)

FIGURE 6.6. *(cont.)*

Conditional knowledge

something. Reiterate that it is important to make predictions and check them while reading because it helps us understand and remember better. Also, we may find more clues in one part of the story than in another part. Therefore, sometimes we can alter our predictions to make better ones based on the new clues.

Model/think-aloud

Read the first three pages or so of the story aloud to the students. Stop and model your thought processes as you encounter information that either confirms or rejects your initial predictions. Also stop and model your thought processes as you encounter information that enables you to make new predictions about what will happen next. Be sure to share not only your predictions but also how

Conditional knowledge

you arrived at those predictions (i.e., what textual evidence and background knowledge helped you make that prediction). List your predictions and clues on the chart.

Guided practice and verbalization

After modeling and thinking aloud, have students share with a partner any predictions they may have and the clues that helped them arrive at that prediction. Students can record their predictions and evidence on their charts.

Modeling

Guided practice

Continue in this manner throughout the text, reading aloud a few pages at a time and stopping at various points to model your own thought processes and then handing the same task over to each pair of students. As information is encountered that confirms, rejects, or causes you to alter your prediction, be sure to stop and record the outcome in the "What Happened" column of the chart. If student predictions are not confirmed, be sure to emphasize that predictions are good guesses based on what we already know and any other

Declarative knowledge

evidence we gather. They are not always "correct" and that is okay.

Conclusion

Verbalization

Once the story is finished, engage students in a discussion in which they talk about how their predictions measured up to what actually occurred in the text. Have students share different ways in which they predicted and how the text influenced their predictions. Have students write a journal entry in which they explain their thoughts about the prediction process and how it affected their understanding of the story.

Assessment

- You will know whether students can make appropriate predictions while reading by their contributions to discussion and the information recorded in the "What I Predict" column
- You will know whether students can indicate what evidence they used to make predictions by their contributions to the discussion and the information recorded in the "Clues I Used to Make Predictions Column."
- You will know whether students are able to monitor their predictions as they read by their contributions to discussion and the information recorded in the "What Happened" column.

(cont.)

FIGURE 6.6. *(cont.)*

Prediction Chart		
What I Predict	Clues I Used to Make Prediction	What Happened

FIGURE 6.6. *(cont.)*

that predictions in the VLP–story grammar activity are initially based on vocabulary, include a great deal of language surrounding strategy use, and are organized by using a story map.

The VLP serves two primary purposes: (1) to preteach vocabulary, using oral language activities that reinforce words' structural and semantic characteristics; and (2) to use vocabulary as a basis for predicting what might occur in the text (Wood & Robinson, 1983). First the teacher studies the text to determine which words are important to understanding the text and which may cause students difficulty. Usually 10–15 total words are identified—but *most* of the words should be familiar to students so that they can draw on their prior knowledge to make predictions. It is preferable to introduce no more than *three* or *four* new or unfamiliar words before reading. Make note of any structural aspects of the words that could be pointed out to facilitate word recognition (i.e., root words, word endings, prefixes). Place each word on a card and place the cards in front of the students. Explain to the students that these words will appear in the text they are about to read. During the language portion of the activity, discussion is focused on developing rich semantic descriptions of new words, making connections among the words, and looking for patterns in words. The key to the language portion is to help students activate appropriate schemata for making relevant predictions. Once students understand the terms, they are taught how to make predictions about what might happen in the text based on these "starter" words. These predictions can be recorded in journals or logs if students are working in pairs or small groups, or they can be recorded on chart paper if the whole class is engaged in the activity.

LOOK What do you see?	THINK What do you know from your experiences?	Make a LINK
	+	=
	+	=
	+	=
	+	=
	+	=

FIGURE 6.7. Sample prediction guide.

Title: _____

Author: _____

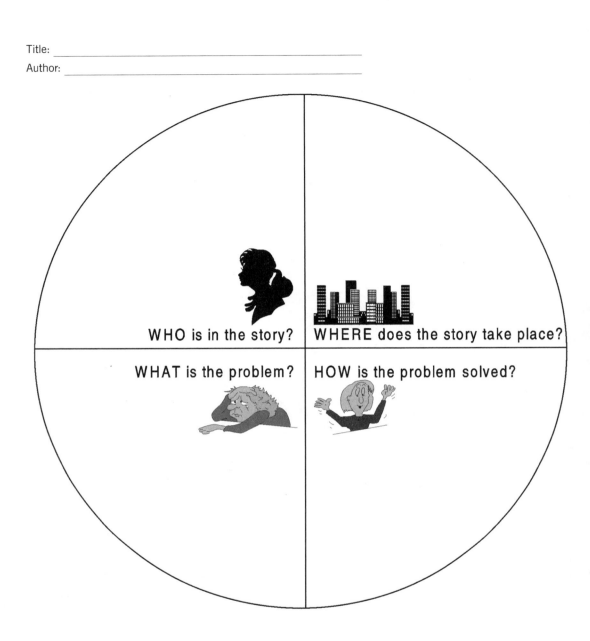

FIGURE 6.8. Story map for use with emergent readers.

Title: _____

Author: _____

Setting	Characters	Problem or Goal	Attempts to Solve Problem or Attain Goal	Solution
	Character Traits			

FIGURE 6.9. Story map for use with upper elementary readers.

When combining the VLP activity with story grammar, it is important that teachers prepare for this activity by choosing a narrative story with a well-defined and explicit story grammar. In the lesson displayed in Figure 6.10, Stephen Mooser's (1978) *The Ghost with the Halloween Hiccups* is used because it contains a clearly identified problem (Mr. Penny has hiccups), explicit attempts to solve the problem, and a clear solution. Students will need to be familiar with story grammar elements to engage in this lesson. Providing story grammar instruction while trying to teach students how to predict may place an unnecessary cognitive burden on them.

Next, it is important to study the text to determine which words are important to understanding the text and which words may cause students difficulty. In the lesson displayed in Figure 6.10, 15 words were selected. Most of these words (12) would be familiar to the second-grade students for whom the lesson was planned. These 12 words provide clues to help students make predictions prior to reading. The lesson includes three words with which students might be unfamiliar (*mayor, worried, hiccups*) to prepare them to encounter the words while reading. The majority of words selected should (1) be within students' spoken, listening, and reading vocabularies; and (2) provide clues to story grammar elements. Figure 6.10's lesson would be located at Points 6 (demonstration phase) and 27 (guided practice phase) of Figure 6.2.

This lesson displays the type of scaffolding that facilitates successful initial attempts at using prediction while reading independently from linguistic text. Students of all ages and abilities have found the VLP–story map activity highly motivating and are eager to read to determine the accuracy of their initial predictions. This activity also provides a visual means of assessing a covert thought process—that of monitoring and updating predictions while reading. Normally this process occurs without any evidence. However, manipulating the word cards and making photocopies of the story map's evolution throughout the reading process provides a tangible means of assessing students' abilities to monitor and update their predictions. The manipulatives also serve as a concrete reminder to students that their predictions can (and should) be altered as warranted by text. This approach is particularly helpful for readers who tend to overrely on background knowledge or who have difficulty focusing their attention on meaning while reading. One teacher, Jaime Quackenbush, noted that teaching prediction served this exact purpose for her student:

> Using the strategy of prediction helped [the student] to become more involved in what he was reading. It was not difficult for him, and it made the reading task more meaningful. I could easily observe his prior knowledge, interest, and experiences at work as he suggested all kinds of possible scenarios and outcomes. He took the strategy and elaborated on everything we read, making me think that this was *really* something he might use in other reading situations. For the first time since I began working with him, [the student] seemed to be really actively reading. He frequently interrupted the reading at points I hadn't intended to stop, saying things such as, "Maybe he's going to . . . " or "I think I know what's going to happen."
> —JAIME QUACKENBUSH, reflective memo

Identifying Text Structure

Text structure refers to the manner in which ideas in a text are interrelated to communicate a message to the reader (Meyer & Rice, 1984). These structures specify the logical

Teacher: Janice F. Almasi

Title: VLP

Topic: Generating predictions while reading

Grade level: 1–3

STAIR hypothesis being addressed:
Students are unaware of strategies that can facilitate their comprehension and recall of text. Students do not read for meaning or monitor comprehension.

Goal of Lesson

Students will learn to:
- Use new and target vocabulary to make relevant predictions about the setting, characters, problems, attempts to solve problems, and resolution of a story
- Indicate the evidence used to make predictions
- Monitor their predictions as they read

Materials

- *The Ghost with the Halloween Hiccups* by Stephen Mooser
- Blank story maps (see Figures 6.8 and 6.9)
- Packets of miniature vocabulary word cards
- Large vocabulary word cards with the following words on them: (*Bert, ghost, Halloween, hiccups, hopping, Laura, major, Mr. Penny, play, scare, sing, tickle, town, water, worried*)
- Chart paper and markers

Introduction

Explanation: declarative knowledge

Begin lesson by telling students that there are certain strategies readers can use to help them understand a story. One of these strategies is making predictions. Predictions are guesses about what you think will happen in the story. Explain that today we will be learning how to make predictions while reading.

Conditional knowledge

Explain that people make predictions before reading and while reading a story. Making predictions can help you understand text because it gives you a reason to keep reading. You read on to find out if your prediction is correct or incorrect. You can also change your predictions as you begin to read and gather more clues.

Procedural knowledge

Explain that you can use the evidence, or clues, in the story and your background knowledge to help make predictions. Today we are going to use some of the words in the story and our understanding of how stories are organized to help us make good predictions.

Description of Instructional Experience

Declarative knowledge

Explain that just as the title, pictures, chapter titles, and headings are clues that help us make predictions, the words in the text help us also.

(cont.)

FIGURE 6.10. Sample lesson teaching students how to predict using a picture book.

Vocabulary development

Conditional knowledge

Display the 15 large word cards on the board. Explain that you have selected 15 words from the story to help us make predictions about what might happen. Discuss the words in a rich, semantic context. Since the word *hiccups* is central to the story, you might begin by drawing a web on the board and placing the word *hiccups* in the center. Explain that it is always a good idea to think about what we already know about the topic of a story before reading and that the story we are going to read today is about hiccups. Have students brainstorm what they know about hiccups and record their ideas on the web. Have students look for ways in which this information might be grouped together. That is, look for superordinate categories, such as description, causes of hiccups, and cures for hiccups. Once background knowledge for hiccups has been activated, explain that talking about hiccups helps us get ready to read the story.

Vocabulary development

Try to make connections between some of the other 14 words and *hiccups.* For example, you might ask students to think about whether you might be "worried" if you had the hiccups. Have students discuss with partners what it means to be worried and why they would/would not be worried if they had hiccups. Then have a brief whole-group discussion of the issue. Other questions to elicit semantic development of concepts might include, "Could a *mayor* get the hiccups? Why or why not?" "Would you be *scared* if you had the hiccups? Why or why not?" "What would happen if you *tickled* someone who had the hiccups?" Each question should foster conversation about, and foster connections between, concepts. This might also be a time to highlight any structural aspects of the words, such as the endings on *worried* and *hopping*, or any other word recognition strategy that would benefit students prior to reading.

Declarative knowledge

Explain that now that we have seen some clues from the story, we can begin to think about those clues and make predictions. Explain that we are going to use a story map as a way of organizing our predictions. Briefly review story grammar elements (i.e., setting, characters, problem, attempts to solve the problem, and solution). Prior to embarking on this lesson, students should already be familiar with these elements. Otherwise the lesson may require too much explicit instruction and place students in a position in which they are cognitively overloaded.

Model/think-aloud

Verbalization

Model/think-aloud

Procedural knowledge

Select a word and model how you would make a prediction about where that word might belong on a story map. "I see the word *town*. I know that a town is like a small city. It's a place. Based on this clue and what I already know about towns, I think that maybe the setting of the story might be a town. I'm going to place my word card under the 'setting' column of my story map. Is there any other place that *town* might fit?" Encourage students to think divergently and consider that it is possible, for example, that the town might be the problem in the story. Be sure to encourage students to share the thinking they used to arrive at a particular prediction and why they think it is legitimate, based on the clues and their prior knowledge. You might also have students look to see if there are other words that might be clues about the setting of the story. Model and demonstrate your thinking with another word or two. Explain that we are going to use these word clues and our background knowledge to help us predict where the words might belong on a story map.

(cont.)

FIGURE 6.10. *(cont.)*

Guided practice

Once you are certain that students understand how to make predictions using the word cards, their prior knowledge, and the story map, pass out packets of miniature word cards and blank story maps. Have students work in pairs to make predictions about where the words might belong on the story map. Encourage students to talk to one another and verbalize their reasons for placing words in certain columns. As students work together, listen carefully to their discussions and take anecdotal notes. It is important that the word cards are not glued onto the story maps. Instead students might gently tape each word to the story map. This will permit students to physically manipulate the word cards later as they read the story and gather further clues that will enable them to update, revise, and alter their predictions.

Verbalization

After students have placed all of the words on their story maps, engage them in a whole-class discussion. The discussion can focus on where various pairs of students placed cards and why they placed them as they did. The discussion should foster the notions that predictions can vary from individual to individual and that there are multiple ways to make predictions. You might have one pair of students come to the board, select a word, read it aloud, place it on the story map where they predict it belongs, and then explain why they placed it there. Follow up by asking whether any pairs placed the same word in a different column and have them explain why they placed it as such.

Assessment

Often this portion of the lesson is sufficient for one day. At this point pairs of students might use their story maps to write a "prediction story" in which they communicate their version of the story before reading Stephen Mooser's version. Pairs of students can then compare their versions with one another. For assessment purposes it is helpful to make a duplicate copy of the students' completed story maps and prediction stories at this point to show what their initial predictions were. This can be compared to their story map versions at later points as they update and revise their predictions based on textual information.

Before beginning to read the story, have students review their story maps. Introduce the story by displaying the book, *The Ghost with the Halloween Hiccups*. Explain that now we finally know the title of the story. This is an additional clue that can help us predict. Often at this point students show outward displays that they are monitoring their predictions. They either begin to move their word cards or begin to discuss with their partner. Capitalize on these moments by encouraging students to share their strategic thinking. "I notice that you are moving your word cards. This is wonderful.

Explanation: declarative and conditional knowledge

Model/think-aloud

This is exactly what good readers do when they read. They make predictions and as they gather new clues and sometimes have to change or alter their predictions. What did this new clue tell you? What kind of adjustments are you making to your story map predictions? Why?" Encourage students to verbalize their reasons for making changes or for keeping their predictions the same. If students do not begin to make adjustments on their own, model and engage in a think-aloud of your own.

(cont.)

FIGURE 6.10. *(cont.)*

Declarative knowledge

Remind students that it is always a good idea to set purposes before reading. Setting purposes helps focus our thinking as we read. At this point students should be primed to read the story and should be anxious to find out what happens. Students usually have little difficulty generating relevant purposes at this point. Have students record their purposes on their story maps.

Guided practice

Assessment

Have students share some of their purposes and remind them that as they read, they should look for clues that might either confirm their story map predictions or cause them to have to change their story map predictions. Encourage students to talk with their partners about these clues as they read. Ask students to begin reading to page 5 of the text. As students read, walk among them and take anecdotal notes to determine whether they are able to use the clues in the text to update and revise predictions when necessary. After reading the first five pages, engage students in a brief discussion that focuses on the clues in the text and how those clues either confirmed their predictions or caused them to alter their story maps. Reiterate that this is what good readers do as they read. They continually monitor and update their predictions.

Have students continue to read further in the story and engage in the recursive process of setting purposes, making new predictions, gathering textual clues, and altering story maps based on the new information. Engage students in a discussion of such processes after completing the story.

Conclusion

Have students complete a student self-assessment in which they respond to the open-ended statements such as, "The word cards _____," "The story map _____," and "My predictions _____."

Engage students in a follow-up discussion in which they share how using the word cards and the story map affected their ability to make predictions. Have students share different ways in which they were able to make predictions and whether making the predictions helped them as they read.

Assessment

- You will know that students are able to use new and target vocabulary to make relevant predictions about the setting, characters, problems, attempts to solve problems, and resolution of a story by their contributions to discussion and by photocopying their initial story maps.
- You will know that students can indicate the evidence used to make predictions by their contributions to class discussion and their discourse with their partner.
- You will know whether students can monitor their predictions as they read by comparing the location of the word cards on their initial story maps to the position of the word cards while reading.

FIGURE 6.10. *(cont.)*

connections among ideas as well as the subordination of some ideas to others. Just as readers have schemata for general world knowledge and content knowledge, they also have textual schemata (Anderson et al., 1977). Textual schemata are mental representations of the ways authors organize different types of text. When readers are able to recognize the manner in which a text is organized, they are able to activate their schemata for that text structure, and comprehension is thereby facilitated (Goldman & Rakestraw, 2000; Pearson & Fielding, 1991; Shanahan et al., 2010).

Text is generally either narrative or expository (i.e., informational), although some texts do contain features of both narrative and expository text. Narrative text is often referred to as *stories* or *fiction*. Text that has an expository structure is informational in nature and may often be referred to as *nonfiction*. Duke (2000) defined informational texts as those written for the purpose of conveying "information about the natural or social world" (p. 205). Students of varying ages are able to distinguish how both genres are organized and are able to use these structures as they read, retell, and write (Langer, 1985).

Narrative text contains story grammar elements (i.e., setting, character, goals, efforts to attain goals, and resolution). Expository text is generally organized according to one of five patterns: cause–effect, comparison–contrast, description–definition, problem–solution, or sequential. When readers are familiar with these text structures, they can anticipate how the text will be arranged and organized (Goldman & Rakestraw, 2000). The ability to anticipate text structure helps readers select and retrieve relevant schemata. For those readers with low prior knowledge, the structure of the text and how well it coheres are very important (Goldman & Rakestraw, 2000; McNamara, 2001). McNamara's (2001) work has shown that, for readers with high prior knowledge, text that is less coherent actually leads them to be more actively engaged in the reading process. As an example, read the following text with the goal of determining what it is about:

> The procedure is actually quite simple. First you arrange things into different groups. Of course, one pile may be sufficient depending on how much there is to do. If you have to go somewhere else due to lack of facilities, that is the next step, otherwise you are pretty well set. It is important not to overdo things. That is, it is better to do too few things at once than too many. In the short run this may be expensive as well. At first the whole procedure will seem complicated. Soon, however, it will become just another facet of life. It is difficult to foresee any end to the necessity for this task in the immediate future, but then one can never tell. After the procedure is completed, one arranges the materials into different groups again. Then they can be put into their appropriate places. Eventually they will be used once more and the whole cycle will have to be repeated. However, that is part of life. (Bransford & Johnson, 1973, p. 400)

Think about how well you understand this passage. On a scale from 1 to 5, with 1 being low and 5 being high, how would you rate your comprehension? Most readers find this to be a difficult passage to comprehend fully. Very few individuals rate themselves at 5. As you read the passage above, you may have been able to determine by the structure of the text that it was describing how to perform some process. Most likely you recognized words that cued you that it was a sequential text structure (e.g., *first, next step, after, then*). Reading these words enabled you to activate your schema for texts that describe how to perform a procedure. Although you were unaware of the topic of the passage, you may have had some minimal degree of comprehension, because you knew at least that the text described a procedure of some form.

In this example, most readers activate a schema or several schemata and try to see how each fits with the textual information. This process quickly becomes frustrating because the text itself is very ambiguous. Comprehending this text presents a *schema retrieval* difficulty because the text is so ambiguous. If the text had been given a title, such as "How to Do Laundry," comprehension would be vastly improved. The cause of this comprehension dilemma is not a reader-based problem but a textual problem. As evidenced in this example, text that is incoherent, poorly organized, or ambiguous can impair comprehension, particularly if the reader has low prior knowledge about the topic. In the remainder of this section we provide sample lessons related to teaching students to recognize text structure and use it as a strategic process to facilitate comprehension. We begin with narrative lessons, followed by lessons focused on expository text structures.

Narrative text structure has a relatively predictable pattern, or story grammar, that readers can sense and use to comprehend the material while reading (Mandler & Johnson, 1977; Stein & Glenn, 1979). Stories generally consist of a beginning, in which the protagonist is introduced in a setting; followed by an initiating event, to which the protagonist responds by establishing a problem or goal; the protagonist then attempts to achieve the goal, which ultimately brings the series of events to an end (Mandler & Johnson, 1977; Stein & Glenn, 1979). Having a schema for narrative structure directs attention to particular aspects of incoming information, helps readers keep track of what they have read, and indicates when a given part of a story is complete or incomplete so that it can be stored or held until more material is encountered (Mandler & Johnson, 1977). Learning about narrative structure enhances students' memory and recall of text (Short & Ryan, 1984) and helps them organize and write stories (Fitzgerald & Teasley, 1986). Like instruction in story grammar, story maps (see Figures 6.8 and 6.9) are teaching tools to help readers develop a sense of story and to assist retrieval and retention of information. Research has shown that when proficient as well as less proficient readers are taught to record story grammar elements on a story map while reading, their comprehension is enhanced (Boulineau, Fore, Hagan-Burke, & Burke, 2004; Idol, 1987; Idol & Croll, 1987). Good strategy users are not only adept at using their prior knowledge of content, but also at using their understanding of the way text is organized to help them understand what they are reading (Shanahan et al., 2010).

The instructional implications are straightforward. Students need to learn how to recognize narrative text structure and to use this knowledge strategically to facilitate comprehension. Story grammar can also be used to assist students when writing narrative texts. When teaching about story grammar, use terms young readers can understand. For example, rather than using the terms *initiating event* and *protagonist*, use words and phrases such as *setting, characters, problems, goals, attempts to solve*, and *solution*. Story grammar can be simplified even further for emergent readers, as in the story map depicted in Figure 6.8. Similar story maps can be used for older students, as in Figure 6.9. Story maps used as a graphic organizer should be employed either *before* reading, to enhance students' ability to predict and set purposes for reading, or *while* reading, to be applied as a cognitive tool that focuses attention and enhances ability to monitor incoming information and compare it to earlier predictions (see the VLP lesson in Figure 6.10).

Unfortunately, in practice many teachers use story maps *after* reading. This use serves only to *assess* students' memory and recall of text. It in no way facilitates strategic processing of text. In the lesson described in Figure 6.11, the teacher, Jaime Quackenbush, teaches her third grader to identify and use story grammar elements to enhance

Teacher: Adapted from a lesson by Jaime Quackenbush

Title: Pizza/Story Parts

Topic: Identifying Narrative Text Structure

Grade level: 2–4

STAIR hypothesis being addressed:
> Students have the ability to comprehend but do not bring meaning to the text unless engaged in a strategy that elicits active thinking while reading.

Goal of Lesson

Students will learn:
- That most stories have a similar structure
- Clues to help identify story grammar elements: setting, characters, goal/problem, action, and outcome

Materials

- *Sylvester and the Magic Pebble* by William Steig
- Blank story maps (see Figures 6.8 and 6.9)
- Story parts chart (see Figure 6.12)
- Miniature vocabulary word cards with words from story that indicate story grammar elements
- Construction paper pizza parts (dough, sauce, cheese, toppings)
- Pictures of various settings and people

Introduction

Explanation: declarative knowledge

Explain that when people write or tell stories, there are certain parts of the story that are almost always there. We need to have all of these parts in order to make a good story.

Reduce processing demands

Create an analogy between needing certain ingredients to make a pizza and needing certain ingredients to make a story. Explain that to create a pizza, you need to have dough, sauce, cheese, and toppings. Explain that to create a story, you also need certain ingredients.

Conditional knowledge

Explain that in this lesson students are going to learn how to identify these story "ingredients" as they read. Explain that being able to identify story parts will help them to remember and understand what they read. Explain that any time they hear or read a fiction story, they should think about and look for these story parts.

Description of Instructional Experience

Explanation: declarative knowledge

Explain that to make a story, you need to have a place where the story happens (the setting). Show several pictures of various settings and explain that the setting involves where the story happens and when it happens. Engage students in discussion of each setting and describe the location and time. During discussion co-construct the story parts chart (see Figure 6.12) with

(cont.)

FIGURE 6.11. Sample lesson teaching students how to identify narrative text structure.

Procedural and conditional knowledge

students by filling in information that defines each element, provides clues to help identify each element in a story, and where to find such information in a story. Use the discussion with the pictures of the setting to elicit the information for the story parts chart. Elicit information that explains that the setting can be determined by looking for clues such as the names of cities or countries, the places people go, time of day, year, and the seasons. Explain that usually the setting is established at the beginning of the story.

Declarative knowledge

Explain that there are also characters in stories. The characters are the people or animals who are in the story (add this onto story parts chart). These characters are placed in the setting. Examine the pictures of characters and describe what types of traits these individuals might have. Engage students in a discussion about how various characters depicted in the pictures might act in a given setting. Explain that characters are recognized by looking for clues such as names, descriptions of people/animals, words such as *boy/girl*, ages of characters, and words that describe the way they think or act. Explain that characters are usually introduced at the beginning of the story.

Procedural and conditional knowledge

Declarative, procedural, and conditional knowledge

Explain that these characters always have a problem or a goal. Explain that it is found by looking for an important event that happens, or by looking for words that tell us something the character is trying to do or get. Explain that the problem or goal is usually presented in the beginning and continues through the middle of the story. Have students select a setting and a main character from the pictures. Engage students in a discussion about what types of problems or goals the character might face in the selected setting.

Declarative, procedural, and conditional knowledge

Explain that the next part of a story occurs as the main character tries to solve the problem or attain the goal. Explain that clues are found by looking for things the characters say or do as they try to solve their problem or attain their goal. Often characters have to try several different ways to solve a problem or attain their goal. Explain that these events usually happen in the middle of the story. Have students brainstorm various ways the character might go about solving the problem.

Declarative, procedural, and conditional knowledge

Explain that in the end the problem is either solved or unsolved, or the goal is either attained or not attained. Explain that clues indicate that the character either no longer has the problem or has accomplished what he or she (or it) was trying to do. Explain that the solution is almost always at the end of the story. Have students think about how the characters in the pictures might solve the problem in their story.

Conditional knowledge

Explain that it is often helpful to use a map when we listen to or read stories to help us focus our attention on the story elements as we read. This helps us understand and remember the story better. Hand out blank story maps to the students. Reiterate each of the story grammar elements and remind students to refer to the story parts chart to help them remember what each element is. Explain that it is also helpful before we read to make predictions about what we think might happen. Engage students in a VLP–story map activity (see Figure 6.10). Present miniature word cards containing words that indicate characters' names, important places, the problem, items and events that happen

(cont.)

FIGURE 6.11. *(cont.)*

throughout the book *Sylvester and the Magic Pebble*. Explain that we are going to use these clue words from the text, and what we know about story elements, to make predictions about where the words might belong on our story map.

Model/think-aloud

Select a word and model how you would make a prediction about where that word might belong on a story map. "I see the word *hill*. I know that a *hill* is a type of landform. It's a place. Based on this clue (refer to story parts chart) and what I already know about *hills*, I think that the setting of the story might be on a *hill*. I'm going to place my word card under the 'setting' column of my story map. Is there any other place that *hill* might fit?" Encourage students to think

Verbalization

divergently and consider that it is possible, "Could a *hill* be a character? Why or why not?" "Could a *hill* be a problem? Why or why not?" Be sure to encourage students to share the thinking they used to arrive at a particular prediction and why they think it is legitimate based on the clues and their prior knowledge.

Model/think-aloud

You might also have students look to see if there are other words that might be a clue about the setting of the story. Model and demonstrate your thinking with another word or two. Explain that we are going to use these word clues and our background knowledge to help us predict where the words might belong on a story map.

Guided practice

Have students work in pairs to make predictions about where the words might belong on the story map. Encourage students to talk to one another and verbalize their reasons for placing words in certain columns. As students work together, listen carefully to their discussions and take anecdotal notes.

Verbalization

It is important that the word cards are not glued onto the story maps. Instead students might gently tape each word to the story map. This will permit students to physically manipulate the word cards later as the story is read and they gather further clues that will enable them to update, revise, and alter their predictions.

Verbalization

After students have placed all of the words on their story maps, engage them in a whole-class discussion. The discussion can focus on where various pairs of students placed cards and why they placed them as they did. The discussion should focus on the clues students used to help them place the word cards and how they were able to make strategic placements.

Verbalization

Have one pair of students come to the board, select a word, read it aloud, place it on the story map where they predict it belongs, and then explain why they placed it there. Follow up by asking whether any pairs placed the same word in a different column and have them explain why they placed it as such.

Create a safe environment

After students have completed their story maps, introduce the story by displaying the book, *Sylvester and the Magic Pebble* by William Steig. Explain that the title of the story provides an additional clue that can help us predict. Often at this point students show outward displays that they are monitoring their predictions. They either begin to move their word cards or begin to discuss with their partner. Capitalize on these moments by encouraging students to share their strategic thinking. "I notice that you are moving your word cards. This is wonderful. This is exactly what good readers do when they read. They make predictions, and as they gather new clues they sometimes have to

(cont.)

FIGURE 6.11. *(cont.)*

Verbalization

Model

Explanation: declarative knowledge

Verbalization

Reduce processing by reading aloud so students can focus on using the strategy

change or alter their predictions. What did this new clue tell you? What kind of adjustments are you making to your story map predictions? Why?" Encourage students to verbalize their reasons for making changes or for keeping their predictions the same. If students do not begin to make adjustments on their own, model and engage in a think-aloud of your own.

Remind students that it is always a good idea to set purposes before reading. Setting purposes helps focus our thinking as we read. Have students record their purposes on their story maps.

Have students share some of their purposes and remind them that, as the text is read aloud, they should look for clues that help them identify various story grammar parts. Encourage students to talk with their partners about these clues as they read. Begin reading the first few pages of the text aloud. As students listen, walk among them and take anecdotal notes to determine whether they are able to use the clues in the text to update and revise predictions when necessary. After reading the first few pages engage students in a brief discussion that focuses on the clues in the text and how those clues helped them identify story grammar elements and what part of the story they heard them in. Refer to the story parts chart, where appropriate, to reinforce and add to each column as warranted by text. Reiterate that this is what good readers do as they read. They use the clues in the text to help them identify story grammar elements.

Continue the read-aloud, stopping at various points in the story to engage in the recursive process of setting purposes, making new predictions, gathering textual clues, and altering story maps based on the new information. Engage students in a discussion of such processes after completing the story.

Conclusion

Bring out the paper pieces of the pizza again and reiterate that, just like a pizza is not really a pizza without all of its parts, neither is a story complete unless it has all of its parts. Reiterate each of the story grammar elements and engage students in a discussion in which they share ways in which using the story map helped them as they listened to the story and aspects that were difficult (or cumbersome) about the process.

Assessment

- You will know whether students know that most stories have a similar structure by their contributions to the discussion.
- You will know whether students can use clues to help them identify story grammar elements (setting, characters, goal/problem, events, and solution) by their ability to place the word cards in the appropriate column of the story map before reading, and by their ability to make appropriate adjustments while reading.

FIGURE 6.11. *(cont.)*

comprehension and recall of narrative text. She begins the lesson by making an analogy between the necessary ingredients for making a pizza and the necessary ingredients authors use to make a story. In this manner Jaime tried to make the notion of text structure more tangible for her student, so he would be able to relate to it better. Other teachers have used the analogy of road maps to help students relate to the concept of story maps. Jaime designed her lesson as a read-aloud so that her student could focus all of his cognitive resources on identifying and using story grammar elements to help him understand the text. The lesson was also conducted in a whole-class environment. Jaime's lesson would be located at Point 4 of Figure 6.2. As well, Jaime developed a story parts chart (Figure 6.12) to remind students of each story grammar element and to provide clues that might help students locate each element in a story.

There are many similarities between Jaime's lesson and the VLP–story map activity lesson depicted in Figure 6.10. The critical difference is that Jaime's lesson is focused primarily on identifying the structure of the text, whereas the previous lesson was focused more on teaching students to generate, revise, and update predictions. Both lessons incorporate similar strategies because the strategies are not easily disentangled during the fluid process that characterizes authentic reading. The difference is in a matter of emphasis. The teacher focuses more of her explicit instruction and explanation (i.e., declarative, procedural, and conditional knowledge) on identifying story grammar elements in the lesson in Figure 6.11, whereas instruction is focused on prediction in Figure 6.10.

	Story Part				
	Setting	**Characters**	**Goal/Problem**	**Attempt to Solve Goal/ Problem**	**Solution**
What It Means	The place and time in which the story occurs	People or animals who are in the story	• What the characters are trying to do or get • The problems the characters face	What happens as the characters try to reach their goal or solve their problem	• What happens in the end • How the goal is reached • How the problem is solved
Clues to Look For	• Names of cities • Names of countries • Places characters go • Time of day • Year • Season	• Names • Descriptions • Ages • Boy/girl • Thoughts • Feelings • Actions	• An important event that affects the characters • What the characters want to do (or have to do) about it	• The things that happen during the story • What the characters do/say	• The problem is solved • The goal is attained • The characters have done or gotten what they were trying to do/get
Where to Find It	Beginning of story	Beginning of story	Beginning/middle of story	Middle of story	End of story

FIGURE 6.12. Story parts chart. Developed by Jaime Quackenbush.

Jaime found that her student was actively engaged and responded well to her lesson:

> I definitely think that knowing the story elements helped [the student] to monitor his reading. Throughout the book we read . . . [the student] was very conscious of the story elements. He acknowledged and considered the different story parts without my prompting; it was an intentional (strategic) thought on his part. He was very much able to complete a story map on his own while listening [to the read-aloud]. This helps him to focus on the various aspects of the story instead of breezing through it. [The student] needs a purpose for reading in order to bring meaning to the text. If he is unsure of the task, he tends to "word call" and understand [nearly] nothing.
>
> —JAIME QUACKENBUSH, reflective memo

Providing instruction that helps readers recognize the underlying structure of narrative text while they read is a beneficial strategy for enhancing comprehension.

Similar instruction is necessary to help students recognize expository text structure as well (Shanahan et al., 2010). Unfortunately, Martin and Duke's (2011) review noted that there are very few studies in which elementary-age students are taught to recognize expository text structure, which may help explain why young children struggle to comprehend informational text (National Center for Education Statistics, 2009). In general, readers have a more difficult time recognizing expository text structures because they are less familiar with them. Duke's (2000) study found that elementary students are exposed to very little informational text and that it is scarce in classroom libraries and rarely used in classroom activities. She found that, on average, only 3.6 minutes of instruction per day is actually spent reading, writing, or listening to informational text. When children do not have the opportunity to even be exposed to informational text, they do not develop an internalized schema for the manner in which authors organize informational material. As well, many authors do not provide cues that help readers identify the structure of the text. Without cues or markers to signal its underlying structure, the text becomes less coherent, which further impacts comprehension (Goldman & Rakestraw, 2000; Kintsch, 1998; Shanahan et al., 2010). Because of these issues, the Common Core State Standards focus on this problem, and recognizing expository text structures is featured prominently in standards related to the craft and structure of informational text (*www.corestandards.org/the-standards/english-language-arts-standards/reading-informational-text*).

Meyer (1975) identified five types of logical relations that operate within expository texts: (1) description (attributes, explanations, definition/example), (2) collection (sequence, enumeration, time order), (3) comparison (similarity/difference), (4) antecedent–consequence (cause–effect relationships), and (5) response rhetorical (problem–solution, question–answer, remark–reply). Authors signal text structure in a variety of ways (Goldman & Rakestraw, 2000). One way is to use introductory headings, sentences, or paragraphs to explicitly tell the reader how the text is organized. Another way is to use explicit connectives (e.g., cue words) that signal text structure via various semantic and syntactic means that link two sentences. When authors use explicit conjunctions, the underlying text structure becomes more obvious to readers. Table 5.3 displayed types of conjunctions that are often used in expository text. Table 6.2 contains the five types of expository text structures, their associated cue words/connectives, and the graphic organizers

TABLE 6.2. Expository Text Structures. *Source:* **Tompkins and McGee (1993).**

Pattern	Description	Cue words	Graphic organizer
Description/ definition/ example	The author describes a topic by listing characteristics and features or giving examples.	*for example, characteristics are*	
Sequence/ time order	The author lists items or events in numerical or chronological order.	Time/temporal connectives: *first, second, third next, then, finally after, before, noon, midnight, when, always,* specific times of day	first ⇒ next ⇒
Comparison– contrast	The author explains how two or more things are alike and/or how they are different.	Contrast connectives: *different, in contrast, alike, same as, on the other hand*	
Cause–effect	The author lists one or more causes and the resulting effect or effects.	Causality connectives: *reasons why, if . . . then, as a result, therefore, because, consequently, so*	Cause → Effect #1 / Effect #2 / Effect #3
Problem– solution	The author states a problem and lists one or more solutions for the problem. A variation of this pattern is the question-and-answer format in which the author poses a question and then answers it.	Concession/adversative connectives: *but, although, however, yet, problem is/dilemma is/puzzle is solved, question posed and answered*	Problem → Solution

Note. Adapted from Tompkins, Gail E., *Teaching Reading with Literature: Case Studies to Action Plans, 1st Edition*, pp. 74–75. © 1993. Adapted by permission of Pearson Education, Inc., Upper Saddle River, NJ.

that visually depict their underlying structure. Larger versions of graphic organizers are depicted in Figures 6.13, 6.14, 6.15, 6.16, 6.17, 6.18, and 6.19.

Englert and Hiebert (1984) found that collection text structures (i.e., sequence and time order) are the most obvious and well defined for young readers to recognize; description and comparison text structures are the most difficult. To explain this difficulty, they hypothesized that, although many elementary school content-related textbooks contain extensive descriptive text, it often occurs in short segments within other structures. Rarely is descriptive text the single organizing framework for an entire text. Text structures embedded within one another make it difficult for readers of any age to easily identify and use the structure of the text to enhance their comprehension.

Text containing ample signals or cues about the underlying structure is said to be "reader friendly." Unfortunately, many authors do not use explicit text structure signals, and their writing is so poorly organized and incoherent that the text is "unfriendly" to readers. At times publishing companies exacerbate the problem. Although the limitations of readability formulas are well known (see Weaver & Kintsch, 1991), publishing

Title: _____

Author: _____

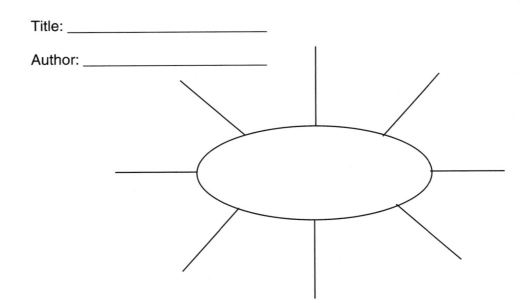

FIGURE 6.13. Graphic organizer for use in recognizing descriptive–definitional text.

Sequence chain for

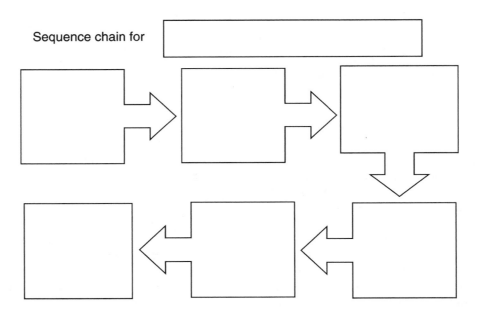

FIGURE 6.14. Graphic organizer for sequence text structure.

Comparison between:

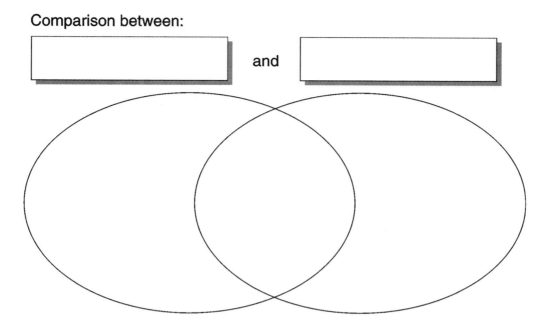

FIGURE 6.15. Graphic organizer for comparison–contrast text structure.

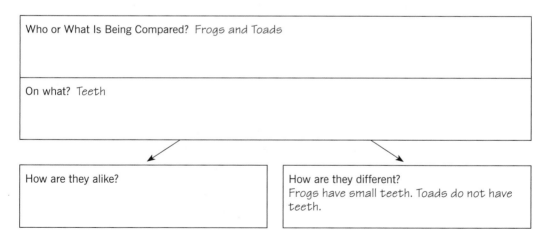

FIGURE 6.16. Comparison graphic organizer using text from Bobbie Kalman and Tammy Evert's (1994) *Frogs and Toads*.

191

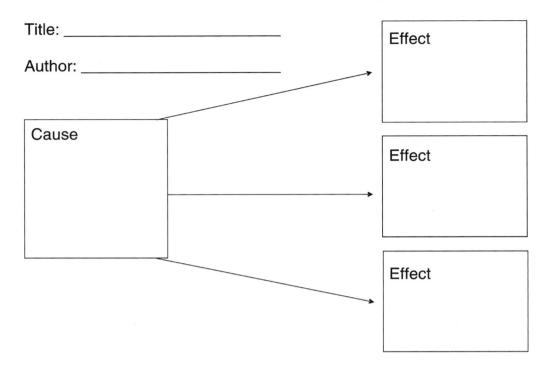

Title: _____

Author: _____

FIGURE 6.17. Graphic organizer for cause–effect text structure.

companies often rely on them to determine the level at which text is written. Such formulas (e.g., Flesch–Kincaid, Fry Readability) often use the number of syllables and sentences in 100-word passages taken from the beginning, middle, and end of a text to determine its readability. Texts that have a large number of syllables have higher readability levels, and texts that have fewer but longer sentences have higher readability levels. A text that has many polysyllabic words and complex or compound sentence structures, rather than simple sentence structures, will have a higher readability. In general, readability levels for expository texts are often far above the grade level for which they are intended. Much of the language within expository text contains polysyllabic content-related words. Typically, these polysyllabic words are repeated over and over within a given passage, thereby artificially increasing its readability. For example, a text on democracy might use the word repeatedly within a 100-word passage. In a text teaching about democracy, the word *democracy* cannot easily be substituted. Hence, editors seek other ways to reduce the readability. They often accomplish the task by simplifying complex sentences and eliminating polysyllabic words (such as connectives) that signal text structure. For example, in the text *Spiders Are Not Insects* by Allan Fowler (1996), the author compares arachnids and insects at the beginning of the text. However, there are no explicit comparison connectives to indicate this text structure:

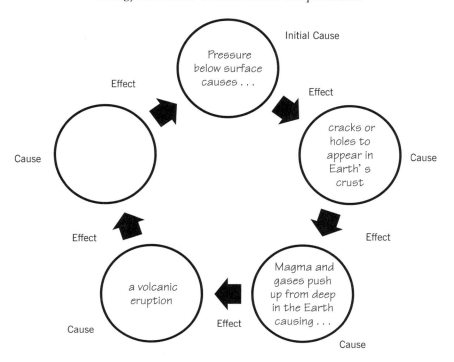

FIGURE 6.18. Alternative graphic organizer for cause–effect cycle using text from Gail Gibbons's (1995) *Planet Earth/Inside Out.*

> Spiders are not insects. They belong to a group of animals called arachnids. Arachnids have eight legs. Insects have only six. Arachnids do not have wings. Insects do. Spiders use hairs on their bodies to sense the world around them. Insects sense things with feelers, called antennae, that grow on their heads. (pp. 6–10)

To signal the comparison text structure more explicitly, the passage could be edited, as follows:

> Many people think spiders are insects. *However,* they are not. They belong to a group of animals called arachnids. Spiders *differ* from insects in many ways. Spiders have eight legs, *whereas* insects have only six. Spiders do not have wings. *However,* insects do. Spiders use hairs on their bodies to sense the world around them. *In contrast,* insects sense things with feelers, called antennae that grow on their heads.

The original text contained 52 words consisting of 73 syllables in nine sentences. The more "reader friendly" text contained 69 words consisting of 100 syllables across nine sentences. The revised text would have a higher readability level because it has more words and more syllables across the same number of sentences. However, it uses comparison connectives (e.g., *however, in contrast, differ, whereas*) to clearly indicate the manner in which the text is structured. Each connective is a polysyllabic word, adding 13 syllables to the text. The addition of the sentence "Spiders differ from insects in many ways" signals that a list of comparisons is forthcoming. Readers should almost be able

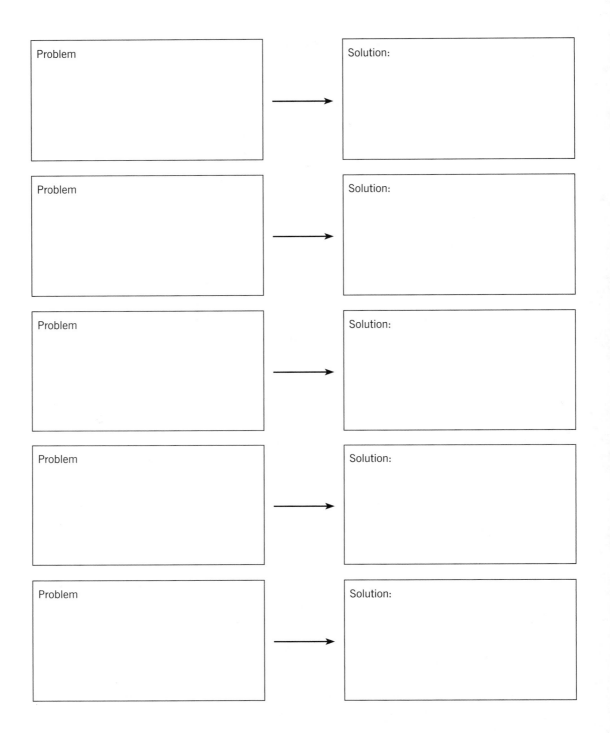

FIGURE 6.19. Graphic organizer for problem–solution text structure.

to visualize a bulleted list of those differences. The original text required readers to infer the underlying text structure—a difficult task for the beginning readers for which this text was intended. Although the revised text would be easier for young readers because it signals the comparison text structure, publishing companies would not use it because the readability would be inflated by the additional numbers of words and syllables.

For those readers who struggle with comprehension, particularly those who have difficulty with semantics, organization, working memory, and monitoring comprehension, their problems are often caused by text that is incoherent, poorly organized, or unsignaled. These problems are further compounded in expository texts (i.e., any informational or nonfiction text) for several reasons. First, students are generally less familiar with the structure of expository text. Narrative is the primary genre to which children are exposed at home and at school. Before even arriving at school, children are often able to internalize the story grammar structure inherent to the narrative genre. Their internalized schema for narrative structure helps them anticipate textual events and enhances their comprehension. Duke (2000) and Pappas (1991) identified three linguistic features of expository texts for children that differ from narrative texts. First, expository texts usually contain present-tense verbs, whereas narratives are primarily written in the past tense. Second, in narrative text characters are introduced in the beginning and referred to using various referents (e.g., *he, his, him*) throughout the text. As discussed earlier, this process is known as "co-reference." Although expository texts do not refer to an animal, place, or object throughout the entire text, the same *class* of animals, places, or objects is continually referred to using referents (e.g., *them, their*). This process is known as "co-classification." Thus, the ways in which common aspects of the text are linked across the text differ. Finally, expository texts use relational processes to indicate text structure, whereas narrative text does not (e.g., *in contrast, however, consequently*).

These linguistic differences make reading expository text a very different experience. Lacking exposure to expository text structure from the time they are very young, children are at a disadvantage. Young students typically are not exposed to expository text until third or fourth grade, when they are reading more fluently. Many students who were previously reading adequately begin to falter with reading at this time. The increased amount of reading from unfamiliar expository text structures becomes overwhelming for these readers, and their comprehension suffers. Much of the early research on text structure found that older and more proficient readers were able to use their knowledge of text structure as an organizational strategy for encoding and storing information gleaned from text. Such knowledge of text structure helps readers better retrieve new information from memory (Englert, & Hiebert, 1984; Hiebert, Englert, & Brennan, 1983; Meyer, Brandt, & Bluth, 1980; Ohlhausen & Roller, 1988; Spivey & King, 1989; Taylor, 1980; Shanahan et al., 2010). Reviews of research have noted that nearly any form of instruction aimed at teaching students to recognize and use text structure (e.g., visual representations of text structure, networking, flowcharting, conceptual frames, mapping, graphic organizers, hierarchical summaries) enhances comprehension and short- and long-term memory of text (Duke & Pearson, 2008; Pearson & Fielding, 1991; Martin & Duke, 2011; Shanahan et al., 2010).

Students are so unfamiliar with expository text structure that any type of instruction will help (Duke & Pearson, 2008). For decades researchers have implored classroom teachers to include more expository text in their instruction from kindergarten on; nevertheless, expository text is still a rarity in elementary classrooms (Duke, 2000). Teachers may ask students to complete a graphic organizer after they read, but such tasks are merely assessment activities unless they are accompanied by the explicit instruction that enables readers to understand and recognize the underlying structure of the text *while* they are reading. Some informational texts use combinations of these patterns, making it even more difficult to recognize the manner in which the author has chosen to communicate information. Again, the organizers serve as a means of helping students anticipate the type of information they will encounter as they read, which helps them set reasonable purposes. While reading the text, students can record information as it is encountered. Although some students find it difficult to read and record information simultaneously, this process helps reduce schema selection–retrieval problems by focusing attention to the text. For students who are "schema imposers" (Wade, 1990)—those students who overrely on their prior knowledge and do not attend to the text—teaching strategies such as setting purposes, making predictions, and identifying text structure helps focus their attention on the text rather than on prior knowledge. The activities described above support such strategy instruction.

The sample lesson depicted in Figure 6.20 teaches students how to recognize comparison text structure. Such instruction provides natural links to writing as well. If students are able to recognize how authors structure text, they can use similar structures to organize their own writing. Armbruster, Anderson, and Ostertag (1987, 1989) suggested that sound instruction about expository text structure should teach students (1) to use format cues such as cue words, headings, subheadings, and paragraphs; (2) to make concrete visual representations of how ideas are organized; (3) common text structures; and (4) how to write using these structures. Each of these elements, in addition to those of the CESI model, is present in the lesson in Figure 6.20.

This lengthy comparison lesson might take place over the course of 2 days. The notion of comparison is initially made using a concrete means. Comparing diagrams of how grocery stores and department stores are organized provided a way of teaching students how to look for similarity and difference in a semiotic text. Comparing two tangible objects is also a way of achieving the same concrete experience (Point 1 of Figure 6.2). The notion of stores and the way they are organized was appealing because of the link that could be made to studying the way various text structures are organized.

Armbruster and colleagues (1987, 1989) suggested that sound text structure instruction should teach students how to record information by using a concrete visual representation of the underlying structure. Organizers serve as a means of helping students anticipate the type of information they will encounter as they read. While reading the text, students can record information as it is encountered. This helps them maintain their focus while reading, and it helps them organize the information they are learning from the text. Although some students find it difficult to read and record information simultaneously, this process helps reduce comprehension problems by focusing attention on the text.

In the lesson depicted in Figure 6.20 the T-chart was used as a graphic organizer; however, many teachers often find the overlapping circles of the Venn diagram (depicted in Figure 6.15) helpful. Some young students find it difficult to understand the notion of similarity that is represented by the overlapping portions of the circles; when permitted to design their own comparison organizers, they often prefer to simply use the T-chart or the comparison diagram depicted in Figure 6.16. Cue words were emphasized by highlighting those in the text *Frogs and Toads* (Kalman & Everts, 1994) and by using cue words in the comparison text that was composed. In this way readers were able to understand how authors construct texts by examining published text and by creating their own. This dual learning exercise emphasizes the connections between reading and writing.

Teacher: Adapted from a lesson by Mike Rock

Title: Grocery Store/Department Store

Topic: Identifying Comparison–Contrast Text Structure

Grade level: 1–3 (for higher grades use age-appropriate texts)

STAIR hypothesis being addressed:
Students are unaware of strategies for identifying expository text structures. Their focus of attention wanes while reading exposition, and they have difficulty recalling what was read.

Goal of Lesson

Students will learn:
• To identify comparison text structure
• To compose comparison text structure
• That awareness of text structure can enhance comprehension

Materials

• *Frog and Toad Are Friends* by Arnold Lobel
• *Frogs and Toads* by Bobbie Kalman and Tammy Everts
• Copies of the store directory for a grocery store
• Copies of the store directory for a department store
• Shopping bags from grocery store/department store
• Word cards containing the phrases (*different, on the other hand, in contrast, unlike, similar, same as, alike, both*)
• Chart paper and markers

Introduction

Reduce processing demands by using maps as text

The lesson will begin by creating an analogy between the manner in which stores are organized and the manner in which texts are organized. Display shopping bags from two different stores (one from a grocery store and one from a department store). Explain that in this lesson, we are going to be thinking about how things are the same and different. "First we are going to think about and describe the types of items we might buy at a grocery store." Draw a T-chart on the board and record students' ideas as they brainstorm things to purchase at a grocery store. Have students think about what type of label this superordinate category might have. Then display the shopping bag from the department store. On the other side of the T-chart, record the information students brainstorm about the types of things they might buy at a department store and label the superordinate category. Explain that although you can buy things at both stores, the types of things within each store are quite different.

Description of Instructional Experience

Explanation: declarative knowledge

Explain that this is similar to when we read books. There are different types of books, and each type of book contains different information. Some tell stories and some tell information.

Explain that stores are also organized in different ways. Pass out copies of the directory for the grocery store. Have students work in pairs or small groups to

(cont.)

FIGURE 6.20. Sample lesson teaching students how to identify expository text structure.

Reduce processing demands by working in small groups

study the directory and describe the way the store is organized. Have students brainstorm why the store is organized as it is. Have students record the organizational features on the directory and the reasons why they are organized in that manner. After students have finished have them share their observations and reasons. Record students' ideas on the T-chart on the board.

Follow the same procedure for the directory of the department store. If you do not have a directory for one of the stores, have students draw their own. In this manner you are engaging them in the process of constructing a visual representation of how a store is organized. This same process can be transferred to text by having students draw their own representations of how texts are organized rather than having them use a pre-made graphic organizer. After students have identified how the department store is organized, engage them in a discussion in which they consider the notion of why it might be important to know how different stores are organized. Gather student responses, leading them toward the conditional knowledge that knowing how a store is organized helps us navigate through the store more easily than if they were to wander around the store aimlessly.

Explanation: conditional knowledge

Explain that just like stores are organized in different ways, so too are the texts we read. Grocery stores are organized in a manner that enables you to move quickly up and down aisles as you gather needed food items. Department stores are organized in a different way. They are organized in clusters that permit you to browse, and lead you from one department to the next. Explain that stores are organized in different ways depending on what they sell and what their purpose is. Texts are also organized in different ways depending on their purpose. Some texts tell a *story*. Display the *Frog and Toad Are Friends* book. Explain that these texts have settings, characters, problems, and solutions. If students are already familiar with these story grammar elements, make that link. Explain that other texts tell *information*. Display the book *Frogs and Toads*. These texts are arranged in a completely different way. Explain that there are five different ways that authors organize texts to tell you information. Knowing how an author organizes a text helps you know what kind of information to expect, and that will help you remember what you read better. Explain that today we are learning about one of the ways authors organize information—by comparison. Explain that the information in the book *Frogs and Toads* tells how frogs and toads are the same and different.

Explanation: declarative knowledge

One effective technique is to gradually create the chart depicted in Table 6.2 over the course of the year as different text structures are studied. The information in each cell can be added as students learn about it. For example, as you explain what comparison text is, add that information into the "Description" column of the chart so students can refer to it. As you introduce, or as students encounter, various cue words that indicate comparison, add them to the chart as well. Students can also add in various ways of organizing comparison information under the "graphic organizer" column.

Explanation: declarative knowledge

Procedural knowledge

Define comparison text as text in which the author explains how two or more things are alike and/or different. Add this description to the chart. Begin by asking the students to think about how they might go about comparing the two stores. "What would you do to see how the stores are the same and different from one another?" Record students' responses on chart paper. Generally

(cont.)

FIGURE 6.20. *(cont.)*

the procedural steps for comparing include some variation of these steps: (1) Observe both objects. (2) Describe the characteristics of each. (3) Carefully study the descriptions and think about how they are the same. (4) Organize the similar ideas. (5) Carefully study the descriptions and think about how they are different. (6) Organize the different ideas. These steps might be written on sentence strips so they can be kept or transferred onto the class chart of expository text structures (Table 6.2).

Model/think-aloud

Model and think aloud about how you might identify similarities between the two stores by looking at the lists of information gathered on each web. You might circle information on each web that is similar. Your discourse might sound something like this: "Hmmm, as I look at the T-chart, I notice that in both stores we can buy things. That is a similarity. I'm going to circle that on both webs." Have students work with a partner to identify other similarities and share with the larger group. Follow the same procedure to identify differences.

Guided practice

Explain that we have now compared the two different types of stores. If we were authors, and we wanted to explain how the stores were the same and different, we could use the notes on our T-charts to help us write about those similarities and differences. Explain that before we write, we are going to see how Bobbie Kalman and Tammy Everts organized their writing when they compared *Frogs and Toads*. Explain that as students listen to the text, they should make a T-chart and label one side "frogs" and the other "toads." Model using chart paper. Begin reading the first paragraph from p. 7, "Frogs and toads look similar, but they are different in some ways." Engage in a think-aloud: "That is a good introductory sentence. It lets me know that the authors are going to tell me how frogs and toads are similar and different. I expect they will tell me about this in the next few sentences." Continue reading, "A frog has smooth, moist skin. . . . " Model how to take notes on the "frog" side of the T-chart: "They are telling me that frogs have smooth, moist skin. I don't need to write that exact sentence. I'll just write *smooth, moist skin* under the 'frog' column." Continue modeling in this manner for several sentences, gradually releasing the responsibility to students by asking them to discuss with their partners what they should record in their charts and then sharing that with the whole group. Use this process while reading pages 7 and 8 aloud.

Model/think-aloud

Reduce processing demands

Model/think-aloud

Guided practice

Verbalization

After taking the notes on the T-chart, examine the structure used by the authors to create the text. It might be helpful to have a transparency copy of both pages so that cue words can be circled. Engage students in a discussion about what the authors did well to signal the comparison text structure and what they would change or alter to make the information even more clear to readers.

Model/think-aloud

Explain that students are now going to think about how they might organize this information about the two different stores to communicate it to others. You might model how to write a paragraph describing the similarities. "First let's think about words we might use to show how two things are the same." Have students brainstorm for cue words (e.g., *same, like, as, similar, both, alike*). As students generate words, create word cards. Begin modeling the writing process. "Just like Bobbie Kalman and Tammy Everts did, it's always good for writers to let their audience know what they are writing about. So, I'm going to

(cont.)

FIGURE 6.20. *(cont.)*

begin by letting my readers know that I'm going to be telling them about how the stores are similar. I guess I could say something like, *Grocery stores and department stores are alike in many ways.* Then I can list the circled items from the T-charts to show how they are similar to one another." Record your topic sentence on chart paper. Use the *alike* word card so students can easily see where the cue words are used. "I see on the web that you can buy things in both stores. So that will be one of the ways they are the same. It says, *Grocery stores and department stores are alike in many ways.* I want to add another sentence that tells one way in which they are the same. I could say, *You can buy things in both stores.* I am using the cue word *both* there, so as I write I'll put that word card in." Continue in this manner until the similarity paragraph is written. Students may be able to work in pairs to construct the remaining sentences.

Guided practice

After modeling, ask students to work in pairs to write a paragraph that describes how the two stores are different. Have students share their paragraphs with one another and explain how they went about writing them.

Conclusion

Students write a self-assessment reflection in their journals with the sentence starter, "Comparison texts _____" and "Using the T-chart _____." After students complete their self-assessment, engage in a whole-class discussion of how to recognize comparison texts and why it is important to be able to do so.

Assessment

- You will know that students are able to identify comparison text structure by observing the manner in which they complete their T-charts while listening to the *Frogs and Toads* text.
- You will know that students are able to compose comparison text structure by the structure of the "difference" paragraphs they write with their partners.
- You will know that students are aware that text structure can enhance comprehension by their contributions to the concluding discussion.

SAMPLE T-CHART

Grocery Stores	Department Stores

FIGURE 6.20. *(cont.)*

Many teachers have found it difficult to incorporate authentic expository text into their classrooms. Some teachers may feel restricted by the limitations of their core reading programs and scripted reading programs. For other teachers the additional time it takes to identify and find such texts may prove challenging. Table 6.3 identifies expository texts that the teachers in our clinical experiences have found useful. The text structures that appear within each, the type of cue words, and any signaling devices (i.e., table of contents, cue words, index, headings) are identified.

Text Maintenance Strategies

Text maintenance strategies include (1) creating mental images, (2) monitoring comprehension by questioning oneself, (3) identifying text structure, and (4) updating and revising predictions. Like text anticipation strategies, good readers use these strategies flexibly and in combination with one another. The key benefit of these strategies is their ability to help focus students' attention while reading. Monitoring is the critical factor in the reading process. If readers are unable, or unwilling, to monitor the incoming information and evaluate whether it matches their mental image, supports or refutes a prediction, provides information about a purpose, or looks like the type of information they would expect to see in a particular genre, then they will not be able to maintain focused attention, and their comprehension will be affected. As noted earlier, readers who have difficulty maintaining focus while reading are often "non-integrators" (Wade, 1990, p. 47) who have difficulty making inferences and integrating information across the text. These readers are frequently word callers who are more focused on accurate word reading than on constructing meaning.

Good readers use several strategies while reading to make sure that their attention is focused on meaning construction. When the text is particularly image-laden, good readers often visualize it. They update and revise these mental images, as warranted by the text. Good readers are also able to monitor their understanding throughout the entire reading process. When they notice that their comprehension is failing, they enact a fix-up strategy to repair their understanding. As mentioned in the previous section, good readers use their textual schema to identify the way in which the text is structured. In addition to fostering schema selection and retrieval, this strategy facilitates schema maintenance as well. Readers use the structure of the text as a guide for anticipating and recording upcoming information as they read. When readers are able to organize, categorize, and store incoming information, memory and recall of text are facilitated. Like identifying text structure, updating and revising their predictions while reading helps students anticipate and focus their attention on the incoming information.

Making Mental Images

Imagery, or visualization, is a strategy in which students are taught to visualize the text as they read. Many struggling readers are unaware that this simple process can facilitate comprehension. Making mental images while reading enhances recall and retention of text, and it might help readers who tend to activate disparate information from each sentence to integrate the information, make inferences, and form a unified picture of the event described in the text (Shanahan et al., 2010). In their review of salient comprehension strategies, Pressley, Johnson, et al. (1989) identified mental imagery as a strategy that is easy to teach. They distinguished between two types of imagery: representational and

TABLE 6.3. Sample Texts That Exhibit Clear Expository Text Structures

Expository text structure type	Sample texts
Description/ definition/ example	**Implicit cues and signaling** Arnosky, J. (1996). *All about deer*. New York: Scholastic. [Uses descriptive text and labeled illustrations to describe deer and their habitat] Asch, F. (1995). *Water*. New York: Harcourt. [Beautiful illustrations and descriptive text describe water] DePaola, T. (1975). *The cloud book*. New York: Holiday House. [Includes index, descriptive text, and some explicit definitions to describe types of clouds] Dussling, J. (1998). *Bugs! Bugs! Bugs!* New York: Scholastic. [Uses descriptive text and vivid photographs to describe insects for elementary readers] Fowler, A. (1995). *The best way to see a shark*. Chicago: Children's Press. [Includes index and descriptive text to describe shark life for young readers] Maynard, C. (1994). *Incredible dinosaurs*. New York: Snapshot. [Includes table of contents, index, and descriptive text to describe dinosaurs]
Sequence/ time order	**Explicit cues and signaling** Aliki. (1992). *Milk: From cow to carton*. New York: HarperCollins. [Uses cue words (e.g., *spring, summer, winter, later, then, after*) to indicate passage of time and explain how milk is produced from field to farm to dairy] Gibbons, G. (1999). *The pumpkin book*. New York: Holiday House. [Uses temporal cue words (e.g., *spring, fall, after, when*) to explain how pumpkins grow] Gibbons, G. (1991). *From seed to plant*. New York: Holiday House. [Uses descriptive text and temporal cue words (e.g., *before, then, when, later*) to explain how plants grow.] Jordan, H. J. (1992). *How a seed grows*. New York: HarperCollins. [Uses temporal cue words (e.g., *now, after, soon*) to indicate time order structure] Kalman, B., & Langille, J. (1998). *What is a life cycle?* New York: Crabtree. [Includes table of contents and index. Uses steps of a cycle that are explicitly numbered to explain various life cycles] Showers, S. (2001). *What happens to a hamburger?* New York: HarperCollins
Comparison– contrast	**Explicit cues and signaling** Kalman, B., Everts, Y. (1994). *Frogs and toads*. New York: Crabtree. [Includes table of contents, index, uses comparison cue words] **Implicit cues and signaling** Fowler, A. (1996). *Gator or croc?* New York: Children's Press. [Includes descriptive text, but primarily comparison text that describes the difference between alligators and crocodiles. Explicit cueing of the comparison structure is not apparent]
Cause–effect	**Explicit cues and signaling** Berger, M. (1983). *Why I cough, sneeze, shiver, hiccup, and yawn*. New York: Thomas Y. Crowell. [Uses question–answer format and descriptive text to explain common reflex actions of the body] Gallant, R. A. (2001). *Rocks*. New York: Marshall Canvendish. [Includes descriptive and cause–effect text structures. Explicit descriptive and causality connectives are used to explain types of rocks and how they were formed] Gibbons, G. (1995). *Planet earth/inside out*. New York: Mulberry. [Includes descriptive, cause–effect, and time/order structures. Explicit causality connectives are used to indicate cause–effect structure]

(cont.)

TABLE 6.3. *(cont.)*

Expository text structure type	Sample texts
Problem–solution	**Explicit cues and signaling**
	Berger, M., & Berger, S. (1999). *Why do flies walk upside down? Questions and answers about insects.* New York: Scholastic. [Includes table of contents, index, and uses question/answer format to explain various questions about insects]
	Prager, E. J. (2000). *Sand.* Washington DC: National Geographic Society. [Uses question–answer format to describe sand]
	Whitfield, P. (1989). *Can the whales be saved? Questions about the natural world and the threats to its survival answered by the Natural History Museum.* New York: Viking. [Uses question/ answer format to explain questions about the living world]
Mixed	**Explicit cues and signaling**
	Gibbons, G. (1995). *Sea turtles.* New York: Holiday House. [Includes descriptive text and sequence text that uses explicit temporal connectives. Also includes a diagram comparing sea turtles and regular turtles]
	Kalman, B. (1997). *How a plant grows.* New York: Crabtree. [Includes table of contents; index; and uses descriptive (pp. 4–7), sequence (pp. 8–11), and cause–effect (pp. 13–27) text structures to explain how plants grow]
	Lauber, P. (1995). *Who eats what? Food chains and food webs.* New York: HarperCollins [Includes some descriptive text, mostly cause–effect structure with some explicit causality cue words; authors also use adversative cue words that give the impression of problem–solution structure]
	Zoehfeld, K. W. (1995). *How mountains are made.* New York: HarperCollins. [Includes some descriptive text, mostly cause–effect structure with explicit causality cue words]
	Implicit cues and signaling
	Branley, F. M. (1988). *Tornado alert.* New York: HarperCollins. [Includes implicit descriptive, problem–solution, and sequence text structures that are implicit]
	Fowler, A. (1996). *Spiders are not insects.* New York: Children's Press. [Primarily descriptive structure, except pp. 6–10, which are comparison; includes index]

mnemonic. Representational images represent and depict the content of the text. That is, readers create pictures of what the author describes in their minds as they read. Gambrell's research (e.g., Gambrell & Bales, 1986; Gambrell & Jawitz, 1993) showed that comprehension is enhanced when students are taught to create mental images while reading. Gambrell and Bales (1986) taught poor readers in the fourth and fifth grades to form mental images as they read. They found that students who were taught to form images as they read were able to identify textual inconsistencies better than their untrained peers. These results suggest that imagery fosters the ability to monitor comprehension while reading.

Other studies have been concerned with the impact of imagery on comprehension and recall of text. Flaro's (1987) study of the use of visual imagery by fourth and fifth graders with learning disabilities showed significant increases on reading comprehension, as did Chan, Cole, and Morris's (1990) study of upper-primary "reading disabled" students and average third graders. Sadoski's work (e.g., Sadoski, 1983, 1985; Sadoski, Goetz, & Kangiser, 1988) examined the impact of imagery and affect on recall. His findings suggest that all three variables are interrelated. That is, when readers have an enjoyable experience with the text, they image more, which affects the amount they are able to recall. Sadoski's findings support Paivio's (1986) dual-coding theory, which contends that "there is a parallel, nonverbal dimension to discourse processing which can be analyzed, and which contributes to the overall comprehension, integration, and appreciation of text" (Sadoski et al., 1988, p. 335).

In contrast with representational images, mnemonic images help readers learn and remember information about unfamiliar concepts. This form of imagery is often used while studying. Readers impose an artificial image onto the textual information to enable them to recall it. Pressley, Johnson, et al. (1989) use an example in which a reader, trying to remember the major exports of a particular country, might create an image of an individual trying to sell particular products in that country. This image is not in the text, nor is it suggested by the text. The reader imposes the image to help him remember the information contained in the text. Pressley, Johnson, et al. (1989) suggested that, although the research on mnemonic imagery has shown that its use produces significant gains in recall, the research has not been clear regarding whether readers are able to apply the strategy on their own, without mnemonic cues provided by researchers.

As shown in Table 6.1, good readers use imagery as a strategy to enhance comprehension with nearly any type of text (see Associated Conditional Knowledge column). Most narrative text contains a great deal of descriptive language that evokes sensory images of the setting and representational images of the characters and their actions. Many expository texts, particularly descriptive/definition/example text, contain similar features that evoke strong images.

The lesson in Figure 6.21 teaches students how to generate representational images as they read. Note that the teacher, Eileen Ludwig, has chosen to begin this lesson by using concrete text (listening to an audiotape) (Point 2 of Figure 6.2) to facilitate transfer and reduce processing demands.

During this lesson Eileen provided a great deal of modeling and thought aloud about the procedures she used to create mental images. She also provided opportunity for her student to try out the process for herself as she listened to Eileen read the text. In this manner Eileen reduced processing and created a safe environment for her student to experiment with a new strategy. The student was able to focus all of her cognitive resources on using the strategy. Eileen also provided ample opportunity for her student to sketch and share her images and describe the procedures she used to create images. In her reflective memo, Eileen noted how well the concrete text she used to begin the lesson helped her student:

> When reading this text [the student] was able to use her own prior knowledge and her senses in order to form images and to understand what she read. Instead of jumping right into written text, we started the lesson off by listening to nature sounds. As we listened to these sounds, we tried to create pictures in our heads and tell what we were seeing. I also believe using a more concrete experience helped [the student] to learn this strategy. After our classroom discussions I realize the importance [of] starting lessons off with concrete events or experiences. . . . I believe this is especially crucial for students . . . who have never had explicit instruction in reading strategies before.
>
> —EILEEN LUDWIG, reflective memo

Teacher: Eileen Ludwig

Title: Imagine It!

Topic: Creating mental images while reading

Grade level: 1–4

STAIR hypothesis being addressed:
Students use some comprehension strategies (e.g., activating prior knowledge, generating predictions) when prompted to do so. However, they do not use other strategies to enhance comprehension.

Goal of Lesson

Students will learn:
- To use the author's language, prior knowledge, and their senses to make mental images and increase comprehension of text
- Why it is important to make mental images while reading

Materials
- *Owl Moon* by Jane Yolen
- Tape player
- Tape of outdoor sounds, including bird and animal sounds
- Modeling clay
- Drawing paper

Introduction

Explanation: declarative, procedural, conditional knowledge

The lesson will begin by explaining to students that when we read, we can make images in our heads. We can use the author's words, what we already know, and our senses to make these images. Just as we use the illustrator's pictures to help us understand what we are reading, we can make our own pictures to help us understand. Good readers paint pictures in their minds as they read to understand what the author is saying. When we read we can think about what we may see, hear, smell, feel, or taste.

Reduce processing demands

Have students close their eyes and listen to a tape of different nature and bird sounds. Ask students to listen very carefully and try to think about what the sounds remind them of. Ask students to try and make pictures in their minds about what they "see" as they listen to the tape.

After playing a portion of the tape, have students draw or depict what they imagined or pictured in their minds as they listened. Then have students share what they imaged with a partner and how they were able to arrive at that image. Engage in a whole-class discussion of these same topics, focusing on the procedural knowledge of *how* students created their mental images.

Verbalization

Share the image that you pictured in your mind as you listened to the tape.

Model/think-aloud

Explain how you got your images by thinking aloud: "On the one part of the tape I could hear the birds chirping and the leaves on the tree rustling. So, I

(cont.)

FIGURE 6.21. Sample lesson teaching students to use mental imagery.

saw birds and a lot of trees in my mind. I also thought that it might be a spring day because the music was very happy and the birds chirped happily. There usually seems to be a lot of birds chirping outside my house during spring. That's why I thought it might be spring. I used my prior knowledge and a few clues from the tape."

Declarative knowledge

Conditional knowledge

Explain that this was the way that *you* pictured the sounds on the tape. Although everyone listened to the same tape, everyone has slightly different images because we all have different background experiences. When we make images while we read, we become more involved in the text and it helps us remember what we read. Emphasize that there is no right or wrong way to make mental images.

Description of Instructional Experience

After introducing the text *Owl Moon* by Jane Yolen, activate prior knowledge, make predictions, and set purposes for reading. Explain that this is a text that is well suited for making mental images because the author uses lots of descriptive language that helps us get a good picture in our minds. Explain that some parts of the text may be easier to make images with than others. Further explain that some stories are better for making images than others because some authors use lots of descriptive language and others use less. Explain that these images help readers activate their prior knowledge in order to understand text. Refer back to the introductory activity to remind students of how we were able to create images based on the sounds we heard.

Conditional knowledge

Reduce processing demands

Model/think-aloud

Model how to use imagery by thinking aloud as you begin to read *Owl Moon* aloud. For example, one part of the text reads: "Then we came to a clearing in the dark woods. The moon was high above us. It seemed to fit exactly over the center of the clearing and the snow below it was whiter than the milk in a bowl of cereal." After reading, engage in a think-aloud that might go something like this: "I picture in my mind a large area that is covered by a lot of newly fallen snow. I also see some light coming off the snow from the reflection of the moon. I picture a very open area in the middle of a forest at night. I picture that it is very cold outside." Explain how you arrived at such images as well. "The author said the snow was whiter than milk in a cereal bowl. I could really picture that in my mind. I think that it might have just fallen or that no other people or animals might have been around because we live in an area where it snows, and I know that the snow does not stay white unless it is very new or nothing else is around to make it dirty. I also know that it is nighttime because the moon comes out at night. I think it might be giving off a reflection because the author says it seems to fit perfectly over the center of the clearing. I also picture that it is a very cold area because I know that it gets very cold out when it snows." Explain how you are able to use the author's words, your own prior knowledge, and some of your senses to make those images in your mind. Explain that these images help you understand what is happening in the story and help you remember because it is easier to remember a picture.

Procedural knowledge

Procedural knowledge

Conditional knowledge

Model/think-aloud

Continue to model and think aloud as you read more of the story aloud. Stop at those places where you naturally image and be sure to communicate what you are imaging and how you were able to create that image. Gradually relinquish

(cont.)

FIGURE 6.21. *(cont.)*

Guided practice

Verbalization

the responsibility for imaging to the students. After modeling in several places, ask students to share their images with a partner and how they arrived at their images, or have some students share their images and how they arrived at them with the whole group. Another option is to have students quickly sketch their images as you are reading. Have students share their images/drawings with a partner and discuss where in the story they imaged, what they imaged, and how they arrived at their images. A whole-class discussion can focus on similar aspects: where students used imagery, what words evoked the most imagery, and how they arrived at their images.

Conclusion

Have students record their feelings about the lesson by having them complete the journal starters, "Creating mental images _____," "While listening to *Owl Moon* _____," or "Listening to the nature tape _____." Engage students in a whole class discussion of what they learned about imagery, whether it helped them as the story was read, and how they were able to image.

Assessment

- You will know that students are able to use the author's language, prior knowledge, and their senses to make mental images and increase comprehension of text by their contributions during class discussion, by their drawings, and by their discussion with their partners.
- You will know that students know why it is important to make mental images while reading by their journal entries at the conclusion of the lesson and the concluding discussion.

FIGURE 6.21. *(cont.)*

Students are able to quickly learn how to create mental images while reading. The challenge is finding ways to transfer such learning to independent use.

Monitoring Comprehension/Questioning Oneself

The ability to monitor one's comprehension is linked to metacognition (Flavell, 1979). To reiterate: Metacognitive awareness consists of knowledge about ourselves, the tasks we face, and the strategies we use (Baker & Beall, 2009; Garner, 1987; Wagoner, 1983). Metacognition makes use of a series of mechanisms aimed at checking, planning, monitoring, testing, revising, and evaluating the strategies we employ (Baker & Beall, 2009; Baker & Brown, 1984). Teaching students to monitor their comprehension while reading involves simply telling them to repeatedly ask themselves "Does this make sense?" as they are reading. The strategy does not involve having students (or the teacher) generate comprehension questions to ask themselves. It is simply an effort to teach students to monitor their understanding as they read. Patty DiLaura George's "stop and go" lesson (see Chapter 2) is an example of teaching very young readers how to stop and think after reading each page to see if the text made sense or not.

Instruction on comprehension monitoring focuses on the reader's ability to oversee her own reading process and to note how well or how poorly her understanding of the text is progressing (Shanahan et al., 2010). Successful readers have an awareness of, and control over, such metacognitive skills, and they actively engage them before, during, and after reading (Baker & Beall, 2009; Brown, 1980). At times during the reading process, readers encounter discrepancies between their schemata and the text. As noted in Chapter 2, Anderson (1980) described this metacognitive awareness that something does not make sense or is hindering comprehension as a "clunk." If the reader is adequately monitoring his comprehension, he will notice the incongruity and attempt to resolve the problem (typically by applying fix-up strategies). Unfortunately, younger and less proficient readers have difficulty monitoring their comprehension (August et al., 1984; Garner, 1980, 1987; Markman, 1977; Myers & Paris, 1978; Paris & Myers, 1981; Yuill & Oakhill, 1991). Successful readers, on the other hand, are more apt to detect inconsistencies in text and routinely readjust their reading strategies and schemata to accommodate such changes (Baker, 1984; Baker & Anderson, 1982; Garner & Kraus, 1981; Garner & Reis, 1981; Winograd & Johnston, 1982). This metacognitive awareness enables readers to comprehend better, particularly if they are able to apply appropriate fix-up strategies for mending comprehension when difficulties are encountered. Good readers purposefully and deliberately apply an array of strategies to maximize their understanding (Paris & Jacobs, 1984; Shanahan et al., 2010).

The ability to monitor one's comprehension is at the heart of strategy instruction. It is an abstract concept that younger and less proficient readers, in particular, have a difficult time learning. However, the research is clear that such readers can be successfully taught to monitor their comprehension. Patty DiLaura George's lesson (introduced in Chapter 2) is a good example of how to teach emergent readers the concept of monitoring. Portions of the text of her lesson appeared in Chapter 2; however, the actual lesson plan is presented in Figure 6.22. Note that she introduced the students to the idea of monitoring by using stop and go signs to indicate whether or not they understood the text. She has also used the clunk and click characters (depicted in Figures 2.2 and 2.3) for similar lessons.

Patty's lesson enabled students to learn how to monitor their understanding, first by listening and then by using a wordless picture book. She also provided a very safe environment in which to learn new concepts (Point 3 of Figure 6.2). As noted in Chapter 2, other teachers created events to simulate the "aha" experience of recognizing when something does not make sense (e.g., Liz Graffeo and Summer Sciandra's Missing Spider Lesson). Once students learn to use a manipulative such as the stop and go or clunk and click tags to monitor their comprehension, the tags can be used as they view videos, during teacher read-alouds, during shared reading, guided reading, and independent reading across the curriculum. By altering the amount of scaffolded support (i.e., the vertical dimension of Figure 6.2) and the textual conditions, the amount of scaffolded support students need to competently monitor their comprehension is gradually reduced. Continued practice under a variety of textual conditions will foster transfer to independence.

Jaime Quackenbush noted that her third-grade student was able to monitor his comprehension on his own after she had focused several of her lessons on comprehension monitoring:

> During our concluding [lesson] I had hoped that [the student] would be able to consciously stop while reading and monitor his understanding. He did so with more focus and intentionality than I'd even imagined! He was not simply following my example or mechanically going through the motions. He was able to explain why he had stopped, where he did, and what he was thinking. I couldn't stop grinning!
> —JAIME QUACKENBUSH, reflective memo

Teacher: Patty DiLaura George

Title: Stop/Go

Topic: Monitoring Comprehension while Reading

Grade level: K–2

STAIR hypothesis being addressed:
Students are unaware that reading is a meaning-getting process. They are unable to recognize when they do not understand what they read.

Goal of Lesson

Students will learn:
• That sometimes when we read the text might not make sense
• To stop and ask yourself whether the text makes sense or not

Materials

• *Good Dog Carl* by Alexandra Day
• "Stop" and "go" tags
• Student self-assessments

Introduction

Explanation: declarative knowledge

Begin lesson by asking students to think of a time when somebody said something to them that didn't make sense. Have students share their experiences. Explain that sometimes when we read, the text might not make sense. Explain that today we are going to learn how to recognize when the text we are reading does not make sense.

Procedural and conditional knowledge

Display sample "stop" and "go" tags. Explain that sometimes when we are reading, things might not make sense. When that happens we should "stop" and think about why it does not make sense. As we are reading today when something does not make sense to us, we are going to turn our tags to the "stop" side to show that something does not make sense. Explain that at other times the text makes perfect sense. During those times we "go" right ahead. Today as we are reading, when everything makes sense to us we will put our tags on the "go" side. Pass out tags to each student. Ask students to turn their tags to the side that will show that they do not understand something. Be sure that students are aware that the "stop" side means they do not understand. Ask students to turn their tags to the side they will show to represent that everything makes sense to them.

Explain that we are going to practice using the tags first by listening to some statements. Some of the statements might make sense to them and some may not. Read a statement to the students. Ask students whether the statement makes sense to them or not. Remind them that if it makes sense, they should turn their tags to "go" and if it does not make sense, they should turn their tags to "stop."

(cont.)

FIGURE 6.22. Sample lesson teaching students how to monitor their comprehension.

Sample statements include:
- I made my husband an ice cream sundae, and I put spaghetti sauce on top of it.
- Last night I dusted and vacuumed my living room.
- I washed my car because it was dirty.
- The flowers in my garden needed a drink, so I gave them some lemonade.
- I watched my favorite television show on the radio.

Model/think-aloud

Model and think aloud after reading the first sentence. You might say something like, "Hmmm, that doesn't make any sense to me. When I stop and think about what you might put on top of an ice cream sundae, I think that I might put hot fudge or strawberry, but I wouldn't put spaghetti sauce. That doesn't make sense to me. I'll turn my sign to the 'stop' side." After reading each sentence, remind students to stop and think about whether it makes sense to them and to turn their tags to either the "stop" or the "go" side. Ask students to share the reasons why a particular sentence made sense to them or not. Be sure to convey acceptance of all responses. Continue in this manner for all sentences.

Guided practice

Verbalization

Explain and remind students that this is the same thing that we do when we read. As we read, we have to stop and think about whether the text makes sense to us or not. If it does not make sense, we need to think about why it does not make sense and use a strategy to help us understand it better.

Description of Instructional Experience

Explain that we are going to use this same procedure as we read the book *Good Dog Carl* by Alexandra Day. Introduce the story and have students activate prior knowledge, set purposes, and make predictions.

Declarative knowledge

Explain that as we read, it is important to stop and think about whether the words and pictures make sense to us. Explain that we will use the "stop" and "go" tags today to indicate whether the words and pictures in this story make sense to us. Explain that this is a unique book because there are very few words. The author has chosen to use pictures to tell the story. Explain that we are going to study those pictures, make the story up in our mind as we read, and stop and think about whether the story they tell makes sense to us or not.

Procedural knowledge

Model/think-aloud

Model and think aloud as you read and display the first pages: "That must be Carl the Dog. It looks like the mother is going away and leaving the dog to watch over the baby. When I stop and think about that, it doesn't really make sense to me that a mother would leave a dog to watch the baby. So, when I stop and think about the story those pictures tell me I am a little confused. I'll turn my sign to 'stop.' That doesn't make sense to me. But that must be what she's doing. I'll just read ahead and see what happens. Maybe I'll understand better as I read more."

Guided practice

Verbalization

Display the next set of pages, encouraging students to study the pictures carefully and to stop and think about whether they make sense or not. Observe and take anecdotal notes on how students respond using their tags. Ask students to share reasons why those pages make sense or do not make sense

(cont.)

FIGURE 6.22. *(cont.)*

Safe environment

to them. Remind students that there are no right or wrong answers. It only matters that they honestly show whether they understand the text or not.

Guided practice

Continue on in this manner, reminding students at the end of each set of pages to stop and think about whether they understand or not. Ask them to turn their tags to the appropriate side and have various students share their thoughts about why a particular page made sense to them or not.

Conclusion

Verbalization

After reading the entire text, have students complete a student self-assessment about using the tags to monitor their comprehension. After completing the self-assessment, engage students in a discussion of the usefulness of the strategy and how they used it. Conclude the lesson by reminding students that we must stop and think about whether the text makes sense while we read all kinds of text. As a follow-up you might continue to use the "stop" and "go" tags during read-alouds, shared reading, guided reading, and independent reading across the curriculum.

Assessment

- You will know whether students understand that text might not make sense when they read by their discourse during class discussion and their self-assessments.
- You will know that students can stop and ask themselves whether the text makes sense or not by observing their ability to manipulate the "stop" and "go" tags and listening to their rationales for why they manipulated the tag in the manner they did.

STUDENT SELF-ASSESSMENT

1. While reading *Good Dog Carl*, stopping and thinking about whether it made sense was:

   very easy   easy   a little hard   very hard

2. While reading *Good Dog Carl*, using the tag to show whether it made sense or not was:

   very easy   easy   a little hard   very hard

3. I think I can use the "stop" and "go" tag to show that I understand what I read:

   all the time   sometimes   never

FIGURE 6.22. *(cont.)*

As students become more adept at monitoring their comprehension under varying conditions, the manipulative stop and go tags can be removed as a scaffold and students taught to use sticky notes or a chart to note those places in the text that were confusing to them. Many teachers find that it is easy to teach students to draw a question mark on a sticky note and place it in the text where they were confused. Students can also jot down what they do not understand on the sticky note. Students can then pair off or form small groups to discuss where they had comprehension difficulties, what caused the problem, and seek help from their peers to understand the text better. These sticky notes serve as an excellent source of agenda items during peer discussions of the text—students can use the sticky notes as a source for discussion topics. Students often begin such peer discussions by saying things like, "On page 37 I was really confused when _____. Can you help me understand that better?" In this manner students show that they are able to monitor their comprehension and actively seek resolution to any problems that arise while they are reading. *Resolution* is the focus of the next section.

Fix-Up Strategies

Fix-up, or repair, strategies are general strategies that good readers deliberately employ after they realize they do not understand what they are reading. These strategies include (1) slowing down and reading ahead for clarification, (2) rereading, and (3) asking about or discussing the confusing portion with someone (see Figure 2.5 for a chart of these strategies). *Slowing down and reading ahead for clarification* is often used when readers encounter new vocabulary or new ideas and they hope that the author will define or explain the unfamiliar or confusing idea in the text that lies ahead; *rereading* involves going back and rereading a word, phrase, sentence, or any portion of text; *asking about or discussing the confusing portion with someone* involves engaging another individual in a conversation in which the goal is to help each other better understand the text. Readers also might consult an outside source such as another text, a video, or a television program to help them better understand what they read. Such consultation clearly takes the reader away from the current reading event; it is often used when a comprehension difficulty exceeds the text's capacity to clarify it. Consulting outside sources is not something that young readers normally do.

The difficult aspect of teaching students to use fix-up strategies is that, like any strategy, it requires an expenditure of time. Many readers, particularly struggling ones, are not eager to reread text. Very often their goal is to "get done" rather than "to understand"; stopping to reread text or slowing down to read ahead carefully only delays them in achieving their goal. These are the circumstances when creating a safe environment for strategy use becomes essential. When students feel as if they must hurry to complete a reading task, there is a reason. They either do not enjoy reading or feel some sort of "assessment burden"—that is, students feel pressure to complete an assessment. If they do not "get done" on time, they may be punished by receiving a poor grade, losing their recess, or having to stay in at recess to complete the assignment. Clearly, there is little reward for slowing down and taking their time to make sure they understand text.

In Chapter 2 the notion of overhauling traditional forms of comprehension assessment was discussed as one means of creating a safer environment for strategy use. This notion is of prime importance here. The lessons described throughout this chapter use authentic and alternative means of assessing students' comprehension and strategy use. These assessment forms do not elicit the same urgency to "get done" because they are linked to the reading process rather than used as postreading assessments of comprehension. The lessons were also designed to show students that there is a "payoff" for expending the cognitive effort required to use strategies. Through the student self-assessments and strategy discussions, the teachers in these lessons attempted to show students that their efforts paid off by enhancing their comprehension. As noted in Chapter 1, experiencing the benefit is essential to creating motivated strategy use.

The best lessons for teaching students how, when, and why they should use fix-up strategies occur during the context of authentic reading experiences. Each strategy can be modeled using think-aloud procedures and practiced during any of the lessons that appear in this chapter. As you are engaged in a teacher read-aloud or modeling, you can "slip in" discourse about using fix-up strategies. For example, as you encounter text that does not make sense, you might say, "Hmmm, that doesn't make sense to me. I think I have to reread to see what the author was talking about. Maybe that will help me understand it better." It is helpful during these think-alouds to refer to a classroom chart, such as the one depicted in Figure 2.5, so students can see and remember the strategies they can use to repair comprehension. It is also helpful to encourage and praise students who engage in a similar process as they read.

One difficulty with teaching students to ask or discuss the comprehension problem with someone is that they may use that strategy at the expense of employing a strategy they can use on their own. It is important to communicate the conditional knowledge that this is a strategy to be used once they have reread or read ahead for clarification. If either of those strategies did not help, *then* they can consider asking someone else or engaging in a discussion. Peer discussions are recommended over teacher-led discussions primarily because teacher-led discussions often become question–answer periods in which the teacher dominates the discourse by asking a series of questions. Cazden (1986) and Mehan (1979) described these interactions as I-R-E (initiate–respond–evaluate) sequences, in which the teacher initiates the discussion by asking a question, students respond to the question, and the teacher follows by evaluating their responses. In my (Janice) comparison of peer discussion and teacher-led discussion environments, I found that 85% of the talk during teacher-led discussions was sustained by such I-R-E sequences (Almasi, 1995). Additionally, these discussions were dominated by the teacher, who was responsible for asking 93% of the questions and for talking 62% of the time. Such environments do not foster student independence and self-regulation—the key to strategic processing.

Peer discussions, in contrast, provide students with the opportunity to set their own agenda for discussion; they explore and discuss questions of interest to them. If students are taught how to set a discussion agenda well, the content of their discussions will likely focus on topics that will help them understand the text better. This process requires that students first be able to recognize when text does not make sense (i.e., monitor their comprehension) and then to actively seek a resolution to their comprehension dilemma. I (Janice) found that students who engaged in peer discussion were better able to recognize and resolve incongruities on their own than comparable students who had engaged in teacher-led discussion (Almasi, 1995). Peer discussion becomes a means for peers to help one another understand the text better (i.e., a fix-up strategy) as well as a catalyst for cognitive, metacognitive, and sociocognitive growth and development.

SUMMARY

This chapter provided teachers with relevant background research, hands-on tools, and resources with which to streamline and facilitate beginning strategy instruction. The chapter began by examining implicit instruction of comprehension strategies, followed by an in-depth examination of explicit instruction. Then sample lessons, based on the CESI model, depicted how to create a safe environment by reducing processing demands, providing opportunities for student verbalization, and providing explicit instruction. The explicit instruction depicted in the sample lessons included explanation, modeling, and guided practice to help students learn particular strategies. Teaching resources are presented for (1) text anticipation strategies (i.e., previewing text, activating prior knowledge, generating predictions, setting purposes, and identifying text structure); (2) text maintenance strategies (i.e., creating mental images, monitoring comprehension, identifying text structure, and updating/revising predictions); and (3) fix-up strategies (i.e., rereading, reading ahead for clarification, asking or discussing it with someone).

CHAPTER SEVEN

Strategy Instruction That Enhances Word Recognition

D eveloping the ability to construct meaning from text is the primary goal of all reading instruction. However, achieving this goal means that readers also must be able to recognize and process words fluently (Pressley, 2000, 2006). Like comprehension, word recognition is a strategic process. For proficient readers, word recognition is almost always skillful and automatic. These readers rarely need to use word recognition strategies because they are able to recognize automatically nearly all words they encounter. That is, nearly all words are sight words for proficient readers and do not require analysis or decoding.

Proficient readers use word recognition strategies only on those rare occasions when they encounter an unfamiliar word. At such times, these readers use one of the following four strategies (or in combination) to recognize the unfamiliar word: (1) analogizing to known words, (2) using letter–sound cues, (3) using orthographic features, and (4) predicting (using context and letter cues) (Ehri, 1991, 1994, 2005). Each of these strategies and related instructional ideas are explained in greater detail later in this chapter. First, the theoretical background related to how readers learn to recognize words is presented. Teachers who understand this developmental process are able to engage in more responsive teaching. That is, they can plan more effective instruction that meets the developmental needs of their students.

HOW DO READERS LEARN TO RECOGNIZE WORDS?

The research evidence supports the existence of developmental phases of word recognition (Blachman, 2000; Ehri, 1991; Juel, 1991; Pressley, 2000; Vellutino & Scanlon, 2002). It is these phases that help us understand how and why readers use particular word recognition strategies over others. Five phases of word recognition development are described below. Ehri's (1998, 2005) terminology is used to denote each phase: (1) prealphabetic phase, (2) partial alphabetic phase, (3) full alphabetic phase, (4) consolidated alphabetic phase, and (5) fluent recognition phase.

Prealphabetic Phase

The prealphabetic phase has also been named the "logographic stage" (Frith, 1985), the "selective-cue stage" (Juel, 1991), and the "emergent stage" (Bear, Invernizzi, Templeton, & Johnston, 2012). Most children are prealphabetic readers prior to entering kindergarten. Readers in this phase of development make use of visual characteristics, rather than letters and their sounds, to recognize words (Ehri, 1998, 2005). Success in reading at this phase is largely contingent on the reader's ability to memorize words and the incidental features associated with them. These readers are not systematic in their use of any particular cue (Bear et al., 2012) and rely mostly on contextual or environmental information, rather than graphic information, to identify words (Juel, 1991). For example, prealphabetic readers may be able to recognize a word such as *McDonald's* not because they can read the word or recognize the letters but because they recognize an environmental cue surrounding the word: the yellow letters on a red background, the golden arches, or the familiar smell as they drive by the restaurant.

Fox (2000) noted that readers in the prealphabetic phase of development often use three types of cues to recognize words: environmental, pictorial, and incidental cues. *Environmental cues* include any salient visual cue in the environment that serves as a clue and helps the reader identify a word or phrase. Masonheimer, Drum, and Ehri (1984) found that preschoolers who used environmental cues did not usually notice when words were misspelled. They also were unable to recognize words when they were removed from their environmental context. That is, a child who is able to recognize the word *McDonald's* when it appeared in its normal environmental context (i.e., white lettering on a red background, with a large yellow *M* in the background) would not be able to recognize the same configuration of letters when printed outside of that context. These readers are able to bring meaning to words only when they are within their normal environmental context.

These readers also use picture cues (illustrations in texts) to help them recognize words and often "read" the text based solely on the pictures. The story they read may bear little resemblance to that contained in the printed words on the pages, for these readers are relying on the pictures to guide their reading. Using picture cues is a good strategy to help bring meaning to text and can often help readers identify unfamiliar words. However, it is not always the most reliable strategy, particularly when text contains few or no pictures.

Fox (2000) described incidental cues as unreliable cues that are subordinate to alphabetic writing. Such cues might include smudges, dog-eared pages, colored inks, the shape of a word, or the shape of a letter. Readers who use these cues to recognize words do not pay attention to the specific letters or sequences of letters in a word to identify it; they rely on some distinguishing aspect such as a single character or double characters. Adult readers are often impressed when beginning readers are able to read "big" words such as *dinosaur, hippopotamus,* or *Halloween.* Very often these young readers are able to recognize these words by their length or their configuration rather than by using letter–sound cues. Configuration cues include the length of the word and the shape, or configuration, its letters make (see Figure 7.1).

Because configuration cues are based on the shape of the letters within a word, they are not reliable with regard to sound. However, they do help readers narrow the field of word choices, except when words have similar patterns of letters. For example, the words *boat, look,* and *toad* in Figure 7.1 all have a similar configuration. In these instances, using configuration cues is not a reliable strategy for identifying words.

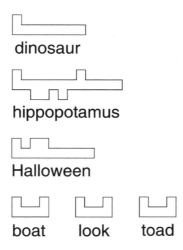

FIGURE 7.1. Using configuration cues to identify words.

Readers also use letter shapes or a salient graphic cue to help identify words. An example from Kevin, a first grader having difficulty with reading, illustrates this point. Kevin could identify the word *my* in isolation and in context. However, while reading, he encountered another word with the letter *m* and responded with excitement, "There go another my!" It soon became apparent that Kevin was only attending to the "mountain-like shape" of *m* as he read *my* for *me, am*, and *mom*; Kevin was using a single character as a salient feature. Learners may also attend to double characters as a distinguishing characteristic. For example, they may recognize the *oo* in *look* and imagine a pair of eyeballs to help them recognize the word. This cue is helpful only for recognizing one word, such as *look*, however. Encountering the words *book, cook, hook*, and *took* may confuse the learner because the words all have the same letter feature.

Prealphabetic readers have difficulty recognizing words outside of their environmental context. These readers encounter difficulties because the associations they form are unsystematic and arbitrary—and therefore hard to remember. Readers in the prealphabetic phase become confused and frustrated because their use of environmental, pictorial, and incidental cues is not consistent or reliable in all contexts. During oral reading, these readers often mistake visually similar words (e.g., *book, look, took*), substituting synonyms or semantically similar words. Readers in the prealphabetic phase must learn to recognize letters and their sounds so they can rely on cues that are consistent. As these children begin to develop letter–sound awareness, they move into the partial alphabetic phase.

We can also recognize prealphabetic readers by examining their writing. These readers have difficulty reading their own writing after a day because their writing is not systematic. Their writing consists of drawings, scribbles, letter-like forms, and random marks on the page (see Figure 7.2). Bear et al. (2012) refer to this as the "emergent spelling" stage. These children may be aware of the convention of directionality, or the notion that writing moves from left to right and top to bottom in English, but they are not aware of the relationship of letters and their sounds until the late emergent stage, at which time there is evidence of using some speech sounds in a representative manner, but there is no representation of word boundaries.

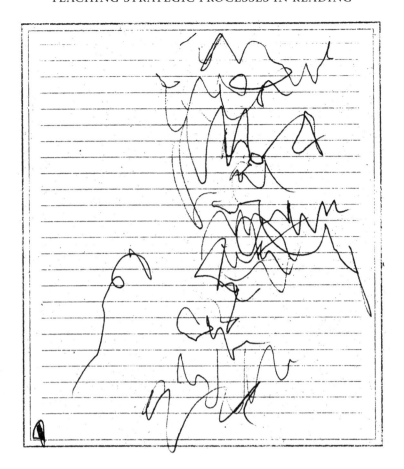

FIGURE 7.2. Example of emergent spelling.

Partial Alphabetic Phase

Readers in Ehri's (1998) partial alphabetic phase are beginning to read words by processing letter–sound relationships, but these relationships are only partial at this point. Learners are beginning to read and write in a conventional manner (Bear et al., 2012). These readers understand that letters are constant symbols that represent sounds, and they are able to use one or two letters to help them identify words. They are aware of the features that distinguish one letter from another, can identify most individual letters consistently, and know the sounds associated with some letters. These readers often use the initial and/or final letter–sounds in words, ignoring the medial sound or providing an approximation when writing/spelling, such as *PT*, *PD*, or *pat* for *pet*. While reading, it is much the same. For example, a beginning reader who is reading an early leveled text such as *My Home* (Melser, 1998), may read the sentence, " 'My *home* is here,' said the bird" as " 'My *house* is here.' " These readers typically rely on context, as well, to identify words. For example, they might read "We ate *pretzels*" as "We ate *pizza*." They notice a /p/ and a /z/ and use the context to think of a word that is a food that begins with a /p/ and has a /z/ somewhere near the end. They then think of a word that fits those criteria and provide an attempt based on those cues. The medial portion of the word is neglected.

Readers in the partial alphabetic phase have an awareness of print conventions such as directionality (e.g., writing in English proceeds from left to right and top to bottom). They have a concept of "word," in that they know that white spaces separate words in writing, and they have the ability to match speech to printed words by pointing to words as they are read (Clay, 1991, 2005; Flanigan, 2007; Roberts, 1992). They also use the context, the pictures, and beginning and/or ending letter sounds to recognize unfamiliar words. These readers are able to read many single-syllable words and can reread books with predictable patterns, but they are likely to confuse words that begin and end alike, and they are likely to ignore the medial portions of words. Their oral reading may be choppy or word by word while they read and "track" the text with their finger (i.e., fingerpointing/voice–print matching/one-to-one matching). The next step for these readers is to become more efficient at using both beginning and ending sounds and then learn to use the letters and patterns of letters in the medial portions of words to recognize them with greater accuracy.

Readers in the partial alphabetic phase are usually semiphonetic spellers (Gentry, 1987) or letter name–alphabetic spellers. Bear and colleagues (2012) explain that writers early in this stage use one or two letters (usually consonants) to represent an entire word. These writers can usually reread what they have written after a day, but their writing is fairly dysfluent. For example, *ISAK* might represent *I saw a cat*. Later in this stage, these writers consistently use beginning and ending consonant sounds to represent words and may even use some medial vowel sounds. Figure 7.3 illustrates a first grader's writing at this stage. The child wrote a riddle in which the reader is supposed to use each clue to guess what the object might be. Notice that the child recognizes the need for white spaces between words, indicating that he or she has a concept of *word*. The child also represents the initial and final consonant sounds in the words and is beginning to represent medial portions. The riddle says: "It is hard. It is hard. It is steel. It has a speaker."

Full Alphabetic Phase

Readers in the full alphabetic phase of development are able to make maximum use of graphic information and use letter–sound relationships to recognize unfamiliar words (Ehri, 1998; Frith, 1985). Juel (1991) referred to these readers as being in the "spelling–sound" stage of development. These readers have a good understanding of letters and the sounds they make and use them to identify words. They also are able to "sound and blend" to recognize individual letters and the sounds they make, blending them together to produce the entire word. Initially the effort to sound and blend is a very overt and deliberate one (Ehri, 1991). Indeed, readers often become "glued" to print at this phase of development, and they may become overly reliant on letter–sound relationships (Chall, 1983; Juel, 1991). Many full alphabetic readers overrely on letter–sound cues to identify words at the expense of context and meaning. These readers often forget that reading is a meaning-making venture. However, much depends on how the teacher structures learning to read within this phase. Careful prompting that reminds learners to "check the word to make sure that it looks right, sounds right, and makes sense" will help them integrate graphophonic cues with syntactic and semantic cues so that they can develop strategies of self-monitoring their own reading.

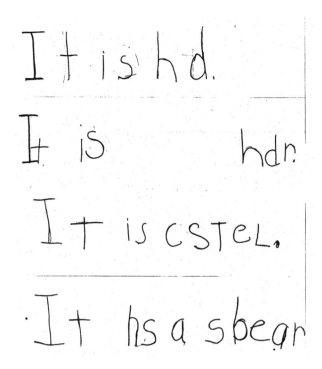

FIGURE 7.3. Example of letter name–alphabetic spelling.

These readers usually spell phonetically (Gentry, 1987). That is, they are able to represent all of the important sounds in the words they write, but these words may not be spelled conventionally. These writers are able to reread their writing fairly fluently. Figure 7.4 displays the writing of a student who is spelling phonetically. This writer is able to represent all of the important sounds in words but still has some difficulty spelling conventionally. For example, he spelled *would* as *wode*, *neat* as *neet*, and *could* as *cold*.

Consolidated Alphabetic Phase

Readers in the consolidated alphabetic phase have sufficient knowledge of the spelling patterns that recur across words and use them to recognize unfamiliar words (Ehri, 1991, 1998, 2005). Frith (1985) described these readers as being in an orthographic phase, in which they are able to instantly process multiletter chunks, or orthographic units, in words rather than letter by letter as in the full alphabetic phase. These readers are beginning to use a variety of spelling patterns to recognize words. They use their knowledge of rimes (i.e., a vowel and any consonants that follow it within a syllable) to recognize recurring spelling patterns in words. For example, if a reader is able to recognize the rime *-est* in words such as *best*, *nest*, *pest*, and *rest*, then she will be able to use that knowledge to help her decode other single-syllable words, such as *chest*, *guest*, and *quest*, and larger and unfamiliar words, such as *interesting*.

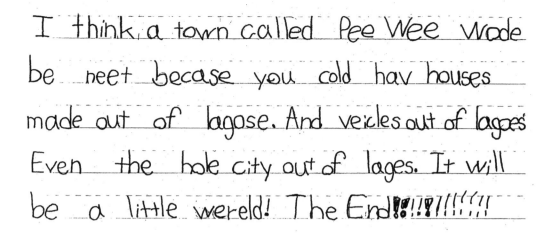

I think, a town called Pee Wee wode be neet becase you cold hav houses made out of lagose. And veicles out of lages Even the hole city out of lages. It will be a little wereld! The End!!!!!!!!!!!

FIGURE 7.4. Example of phonetic spelling.

Readers in the consolidated alphabetic phase also are beginning to recognize and use affixes (i.e., prefixes and suffixes) as multiletter chunks. In the previous example, a reader might quickly notice the *-est* rime and then the *-ing* ending in *interesting*. In essence, these readers are "consolidating" the reading process by having to process less information. Instead of having to sound and blend each of the 11 letters in the word *interesting*, these readers would only have to process four multiletter chunks. Ehri (1991) noted that this process helps readers (1) decode polysyllabic words (i.e., words with more than one syllable), (2) set up access routes in memory for recognizing words by sight, and (3) speed up the process of accessing these sight words. Consolidated alphabetic readers are able to recognize many words by sight, their reading is fluent, and they are able to read silently (Bear et al., 2012). These readers are able to recognize most words but they may have difficulty decoding polysyllabic words. These readers are usually transitional (Gentry, 1987) or within/word pattern (Bear et al., 2012) spellers. These writers are able to spell most words conventionally; however, they may use variants or alternate spellings. For example, they may spell *awake* as *awaik* or *driving* as *driveing*.

Fluent Recognition Phase

Readers who are able to fluently and automatically recognize all of the words they normally encounter in everyday reading and who proficiently use the orthographic patterns in words to read the occasionally unfamiliar word are in the fluent recognition phase (Ehri, 1998). These readers are able to read fluently nearly any form of text at any level. When these readers do encounter a technical word in a high school or college content-area textbook, or a professional journal, they are able to use a variety of word recognition strategies to fluidly decode the new word. These readers are usually conventional spellers (Gentry, 1987) who spell most regular and irregular words correctly and use their knowledge of letter–sound relationships and orthographic patterns to spell unfamiliar words.

WHAT STRATEGIES DO READERS USE TO RECOGNIZE WORDS?

The primary goals of word recognition instruction are to teach readers how to recognize unfamiliar words rapidly and independently and how to use multiple strategies for dealing with unknown words. Research evidence strongly supports the view that readers should be taught to approach word recognition and word solving in a variety of ways (Berninger et al., 2003; Ehri, Satlow, & Gaskins, 2009; Mathes et al., 2005). Furthermore, different children will benefit from different types of instruction (Gaskins, 2011).

Awareness of the developmental phases involved in learning to recognize words helps teachers understand why some readers use, or rely on, particular strategies. Such awareness also provides teachers with an understanding of what readers are currently able to do and where instruction should lead them. That is, recognizing that a reader is in the prealphabetic phase of development (1) informs the teacher about what types of strategies the child is currently able to use to recognize words (i.e., possibly environmental cues, pictorial cues, and incidental cues) and (2) suggests a focus on those particular strategies that will best help the reader begin to recognize words more reliably.

Modeling, Demonstrating, and Highlighting Strategies to Help Learners Problem-Solve Unknown Words

During both whole-class and small-group lessons, shared reading, originally called the shared book experience (Holdaway, 1979), can be used to support the development of strategic processes to solve unknown words. This technique, which simulates the "lap reading" experience that occurs in many homes, has proven to be an effective means of enhancing young children's word analysis, comprehension, vocabulary, and fluency development (Eldredge, Reutzel, & Hollingsworth, 1996). The value of such activities should not be underestimated because they provide readers with ample opportunities to orchestrate strategic processes within continuous text, yet there are also carefully selected opportunities to zero in on specific words and strategies. With younger readers, it may be important to highlight individual strategies within demonstrations, but it is also important to show how these strategies work together in a flexible manner—when one strategy proves ineffective or insufficient, readers may need to try something else. As a part of the demonstration during shared reading, the teacher does the following:

1. "Highlights" the strategy or strategies chosen and explains to learners when and why they are useful.
2. Shows the students how to use each strategy with the shared reading text.
3. Provides practice opportunities for the students to employ strategies as the text is read together.
4. Reminds students to use the strategies when they are reading on their own.
5. Praises and labels the student's strategic behavior and context while observing and listening while he or she reads.

As noted, opportunities to practice the strategies can occur in repeated shared reading events, and teachers can also return to these same strategies that have been highlighted during whole-group instruction while working with students individually or during small-group instruction.

In the section that follows, connections are drawn between instructional practices, the developmental phases of word recognition, and their impact on strategy use. Five word recognition strategies are described in detail: (1) recognizing words by sight, (2) analogizing, (3) using letter–sound cues, (4) using orthographic features, and (5) using context cues. Each description is accompanied by instructional suggestions and sample lesson plans.

Recognizing Words by Sight

Ehri (1991) noted that speakers of any language possess a lexicon, which stores words held in memory. When people are able to read words by sight, they use information they remember from their prior experiences with those words. When reading, we notice the features of a given word and access the identity of the word from memory. A word's features include its (1) pronunciation, (2) meaning (i.e., semantic characteristics), (3) syntax (i.e., the grammatical role it plays in sentences), and (4) orthography (i.e., information about its spelling and the way it is written). Those words that are encountered frequently in our reading are more likely to be read by sight than those that occur infrequently. After repeated encounters, accessing the features of the word from our lexicon occurs with increasing speed. Eventually, after many encounters with the same word, it is recognized automatically.

Initially, emergent readers are able to recognize a small number of words by sight. These are usually the words that appear most frequently in their reading, such as *I, and, the, a, to, see, in, it, on, my, is, not, go, look,* and *like.* Readers are often in the prealphabetic or partial alphabetic phases as they begin to recognize words by sight. This means that they remember the words based on incidental or configuration cues, not on orthographic or alphabetic features. This method of learning sight words works for a while, but as noted above, these readers often become confused when words have similar features. For example, they may confuse visually similar words such as *in* and *is, here* and *home,* or *that* and *they.* Letter–sound correspondences are required at some point to achieve competent sight word recognition. It is this point at which readers must learn a more reliable strategy, such as using letter–sound cues or analogizing.

Individuals who read words by sight possess several characteristics that distinguish them from readers who use other strategies to recognize words. First, they recognize words automatically. If they are emergent readers, they either "know" the word or they do not, and they will tell you so. They recognize sight words as a whole unit without pauses between phonemes (i.e., the smallest unit of sound) or syllables. Words that are recognized by sight are read rapidly. Readers who have been taught to read words by sight are usually able to distinguish correct spellings of words from homophonous ones. That is, because they learned to recognize the word by its visual features rather than its phonemic features, they are able to recognize that *wait,* rather than *wate,* is the conventional spelling. When these readers encounter unconventional spellings, they often say, "That doesn't *look* right." These readers also are able to pronounce irregularly spelled words correctly rather than phonetically. For example, sight-word readers would be able to pronounce *cough* as /kof/ rather than /kouf/, /koug/, /ko/, or /kog/.

Learning words by sight is not really a strategic process. When one encounters an unknown word, one would not think, "Hmmm, I think I'll try to read this word by sight." Sight words are either known or not known. It is not a strategic or deliberate choice to employ recognizing sight words. Sight-word recognition is skillful and auto-matic. However, there is an important relationship between strategic activity and aware-ness of whether or not the word is known. Clay (1991) has referred to these known words as "islands of certainty in a sea of print." These known words or sight words have stra-tegic value, serving as "visual signposts" to help learners fingerpoint or match speech to print, in turn, helping them to locate or monitor their own knowledge of what is known. Through this early awareness, learners begin to monitor whether the word "looks right" (as a known word). Monitoring is foundational to early strategic activity (Clay, 1991, 2001; Schwartz, 1997) and serves as a precursor in problem solving unknown words.

It is the ultimate goal for every reader to be able to recognize by sight nearly every word encountered. Early in their literacy development, readers must learn initial basic-function words that are a critical part of their sight-word core. Adams (2011) points out that these frequently occurring words pose two difficulties: (1) The words are not always clearly discernible in the speech stream (e.g., "*uh book*" for *a book*) and often have irreg-ular spellings. We would add that they typically have limited meaning in isolation. Exam-ples include *the, a, of, to, in, for, with, and, but, my, it, are, did.* (See Adams, 2011, for additional examples.) Adams suggests language and writing activities for kindergarten-ers *before* reading to develop understanding of usage and spelling. In addition to shared reading, writing activities can promote enhanced word recognition. Activities such as the language experience approach and other shared or interactive writing activities will help to develop usage because the stories or sentences developed collaboratively are linked directly to a child's recent experiences, language, and knowledge. As the teacher and children work together, children have opportunities to contribute their ideas to construct the story, so the text becomes their language.

With shared writing, teachers model conventional spelling and children have an opportunity to read what is written. If interactive writing is used, learners can contribute and share the pen jointly with the teacher, taking turns writing the sight words or even partial words or letters that they know. In the example below, the teacher supports a first grader, Bailey, in an individual interactive writing experience that followed a read-aloud of *Goldilocks and the Three Bears.* Bailey dictated the sentence, and the teacher shared the pen while scaffolding Bailey's attempts to write the words. The underlined portions show the word or letters that Bailey was able to contribute independently or with the help of the teacher, prompting the child to say the word slowly and write what she heard. *P* indicates where the teacher prompted. The teacher modeled all portions that are not underlined.

```
          P          P        P  P            P
The  g ir l  w en t  to  sl ee p  in  the  b a b y  bear's  b ed.
```

Bailey is also learning that she must go back and reread what she has written in order to recall the next word she intends to write. Such writing and rereading provide numerous exposures to how a word looks in print, helping to facilitate and reinforce word recogni-tion and spelling.

As just indicated, recognizing words by sight requires many exposures, so text selec-tion is critical to instruction. Texts that have predictable or repetitious patterns are ideal. One type of predictable text has predictable words. Often these texts have a rhyming pattern and repetitious phrases that permit the learner, to predict upcoming words in text. For example, in Deming's (1993) book, *Who Is Tapping at My Window?*, a little girl hears a tapping at her window and asks, "Who is there?" Various farm animals respond, "It's not I." Eventually she discovers that it is the rain tapping at her window. The repetition of the phrases throughout the text, "Who is there?" and "It's not I," is ideal for enhancing sight-word recognition. In addition, the text offers rhyme in the names of each pair of animals that responds (e.g., the loon's response is followed by the raccoon's, the dog's response is followed by the frog's). Rhyming helps children anticipate what an unfamiliar word might be by using the rhythm of the text.

Another type of predictable text features repetitious phrases. An example is Mirra Ginsburg's *The Chick and the Duckling* (1988). In this text, the duckling has a busy day filled with many adventures (digging, climbing, running). The duckling uses the same phrase to tell the chick what he is doing, "I am _____ing," to which the chick always responds, "Me too." The chick follows the duckling on every adventure but soon finds, when the duckling decides to go swimming, that this is not always wise. The duckling must save the chick, and the chick learns his lesson. The next time the duckling decides to go swimming, the chick responds, "Not me." This text is well suited for sight-word instruction. It tells a simple story using repetitious language. Emergent readers can easily use the language patterns to recognize the repeated words (*I, am, said, the, duck, me, too, chick*). Those words that vary are all verbs with an *-ing* ending (*digging, climbing, running, swimming*). Although these readers may have difficulty with the unfamiliar words, the pictures vividly depict the action, providing picture cues for decoding them.

Books with a cumulative pattern add one new phrase (usually a new character or a new event) as every page is turned. As the story progresses, all of the characters (or events) are repeated each time a new character is encountered. Steven Kellogg's *Chicken Little* (1987) tells the classic story of the chicken that becomes alarmed when an acorn hits her on the head, and exclaims, "The sky is falling! The sky is falling! I must tell the king!" On her way to inform the king, she meets a succession of animals that join her (Henny Penny, Ducky Lucky, Goosey Loosey, and Foxy Loxy). As each animal is encountered, Chicken Little repeats the story, and that animal joins the group on their journey to the king. Other tales with cumulative patterns include Verna Aardema's (1983) *Bringing the Rain to Kapiti Plain*, Rodney Peppe's (1985) *The House That Jack Built*, and Maurice Sendak's (1962) *Chicken Soup with Rice*; however, these texts are much too difficult for prealphabetic and partial alphabetic readers. Table 7.1 provides a list of texts that can be used during explicit instruction to teach various word recognition strategies. Texts for use during sight-word instruction can also be drawn from children's own language as they produce stories during the language experience approach, shared or interactive writing, or shared reading of songs, chants, nursery rhymes, and poems.

In addition to selecting an appropriate text to use during instruction, there is a number of other factors that should be considered when teaching children to read by recognizing sight words. First, only a limited number of sight words should be taught at one time. Typically, for shared reading, three to five words might be selected; if we are working with the whole class, the number and variety of words already known or partially known are likely to vary a great deal, so we broaden the scope. If we are working with a small group (as in guided reading), we may narrow the scope and select only a few words, no more than three or so, since we are tailoring the instruction to the unique characteristics and knowledge of those in the small group. In either case, we may also focus on one or two additional words that have been introduced previously in an attempt to consolidate and reinforce learning. In most cases, the words chosen should be frequently occurring words within the text selected. In the example above, in which Ginsburg's (1988) *The*

TABLE 7.1. Texts for Use in Word Recognition Lessons

Strategy and Texts	Instructional Use
Recognizing words by bight	
Cole, J. (1989). *101 jump-rope rhymes.* New York: Scholastic.	Over 100 rhymes that use repetitious phrases and rhymes.
Cole, J., & Calmenson, S. (1990). *Miss Mary Mack and other children's street rhymes.* New York: Morrouno.	These rhymes involve hand-clapping, ball-bouncing, and counting-out rhymes that involve rhyme, repetitious phrases, and alliteration.
Deming, A. G. (1994). *Who is tapping at my window?* New York: Penguin.	A young girl hears a tapping at her window and repeatedly asks, "Who is there?" Various animals each respond, "It's not I." Each animal pair rhymes (e.g., the dog's response is followed by the frog's).
Eastman, P. D. (1960). *Are you my mother?* New York: Random House.	Tells the tale of a baby bird going on a long journey to find his mother.
Florian, D. (2000). *A pig is big.* Singapore: Greenwillow.	Rhyming text is used to explain the concept of size from pigs to cows to cars, and finally to the universe.
Galdone, P. (1968). *Henny Penny.* New York: Scholastic.	Classic cumulative tale in which an alarmed hen believes the sky is falling when an acorn hits her on the head. On her way to tell the king, she meets a variety of animals that join her.
Ginsburg, M. (1988). *The chick and the duckling.* New York: Macmillan.	Uses repetitious phrases at an emergent reader level to tell the story of a chick that mimics a duckling's every move—until the duckling decides to take a swim.
Hutchins, P. (1968). *Rosie's walk.* New York: Macmillan.	Rosie the hen goes for a walk and unwittingly leads a fox, who is after her, into multiple disasters. Uses directionality words (e.g., *over, around, past, through, under, into, across*).
Kalan, R. (1981). *Jump, frog, jump!* New York: Greenwillow.	Cumulative tale of a frog trying to catch a fly without getting himself caught.
Langstaff, J. (1974). *Oh a-hunting we will go.* New York: Atheneum.	Uses rhyme and repetitious phrases to tell the story of a group that catches various animals (e.g., a fox is put in a box) and then lets each one go.
Martin, B. (1993). *Brown bear, brown bear.* New York: Holt, Rinehart & Winston.	Beloved story that uses repetitious phrases ("Brown Bear, Brown Bear what do you see? I see a _____ looking at me.") to describe the various animals that are seen.
Marzollo, J. (1989). *The teddy bear book.* New York: Dial.	These poems about teddy bears are adapted from songs, jump rope rhymes, cheers, and poems. Each uses repetitious phrases and rhyming.
Otto, C. (1991). *Dinosaur chase.* New York: HarperCollins.	Minimal text and rhyme tell the story of a dinosaur chase that ensues after a valuable necklace is stolen.
Raffi. (1989). *Five little ducks.* New York: Crown.	Repetitious phrases and rhyme are used to tell the story of five little ducks who disappear one by one until their mother finds them.
Shaw, C. (1947). *It looked like spilt milk.* New York: Harper.	Repetitious phrases ("Sometimes it looked like _____, but it wasn't _____.") are used to pique children's creative ideas about what a cloud might look like.
Silverstein, S. (1964). *A giraffe and a half.* New York: HarperCollins.	Uses rhymes and cumulative patterns to explain what happens when a giraffe is "stretched another half."
Taback, S. (1997). *There was an old lady who swallowed a fly.* New York: Penguin.	Classic cumulative tale of an old woman who swallows a series of creatures. Uses repetitious phrases and rhyme.

(cont.)

TABLE 7.1. *(cont.)*

Strategy and Texts	Instructional Use
Using letter–sound cues	
Base, G. (1986). *Animalia.* New York: Harry Abrams.	Uses alliteration and fanciful illustration to provide a variety of images for each letter of the alphabet.
Brown, M. W. (1993). *Four fur feet.* New York: Doubleday.	Reader is drawn to the /f/ sound. The phrase *four fur feet* is repeated in every sentence as the furry creature walks through different places (along a river, into the country, etc.).
Ehlert, L. (1989). *Eating the alphabet: Fruits and vegetables A to Z.* San Diego, CA: Harcourt Brace Jovanovich.	Various fruits and vegetables are depicted for each letter of the alphabet.
Gordon, J. (1991). *Six sleepy sheep.* New York: Puffin Books.	Reader is drawn to the /s/ sound as six sheep try to fall asleep by slurping celery soup, telling spooky stories, singing songs, and sipping simmering milk.
Hague, K. (1984). *Alphabears.* New York: Henry Holt.	26 teddy bears introduce the alphabet using alliteration (e.g., "Teddy Bear John loves jam and jelly").
Van Allsburg, C. (1987). *The Z was zapped.* Boston: Houghton Mifflin.	Depicts each letter of the alphabet engaged in an alliterative misfortune.
Analogizing	
Degan, B. (1983). *Jamberry.* New York: Harper.	Uses rhyme to share the joys of berry picking.
Fortunata. (1968). *Catch a little fox.* New York: Scholastic.	A group of children goes hunting and talks about what they will catch and where they will keep it. Each phrase rhymes (e.g., "a frog will be put in a log"). In the end the animals capture the children and put them in a ring to hear them sing.
Hawkins, C., & Hawkins, J. (1986). *Tog the dog.* Putnam.	The use of the *-og* rime is prevalent in this tale of the adventures of Tog the dog who likes to jog, gets lost in the fog, etc.
Hawkins, C., & Hawkins, J. (1985). *Jen the hen.* Putnam.	The use of the *-en* rime is prevalent in this tale.
Hawkins, C., & Hawkins, J. (1984). *Mig the pig.* Putnam.	The use of the *-ig* rime is prevalent in this tale.
Hawkins, C., & Hawkins, J. (1993). *Pat the cat.* Putnam.	The use of the *-at* rime is prevalent in this tale.
Hepworth, C. (1992). *Antics: An alphabetical anthology.* New York: Putnam.	Uses intriguing illustrations of various ants as they engage in activities or with objects containing the *-ant* rime (e.g, antique).
Most, B. (1999). *There's an ant in Anthony.* New York: Econo-Clad Books.	Polysyllabic words containing the *-ant* rime are present throughout as Anthony tries to find "ants" in everyday objects.
Most, B. (1981). *There's an ape behind the drape.* New York: Morrow/Avon.	The *-ape* rime is prevalent in this tale.
Rosen, M. (1995). *Walking the bridge of your nose.* New York: Kingfisher.	Collection of poems, riddles, and rhymes.
Shaw, N. (1986). *Sheep in a jeep.* Boston: Houghton Mifflin.	Use of the *-eep* rime is prevalent in this tale.
Shaw, N. (1989). *Sheep on a ship.* Boston: Houghton Mifflin.	Rhyme and alliteration abound in this story of sheep on a deep sea voyage. Uses rimes *-ip, -ap, -orm, -ail, -ide, -aft,* and *-ift.*

(cont.)

TABLE 7.1. *(cont.)*

Strategy and Texts	Instructional Use
<u>Analogizing</u> *(cont.)*	
Shaw, N. (1992). *Sheep out to eat.* Boston: Houghton Mifflin.	Rhyme and alliteration are used to tell the tale of sheep in a tea shop who have trouble finding something palatable to eat. Uses rimes *-op, -eat, -urp, -ard, -ite, -ake, -ash, -out, -unch, -ip.*
Silverstein, S. (1974). *Where the sidewalk ends.* New York: HarperCollins.	Classic collection of poems that use rhyme and alliteration.
Seuss, Dr. (1974). *There's a wocket in my pocket.* New York: Random House.	Uses manipulatives of onsets with rimes (*zlock/clock*) to tell the zany tale of a character who meets a variety of pleasant and unpleasant characters (*yottle/bottle*).
Seuss, Dr. (1957). *The cat in the hat.* New York: Random House.	A variety of rimes is used to tell the story of the Cat in the Hat as he comes to entertain the children on a rainy day.
Seuss, Dr. (1960). *Green eggs and ham.* New York: Random House.	Uses (*-am, -ouse, -ox, -ere*) to tell the cumulative tale of Sam, who tries to convince his friend to eat green eggs and ham.
Seuss, Dr. (1963). *Hop on pop.* New York: Random House.	Uses a variety of rimes (-up, -ouse, -all, -ay, -ight, -im, -ee, -ed, -at, -ad, -ing, -ong, -alk, -op, -own, -ack).
Winthrop, E. (1986). *Shoes.* New York: HarperTrophy.	Describes various types of shoes using repetitious phrases and rhyming.

Chick and the Duckling was used, the words *I*, *am*, *said*, *the*, *me*, and *too* recur most frequently. The words *I* and *the* are likely to be known by many of the students if they have been exposed to shared reading activities previously; however, we would continue to reinforce these words for students who may have confusion or lapses. Three to four of the remaining frequently occurring words (*am*, *said*, *me*, *too*) would be appropriate for focused sight-word instruction. With prealphabetic and partial alphabetic readers, it is especially useful to scaffold their development through shared reading. The sample lesson depicted in Figure 7.5 uses this instructional method and focuses on other comprehension and word recognition strategies in addition to sight-word recognition.

Notice that during this lesson, the sight words were taught using a direct teaching method. Sight words should be introduced using a predictable method to which students become accustomed. Notice also that the teacher incorporated comprehension strategies and links to other word recognition strategies when possible. The lesson began by engaging students in the comprehension strategies of previewing the text, thinking about what they already know about chicks and ducklings, and making predictions. As the sight words were taught, the teacher pointed out some of the structural features of each word. Although these readers may be in the prealphabetic and partial alphabetic phases of development, this does not preclude them from being introduced to letter–sound cues or other cues that might help them distinguish one word from another. These readers may not fully understand or use these cues to identify words yet, but they should begin to hear the strategic language associated with their use. In reality, these readers may be able to recognize *me* as the small word and *chick* as the long word, but as they continue to read and reread the same text and other texts, they will notice other features of those words—which is another reason why sight-word instruction should provide ample practice in a variety of strategies.

Teacher: Janice Almasi

Title: Sight Words

Topic: Recognizing words by sight

Grade level: K–2

STAIR hypothesis being addressed:
> Students are partial alphabetic readers who are just beginning to learn to read. They are able to use environmental cues and pictures cues to read words and are able to "read" text they have memorized. Students are beginning to recognize the relationship between letters and the sounds they make and use initial consonant sounds and some ending sounds to represent words in their writing. Students need to develop a bank of words they can recognize quickly and automatically by sight.

Goal of Lesson

Students will learn:
- To recognize the words *me*, *too*, *said*, *am*, by sight
- That sentences are read from left to right and end with a period

Materials

- *The Chick and the Duckling* by Mirra Ginsburg (big book version)
- Sentence strips
- Word cards with the words *am*, *said*, *me*, and *too* on them
- Pocket chart
- Paper (or felt) representations of the chick and the duckling depicted in the text

Introduction

Declarative and conditional knowledge about comprehension strategies

Introduce the story *The Chick and the Duckling* by having the students look at the pictures on the cover. Ask students to describe what they see. Read the title to the students and have them make predictions about what the story might be about. "Today we are going to read a story. Before we read any story it is always a good idea to look at the pictures on the cover and think about what it might be about. So let's study the picture on the cover. What do you see?" Have students share their observations and predictions about what the story might be about. Then read the title to the students and have them refine their predictions and observations further.

Declarative and conditional knowledge about comprehension strategies

Remind students that it is always a good idea to think about what we know about the subject of a book before we read it. This helps us get ready to read. Have students think about what they know about chicks and ducklings. Try to guide their thoughts to things that chicks and ducklings do, as this is the focus of the text. As students share their thoughts, record their ideas about what chicks do on one semantic web and their ideas about what ducklings do on another. Have students think about and share what they might like to find out as you read the book.

(cont.)

FIGURE 7.5. Sample lesson teaching students to recognize words by sight.

Begin reading the book aloud to the students. Since the text has repetitious language, encourage the students to join in once they pick up the pattern or after reading the lines in which the duckling says, "I am ___ing." Ask the students, "What do you think the chick might say?" and have them join in chorally as you read the chick's response, "'Me too,' said the chick."

After reading the text aloud once, engage students in a brief discussion in which they stop and share their reactions to the book with a partner. Ask students to think and talk about whether the ideas they had about what chicks and ducklings do matched the author's ideas.

Description of Instructional Experience

Explain that the author, Mirra Ginsburg, uses many of the same words over and over throughout the story. Ask students if they remember any of the words that were used over and over again. Often students remember the phrase, "Me too, said the Chick." Place a sentence strip with that phrase written in black marker in the pocket chart. Point to each word as you reread the sentence aloud for the students. Explain that today we are going to learn to read a few new words that the author used over and over again in the story *The Chick and the Duckling*.

Direct teaching of sight word:
1. *Look at word and say it*
2. *Tell the meaning*
3. *Analyze the word's structure*
4. *Discuss the word and use in context*

Show students a word card with the word *me* written in red on it. Say the word. Point out various features of the word. "Listen to the sounds in the word *me*." Pronounce the word very deliberately, emphasizing the sounds /m/ and /ē/. Have students think about other words that begin with the same /m/ sound. "The word *me* has the same sound at the beginning as lots of other words. M-m-m-m-e. What other words do you know that start with an /m/ sound?" Have students share those words. "Yes, all of those words (*repeat the words*) begin with the /m/sound. The word *me* starts the same way. The letter that makes the /m/sound is *m*. Notice that the word *me* has an *m* at the beginning. It also has an /ē/ sound at the end. M-e-e-e-e. Do you know any other words that end with an /ē/ sound?" Have students share words. They may have difficulty with this concept. You may have to model and share rhyming words such as *be, see, knee, tree, pea,* and *we*. Discuss the word's meaning and how it is used in sentences. Have students use the word in sentences.

Guided practice

Pronounce the word again and have one student place it on top of the word *Me* in the sentence in the pocket chart. Pass out envelopes containing each of the four target sight words in them (*me, too, said, am*). Ask students to spread out their word cards and find the word *me*. Follow the same procedure to teach the other four sight words.

Model/think-aloud

Explain that now that we know several words, we can use them to build sentences. Model and demonstrate how to build the sentence from *The Chick and the Duckling*. Engage in a think-aloud as you explain that when we read in English, the words always start on the left and go to the right. Place the sentence strip with the phrase, "'Me too,' said the Chick," written in black in the pocket chart. Model how to rebuild the sentence by placing the red word cards over top of the black words. Try to use strategic language to help students learn to distinguish between the sight words. "I know the sentence

(cont.)

FIGURE 7.5. *(cont.)*

says, 'Me too, said the Chick.' I have to find the word *me* first. *M-m-m-m-e.* Hmmm, it starts with an /m/ sound. I know that the letter *m* makes an /m/ sound, so I have to find a word that starts with *m.* Okay, I see one." Pick up the red word card *me* and as you say it place it on top of the black *me* on the sentence strip. Continue in this manner, placing the rest of the red word cards on top of the sentence strip. Remind students that a period marks the end of this sentence. Place a period word card as the last word card in the sentence. Ignore the quotation marks for now, unless students ask about them. If they do ask, use the teachable moment to explain quotation marks.

Guided practice

Pass out a sentence strip containing the phrase, " 'Me too,' said the Chick," to pairs of students. Have them work together to rebuild each sentence using their word cards. Make sure students pronounce each word as they lay it on top of the identical word in the sentence. As students engage in this activity, observe their progress by making anecdotal records. You may stop and ask each pair of students how they knew a particular word to try to gauge what strategies they are using to recognize the sight words. "How did you know that word was _____ ?" Record students' responses in notes. Make sure students mix up the word cards each time they rebuild the sentence. As a challenge you can have them remove the sentence strip to see if they can build the sentence without the sentence strip as a guide.

Reread

Guided practice

After students have practiced for awhile, gather them together to reread the story. Explain that you are going to reread the story and that the students can join in with the reading at any time now that they are more familiar with some of the words. Begin rereading the story and encourage students to join in chorally, reading those parts with which they feel comfortable. If students did well with the sentence rebuilding, you might have them place their word cards on top of the phrase, or build it on their own, each time it is reread in the story.

Conclusion

Have students complete a self-assessment using their three faces on craft sticks. One craft stick has a circle with a smiley face on it, one has a frowning face on it, and one has a straight mouth on it. Each student should have their own set of craft sticks. Ask students the following questions. "Which face shows how you felt about the story *The Chick and the Duckling*?" Have students hold up the appropriate face and take anecdotal notes on their responses. "Which face shows how well you were able to learn the new words *me, too, said, am*?" Have students hold up the appropriate face and take anecdotal notes on their responses. "Which face shows how well you were able to rebuild the sentence?" Have students hold up the appropriate face and take anecdotal notes on their responses. After each response engage students in a discussion about their responses (e.g., "Why was it hard to recognize some of the words? Why was it easy to rebuild the sentence?").

An alternative is to type the questions on a piece of paper and draw the three faces after each question. Each student receives his or her own self-assessment to complete. As you read each question, have students think about their responses and circle the appropriate face. This procedure takes a bit more time but eliminates the need to take anecdotal notes.

(cont.)

FIGURE 7.5. *(cont.)*

Assessment
- You will know whether students are able to recognize the words *me, too, said, am,* by sight if they are able to pick up the appropriate word when it is read aloud and place it on the sentence strip.
- You will know whether students know that sentences are read from left to right and end with a period if they are able to rebuild the sentence using their word cards going from left to right and ending them with a period word card.

Follow up
Students can identify those sight words from the story they know automatically. These words can be added to their personal word banks for use in word hunts, concept sorts, and writing activities (see Bear, Invernizzi, Templeton, & Johnston, 2012, for many more word bank activities). Word hunts require students to search through their word banks for words that have a given feature (e.g., words that begin with a /k/or end with /t/). Concept sorts require students to find words from their word banks that fit a particular category (e.g., words that are movements [*kick, jump, fly*], words that are animals). Word banks can be used to help students as they write, or students may try to generate sentences using words from their word banks.

FIGURE 7.5. *(cont.)*

Students should use the new words they have learned in their writing, their oral language, and their reading. For example, after rereading the text over the course of several days, students might work in small groups or with a partner to create an alternate version of the text. Each group or pair of students might add an adventure for the chick and the duckling. That is, they might add their own sentence about the duckling doing something and the chick responding, "Me too." The teacher might encourage students to draw from their original list of duckling actions that was brainstormed and webbed prior to reading the story. If students noted that ducklings "jump," then they might add the adventure, " `I am jumping,' said the Duckling. 'Me too,' said the Chick." Each pair of students can illustrate their adventure on a large piece of paper, with its description written on the bottom. After each pair completes the new adventure, the entire new version can be bound into a book. Each pair of students can read their page of the new book. To give them practice in using the new sight words orally, students might also dramatize their new story or the original story.

New sight words to which students have recently been introduced could be used in shared writing, interactive writing, and language experience stories; students should also be encouraged to use the new sight words in their own individual writing. Sentences can be written on sentence strips by the teacher, leaving a blank where one of the newly introduced sight words belongs. Place the sentence strip in the pocket chart and read the sentence to the students. Students can use their individual word cards to hold up the sight word they think makes sense in the blank. In this way, students use their semantic and syntactic knowledge as well as their graphophonemic knowledge to help them determine which sight word fits in a sentence. Given that these sentences differ from those in the original story, students learn to recognize words outside of their initial context. Table 7.2

TABLE 7.2. Teaching Readers to Recognize Words by Sight

1. Teach a limited number of sight words at a time (three to five words).

2. Select those words that recur most frequently in the text you are using for instruction. Be sure that the text is developmentally appropriate for your students. Most texts for sight-word instruction contain predictable patterns: repetitious words or phrases, cumulative patterns, or rhyme.

3. Use a direct and predictable teaching method for sight-word instruction:

   a. Look at the word and say it.
   b. Explain the meaning of the word.
   c. Analyze the word structurally.
   d. Discuss the word and use it in context.

4. Provide ample practice in a variety of authentic ways.

5. Encourage students to use the word in their oral and written work.

6. Use a pocket chart with slotted sentences from stories and other text with which children are familiar, so that students can use their background knowledge and knowledge of sentence structure (i.e., syntax) to take educated guesses about the word.

highlights those elements that are most essential to remember when teaching students to recognize words by sight.

Using Letter–Sound Cues

Readers who use the letter–sound strategy are able to recognize unknown words by looking at letters and groups of letters in a word, thinking about the sounds associated with those letters, and blending those sounds together to form a spoken word. Readers in the partial alphabetic phase of development are beginning to use letter–sound cues to recognize unknown words. That is, they look at the letters in a word, associate sounds with those letters, and use that knowledge of letters and sounds to read words. As noted earlier, readers in this phase of development normally use the letter–sound cues they glean from the beginning and end of the word and search their mind for a word that begins and ends similarly. They take an "educated guess" at the word, based on the letter–sound cues, the context, and their schemata. Readers who are at the alphabetic phase of development are able to use letter–sound cues to decode the entire word.

Intrinsic to the ability to recognize letter–sound correspondences is *phonological awareness*, a superordinate term referring to the ability to attend to, identify, and manipulate the sound segments of speech (Bear et al., 2012; Blachman, 2000). Recognizing alliteration, rhyme, and syllables requires phonological awareness, as does the ability to segment words into their constituent sounds and blend those sounds into words. *Phonemic awareness*, a subcategory of phonological awareness, refers only to the ability to identify and manipulate individual phonemes within words. For example, when the word *cat* is pronounced, a child with phonemic awareness would be able to identify each phoneme in the word *cat* (/k/, /a/, /t/) and blend the sounds together to say the word. The child would also be able to manipulate those sounds. That is, if you asked her to substitute the /k/ sound in *cat* with an /s/ sound, the child would be able to identify the phonemes /s/, /a/, /t/ and blend them together to say the word *sat*. There is convincing research evidence that phonological awareness is a predictor of future success in reading (Blachman, 2000). There also is evidence that many children develop such understanding naturally by playing rhyming games, oral language games, singing, chanting, and connecting speech to print during read-alouds (Murray, Stahl, & Ivey, 1996). For these children, explicit instruction and training in phonological awareness are *not* necessary. However, those children who do not develop phonological awareness on their own by playing with oral language require more explicit instruction.

Phonological awareness and phonemic awareness refer only to the *sounds* in words and therefore are *not* equivalent to *phonics*, which refers to the relationship between *letters* and the *sounds* that make them. Blachman's (2000) review of the research noted that when instruction links phonological awareness to the letters that represent those sounds (i.e., letter–sound correspondences, phonics), word recognition is enhanced. Thus letter–sound relationships are critical to becoming a proficient reader in English. The sounding and blending process that readers who use letter–sound cues employ to read unfamiliar words is often a slow, deliberate one (Ehri, 1991). Fox (2000) noted that as readers become facile with letter–sound cues, they begin to recognize letter–sound "neighborhoods"—a letter sequence that represents one or more sounds in a word. For example, the *c* in *cat* is a letter that represents one sound, /k/, but the *ch-* in *chat* is a letter–sound neighborhood (i.e., a consonant digraph) that represents one sound, /ch/. The *-augh* in *caught* is also a letter–sound neighborhood. It is a sequence of letters that recurs in English words to produce an /aw/ sound. As students read more, they become more familiar with these letter–sound combinations. Eventually the sounding and blending process speeds up, but it is always a slower process than recognizing words by sight or than using orthographic cues.

The success of using letter–sound cues to recognize unfamiliar words depends on the regularity of the letter–sound correspondences in a word (Ehri, 1991). For example, the sequence of letters *-ough* can have multiple pronunciations in the English language, as in the words *tough*, *bough*, *cough*, and *dough*. These inconsistencies make it difficult for emergent readers to use letter–sound cues. Those readers who have auditory difficulties are further impeded when trying to use letter–sound cues. Many struggling readers have had some form of auditory difficulty (i.e., hearing loss, tubes in ears, ear infections) at the time when they were learning to read.

Children who have learned to read using primarily letter–sound strategies (i.e., phonics) often make miscues, or reading errors, that produce nonsense words (i.e., mispronunciations). For these students, reading has become more a matter of word calling than meaning getting. It is essential for these readers to engage in "cross-checking" as they use letter–sound strategies to decode words (Clay, 1991; Fox, 2000). As shown in Table 7.3, readers should be taught to strategically cross-check the letter–sound cues that they have used in print with the context or meaning. As readers problem-solve unknown words using letter–sound cues, they must monitor to determine that what they have read is a real word and that it makes sense and sounds right in the context of what is being read.

Several instructional principles for teaching letter–sound cues foster a safe environment for using this strategy. First, instruction should occur within an authentic reading context rather than in isolation. *Isolation* refers to activities and instruction that are not linked in any way to text. Sometimes teachers design word recognition instruction in kindergarten and first grade around a "letter of the week." Unfortunately, such instruction introduces letters and sounds without relating them to authentic reading and writing contexts (Wagstaff, 1997–1998). Even when such instruction features rich language development around many different words that begin with the featured letter of the week, and even when such instruction is linked to alphabet books, readers are left with no understanding of the *strategic processes* that underlie the application of using letter–sound cues to decode unfamiliar words (Stahl, 1992). Teaching letter–sound cues outside authentic reading contexts creates greater opportunity for failure that lowers self-esteem. Without authentic contexts, readers have no other cues to rely on to help them with the word recognition process. Texts that are most appropriate for beginning reading instruction are those, as in sight-word instruction, that have predictable and repetitious patterns of language. These texts—which include familiar nursery rhymes, poems, and jump-rope chants as well as books—provide a more supportive context for readers to use letters and sounds as a strategy for recognizing unknown words.

The idea of teaching word recognition more as a strategy than a skill is one that our graduate students find particularly challenging. Fluent adult reading is comprised entirely of skillful reading, which makes it very difficult to even see the need to be strategic during the word recognition process. In the sample lesson in Figure 7.6, a model of explicit instruction in using letter–sound cues as a *strategy* is presented. This lesson, like the lesson on sight-word instruction, uses the shared reading or shared book experience (Holdaway, 1979) as a methodological framework.

The major distinction between this lesson and those that are more skills-based is that the teacher provides explanations of the declarative, procedural, and conditional knowledge associated with using letter–sound cues as a word recognition strategy (see Table 7.3). The lesson also relates this instruction to authentic texts. Once students have been introduced to the strategy, they can be encouraged to use it in their independent reading. This usage can be modeled for students during read-alouds as well as during shared reading experiences. For example, during independent reading time (e.g., Drop Everything and Read, sustained silent reading), students can be encouraged to jot down any words they did not recognize automatically. Some teachers find that providing students with a chart, such as the one depicted in Figure 7.7, is helpful for such tasks. As students read, they record any words they do not know automatically, then place checkmarks next to the strategy (or strategies) they used to problem-solve the unknown word. Students can circle any words that they were unable to figure out. It is important that teachers model using this chart prior to asking students to use it during their independent reading time. Modeling can be done during a read-aloud. As the teacher encounters a word that might be difficult for students to decode, he can think aloud about the strategies he would use to decode the word. While engaged in the process, the teacher would model how to complete the chart. As students use the chart for the first few times, the teacher would monitor and scaffold its use. After independent reading time, the teacher may provide time for students to share a word they problem-solved or attempted to problem-solve in its context and share what they tried. Other students and the teacher may offer other strategies for figuring out the word. This strategic discourse is as essential to learning how to use word recognition strategies as it is to using comprehension strategies. Students need opportunities to verbalize the strategies they use and listen to how others strategically approach words.

Again, as with any strategy instruction, it is essential that students feel safe and secure in their learning environment, if they are to be willing to share their frustrations and their attempts to resolve them. It is important during this time to praise and celebrate students' efforts, even when they are unsuccessful at actually decoding the unknown words. Taking risks by trying to use strategies is the primary goal.

(text resumes on page 240)

TABLE 7.3. Declarative, Procedural, and Conditional Knowledge Associated with Word Recognition Strategies

Word recognition strategy	Associated declarative knowledge	Associated procedural knowledge	Associated conditional knowledge
Using letter–sound cues	Readers need to know *that*: • Words are composed of letters. • Letters represent sounds. • Sounds can be blended together to form spoken words. • Consonant sounds are more reliable than vowel sounds.	*How* to use letter–sound cues: • Look at the beginning of the word. • Think about what sound the letter(s) at the beginning of the word makes. • Look at the next group of letters. • Think about what sound(s) the letter(s) makes. • Blend the sounds together. • Cross-check to make sure the sounds blended together form a real word that makes sense in the context. • If the blended word does not make sense, reblend it, trying different sounds with the same letters, and cross-check; or regroup the letters, reblend, and cross-check.	*When* is it helpful to use letter–sound cues? • Readers can recognize words that are in their spoken vocabulary but not in their reading vocabulary. *Why* is it helpful to use letter–sound cues? • Provides readers with a more reliable means of decoding unfamiliar words. • Enables readers to read sight words with increased accuracy (Ehri, 1991).
Analogizing	Readers need to know *that*: • Words share common letter patterns (e.g., rimes). • Beginning sounds can be added to those common letter patterns. • Blending beginning sounds with the common letter patterns can create new words. • Analogizing is helpful when decoding polysyllabic words.	*How* to analogize: • Look for a familiar letter pattern in the word (e.g., rimes). • Pronounce the letter pattern. • Look at the letters that come before the letter pattern (e.g., "onsets"). • Think about what sounds the letters make. • Blend the beginning sounds together with the letter pattern. • Cross-check to make sure the blended sounds form a real word that makes sense in the context. • If the blended word does not make sense, reblend it, trying different sounds with the same letters, and cross-check; or regroup the letters, reblend, and cross-check.	*When* is it helpful to use analogizing? • When reading single-syllable and polysyllabic words. *Why* is it helpful to use analogizing? • Readers who use analogizing expend less mental effort in recognizing unfamiliar words than readers who decode letter by letter (Fox, 2000). • Blending onsets and rimes is easier than blending individual sounds in words. • Remembering rimes makes it easier to learn vowel variants and eliminates the need to learn exceptions to vowel rules.

	Readers need to know *that*:	*How* to use orthographic cues:	
Using structural analysis cues (Chunking)	• Spoken words can be divided into small and large sound units. • The same sound units, or letter patterns, recur in many words. • Some of the multiletter chunks in words are meaningful and some are not. • Recognizable multiletter chunks include prefixes, suffixes, root words, compound words, contractions, and syllables.	• Look carefully at the word. • Look at the beginning of the word for a prefix. If there is one, pronounce it. • Look at the end of the word for a suffix. If you see one, pronounce it. • Now look for a smaller word or a root word within the word. Think about its meaning. • Look for ways to divide the word into syllables. • Blend the chunks together. • Cross-check to make sure the word is pronounceable. Can I pronounce the word? Does it look right? Does it make sense? • If the word does not make sense or does not sound right, then rechunk the word by dividing it into different multiletter chunks. • Reblend the chunks. • Cross-check. • If the word still does not make sense, use the letter–sound cue or the analogy strategy.	*When* is it helpful to use orthographic cues? • When reading polysyllabic words *Why* is it helpful to use orthographic cues? • These cues facilitate decoding unfamiliar words, particularly polysyllabic ones (Ehri, 1991). • Readers who use chunking expend less mental effort in recognizing unfamiliar words than readers who decode letter by letter (Fox, 2000). • Blending chunks is easier than blending individual sounds in words. • These cues enable readers to set up access routes in memory for reading words by sight (Ehri, 1991).
Using context cues	Readers need to know *that*: • When they come to words they don't know, they can use the pictures and surrounding words to help them. • They must be able to read most of the surrounding words in order for context cues to be effective. • Sometimes there are not enough cues in the context to help readers figure out an unknown word.	*How* to use context cues: • When an unknown word is encountered, stop and think about what word might make sense in that space. • Reread the words in that sentence and the sentences before and after it for contextual help. • Look at the clues in the pictures. • Make a list of words that might make sense in the space. • Look carefully at the letters in the word and the sounds they make to see if any of the words in the list have those letters and sounds in them.	*When* is it helpful to use context cues? • When an unknown word has a supportive context (i.e., pictures and words) *Why* is it helpful to use context cues? • They help bring meaning to the reading event.

Teacher: Janice F. Almasi

Title: Letter–Sound Cues

Topic: Recognizing words using the letter–sound cue strategy

Grade level: 1–2

STAIR hypothesis being addressed:
> Students are partial alphabetic or alphabetic readers. They are able to identify the sounds in a spoken word and are beginning to use initial and final letters to help them recognize unfamiliar words.

Goal of Lesson

Students will learn:
- To identify words that begin with /f/, /fl/, /fr/
- To identify words that begin with /sn/, /sw/, /sl/ (if students are ready)

Materials

- *Jump, Frog, Jump!* by Robert Kalan
- Words cards with the words *fly, frog, fish*
- Pocket chart
- Chart paper

Introduction

Declarative and conditional knowledge about comprehension strategies

Introduce the story *Jump, Frog, Jump!* by Robert Kalan by having students look at the pictures on the cover. Ask students to describe what they see. Read the title to the students and have them make predictions about what the story might be about. "Today we are going to read a story. Before we read any story, it is always a good idea to look at the pictures on the cover and think about what it might be about. So let's study the picture on the cover. What do you see?" Students might notice the fly, fish, frog, snake, and turtle on the cover and make predictions about how those characters might be related to the title. Have students share their observations and their predictions about what the story might be about. Then read the title to the students and have them refine their predictions and observations further.

Declarative and conditional knowledge about comprehension strategies

Remind students that it is always a good idea to think about what we know about the subject of a book before we read it. This helps us get ready to read. Have students gather into five small groups and ask students in each group to think about what they know about the habits and habitat of one of the characters. Each group can record ideas on a web or brainstorm ideas. As each group shares thoughts, record the ideas on a semantic web for each creature. Have students think about and share what they might like to find out as you read the book.

Declarative knowledge

Draw students' attention to the names of each character depicted on the cover. Explain that sometimes the first letter in a word is the same, as in *fish, fly,* and *frog*. Explain that today we are going to be learning how to use the other letters and sounds in words to help us recognize them.

(cont.)

FIGURE 7.6. Sample lesson teaching students to use letter–sound cues as a strategy for recognizing unknown words.

Description of Instructional Experience

Read the book aloud to students. Stop at various points to have students discuss their predictions with a partner to determine whether their predictions were verified or rejected. Once the book is completed, have students share their thoughts and reactions with a partner and then hold a brief whole-group sharing of those reactions to the text. Make links between the students' initial webs and what habits the creatures actually exhibited in the text.

Declarative and conditional knowledge

1. Draw attention to students' use of the words *fish, fly,* and *frog* and ask how we might be able to tell the difference between those words when we are reading them, since they all start with the same sound, /f/. Explain that although using the beginning letter of a word is very helpful in reading words, sometimes words start with the same letter. Explain that when this happens, we have to look more carefully at the rest of the word to tell them apart.

Model/think-aloud

Display word cards with the words *fish, fly,* and *frog* on them. "Hmmm, as I look at the words *fish, fly,* and *frog,* I notice that they all start the same way, with an *f.* I'd better look more carefully at the next letters to see how they are different." Model and think aloud as you pronounce the individual phonemes in each word and then blend them together to pronounce the entire word.

Procedural knowledge

Next, model how to cross-check to make sure the blended word is a real word that makes sense. Continue in this manner, thinking aloud as you examine the graphic and phonemic differences between the three words. Have students share their insights as to how they may be able to distinguish among the three words as well. Explain that sometimes two consonants work together to make sounds. Explain that in the beginning of the word *fly* the *f* combines with the *l* and we hear two sounds. Explain that there are lots of words that begin with *fl.* Share a couple of examples and have students share others. Add these words onto the class word wall under *fl.* Follow same procedures for *fr.*

Verbalization

Guided practice

Explain that as we reread the story *Jump, Frog, Jump!,* there will be several times when we hear words that begin with /f/, /fl/, and /fr/. Pass out word cards with *fish, fly,* and *frog* on them. As the story is reread, have students hold up a word card each time they hear a word that starts the same way as *fish, fly,* or *frog.* Reread text, stopping as students hear words with the /f/, /fl/, or /fr/sound in them. Have students share how they could tell that the word on the card had the same beginning sound as the word in the text. Students can then engage in a word sort activity in which they sort a number of different word cards, each word beginning with /f/, /fl/, or /fr/. Students group the words into categories by comparing the similarities and differences within and across the words.

Verbalization

2. If students seem fairly successful with the previous portion of the lesson, they might be able to consider other consonant blends as well. If they are not, then it would be wise to move on to step 3. Ask students if they noticed any other words that started with two consonant sounds. For example, students may notice that *swallowed* and *swam* both begin with /sw/, that *snake* begins with /sn/, or that *slid* begins with /sl/. Write each word on a word card and engage in a think-aloud in which you point out the graphic and phonemic features of the words. Explain that we can add an *sw, sn,* and an *sl* section to our word wall. Then say, "as we reread let's listen to see if we hear the words that start with /sw/, /sn/, and /sl/." Pass word cards out to students and have

Model/think-aloud

(cont.)

FIGURE 7.6. *(cont.)*

Guided practice

students continue to listen, holding up *swam*, *snake*, or *slid* each time they hear a word that starts with those sounds. Again, a word sort activity using words with initial consonant blends /sw/, /sn/, and /sl/could be used at this point to help children compare and contrast the features of words beginning similarly.

3. At the conclusion of the rereading, note the words that were added to the word wall. Explain that there are many other words that we might encounter as we read that begin with /f/, /fl/, and /fr/. Have pairs of students engage in a word hunt in which they look through magazines for pictures of words that start with /f/, /fl/, or /fr/; or they can look through their word banks, writing folders,

Guided practice

or familiar texts they have already read to find words that start with *f*, *fl*, and *fr*. Materials should be ones with which students are familiar. As students locate words and pictures, they can add them to the sheet of paper that has the appropriate consonant or consonant blend on the top and the keyword from the story (e.g., /fl/ *fly*). If students cut out pictures, they should also be asked to label each picture as they paste it onto the appropriate paper.

Verbalization

4. Once students have completed their hunt, the groups can gather together to engage in a discussion, listing the words and pictures they found that represent each sound. Discussion should focus on verbalizing why particular words fit into particular categories. Words can then be added to the class word wall under *f*, *fl*, and *fr* columns.

Conclusion

Have students share what they should do when they come to a word they don't know how to pronounce during reading. Have students share whether it was easy or difficult to find words that started with /f/, /fl/, and /fr/. Have students

Verbalization

explain how they can tell the difference between these words, given that they all start with *f*.

Assessment

- You will know whether students are able to identify words that begin with /f/, /fl/, /fr/or /sn/, /sw/, /sl/ if they are able to locate pictures and/or words from familiar texts that begin with those sounds.

FIGURE 7.6. *(cont.)*

Analogizing

Skilled readers do not recognize unfamiliar words letter by letter or sound them out letter by letter, as is done when using the letter–sound cue strategy (Pressley, 2000). As readers mature, they are able to recognize common letter patterns and have a store of known words that they are able to read by sight. Therefore, instead of reading words sequentially in a letter-by-letter fashion, they recognize common letter chunks and, when reading unfamiliar words, blend the chunks together. This method makes word recognition a quicker, more automatic process (Clay, 2005; Ehri, 1991; Fox, 2000; Goswami & Bryant, 1990; Goswami & Mead, 1992).

Unknown Word	Page Number	Word Recognition Strategy Used			
		Letter–Sound Cues	Analogizing	Chunking	Context Cues

FIGURE 7.7. Sample sheet for recording word recognition strategies used during independent reading.

When readers use analogizing to recognize unknown words, they are making use of familiar letter (spelling/orthographic) patterns to help them read unfamiliar words. These letter patterns provide readers with a stable and regular system for decoding. For example, if a reader knew the *-ust* letter pattern, he could use that knowledge to read the words *rust, trust,* and *disgust.* As noted, the *-ust* letter pattern is called a *rime* or a phonogram. Rimes are the vowel(s) and consonant(s) at the end of a syllable. In the example above, the vowel *u* and the consonants that follow it, *st*, comprise the *-ust* rime. The consonants that come at the beginning of a syllable are called *onsets.* In the example above, *r* is the onset in *rust* that is attached to the *-ust* rime. Onsets can consist of single consonants (e.g., *b, d, g, j, r*), consonant blends (e.g., *cr, tr, thr, scr*), or consonant digraphs (e.g., *sh, wh, ch, th*). Some refer to the words that are derived from onsets and rimes as *word families.* Thus the *-ust* word family would consist of single-syllable words (e.g., *bust, crust, dust, gust,* *just*, *rust*) and polysyllabic words that contain the -*ust* rime somewhere within them (e.g., *disgust*, *distrust*, *encrust*, *entrust*, *sawdust*). When words end with similar rimes (e.g., *just*, *trust*), they usually rhyme.

Rimes can also consist of a single vowel, as in the -*y* family (e.g., *by*, *cry*, *dry*, *fly*, *my*). Some rimes consist of letter patterns (found in sight words) that can stand alone without an onset (e.g., -*an*, -*it*, -*on*, -*in*) or can be combined with onsets. These usually make the best rimes for beginning analogizing instruction, because they are sight words containing letter patterns that readers internalize and remember quickly. Ehri (1991) noted that older readers are more likely than younger readers to use analogizing to read unfamiliar words. For it to help younger readers, analogizing must be taught more formally. Ehri's review of research also noted that, for younger readers to be able to use analogizing, they must be able to segment words into onsets and rimes, and they must have some ability to use letter–sound cues. Thus, for readers to successfully use analogizing, they should at least be in the partial alphabetic or full alphabetic phase of development. A list of 37 high-frequency rimes in the English language is presented in Figure 7.8.

The underlying principle of analogizing is that if readers can automatically recognize a letter pattern or rime, such as -*end*, and if they are able to blend onsets onto that rime, then they should be able to read a multitude of words even if they are unfamiliar (e.g., *bend*, *blend*, *fend*, *lend*, *mend*, *send*, *amend*, *commend*, *comprehend*). Sometimes readers can use their knowledge of a familiar letter pattern in a sight word and analogize the letter pattern to an unfamiliar word. For example, suppose a reader could not recognize the word *twig* in the sentence, "There was a twig on the ground." However, the reader does know the word *big* and is able to manipulate the sounds in a word. Therefore, she can use her knowledge of the -*ig* rime and substitute a /tw/ for the /b/ to help her recognize the unknown word. The reader's thinking process might be: "I don't know that word, but it ends the same way that *big* does. Maybe it sounds the same as *big*. I'll substitute a /tw/ sound for the /b/." The reader then pronounces the /tw/, blends it to the -*ig* rime, and cross-checks to see whether the word she has blended sounds like a real word that makes sense in the sentence.

Analogizing places fewer cognitive demands on readers than using letter–sound cues, because readers only need to blend the onset and the rime—as opposed to sounding and blending each individual letter and sound (Fox, 2000). Fewer cognitive demands make analogizing an ideal strategy to teach younger and less experienced readers. The consonant sounds in onsets are usually very reliable, but vowel sounds are much less reliable. When vowel sounds are present in a rime, however, their sounds are much more reliable. This reliability provides emergent readers with more dependable cues for decoding than having to remember all of the various vowel sounds and their associated rules and exceptions when using letter–sound cues as a decoding strategy. (See Table 7.3 for the declarative, procedural, and conditional knowledge associated with using analogizing as a word recognition strategy.)

Students who benefit from learning how to use analogizing as a strategy are those who understand letter–sound relationships but who may not know that words also contain common letter patterns. Eileen Ludwig, one of our graduate students, described her student's reading ability in the following manner:

> In one of my sessions with [the student] I conducted a miscue analysis. I feel as though I learned quite a bit about [the student's] decoding strategies even before analyzing the data. As I observed [the student's] behaviors and decoding strategies

-ack

back, black, clack, crack, hack, lack, knack, pack, quack, rack, sack, shack, smack, snack, stack, tack, track, whack, attack, backpack, bushwhack, Cossack, cutback, drawback, haystack, hijack, horseback, knapsack, piggyback, racetrack, ransack, rickrack, setback, skyjack, tamarack, thumbtack, tieback, wisecrack, zwieback

-ail

bail, fail, grail, hail, jail, mail, nail, pail, quail, rail, sail, snail, tail, trail, airmail, assail, bewail, bobtail, coattail, contrail, curtail, derail, detail, entail, fingernail, handrail, hangnail, hobnail, monorail, ponytail, prevail, retail, toenail, topsail, travail

-ain

brain, chain, drain, gain, grain, main, plain, sprain, stain, train, abstain, appertain, ascertain, attain, complain, constrain, contain, detain, disdain, domain, entertain, eyestrain, explain, ingrain, maintain, ordain, pertain, refrain, restrain, sustain, terrain

-ake

bake, brake, cake, fake, flake, lake, make, rake, shake, snake, stake, take, wake, awake, cheesecake, clambake, cupcake, forsake, fruitcake, grubstake, handshake, keepsake, mistake, muckrake, namesake, overtake, pancake, partake, snowflake

-ale

bale, dale, gale, hale, kale, male, pale, sale, scale, shale, stale, tale, vale, wale, whale, exhale, female, impale, inhale, regale, resale, baler, azalea, salesman

-ame

blame, came, fame, flame, frame, game, lame, name, same, shame, tame, became, mainframe, nickname, overcame, surname

-an

bran, can, fan, man, pan, plan, ran, scan, span, tan, than, van, afghan, airman, bedpan, began, caravan, divan, dustpan, fireman, mailman, rattan, sampan, seaman, sedan, suntan, toucan, wingspan

-ank

bank, blank, clank, crank, dank, drank, flank, frank, lank, plank, prank, rank, sank, shank, shrank, spank, stank, swank, tank, thank, yank, gangplank, outflank, outrank, riverbank, sandbank

-ap

cap, clap, flap, gap, lap, map, nap, scrap, slap, snap, strap, tap, trap, wrap, bootstrap, burlap, catnap, entrap, firetrap, gingersnap, handicap, hubcap, kidnap, mishap, mousetrap, overlap, pinesap, stopgap, thunderclap, wiretap

-ash

bash, cash, dash, gash, hash, lash, mash, rash, sash, abash, brash, clash, crash, flash, gnash, slash, smash, stash, trash, potash, rehash, splash, thrash, cashew, cashier, fashion, dashboard

-at

bat, cat, chat, fat, flat, gnat, hat, mat, pat, rat, sat, scat, slat, spat, that, acrobat, bobcat, brickbat, bureaucrat, butterfat, chitchat, combat, copycat, democrat, diplomat, doormat, format, habitat, hemostat, muskrat, nonfat, Photostat, rheostat, wildcat

-ate

crate, date, fate, gate, late, mate, plate, rate, sate, skate, slate, state, abate, calculate, candidate, create, debate, disintegrate, dissipate, donate, elate, elevate, estimate, excavate, inmate, irate, irritate, locate, migrate, motivate, mutate, negate, notate

-aw

caw, haw, jaw, law, man, paw, raw, saw, claw, draw, flaw, gnaw, slaw, thaw, bylaw, macaw, squaw, straw, bawdy, brawl, crawl, drawl, shawl, trawl, dawn, fawn, gawk, hawk, lawn, pawn, tawny, yawn, dawdle, lawman, lawyer, tawdry, jawbone, rawhide, sawdust, sawmill

-ay

bay, clay, day, gay, gray, hay, lay, may, pay, play, ray, say, stay, stray, sway, tray, way, allay, anyway, ashtray, away, betray, birthday, castaway, dismay, doorway, foray, freeway, gateway, hearsay, holiday, mainstay, payday, portray, relay, someday, subway

-eat

beat, bleat, cheat, cleat, heat, meat, neat, peat, pleat, seat, treat, wheat, browbeat, buckwheat, defeat, downbeat, drumbeat, entreat, heartbeat, mincemeat, offbeat, overheat, repeat, retreat, upbeat

(cont.)

FIGURE 7.8. Thirty-seven high-frequency rimes in the English language. *Based on* Wylie and Durrell (1970) and Fox (2000).

-ell
bell, cell, dell, dwell, fell, quell, sell, shell, smell, spell, swell, tell, well, yell, barbell, befell, bluebell, bombshell, doorbell, eggshell, farewell, foretell, inkwell, nutshell, oversell, stairwell

-est
best, chest, crest, guest, jest, lest, nest, pest, quest, rest, vest, west, wrest, zest, armrest, arrest, attest, bequest, congest, conquest, contest, detest, digest, divest, infest, ingest, invest, request, suggest

-ice
ice, dice, lice, mice, nice, rice, vice, price, slice, spice, trice, twice, advice, device, entice, splice, thrice

-ick
brick, chick, click, crick, flick, kick, lick, nick, pick, prick, quick, sick, slick, stick, thick, tick, trick, wick, airsick, derrick, gimmick, handpick, homesick, limerick, lipstick, maverick, sidekick, rollick, seasick, yardstick

-ide
bride, chide, hide, pride, ride, side, slide, stride, tide, wide, abide, aside, astride, bromide, chloride, collide, confide, decide, dioxide, divide, fireside, fluoride, outside, oxide, peroxide, preside, provide, reside, roadside, subside, suicide, sulfide

-ight
bright, fight, flight, fright, knight, light, might, night, plight, right, sight, slight, tight, airtight, alright, copyright, daylight, delight, firelight, fortnight, headlight, highlight, hindsight, limelight, midnight, skylight, spotlight, starlight, stoplight, tonight, twilight

-ill
bill, chill, dill, drill, fill, frill, gill, grill, hill, kill, mill, quill, sill, skill, spill, still, swill, thrill, till, twill, anthill, distill, doorsill, downhill, fiberfill, foothill, freewill, fulfill, goodwill, handbill, instill, landfill, playbill, sawmill, treadmill, windchill, windmill

-in
chin, grin, pin, skin, spin, thin, tin, twin, win, akin, begin, chagrin, doeskin, kingpin

-ine
dine, fine, line, mine, nine, pine, sine, tine, vine, wine, brine, shine, spine, swine, thine, twine, whine, alpine, bovine, byline, canine, cosine, define, devine, equine, feline, iodine, refine, recline, shrine, supine, ninety, winery, dinette, nineteen

-ing
bring, cling, ding, fling, king, ring, sing, sling, sting, string, thing, wing, wring, zing, anything, awning, bedspring, bowstring, bullring, downswing, drawstring, earring, hamstring, handspring, latchstring, offspring, plaything, shoestring, upswing, wellspring

-ink
ink, blink, brink, chink, clink, drink, fink, kink, link, mink, pink, rink, shrink, sink, slink, stink, think, wink, hoodwink

-ip
chip, clip, dip, flip, grip, hip, lip, nip, quip, rip, ship, sip, skip, slip, snip, strip, tip, trip, whip, zip, airship, catnip, equip, fingertip, flagship, kinship, outstrip

-ir
fir, sir, stir, whir, astir, nadir, tapir, birch, bird, birth, circa, dirge, dirt, dirty, firm, first, girl, girth, mirth, circle, circuit, giraffe, girdle, mirage, piranha, sirloin

-ock
block, clock, crock, dock, flock, frock, knock, lock, rock, shock, smock, sock, stock, bedrock, deadlock, gamecock, hemlock, livestock, o'clock, padlock, peacock, roadblock, shamrock

-oke
awoke, broke, choke, coke, joke, poke, smoke, spoke, stoke, stroke, woke, yoke, artichoke, backstroke, bespoke, cowpoke, evoke, heatstroke, invoke, keystroke, provoke, slowpoke, sunstroke

(cont.)

FIGURE 7.8. *(cont.).*

-op	-or	-ore
chop, crop, drop, flop, hop, mop, pop, prop, shop, stop, top, airdrop, backdrop, bellhop, blacktop, dewdrop, doorstop, gumdrop, hardtop, hilltop, lollipop, outcrop, raindrop, rooftop, tabletop, teardrop, treetop, workshop	for, nor, born, cord, cork, corn, ford, fork, form, horn, lord, morn, pork, torn, worn, acorn, adorn, chord, flora, glory, scorn, shorn, short, snort, sport, stork, story, sword, sworn, thorn, décor, abort, aorta	chore, more, score, shore, snore, spore, store, tore, wore, adore, anymore, before, bookstore, carnivore, commodore, deplore, drugstore, encore, explore, folklore, herbivore, ignore, implore, seashore, semaphore, sophomore, therefore

-uck	-ug	-ump
buck, chuck, cluck, duck, luck, pluck, snuck, struck, stuck, suck, tuck, truck, amuck, awestruck, mukluk, potluck, woodchuck	bug, chug, dug, drug, hug, jug, lug, mug, plug, pug, rug, shrug, slug, smug, snug, thug, tug, bedbug, earplug, firebug, fireplug, humbug	bump, chump, clump, dump, frump, grump, hump, jump, lump, plump, slump, stump, thump, trump, mugwump

-unk
bunk, chunk, clunk, drunk, dunk, flunk, funk, hunk, junk, plunk, punk, shrunk, skunk, slunk, spunk, stunk, sunk, trunk, debunk, chipmunk

FIGURE 7.8. *(cont.).*

while she read the passage, I believe I gained a greater insight to what she does or does not do when she reads. As [the student] read the passage, she worked extremely hard at sounding out words that she did not recognize. Rather than chunking words or analogizing unknown words to known sight words, she sounded out each letter in order to decode a word. For example, when she came to the word *corner*, she worked very hard at sounding out the word letter by letter. She then read the word as *cormer*. She also substituted *what* for *was*. Since *cormer* is very similar to *corner*, and *what* is somewhat similar to *was*, I do feel that [the student] used visual information in order to help her figure out some words. During our lessons I noticed that [the student] would try to sound out words but would then take a guess if she thought it was taking her too much time. However, when she read this [passage], she spent much more time trying to sound out each individual letter in order to form a word. Even though she did take more time trying to sound out letters, there were some words in which she could only pronounce certain sounds. Most of these included initial consonant sounds. For example, she substituted *what* for *was*, *after* for *afraid*, and *wouldn't* for *wasn't*.

—EILEEN LUDWIG, reflective memo

Eileen's insights from her observations and miscue analysis reveal a child who is relying on letter–sound cues to decode unfamiliar words because she has no other strategies to use. Eileen noted that much of the child's previous classroom instruction was focused primarily on phonics-based approaches to learning to read in which much of the instruction focused on completing phonics workbooks. Thus the strategies she employed were consistent with those to which she had been exposed. Eileen's hypotheses focused on broadening the child's repertoire of available word recognition strategies to include learning to recognize common word patterns and using them to facilitate decoding. Analogizing is an ideal strategy to teach these readers, who recognize the beginning and sometimes the ending sounds in a word and "guess" at the medial portion. Sometimes teachers analyze such students' miscues and determine that they should be learning vowel sounds and vowel combinations (i.e., digraphs, diphthongs, *r*-controlled vowels) because it is the medial portion with which they are having difficulty. However, it is more helpful, as noted above, to teach these readers about rimes and onsets than specific vowel sounds because the vowel sounds in rimes are more reliable than teaching them separately as one would when teaching them as part of the letter–sound cue strategy.

The sample lesson in Figure 7.9 was derived from Eileen Ludwig's and Keli Garas-York's lessons. The sample lesson provides a large amount of scaffolding for students, as teachers model and demonstrate how to sound and blend onsets with the -*ape* rime to recognize unfamiliar words in Bernard Most's (1986) *There's an Ape Behind the Drape*. Before reading the text, the students are engaged in word work that involves manipulating letter tiles to build the -*ape* rime. After the reading, they add consonants to the beginning of the rime. They hunt for words containing the -*ape* rime. As children develop these rimes, they are encouraged to remind themselves, "If I know *ape*, I can read *cape*. If I know *cape*, I can read *drape*. If I know *drape*, I can read *grape*." (If the children are writing or making the words with magnetic letters, they might say *spell* instead of *read*.) During the read-aloud of the text the teacher has the primary role as she models and demonstrates what it would look like and sound like to use the analogizing strategy. In essence, the teacher is teaching students the Discourse of a new word recognition strategy. Internalizing this Discourse and engaging in similar actions and thoughts as students read is the long-term goal. With practice, students will be able to recognize common rimes in larger words and use their knowledge of those rimes to help them decode unfamiliar words.

When teaching word recognition strategies, it is important to embed and link the instruction to authentic literacy contexts, such as the text featured in this lesson, as well as authentic writing experiences. This lesson provided students with the opportunity to use the -*ape* rimes in their writing before reading the text, as they wrote prediction sentences about what might happen in the story, and after reading the text, as they created their own stories using the -*ape* rimes they had gathered during their word hunt. Authentic reading experiences were linked to the text *There's an Ape Behind the Drape* (Most, 1986), which featured several opportunities for the teacher to model how to use the -*ape* rime to help decode unknown words.

After teaching this lesson, one of the teachers, Keli, noted how important the teacher modeling during the read-aloud was for her student:

> I think the most important thing that I learned in this lesson is the benefit of reducing processing demands. When I was reading the book, *There's an Ape Behind the Drape*, [the student] was more focused on the -*ape* words in the story rather than trying to decode every word in the book. She also seemed more at ease during the rest of the session.
>
> —KELI GARAS-YORK, reflective memo

Keli also grappled with the question of how much to include in one lesson. In preceding lessons she had tried to teach several word families at once, hoping that her student would be able to use them all in the texts that were chosen; however, the struggling reader

Teacher: Adapted from lessons by Keli Garas-York and Eileen Ludwig

Title: Analogizing

Topic: Recognizing words using the analogy strategy

Grade level: 2–4

STAIR hypothesis being addressed:

> Students are in the alphabetic phase of development. They are able to identify the sounds in a spoken word and are able to use initial and final letters to help them recognize unfamiliar words, but they have difficulty with medial portions of words and vowel sounds.

Goal of Lesson

Students will learn:

- To identify unknown words using onsets and rimes (long-term goal); specifically, they will learn to recognize unknown words having an *-ape* rime
- To blend onsets and rimes to recognize unknown words (long-term goal); specifically, they will learn to blend onsets with the *-ape* rime to recognize unknown words
- To cross-check to make sure that identified words make sense (long-term goal)

Materials

- *There's an Ape Behind the Drape* by Bernard Most
- Chart paper, markers
- Pocket chart/alphabet letters, letter tiles, or magnetic letters
- Hidden Pictures from *Highlights for Children* magazine

Introduction

Reduce processing by using concrete example

The lesson will begin by displaying a "Hidden Picture" from the *Highlights for Children* magazine. Ask students to study the large picture to see if they can find any other pictures hidden within it. Have students share the pictures they find and explain *how* they were able to locate the pictures. As students share the procedures they used for finding the "hidden" pictures within the larger picture, write them down on chart paper. Explain that sometimes when we are reading and come to a word we do not know, we can use the same process to help us figure it out. Instead of looking for small pictures within a big picture, we can look for smaller words, or letter patterns, within a bigger word. Explain that today we are going to learn how to look for these letter patterns in bigger words to help us read them.

Procedural knowledge

Declarative knowledge

Description of Instructional Experience

Model/think-aloud

Since students are familiar with compound words, the lesson will begin by showing some compound words. Explain that when you look at these words, you can see smaller words inside them, just like we could see hidden pictures inside the larger picture. Model and think aloud using some examples such as

(cont.)

FIGURE 7.9. Sample lesson teaching students to use analogizing as a strategy for recognizing unknown words.

Declarative knowledge

Conditional knowledge

Procedural knowledge

Declarative knowledge

Declarative knowledge

Model/think-aloud

Procedural knowledge

Model/think-aloud

Guided practice

Verbalization

Declarative and conditional knowledge about comprehension strategies

snowman. Explain that *snowman* is one word, but it has smaller words inside it. Explain that sometimes when we are trying to read big words and small words, it helps to look inside the word and study it to see if there are smaller words or parts of words in it. Explain that this strategy is a good one to use for small words, but it is also very helpful in reading big words.

After reviewing a few examples, note the process you used during the think-aloud to locate the smaller words. Compare your process to that which the students used to locate the hidden pictures in the larger picture. The goal here is to try to verbalize the procedural knowledge associated with recognizing smaller word parts in larger words. For example, you might explain that there are certain steps we can follow to help us recognize unknown words. First, we should look carefully at the word. As we look, we can look for smaller words or chunks inside the bigger word. Say each word chunk and then blend the chunks together. Finally, we need to cross-check to make sure the word makes sense. Ask yourself "Can I pronounce the word?" "Does the word look and sound right?" "Does the word make sense in the sentence?" Explain that it is important to cross-check to make sure that what you read makes sense.

Explain that just as some big words have small words within them, there are also common word parts that we can look for too. Explain that these word parts are called *word families.* Just like people in families have similar last names, words in word families have similar letter patterns. Explain that one word family is the *-ape* family. Build the rime *-ape* using letter tiles or magnetic letters. Pronounce the rime and then explain that we can add sounds to the beginning to make different words in the *-ape* family. Explain that all of the words will have the common letter pattern *-ape* so they will all rhyme. Add single letters (*c, g, t*), blends (*gr, scr*), and digraphs (*sh*) to the rime and model and demonstrate the process of blending the onsets with the rime. Be certain to think aloud and reiterate the procedural steps used above to blend the onsets and rimes. For example, if you were reading the word *tape*, you might say, "I see the little word *-ape* inside that word. I see a /t/ sound at the beginning. Those letters make a *t* sound. *T* and *ape. Tape.* Let me think, is that a word? *Tape.* Yes, I've heard of *tape* before. It's something you use to hold things together. If I were reading, I'd want to make sure that *tape* made sense in the sentence I was reading. Yes, the word *tape* makes sense." Model using another letter tile as an onset and then have students work with a partner using their own letter tiles (or paper letters) to build the *-ape* word family and add various consonants and consonant clusters to build real and nonsense words. Have students talk about whether they were able to blend the onsets and rimes and what part of it was difficult.

Explain that we will be using this strategy and the *-ape* word family while reading the book *There's an Ape Behind the Drape* by Bernard Most. Have students look at the cover and make predictions. Ask students to describe what they see. Read the title to the students and have them make predictions about what the story might be about. "Today we are going to read a story. Before we read any story, it is always a good idea to look at the pictures on the cover and think about what it might be about. So let's study the picture on the cover.

(cont.)

FIGURE 7.9. *(cont.)*

*Declarative and
conditional knowledge
about comprehension
strategies*

What do you see?" Have students share their observations and predictions about what the story might be about. Then read the title to the students and have them refine their predictions and observations further. Using the *-ape* words that were generated prior to introducing the story, have students work with a partner to write sentences using the *-ape* words to predict what the story might be about. For example, students might predict that the *ape* is wearing a *cape* as he stands behind the *drape*. Students might choose to use a story map to help them generate predictions about the characters, their goals/problems in the story, and how they might go about solving those problems.

Remind students that it is always a good idea to think about what we know about the subject of a book before we read it. This helps us get ready to read. Have students think about and share what they might like to find out as you read the book.

Reduce processing

Model/think-aloud

Guided practice

Explain that as we read the book, we will see if there are places where we can use the analogizing strategy to read the *-ape* words. Begin reading the book aloud and thinking aloud as you read. When you come to the first *-ape* word, model and think aloud using the procedures for sounding and blending onsets and rimes. Be sure to cross-check the blended word to make certain that it makes sense in the sentence. As the reading continues, model and have students assist with this sounding and blending process when *-ape* words are encountered.

Verbalization

After reading the story, have students discuss how well their predictions and prediction sentences compared to Bernard Most's version. Engage students in a whole-class discussion of their thoughts about the story, their predictions, and how well the analogizing strategy worked.

Guided practice

Explain that we might even find the *-ape* family in larger words such as *landscape, skyscraper,* and *shipshape*. Have pairs of students engage in a word hunt in which they look through their word banks, writing folders, and familiar texts they have already read to find words that have *-ape* in them. Materials should be those with which students are familiar. As students locate words and/or pictures, they can record them on a sheet of paper. Once students have completed their hunt, the group can gather together to engage in a discussion and listing of the words and pictures they found that have *-ape* in them. Each new *-ape* word can be added onto the word family wall. Students can then work with a partner to create their own *-ape* story using the words added to the *-ape* section of the word family wall.

Conclusion

Verbalization

Students will write their responses to the lesson and what they have learned about using analogizing as a strategy for recognizing unknown words. Students should be encouraged to write about their understanding of *what* the analogizing strategy is, *when* they might use it, and *why* they should use it.

(cont.)

FIGURE 7.9. *(cont.)*

Assessment
- You will know whether students are able to recognize unknown words having an *-ape* rime as they use the letter tiles to build words with *-ape* in them, by their participation and discussion during the read-aloud, and by their ability to locate *-ape* words as they hunt through their writing folders and familiar texts.
- You will know whether students are able to blend onsets and rimes to recognize unfamiliar words with *-ape* in them by their ability to use the letter tiles to build, sound, and blend words with *-ape* in them.
- You will know whether students are able to cross-check to make sure that identified words make sense as they assist during the cross-checking procedures of the read aloud.

FIGURE 7.9. *(cont.)*

with whom she was working was not able to process so much material, and she was having difficulty understanding the concept of blending the onsets and rimes. Therefore, Keli focused her ensuing lessons on only one word pattern/family to make certain that her student understood the concept of blending onsets and rimes. She also selected texts that featured that particular word family. In Keli's summation:

> This lesson went very well. I'm glad that I just focused on one word family. [The student's] use of the analogy strategy was more prevalent and more immediate while she was reading *Sheep in a Jeep* (Shaw, 1988) than in other readings she has done after instruction. I counted the number of times she correctly identified an *-eep* word. Out of 29 *-eep* words in the story, [the student] correctly identified 20 of them. She often substituted *truck* for *jeep*. I am thinking that she is overrelying on the pictures, or, on a positive note, she is bringing meaning to the text.
> —KELI GARAS-YORK, reflective memo

Eileen Ludwig also felt that her student responded well to similar instruction. She noted:

> According to Fox (2000), readers who use analogous onsets and rimes put less mental effort into word identification than do readers who decode words letter–sound by letter–sound. Blending onsets and rimes is much easier than blending individual sounds because with onsets and rimes there are usually only two items. Since [the student] does have auditory processing difficulties, I thought that this may be a good strategy for her to use. With this strategy, [the student] did not have to concentrate so much on sounding out each letter. I did feel that this strategy did put much less stress on her and did increase her learning. Walker (2012) states that a diagnostic teacher adjusts instruction to incorporate what students know and what students can do. The teacher can reduce the student's stress by using a student's strengths. I feel that in this lesson I was able to use one of [the student's] strengths in order to help her read the text. Through observation during the lesson, I found that [the student] did recognize similar patterns and was able to identify words that she would

not have been able to recognize without using this particular strategy. More importantly, I believe that [the student] was able to see the success she was having. She even said, "Wow, I can do this." Furthermore, with a great deal of modeling, guided practice, and feedback, [the student] started to use the cross-checking strategy.

—EILEEN LUDWIG, reflective memo

The students involved in these lessons were quickly able to use the strategy to help them read unfamiliar words. The texts that are selected for such lessons are critical. Texts should support the instruction so that readers can actually use what they are learning to help them read the text. Table 7.1 provides a list of texts our teachers have used successfully in their lessons. Many of the titles indicate the rime that appears most frequently in the text. Included are books of poetry, jump-rope chants, and nursery rhymes—all of which are very appropriate for use in teaching readers how to recognize rimes and onsets while analogizing.

The sample lesson in Figure 7.9 focused more on using analogizing to recognize unknown words of one syllable. For those readers approaching the end of the full alphabetic phase of development and transitioning into the consolidated alphabetic phase, lessons that focus more on using analogizing as a strategy to help read unfamiliar polysyllabic words would be appropriate. Texts such as Cathi Hepworth's (1996) *Antics: An Alphabetical Anthology* and Bernard Most's (1992) *There's an Ant in Anthony* are very appropriate because the *-ant* rime is clearly apparent in many polysyllabic words in both texts. Cathi Hepworth's alphabet book uses intriguing illustrations of various ants. For example, the first page contains the word *antique* and a picture of an old ant in a rocking chair listening to an antique record player. The limited amount of text and the vivid illustrations make it an ideal way of reducing processing demands for readers who are just beginning to learn that rimes occur in polysyllabic words.

Bernard Most's text (1992) *There's an Ant in Anthony* is also a perfect accompaniment in that it features a young boy (Anthony) who discovers that the word *ant* appears in his name. He then goes on a search for *-ant*s in other objects. He finds that there is an *-ant* in a *plant* and in many other objects. The author highlights the *-ant* in each word by using red ink, which makes the *-ant* rime very obvious and easy for readers to locate. As the story progresses, the *-ant* rime turns up in many polysyllabic words. The book is ideal for introducing students to the notion that big words are not as mysterious and difficult as they may appear, because they are comprised of familiar letter patterns and chunks.

Using Structural Analysis (Chunking)

Structural analysis involves using meaningful and nonmeaningful multiletter chunks to recognize unknown words (Fox, 2000). Using structural analysis, or chunking, is most helpful when reading polysyllabic words. Meaningful multiletter chunks provide the reader with root words, prefixes (e.g., *pre-, un-, dis-*), suffixes (e.g., *-able, -or*), contractions (e.g., *isn't, wasn't*), and compound words (e.g., *houseboat*), all of which may yield insight into meaning and sound. Nonmeaningful multiletter chunks only help readers with sound and may consist of syllables, accents, and other units of pronunciations such as rimes. For example, the word *table* consists of two syllables (*ta* and *ble*). These syllables do not carry any meaning. They are simply letter patterns that commonly recur in words.

When readers recognize or use the same multiletter chunks repeatedly, in time they internalize these letter patterns and recognize them as intact units (Fox, 2000). The ability to recognize multiletter chunks streamlines the word recognition process and greatly reduces a reader's cognitive burden. Fox noted that when readers decode words letter by letter (as in phonics), they must hold each individual letter–sound correspondence in their short-term memory. This method becomes an enormous burden when reading longer words. For example, if a reader were trying to pronounce the word *unavailable*, he would have to identify and consider 11 individual letters. This length overburdens short-term memory, which is only capable of holding between five and seven thought units at one time. When short-term memory is overburdened, some thought units are lost or forgotten. If this happens during reading, it inevitably means that the letters that were sounded out at the beginning of the word are most certainly forgotten, and by the time the entire word is sounded out, comprehension is affected as well. Thought units can consist of a single letter or a group of letters. Thus recognizing a group of letters as a whole chunk makes word recognition more efficient. For example, if a reader is able to recognize automatically the prefix *un-* as one multiletter chunk, the root word *avail* as another chunk, and the suffix *-able* as a third, then the burden on short-term memory is limited to three thought units. Recognizing multiletter chunks reduces the amount of mental effort expended and accelerates the word recognition process. The reduced burden on short-term memory also means there is less disruption to comprehension.

The chunking strategy is similar to analogizing in that both methods involve recognizing and using common letter (spelling/orthographic) patterns in words. However, readers who use meaningful and nonmeaningful multiletter chunks to recognize unfamiliar words are at the consolidated alphabetic phase of development (Ehri, 1998). Indeed, the word *consolidated* is used to describe this phase of development because these readers are aware of letter–sound relationships to such an extent that they have consolidated various letter sequences into chunks that they recognize as intact units, rather than decoding letter by letter, as occurs with readers in the full alphabetic phase of development. These readers are, therefore, proficient with alphabetic phase reading (Ehri, 1991, 2005). Readers in the consolidated alphabetic phase know that spoken words can be divided into large and small sound units, and they can separate spoken words into their constituent sounds and blend them together to form words. (See Table 7.3 for the declarative, procedural, and conditional knowledge associated with this strategy.) These readers also know that some multiletter chunks yield meaning and pronunciation (i.e., meaningful chunks), and some are helpful only with pronunciation (i.e., nonmeaningful chunks). Much of this development begins to occur for most children in second grade, as they begin to acquire sufficient experience reading words to recognize standard spelling patterns in English (Ehri, 1991, 2005; Fox, 2000).

When using the chunking strategy, readers are likely to recognize different multiletter chunks, depending on their background knowledge (Fox, 2000). For example, one reader may not recognize the word *disappointment* while reading. He knows that it is a large word and that using the chunking strategy would be helpful, but he is not aware that *disappoint* is a root word. Instead he notices the multiletter chunk *dis-* (even though it is not a prefix), the suffix *-ment*, the smaller word *point*, and the *-ap* syllable. As he blends the chunks together, he is still able to blend a word that makes sense, even though he may not recognize the actual root word. This is part of what makes using chunking strategic. Different users approach the task in different ways. They may all accomplish the same goal of recognizing the word, but they may not all go about accomplishing the goal in the same manner.

When teaching students to use chunking as a strategy, it is helpful to focus instruction on those multiletter chunks that recur most frequently in English words. It is especially important to focus on those prefixes and suffixes that occur most frequently. White, Power, and White (1989) noted that the number of words with prefixes and suffixes encountered by students doubles from fourth to fifth grade, and doubles again by seventh grade. Four prefixes account for 58% of the prefixed words students encounter in grades 3 through 9 (White, Power, et al., 1989). These prefixes are *un-*, *re-*, *in-* (meaning *not*), and *dis-*. The prefix *un-* is the most frequently occurring, found in 26% of all words with prefixes. It is most worthwhile to focus instruction initially on these four prefixes.

According to White, Sowell, and Yangihara (1989), those suffixes that occur most frequently in English words are *-s* (*-es*), *-ed*, *-ing*, *-ly*, and *-er*. The suffixes *-s* (*-es*), *-ed*, and *-ing* make up 65% of the suffixes readers in grades 3 through 9 encounter. Therefore, the most beneficial instruction occurs regarding these word endings. Many readers are aware of these three word endings by the end of first grade because authors use them so much in their writing. The remaining high-frequency suffixes are usually familiar to most readers by the end of second grade (Fox, 2000). Young readers also find it easy to recognize and break compound words into meaningful chunks. Thus readers' ability to begin to recognize multiletter chunks can occur early on; however, these young readers may not be fully able to recognize these intact multiletter chunks as quickly as older readers who are in the consolidated alphabetic phase.

A sample lesson teaching students how to use structural analysis cues, or chunking, to recognize unfamiliar words is presented in Figure 7.10. Because the lesson focuses on teaching readers to look for the most recognizable suffixes, it is probably best suited for students in the late full alphabetic or early consolidated alphabetic phases of development. Similar lessons can certainly be used with prefixes, other suffixes, root words, or compound words. One of the key features to note in this lesson is how the concept of chunking is linked initially to a concrete analogy of adding and removing cars from a train, thus making the process more tangible. In addition, the lesson features brief texts (poems) that have several chunkable words in them (e.g., *-s*, *-ed*, and *-ing* suffixes) on which the instruction focuses. Finally, the lesson features modeling and demonstration by the teacher and affords students the opportunity to try chunking during guided practice with a partner. The "Chunkable Words" sheet that students complete as they read reiterates the procedural steps involved in chunking and provides the teacher with a means of assessing students' ability to recognize those words that are chunkable and to decode them using the strategy.

Using Context Cues

Context cues enable readers to form an expectation about the text (Ehri, 1991). These cues may come from the pictures, headings, subheadings, or text that surrounds a given word. Context cues enable readers to make a guess at what words would make sense in a given context—or at least to narrow down the range of possibilities.

In her review of research on word recognition, Juel (1991) noted that although the use of context has been shown to facilitate comprehension processes, the research supporting its use for word recognition is not substantive. Research has consistently shown

Teacher: Adapted from lessons by Kristin Zahn and Anita Brocker

Title: Chunking

Topic: Recognizing words using structural analysis cues (chunking)

Grade level: 2–4

STAIR hypothesis being addressed:
    Students are in the consolidated alphabetic phase of development. They are able to use letter–sound correspondences to decode words, but they have difficulty decoding polysyllabic words.

Goal of Lesson

Students will learn:
- To decode unfamiliar words that are big by chunking the words into smaller pieces and blending the pieces together
- Why chunking is helpful for reading unfamiliar words
- To look for suffixes in words and use them to decode unfamiliar words
- To cross-check to make sure that identified words make sense

Materials

- "The Invitation," a poem by Shel Silverstein in *Where the Sidewalk Ends;* written on chart paper
- "Spring," a poem by Karla Kuskin; written on chart paper
- Chart paper, markers
- Sticky notes
- Word wall
- Word cards with sample root words and suffixes (-s, -es, -ed, -ing)
- Model train
- "Chunkable Words" sheets

Reduce processing demands

Introduction

Show students the model train and explain that trains are comprised of lots of different cars. Demonstrate how you can add cars on and take them away to make the size of the train bigger or smaller. Explain that words are kind of the same. Big words, like trains that are really long, are usually made up of smaller words or word parts. Explain that today we are going to be learning how to add and delete word parts from big words to make them easier to read.

Declarative and conditional knowledge

Description of Instructional Experience

Declarative knowledge

Explain that today we will be learning a strategy called chunking that helps readers figure out unknown words. Note that the strategy works especially for big words. Explain that chunking involves breaking a word into smaller pieces and then blending the pieces back together again, just like pulling some of the cars off of a train and adding others.

(cont.)

FIGURE 7.10. Sample lesson teaching students to use structural analysis cues to recognize unknown words.

Declarative knowledge	Explain that today's lesson will focus on parts of words that get added to the end. Explain that a suffix is kind of like the caboose on the end of a train. These word parts are called suffixes. Explain that a suffix is a word part that can change the meaning of a word or add information about the word. Place a word card with a root word on it (e.g., *play*) on one of the cars on the train.
Declarative knowledge *Model/think-aloud* *Procedural knowledge*	Explain that the cars of the train are kind of like the root words in a word. Explain that the suffixes would go on the caboose, or at the end, of the train. Place a word card with the suffix *-s* on the caboose. Model and think aloud how you blend the word parts together. "If I didn't know this word when I first saw it, I'd look carefully at the whole word. Then I'd look at the beginning of the word for a prefix. I don't see one on this word. Then I look at the end of the word for a suffix. I do see an *s* added to the end of this word. So, I'm just going to 'chunk' it. That means I'm going to remove that word part to make the word smaller. This helps make the word easier to read. Now I see that the word I'm left with is *play*. Now that I've chunked the word into two parts, I have to blend it back together." Demonstrate how to blend each word part back together. "Now I have to cross-check to make sure it makes sense. *Plays*. That is a real word that makes sense." Now demonstrate how the meaning changes by adding a different suffix (*-ed* or *-ing*) to the end. Use the words in sentences to demonstrate the differences in meaning.
Conditional knowledge	Explain that we just added suffixes to the end of the root word, but when we are reading and see really long words that we can't read, we temporarily chunk off the suffixes so we can see all of the word parts. Then we blend them back together.
Model/think-aloud *Procedural knowledge*	Explain that we can use this strategy as we read. Explain that we are going to try using it while reading a poem entitled "Invitation." Have students think about what they know about invitations and make predictions about what the poem might be about. Display the poem "Invitation" on chart paper. Model and think aloud while reading the poem. As you encounter "chunkable" words containing the suffixes *-s*, *-es*, *-ed*, or *-ing*, stop and model the process of how you might go about reading the big word. Model the procedural knowledge of how to chunk the word and use the sticky notes to cover up the suffix temporarily so that you can focus on the root word. During the reblending step, uncover the suffix. Be sure to also model the cross-checking procedure in which you monitor the reblended word to make sure that the word is pronounceable and makes sense in the sentence. Continue modeling and thinking aloud in this manner as the rest of the poem is read.
	After reading the entire poem, have students engage in a discussion with a partner about how well their predictions matched the text. Then begin a discussion focused on the "chunkable" words. Add each new word to the word wall under the appropriate suffix (*s*, *-es*, *-ed*, or *-ing*) and reiterate how chunking helps when reading longer words.

(cont.)

FIGURE 7.10. *(cont.)*

*Guided practice
using comprehension
strategies*

Explain that students will now have an opportunity to use the strategy with a partner as they read a poem called "Spring" by Karla Kuskin. Have students share what good things they know to do before reading (read the title, think about what they know about spring, make predictions about what the poem might be about). Have each pair of students brainstorm and record their background knowledge and predictions on a web.

*Guided practice using
chunking*

Provide each pair of students with a copy of the poem, a sheet entitled "Chunkable Words," and sticky notes. Explain that as students read, they should watch for "chunkable" words and use the sticky notes to "chunk" them into readable portions before blending the word back together. Have students record their "chunkable" words on the sheet. The sheet should also serve to help students engage in all of the procedural steps involved in chunking. Explain that students can leave the sticky notes on the words that they chunked. After reading the poem, have students discuss their responses to, and predictions about, the poem.

Conclusion

Verbalization

Engage the whole group in a discussion in which students share their "chunkable" words and discuss which words they chunked, *how* they chunked the words, and *why* those particular words were chunkable. Have students explain and share whether the chunking strategy was helpful for them or not. Have students add the newly chunked words onto the word wall under the appropriate suffix.

Students can also look for chunkable words during their independent reading using this same procedure.

Assessment

- You will know whether students are able to decode unfamiliar polysyllabic words by chunking them into smaller pieces and blending the pieces together by observing their work with their partner as they read the poem and complete the "Chunkable Words" sheet.
- You will know if students know why chunking is helpful for reading unfamiliar words by their responses during the concluding discussion.
- You will know whether students are able to look for suffixes in words and use them to decode unfamiliar words by observing their work with their partner as they read the poem and complete the "Chunkable Words" sheet.
- You will know whether students are able to cross-check to make sure that identified words make sense by observing their work with their partner as they read the poem and complete the "Chunkable Words" sheet.

(cont.)

FIGURE 7.10. *(cont.)*

CHUNKABLE WORDS SHEET

Chunkable word (word and page number)	Is there a prefix?	Is there a root word?	Is there a suffix?	Cross-check	
				Can I pronounce it?	Does it make sense in the sentence?
[example] playing, 2	—	play	*-ing*	yes	yes

FIGURE 7.10. *(cont.)*

that poorer readers tend to rely on context for word recognition. Both Ehri (1991) and Juel (1991) noted that when a reader's ability to use graphic information (i.e., letter–sound cues) is limited, the reader compensates by relying on background knowledge and contextual information. Thus, the use of context cues as a word recognition strategy is recommended with caution.

Instruction focusing on context cues must emphasize that in order for the strategy to be helpful, the surrounding words must be known. That is, the unknown word must be surrounded by a known meaningful context. If the student is struggling to read a large portion of the text, there will not be a sufficient number of recognizable words to make the strategy successful. Likewise, if the surrounding context is not supportive, then students will have difficulty using contextual cues. For example, suppose a student came across the sentence "It was oppressive" in the course of reading. If the student has difficulty reading the word *oppressive*, and there are no other cues available to help him bring meaning to the word, then using context cues is certainly not a beneficial strategy for decoding the word. However, if the sentence were surrounded by other sentences that gave an indication of the meaning, then context cues might be more helpful: "It had been over ninety degrees every day for the past 2 weeks. The sun's rays were relentless, there was no trace of wind, and our air conditioner was broken. It was *oppressive*." In the second circumstance the sentences leading up to the unknown word provide the reader with meaningful cues (assuming the reader knows all of the words in those surrounding sentences). If the unknown word is not in the reader's spoken or listening vocabulary, then it is possible that not even a supportive context would help the reader decode the unknown word. That is, the reader may be able to gain a vague notion of what the word *oppressive* means by the surrounding context, but if he has never heard the word before, then even a highly descriptive context may not help him decode it. He may decide to skip over the word, having but a vague notion of the word's meaning and pronunciation.

During strategy instruction, these aspects of using context cues as a strategy for word recognition must be communicated to readers. They need to know under which conditions the strategy might and might not work (i.e., conditional knowledge), and they need to know that using context cues is not the way that readers recognize most unknown words. It is an additional strategy that comes in handy in those circumstances in which there is a very supportive context and in which most of the surrounding words are known.

Students who benefit most from instruction that focuses on using context cues are those who overrely on letter–sound cues to decode unknown words, as in the sample lesson in Figure 7.11. These students often mispronounce words when they are reading, and their miscues are nonsense words rather than real words (e.g., reading the word *corner* as *cormer*). Thus teaching these students to use context cues provides them with a strategy that helps them focus more on meaning than solely on graphic information to read unknown words. This is precisely the type of student that AnnaMaria Figliomeni had in mind when she designed the sample lesson in Figure 7.11. In her reflective memo she noted that although her student said that he sounded out words and used context cues when he came to unfamiliar words, her observations revealed that he relied solely on letter–sound cues and was not reading for meaning. Based on these observations, she designed lessons that would focus on teaching her student how to use context cues in conjunction with letter–sound cues to decode unknown words.

In the sample lesson the teacher began by using a concrete experience that would help her student link the use of context cues to building a puzzle. After teaching the lesson AnnaMaria noted:

> When [the student] assembled an unfinished Clifford [the dog] puzzle, I asked him to explain his thinking to put it together. Such thoughts as, "I knew this piece went here because his eyes are at the top" and "I'll put this piece back for later" were shared. Unknown to me at the time of planning my lesson was that his comments would serve as a springboard to analogize this process of putting a puzzle together with using context clues. The full impact of this experience was realized in my past session with [the student] when he stated, "I didn't know that before" and began applying [the context cue strategy] as he read. For example, while reading *Harry and Willy and Carrothead* [Caseley, 1991], [the student] came across the word *cooed*. At first he used a [sticky] note to indicate it was a CLUNK word, a word he could not say. However, he later removed the [sticky] note when he reached the end of the sentence. When asked how he got the word, [the student] replied, "It looked like *cooled* but it doesn't have the *l* and it wouldn't make sense, 'He cried and *cooed* and waved his arms like any baby.' "
>
> —ANNAMARIA FIGLIOMENI, reflective memo

Teacher:	Adapted from a lesson by AnnaMaria Figliomeni
Title:	Puzzle
Topic:	Recognizing words using context cues
Grade level:	1–4 (for higher grades alter text accordingly)

STAIR hypothesis being addressed:
Students rely on letter–sound cues as their primary decoding strategy at the expense of comprehension. Students may also have difficulty monitoring their understanding while reading.

Goal of Lesson

Students will learn:
• To decode unfamiliar words by using context cues along with letter–sound cues

Materials

• *There Was an Old Lady Who Swallowed a Fly* by Simms Taback (big book and little books)
• Sticky notes
• Puzzle
• Paper
• Markers

Reduce processing demands by using concrete experience

Verbalization

Introduction

Begin by presenting students with a puzzle that is partially completed. As students work to complete the puzzle, ask them to explain what they are thinking as they select pieces and fit them into place. The goal of this think-aloud is to get students to verbalize the process they use while working on the puzzle.

Description of Instructional Experience

Declarative knowledge

Procedural knowledge

Explain that when we put together a puzzle, we have to use the surrounding pieces to help us determine which pieces fit in the empty spots. Explain that when we read, using context cues is similar to this process. "When readers come to words they don't know, they can use what they do know and what they see in the text to help them figure out the words, much like you used the completed parts of the puzzle to help you fit in the missing pieces. This is called using context clues. By *context* I mean the other words in the sentence or even the pictures on the page. These other words and pictures can help you figure out what an unknown word is. So, if you see come across a 'clunk word' or a word that you don't know, think about how the words fit together in the sentence to make sense. First it is important to get an idea of what you are reading about. Skip the word you don't know and think about what kind of word might make sense in the sentence. If the other words in the sentence don't help, the pictures might. You can even look at the letters and sounds in the word you don't know to help you. All of these things can work together to help you figure out the word."

(cont.)

FIGURE 7.11. Sample lesson teaching students how to use context cues to recognize unknown words.

Model/think-aloud

Model the process of using context cues with the book *There Was an Old Lady Who Swallowed a Fly*. Begin by glancing at the cover and reading the title. For example, you might model what you would do if you did not know the word *lady* in the title. "I know an old . . . hmmm I don't know that word. I know an old BLANK who swallowed a fly. Hmmm, what word would fit in the title and make sense?" Cover the unknown word with a sticky note so students can see how you would focus on meaning first and then use letter–sound cues to verify

Procedural knowledge

your context-based guesses. Have students generate a list of words that might possibly fit in the blank and list them on the board. "The only context I have is the rest of the words in the title and the picture. When I look at the picture, I see two children and an old woman. The title 'I know an old BLANK' gives me the clue that there is something or somebody old. The only old person I see in the picture is an old woman. Let's see if that fits, or makes sense, in the title 'I know an old *woman* who swallowed a fly.' Yes, that makes sense. Let me look at the first letter of the word to see if it begins with /w/." Reveal the first letter by moving the sticky note over. "Oh, the first letter is *l*. Now I need to think if I know a word that means the same thing as 'woman' that begins with *l*. Can anyone think of a word that means 'woman' that beings with *l*?" Have students think about words that might fit those two clues. List the words on the board or on chart paper. Then reveal the remaining letters in the word and cross-check with the words on the board to see where it occurs.

Conditional knowledge

Explain that this process is similar to the way we determined which puzzle pieces fit into the empty spaces. Explain that we can only use context cues to help us if we can read or carefully observe all of the cues in the words and pictures surrounding the unknown word.

Before continuing with the book, have students make predictions about what might happen in the book based on the title and picture clues. After sharing their thoughts with a partner, students can write their predictions in their prediction logs. Begin reading the book aloud, stopping to model in places where there might be a word that students cannot recognize. After modeling a few more words using this procedure, have students work with a partner to continue reading the story. Have students use sticky notes to cover up words they do not know and then think aloud with their partner as they work to use context cues to figure out their unknown words. As students work together, carefully observe and take anecdotal notes on their ability to use the context cue strategy.

Model/think-aloud

Guided practice

Verbalization

Once students finish reading the book, have them share their thoughts and reactions about the book with their partner. Encourage students to discuss how well their original predictions matched the text.

Conclusion

Procedural knowledge

Gather students together and have them share some of the unknown words in which they tried to use context cues to help them deduce the word.

(cont.)

FIGURE 7.11. *(cont.)*

Verbalization	Have students explain the procedure they used and how well it worked. Students might elect to actually model the procedure they used, explaining how it worked by using the big book version of the text and a sticky note. Be sure to talk about those conditions under which using the context cues may not have worked as well as those that did. This will help students understand that sometimes the context is not always helpful for recognizing unknown words.
Verbalization	
Verbalization	Have students share what they learned about using context cues and use this discussion to review the declarative, procedural, and conditional knowledge associated with its use.

Assessment

- You will know whether students can decode unfamiliar words by using context cues along with letter–sound cues by observing them as they work with their partners, using sticky notes and verbalizing their thinking about context cues while completing the reading of the book.

FIGURE 7.11. *(cont.)*

AnnaMaria's reflections show that sometimes strategy use takes a while to gel. Her first lesson on using context cues was taught in early March, but her student was not able to begin using the strategy on his own until several weeks later, after consistent modeling, demonstration, and guided practice in a variety of contexts.

COORDINATING FLEXIBLE USE OF SETS OF STRATEGIES

AnnaMaria's lesson in Figure 7.11 also features the coordinated use of context cues and letter–sound cues. This coordination is essential for all strategy use. Strategies are rarely used in isolation. They are coordinated as sets that are used flexibly and in conjunction with one another. Thus instruction must provide students with the opportunity to see how strategies are used together and how they are mutually supportive. Making this coordinated use of strategies visible requires a great deal of modeling, demonstration, and thinking aloud about the thought processes that occur while reading.

The Chunkable Words sheet in Figure 7.10 is useful for students to complete as they are learning how to use strategies flexibly. As they begin to make their lists of unknown words and the strategies they used to decode them, discussions can revolve around the conditions under which various strategies worked and did not work. As well, students can study the types of words that lent themselves to decoding using a particular strategy. Such study and reflection can help students realize that polysyllabic words lend themselves better to decoding by chunking than by letter–sound cues. Even though our instruction might directly communicate this information, sometimes it takes extensive use of strategies, and reflection on such use, before students begin to understand fully the conditional knowledge associated with each strategy.

SUMMARY

This chapter provided an overview of relevant research, sample lessons, and guidelines for instruction in teaching readers to use word recognition strategies. Relevant theory pertaining to the phases of reading development was discussed and connected to authentic teaching contexts and sample lessons. These phases of development are the prealphabetic phase, partial alphabetic phase, full alphabetic phase, consolidated alphabetic phase, and fluent recognition phase. The sample lessons focused on five ways that readers learn to recognize words: using sight words, using letter–sound cues, analogizing, using structural analysis (chunking), and using context cues.

CHAPTER EIGHT

The Path to Becoming
a Successful Strategies Teacher

" It is not easy to be a strategic teacher." These words appeared repeatedly as Janice read and reread her graduate students' reflective memos and portfolios. She told them that it wasn't easy at the beginning of the semester, when they began learning about teaching strategic reading processes. It is a long and difficult journey—one that many teachers do not embark upon in their careers. The intense reflection and personal growth that must accompany strategy instruction is often painful. The goal of this chapter is to explore this growth process. Research-based descriptions of teachers' growth and progress are presented, followed by an examination of their triumphs, difficulties, and emotional reactions as they learned to teach strategic processing.

GROWTH AS TEACHERS OF STRATEGIC PROCESSING

Research to date has suggested conclusively that learning to become an effective teacher of strategic processing takes time (Anderson, 1992; Anderson & Roit, 1993; Brown & Coy-Ogan, 1993; Duffy 1993a, 1993b; El-Dinary & Schuder, 1993; Pressley, Schuder, SAIL Faculty and Administration, Bergman, & El-Dinary, 1992). It is a lengthy process that takes years before teachers feel comfortable implementing it. One reason may be, as Anderson and Roit (1993) noted, that "it is a learning-based rather than activity-based way of teaching, and thus, teachers must understand it at a deeper level" (p. 133).

Although Anderson and Roit (1993) noted that the teachers in their study took up to two years to learn to teach strategies comfortably and flexibly, several studies of teachers learning to teach transactional strategies instruction (TSI) reported that this process can take up to 3 years (Pressley, El-Dinary, et al., 1992). Brown and Coy-Ogan (1993) found that becoming an effective strategy teacher was a long and difficult process and that the teacher in their case study progressed through similar phases of development as her students did, as they learned to become independent strategy users. Brown and Coy-Ogan also found that the teacher's growth and development followed a pattern similar to Hall and Hord's (1987) concerns-based adoption model of teacher change. Initially, teacher implementation of strategy instruction was mechanical and routinized. This stage was followed by one of experimentation, in which the teacher altered her procedures and tried variations of the more routinized ones with which she began. Finally, she internalized and personalized her instruction. Anderson (1992) found that the teachers in her experimental study also followed a similar pattern of growth.

In their study of teachers' acceptance of TSI, El-Dinary and Schuder (1993) found that for effective professional development, teachers must (1) experience a safe, supportive environment in which to learn; (2) be respected as professionals; (3) receive explanations and modeling of what good instruction looks like; and (4) engage in interactive coaching to help them solve instructional difficulties. Like other researchers, El-Dinary and Schuder found that it took years of development before their teachers felt comfortable implementing strategy instruction.

Duffy (1993a, 1993b) examined 11 teachers' growth and development across a 5-year period, as they became expert strategy teachers. Duffy (1993a) described strategies as "plans for solving problems encountered in constructing meaning" (p. 232). He further described a good strategy user as someone who "consciously adapts individual strategies within an overall plan for constructing meaning" and "who uses *sets* of strategies, *coordinates* those strategies, and *shifts* strategies when appropriate" (p. 232, emphasis original). Duffy's definitions suggest that teaching students to be strategic involves much more than teaching students individual strategies such as predicting and setting purposes. Teaching students to be strategic means teaching them a way of thinking about what it means to be strategic, and teaching them how to adapt and use individual strategies flexibly, in combination with one another, as an integrated set with which to construct meaning.

Points of Progress

Duffy (1993b) conducted two interviews with each teacher each year and wrote descriptions of each teacher's experience based on these interviews. Teacher interviews and transcripts were then analyzed using qualitative methods of analytic induction, in which interviews were read and reread to identify any recurring comments and themes. These recurring comments and themes were grouped together to form categories. The teacher descriptions were rewritten, using the teachers' words as much as possible. Duffy found that the teachers in his longitudinal study experienced nine "points of progress" (p. 113) as they grew in their ability to teach strategic processing. He cautioned that these points of progress were not to be viewed as linear developmental stages but as a recursive process that was affected by social, cultural, and experiential conditions. Each point of progress is briefly described below.

Point 1: Confusion and Rejection

Duffy (1993b) noted that teachers generally experienced confusion and rejection at this point in the beginning of the project. As in other staff development projects, the teachers expected to receive a set of materials to follow; however, in this case they were expected to create their own program. Many teachers suggested that they could not create their own program because they were expected to follow their basal textbooks. It was inconceivable to them that they could create their own program, based on the needs and interests of their students.

Point 2: Teacher Controls the Strategies

At this point teachers used individual strategies in conjunction with the stories in their basal textbooks or with children's literature or content-area lessons. During these lessons, the teacher engaged students in using strategies (i.e., setting purposes, making predictions, tapping into background knowledge); however, only the teacher was aware of the strategic processing. The students passively responded to the teacher's request to activate background knowledge or set purposes. The teacher was doing all of the active processing and decision making regarding *where* and *when* strategies would be used. Strategy use was implicit, and the teacher did not explain the declarative, procedural, or conditional knowledge associated with strategy use. Students were not involved in actively planning or initiating strategy use. Duffy (1993b) noted that postlesson interviews with students revealed that better readers were able to glean information about strategy use from such implicit lessons, but poorer readers were completely unaware of the strategies.

Point 3: Trying Out

Teachers at this point realized that less proficient readers needed more explicit instruction to become aware of strategies. These teachers were interested in acquiring lists of strategies recommended by experts. Their lessons often focused on explicit instruction of strategies in isolation and were taught without texts at the end of the reading period. These teachers named strategies (e.g., predicting), made generic statements about their importance, and gave specific steps to follow to perform the strategy. Teachers did not relate strategies to one another or talk about an overall strategic approach to constructing meaning. Strategies were taught individually, using worksheets, and they were taught apart from real-world literacy situations. After these lessons, students could identify the strategies they had learned and provide a generic statement about their importance, but they could not describe the conditional knowledge associated with *when* they should be used or the declarative knowledge of *what* function was served by each strategy.

Point 4: Modeling Process into Content

Teachers at this point were still concerned about teaching the "right" strategies, but they were more concerned about helping their students gain metacognitive control of the strategy process. They shifted to teaching strategies before students read texts, and they explicitly related strategy use to the text rather than teaching it in isolation or at the end of the reading period. However, teachers at this point did not embed instruction in authentic literacy tasks. They also modeled the thinking associated with the given strategy by performing think-alouds. Students were much better able to express the function of strategies and the thinking that occurred when using each, but they were not aware of *why* they were learning a particular strategy or *when* to use it (i.e., conditional knowledge).

Point 5: The Wall

At this point teachers began to realize that modeling strategic thinking and providing explicit instruction were not enough. They noticed that students thought only in terms of individual strategies, rather than sets of strategies, as they read authentic texts, and the teachers felt the need to make strategy use more genuine and useful. These teachers, who were once euphoric and confident, now felt emotionally drained and guilty because they were not doing enough for their students. Duffy (1993b) noted that this was a pivotal point in teachers' progress. Many sought ways to simplify strategy teaching. They yearned for lists of strategies, commercially prepared materials, packaged programs, and directives from staff developers that would enable them to fit strategy instruction within the traditional school framework. These teachers still wanted to exert some measure of control over the curriculum.

Point 6: Over the Hump

Teachers at this point realized that strategy instruction is much more complex than teaching individual strategies. They were less concerned about a list of "approved" strategies to teach and focused instead on teaching students to approach text strategically as independent problem solvers. They realized that there is no one way to make sense of text or to approach text and sought ways to impart the flexibility inherent in this understanding to students. Teachers integrated reading and strategy use into authentic contexts in which students had a goal to achieve, a problem to solve, or a product to create. These integrated units were keyed to students' interests, which further motivated them to make sense of the texts through strategy use, thereby accomplishing the task. Students in these lessons began to talk about strategy use as a means to an end rather than as the end product of a lesson.

Point 7: "I Don't Quite Get It Yet"

Teachers at this point were characterized as still holding onto the belief that there is a "right" way to teach strategies. These teachers were uncomfortable modifying strategies in relation to their students, the texts, and the contexts in which the strategies were used. They continued to seek out authorities to "approve" their methods rather than creating their own variations.

Point 8: Creative–Inventive

These teachers were comfortable and secure with their understanding of strategic processing and how to teach it and were able to create, revise, or invent strategies. They observed and listened to their students carefully to determine the direction in which instruction needed to go. There was no preplanned agenda or curriculum, and they no longer sought out lists of "approved" strategies. Their students engaged in authentic reading and writing that centered on units of interest to them and used strategies to construct meaning. As teachers observed their students, they noticed when explicit instruction on a given strategy or set of strategies might be helpful and provided it.

Duffy (1993b) noted three conditions associated with teachers at Point 8: They gave control to students, were willing to fail, and tolerated ambiguity. These teachers provided opportunities for students to direct the course of their own learning but stood alongside them to provide scaffolded support when necessary. When their efforts or their lessons failed, they viewed these failures as learning opportunities. Now comfortable with the complex nature of strategy instruction and the ambiguity that goes with such instruction, they often realized that the lessons they had planned were not needed or appropriate, and they were flexible enough to make adjustments and to be responsive to their students' needs. They comprehended the dynamic, changing nature of strategy instruction and were able to communicate this process to students, as they engaged in authentic reading and writing.

Point 9: Unnamed

Duffy (1993b) did not observe Point 9, but he and the teachers with whom he worked expected to continue to grow and develop. They assumed that they were not at an end point in their understanding of strategy instruction.

This type of growth and development are difficult to accomplish in teacher preparation programs primarily because of the finite nature of semester-long courses that are often devoid of authentic teaching experiences. The teachers in Duffy's (1993b) study felt that teacher education about strategy instruction needed to occur in classrooms where teachers could see strategy instruction in action and use what they were learning. They felt that learning to write lessons for the professor was inauthentic, that lessons needed to be planned for real students in real contexts. Duffy's teachers also felt that professors and teacher educators needed to attend not just to the cognitive dimensions of teacher development but the affective dimensions as well.

Teaching Shifts

Although Duffy's (1993b) points of progress provide useful markers for teachers to see how their development is progressing over the long-term, it is also important to look at development at a more local level. That is, Duffy's (1993b) points of progress illustrate holistic changes in teachers, but it is also important to see what kinds of changes happen on a smaller scale in terms of the way teachers talk and in terms of what they include in their lessons on strategic processing. Some researchers have therefore examined the shifts that occur as teachers learn to teach strategic processing.

Anderson and Roit's (1993) study of middle and high school teachers identified 20 teacher shifts observed over a 3-month time period as teachers learned to implement strategies instruction. Teacher shifts were defined as "changes that need to be made in teaching to encourage active reading" (p. 131). Teachers in the experimental group were taught how to implement collaborative strategy instruction with small groups of students, and teachers in the control group taught small groups of students as they normally would. Teachers' lessons were observed and videotaped and rated on several shift dimensions. The dimensions represent the principles for fostering active, strategic reading that were taught during the professional development sessions. Table 8.1 displays the dimensions and how each of the 20 types of shifts is related to the varied dimensions. The teachers who learned how to implement collaborative strategy instruction displayed significantly greater numbers of shifts than control teachers. Their initial lessons tended to exhibit behaviors in the "Teacher Shifts From" column in Table 8.1. Three months later teachers' lessons exhibited shifts reflected in the "Teacher Shifts To" column. These shifts represent substantive changes in the ways teachers approached instruction. Their instruction began to focus more on the reading process and less on products, more on students learning how to be strategic and less on students getting the right answers, more on developing students' ability to control the strategic process and less on teacher guidance and control, and more on student collaboration and less on individual student growth.

TABLE 8.1. Anderson and Roit's (1993) Dimensions of Teacher Shifts

Dimension	Teacher shifts	
	From . . .	To . . .
Treat reading problems openly as objects of inquiry	1. Focusing on smooth and errorless reading.	1. Welcoming reading problems as objects of inquiry.
Focus on how to solve problems: Emphasis of instruction is on process rather than product; on learning how to do something rather than simply getting answers right; on learning strategies to help reading (learning goals) rather than simply understanding the content of a particular text (task goals).	2. Focusing on and provides "right" answers.	2. Focusing on how to solve problems.
	6. Teaching a strategy in the same way even after it is mastered.	6. Introducing increasingly complex strategy use.
	12. Focusing on content recall.	12. Focusing on understanding.
	13. Avoiding teaching during actual reading.	13. Teaching during reading to ensure understanding.
	18. Teaching the same approach to all texts.	18. Fitting strategies to appropriate texts.
Emphasis should be placed on new learning rather than on what the students already know.	5. Focusing on what students know.	5. Focusing on new learning.
	4. Focusing on students' interests, assuming that learning takes place.	4. Focusing on what students are learning, keeping interests in mind.
	10. Emphasizing getting reading finished.	10. Emphasizing learning from and about reading.
Emphasis should be placed on keeping the students informed of purposes, problems, and progress.	11. Not informing students of purposes.	11. Telling students what they will be learning and why it is worth learning.
Provide models of thinking	7. Modeling answers.	7. Modeling and encouraging students to model thinking.
Ask thought-provoking questions	3. Asking content-based questions that apply only to the present text.	3. Emphasizing asking content-free questions that apply to many texts.
	15. Beginning session with motivators; ends with questions.	15. Beginning session with goal setting/predictions; ends by returning to them.
	20. Presenting only very easy material.	20. Presenting somewhat challenging material.
Allow student control	8. Maintaining control of what is to be learned.	8. Letting students take control of what is to be learned.
	9. Doing most of the hard thinking.	9. Teaching students to do the hard thinking.
	14. Beginning session by asking questions or telling about the text.	14. Beginning session by having students skim to form their own impressions and goals.

(cont.)

TABLE 8.1. *(cont.)*

Dimension	Teacher shifts	
	From . . .	To . . .
Allow student control (cont.)	16. Deciding which words and ideas in a text will be difficult.	16. Teaching students to determine difficult words and ideas.
Focus on group collaboration Acquiring reading know-how should be a collaborative enterprise between students and teacher, with the collaborators sharing their discoveries, insights, problems, and strategies and working together to attain reading/learning goals.	17. Focusing on individual performance and success. 19. Encouraging homogeneity so that everyone will show the same accomplishments.	17. Focusing on group collaboration. 19. Encouraging different competencies so that students can share ideas.

Note. Adapted from Anderson and Roit (1993). Copyright 1993 by the University of Chicago Press. Adapted by permission.

Brown (2008) was also interested in the changes that occurred in teachers' instructional practice. She examined how teachers who were learning to implement TSI differed from those teachers who were not trained to use TSI. She found that teachers differed primarily along three dimensions: (1) how they communicated information about strategic processing to students, (2) the strategies on which they focused, and (3) the manner in which they evaluated students. In terms of communicating information about strategic processing, TSI teachers tended to provide overt, explicit explanations of strategic processing and modeled their thinking by verbalizing their reasoning. As well, the TSI teachers tended to explain strategic benefits. Non-TSI teachers, however, tended to deliver information without explaining processing or modeling.

The TSI teachers also differed in terms of the strategies on which they focused. TSI teachers focused on a much wider range of comprehension strategies, including predicting, making connections to prior knowledge, summarizing, visualizing, and clarifying confusions. On the other hand, the non-TSI teachers focused primarily on predicting and making connections to prior knowledge.

Finally, the manner in which students were evaluated differed. The non-TSI teachers tended to ask more text-based questions, evaluated the correctness of students' responses, and complimented students' responses. Because strategic processing varies from reader to reader, evaluation does not tend to have "right" or "wrong" answers. Instead, teachers attempt to teach students to evaluate their own progress. Thus, TSI teachers did not engage in as much evaluative behavior related to asking questions, evaluating students' responses, or praising students' responses.

Sailors and Price (2010) examined teachers' instructional changes also, but they were more interested in how the type of professional development related to strategy instruction affected teachers' instruction and their students' achievement. Their research examined whether simply attending a traditional 2-day summer workshop (partial intervention) or attending the 2-day summer workshop followed by classroom-based support from a reading coach (full intervention) had a greater impact on teachers' strategy instruction and students' achievement. Observations revealed that teachers in both groups were able to implement strategy instruction to some degree. However, those teachers who received the additional coaching provided significantly more opportunities to engage in intentional comprehension strategy instruction in class. Like the TSI teachers in Brown's (2008) study, the teachers receiving coaching provided significantly more opportunities for explicit explanations of strategic processing that included declarative, procedural, and conditional knowledge. The students in the full intervention classes also scored significantly higher on standardized tests of reading comprehension than students in the partial intervention classes.

EXAMPLES OF TEACHERS' GROWTH AND DEVELOPMENT

Although learning to become a "strategies teacher" is a lengthy process, the studies reviewed above suggest that instructional changes are obvious and student achievement is enhanced. With these thoughts in mind, Janice began rethinking her own graduate courses while she was teaching at the University at Buffalo. The course that she taught on strategic reading processes was an elective in the master's program in literacy at the University at Buffalo. Teachers entering the course had at least two graduate courses in literacy that focused on childhood literacy methods and assessment. Some had many more literacy courses. Teachers in the master's program in literacy education at the University at Buffalo at that time had two options. They could pursue a 36-credit program that produced graduates who have a master's degree in education and certification as a literacy specialist in the state of New York, or they could pursue a 33-credit program that produced graduates who have a master's degree in education with an emphasis in literacy education. The latter program did not yield certification as a literacy specialist. Its goal was to provide classroom teachers with additional courses in literacy education (18 credits), but it did not include all of the clinical work that was required in the literacy specialist program. Both programs, however, required teachers to be involved in a 3-credit supervised school-based literacy practicum. The 6-week school-based practicum was held in the summer in a local school district and required teams of graduate students (usually a literacy specialist and a literacy emphasis student) to work with small groups of struggling readers. At the conclusion of the practicum, students wrote case study reports of each child with whom they had worked. The case study detailed each child's strengths and needs, described the program of instruction that was developed based on those strengths and needs, and summarized how the child responded to the instruction. These case study reports were given to school administrators, teachers, and parents.

    The intent of the practicum was to imitate the context in which the graduate students might find themselves when working as teachers in schools. They learned to plan and implement instruction for struggling readers, but they also learned how to work with colleagues. In this sense, we tried to imitate the "push-in" model of instruction, in which the literacy specialist worked collaboratively with the classroom teacher to plan and implement instruction in the classroom (see Klenk & Almasi, 1997, for further explanation). Working in pairs enabled teachers to learn how to plan collaboratively and to serve alternately in the classroom as instructor or observer.

    The course in teaching strategic reading processes was an elective that teachers often took just prior to participating in this intense school-based practicum. In the course teachers began learning what was involved in strategic processing and how to teach and assess it. In the spring of 2000 before the first edition of this text was written, they were required to work one on one with a struggling reader as a way to implement what they were learning about teaching strategic processes. The course requirements included planning at least eight 1-hour lessons with a struggling reader. These lessons operated within the framework of ongoing assessment described in Chapter 4, in which observation, assessment, and instruction inform one another simultaneously. Using the STAIR model described in Chapter 4, teachers learned to generate hypotheses based on these observations, assessments, and instruction. Teachers wrote full lesson plans similar to those presented in Chapters 6 and 7. They were expected to provide the marginal glosses on the sides of their lessons to indicate each element of the CESI model that was operating in their lesson. The intent of this part of the assignment was to help them become more metacognitively aware of critical elements of strategy instruction as they planned. In contrast to the lessons in Chapters 6 and 7, students' lesson plans also included a research-based rationale for their instruction, and they had a concluding section in which they tried to anticipate instructional challenges.

After each lesson, teachers wrote a reflective memo that detailed what they had learned during their observations and experiences with their case study students. The goal was to articulate and share discoveries, insights, and reflections that occurred to them about the process of teaching strategic processing to students, as they attempted to integrate the course readings with their experiences. The focus in these reflective memos was on *their* growth and development as a *teacher* of strategic processing, rather than on their students' growth.

The final course requirement was a process portfolio in which students displayed, reported, and detailed their growth as a learner and teacher of strategic processing. Their portfolios included the reflective memos from each meeting with their case study student as well as any other evidence of their progress as a learner and teacher of strategic processing (e.g., data from case study student, audiotapes, videotapes, artwork, music, narratives, articles that had had a significant impact, pictures, graphic organizers). Teachers were asked to find a creative means of collecting, organizing, and presenting their development. They wrote a metacognitive analysis of their development in terms of their strengths, areas of growth, and areas of improvement; they were encouraged to make connections to texts read, class discussions, and their work with their case study student to illustrate how their growth and development were affected by those external influences.

It is the work of these 19 former graduate students that informs the remainder of this chapter. As recommended by the research of El-Dinary and Schuder (1993), Janice designed the course to be taught in the same flexible manner that strategy instruction should proceed. Thus, although there was an initial syllabus, the content of the course was altered and modified continually, based on the needs of her students. She tried to model the process of good strategy instruction in which the teacher responds to students' needs on a moment-by-moment basis. This meant that, at times, what she had planned for a 3-hour class needed to be altered considerably. Although they closed each weekly class by creating the following week's agenda together, the teachers found that as they read their assignments and worked with their students throughout the week, they needed assistance in areas other than what we had previously planned. Sometimes teachers requested alterations to the planned agenda even at the beginning of class. Janice often found herself going back to her office during their small-group discussions or during a break to gather the necessary materials to quickly adjust to their needs.

Janice also read and responded to their lesson plans and reflective memos as they were submitted, and she responded to portions of their case study reports prior to their final due date. However, she did not read or respond to their process portfolios until they were completed. Janice then analyzed all of these written documents, using analytic inductive methods. That is, she read and reread all documents (152 lesson plans, 152 reflective memos, 19 case study reports, and 19 process portfolios) and her own comments on them on multiple occasions. As she reread these documents, she made notes regarding strengths, weaknesses, and growth patterns for each student. She color-coded relevant portions of these documents to highlight various strengths and weaknesses and grouped them into categories. She then recorded the categories on a grid and mapped out each student's growth and development across the eight lessons and his or her final portfolio reflection. As she repeatedly read and reread the documents, patterns and trends emerged regarding the aspects of strategies instruction that were relatively easy and painless for teachers to implement and those aspects that were more challenging. This chapter concludes with examples of their responses, "In Their Own Words," as they learned to teach strategic processes.

PAINLESS ASPECTS

Although the teachers encountered difficulties and frustrations, they also experienced their share of successes and triumphs. Many teachers found that they learned and grew the most in those areas in which they had had difficulty. In this sense they (and Janice) considered such growth a triumph. However, there were two areas in which they met with success from the onset: (1) creating a safe environment that fostered student motivation and self-esteem, and (2) being flexible and maintaining an open mind. Both of these triumphs are described below, using the teachers' own words whenever possible.

Creating a Safe Environment

Although the teachers had difficulty learning how to reduce processing demands and designing guided practice so that a safe environment was nurtured, from the beginning they recognized the importance of creating an environment in which students would feel comfortable taking risks. Some of the teachers immediately recognized their students' passivity, lack of motivation, or negative attitude while reading and worked diligently to gain each student's trust. They found the course readings helpful in gaining an understanding of the theoretical reasons why students have low self-esteem, low motivation, and negative attitudes. In her final portfolio reflection, one teacher noted:

> The Johnston [and Winograd] (1985) article was a real eyeopener for me. It states that less successful children are treated differently from more successful children in several ways, which make it easy for less successful children to attribute their failure to low ability (p. 285). I believe this is true especially from what I am observing in middle school. The teachers are giving me the impression that the lower achieving kids are not putting in enough effort. They may not be putting in effort because they are not being motivated in the right way. The teachers seem to not even consider the affective domain. I do not see them trying to create a safe environment for the students.

The teachers often noted that, during the lessons, their students would say things like, "Wow, I can really do this." They noticed their students smiling more, exuding a relaxed posture, and verbalizing more as they gained trust in one another. One teacher, who had been working with a quiet child who viewed reading very negatively, noted in her final portfolio reflection that creating a safe and relaxed environment for her student was an area in which she had had great success by reducing processing demands, engaging the child in motivating activities that taught her how to be strategic, and sharing her own (the teacher's) difficulties while reading. One very successful incident occurred during her fourth lesson when she detected the fragility of the student's self-esteem through an unplanned, informal conversation and was able to gain her trust and respect by sharing how she struggles when she reads difficult texts:

> While talking with [the student] I was telling her what I do if I am not sure about a word or what something means. She said, "I'm sure you probably know all the words already. You probably don't have to do anything." I found this to be the perfect opportunity to pull out my articles and notebook from this class. I showed her how I have to underline things I think are important, how I put notes in the margins, how I constantly reread, and how I ask questions in class in order to understand what I have to read for my class. I think that she was very surprised to see how much I have to do in order to understand what I read. [The student] then began to tell me whatever she does is not good enough for her parents, so she feels as though she shouldn't do anything. She made several other comments to me that revealed her negative attitudes and lack of self-confidence toward reading, especially when it comes to academics. [The student] was much more open and talkative than she had been in the past. Since I got to the school early, and it was during her snack and free time, I spent this time talking with her and her friends. I think that this really made her feel a lot more comfortable and contributed to her openness when it actually came time to do a lesson. In the future, I am going to try and arrive to the school a little early so that [the student] can have the opportunity to become more relaxed before working with me on the lesson. It seemed as though something as simple as this made a difference when working with her.

This teacher used skillful observation and quick thinking to make the most out of this situation. In so doing, she was able to help her student understand that good readers need to work hard to make sense of text—constructing meaning is difficult for everyone. This insight enabled her student to feel a little better about her own struggles and helped her see her teacher as someone with whom she could talk openly and candidly.

Many of the teachers in the class had never worked intensely with struggling readers in a one-on-one situation; they had never had the type of intimate contact with a struggling reader that would help them understand the frustration. One teacher shared an experience that she'd had with her student, in which she realized how motivation affects students' attitudes: "I think the greatest lesson I learned was that motivation is definitely an important component when working with struggling readers. When I took the book out for my student to start reading, her whole attitude changed. She became reluctant and quiet, and I felt that I was pulling responses or answers out of her." This teacher was observant and noticed the affective changes in her student as they switched gears from using strategies with more concrete (i.e., semiotic) texts to using them with more abstract (i.e., linguistic) texts. We often miss these subtle behavioral changes when working with students in a whole-class atmosphere. Near the end of the semester, after the teacher had successfully captivated and motivated her student by reducing processing demands and linking strategy instruction to authentic contexts, this same teacher was able to understand her student's initial frustration and lack of motivation by comparing it to her own frustrations as she struggled to learn about strategy instruction:

> I keep thinking about how I felt throughout the course of this semester and all of the emotions that I have gone through at one time or another. Then I think about [the student] and how it must feel to sit in class day after day and really struggle with reading. I think that I gained the important perspective of a student rather than a teacher over the past few months. To be an effective reading teacher I think that a person has to look past all of the best methods and ideas at times and really take a look at the student. This lesson also made me rethink the effect that motivation can have on a student. [The student] went from almost not wanting to participate in this lesson to almost not wanting this lesson to come to an end. That was a huge difference in attitude than when we first started working together. I think that in the beginning her motivation was that her mom was telling her that she was going to be working with me. Now I feel like she (almost) looks forward to working with me because she wants to see what I will do next. I think that this has definitely helped her to make some of the progress that she has made.

These teachers' comments show their success at capturing their students' attention and creating a safe environment in which to try out new strategies. They were able to motivate their students and gain their trust. At the beginning of the course, Janice emphasized how crucial the environment was for successful strategy instruction. Without a safe environment, students do not feel comfortable exposing their inadequacies or exploring new ideas. Although the teachers struggled with many aspects of strategy instruction, they were very successful in the area that is truly the most important and fundamental aspect of CESI—creating a safe environment.

Flexibility and Open-Mindedness

The teachers in Janice's class were also very successful at demonstrating flexibility and open-mindedness. They felt that their growth as strategy teachers was due, in large part, to their "willingness to try new things" and to be "flexible enough to modify their thinking," as one teacher put it. They noted the importance of seeing themselves as lifelong learners and viewed their growth as strategy teachers to be unfinished. In short, they recognized how difficult strategy instruction is and realized that, after working diligently and reflecting deeply on their practice, they still were not quite "there" yet. They grew accustomed to the ambiguity and uncertainty that accompany strategy instruction and realized that, instead of trying to control the process, they had to be flexible and open-minded to understand it better. One teacher noted that she was used to being a passive learner who took notes and waited for information to be given to her. She found that being a strategy teacher required something different of her—there were no neat and tidy answers or solutions. To teach strategies, one had to be strategic—which meant taking an active part in one's own learning:

> The reason that I felt like I was muddling through the first few lessons was that that is what I was actually doing. I was teaching lessons using the pieces of knowledge

that I had and not really making any connections between the two parts—the information/ideas and the actual putting it into practice. I believe that this is what led me to have the feelings of confusion and frustration that I did. I thought that the pieces were going to naturally fall into place. Once I realized that this was not going to happen, and that I had to be the one that took some initiative to make some of the pieces come together (make connections), I had to go from being a passive learner to an active one who had to try and connect the information that I had.

This is exactly what we must teach children to do as they learn to become strategic. They must be actively involved in their own learning in authentic situations, so that they learn how to solve problems in the contexts in which they encounter them. It is much easier and more comfortable to sit passively and absorb information. The class in which Janice's graduate students were enrolled required them to be active participants in their own learning. Although difficult and different for many of them, they accepted the challenge (albeit, reluctantly for some), and this acceptance became one of their biggest triumphs.

The teachers showed that they were able to adjust their instruction flexibly, in response to their students' needs. They grew into this area of strength because of their desire to help the children with whom they worked. Many of the teachers noted this point in their final portfolio reflections. One teacher described this process in the following manner:

> As I continued to work with my student, I realized that it was much more important to make sure that she understood the concept being taught than just getting through the entire planned lesson. For example, there were many times that I had to change what we were going to do when we were in the middle of a lesson. I would realize that another strategy had to be reinforced or that she just wasn't getting it. In the beginning of the semester changing plans midway flustered me; I wanted to cover as much as I could possibly cover in the plan. By the time I taught the third lesson, I realized the importance in making sure my student understood what the strategy was, how it could be utilized, and when and why it would be appropriate rather than just trying to get through a lesson because that was the initial plan. Therefore, I feel that this experience has made me much more flexible in adjusting instruction *while* I am teaching.

While working with their students, the teachers realized that they had to "be flexible, open-minded, and willing to do whatever it takes to help." Coming to this realization is another great triumph because it shows that these teachers were forming habits of mind for teaching that are not discernible from written lesson plans and are possible only because of the fabric of one's being.

CHALLENGING ASPECTS

Teachers' difficulties and frustrations were manifested primarily via their lesson planning, their reflective memos, and their process portfolios. Often what initially was a difficulty or a frustration became a triumph over the course of the semester. Although a total of 20 distinct difficulties emerged from the analysis, only the 5 most common difficulties are presented below; the other difficulties did not occur with enough frequency to warrant any sort of generalizability. Student teachers had difficulty with:

- Explicit instruction
- Reducing processing demands
- Unfocused lessons
- Planning coherent lessons
- Distinguishing between skills, strategies, and activities

Explicit Instruction

The teachers initially had great difficulty including explicit instruction in their lessons. The element that gave them the most difficulty was communicating the underlying declarative, procedural, and conditional knowledge associated with strategic processing. The second aspect of explicit instruction that was problematic was providing enough modeling and guided practice to facilitate students' successful implementation.

Communicating Declarative, Procedural, and Conditional Knowledge

Understanding the concepts underlying declarative, procedural, and conditional knowledge presented the greatest difficulty for Janice's graduate students. Although 12 of the 19 teachers had taken their previous childhood literacy methods course with Janice, where they were introduced to the notion of strategy instruction and the importance of declarative, procedural, and conditional knowledge to such instruction, 18 of 19 students were confused about the terms and experienced difficulty including these three types of knowledge in their instruction throughout the semester. Janice introduced these terms by defining them and linking them to authentic contexts, similar to the manner in which the terms were introduced in Chapter 1. Throughout the semester, Janice continually used the terms and made connections in varied contexts whenever possible. In addition, as noted, teachers were required to make marginal glosses on their lesson plans to note where they had included each type of knowledge in their lessons. These marginal glosses were intended to help teachers remember to include the three types of knowledge in their instruction, and to serve as a way for Janice to assess whether they understood and could use the terms appropriately.

The type of knowledge that was most problematic for teachers was procedural knowledge. Most often teachers simply neglected to include information about *how* to perform a given strategy or set of strategies in their instruction. They would include information related to what the strategy was (declarative knowledge), when to use it, and why it was important (conditional knowledge), but they never actually taught students the procedural knowledge related to *how* to perform the strategy. Similar to the difficulty that Anderson and Roit (1993) noted in their study, some teachers thought they were including procedural knowledge, but were actually teaching students how to perform an *activity* rather than engage a *strategic* mental process. For example, they taught students how to complete a K-W-L chart (Ogle, 1986) but did not teach the related strategies of how to tap their background knowledge or set purposes while reading. Thus, in the early stages of the semester it was also clear that teachers had difficulty distinguishing between strategies, skills, and activities. Such confusion would obviously make it difficult to convey the relevant declarative, procedural, and conditional knowledge to their students.

It was not surprising that these three types of knowledge would prove difficult for teachers to understand and include in their teaching. Good readers never consciously think about the abstract concepts involved in the *process* of reading as they read. Janice began to realize that the teachers were having difficulty including this knowledge in their lessons because they themselves were not really sure what types of declarative, procedural, and conditional knowledge were associated with particular strategies and sets of strategies. Although she had always balked at "giving" them such information, she sensed their anxiety and frustration. Thus, she and her students decided to spend part of one class thinking about each type of knowledge in relation to particular strategies. The students were elated. They worked in small groups to discuss the type of declarative, procedural, and conditional knowledge that might be associated with various strategies. Their collaborative thinking helped produce charts similar to those displayed in Tables 6.1 and 7.3. In fact, they told Janice that she must include these charts in this text because it was so helpful for their planning.

Duffy (1993b) would describe this type of thinking as indicative of Point 3 teachers who were "trying out" strategy instruction. The focus was on specific strategies and teaching students names of strategies (declarative knowledge), how to perform strategies (procedural knowledge), and the importance of the strategy (conditional knowledge). Such instruction often promotes use of individual strategies rather than the coordinated, flexible use of sets of strategies that typifies mature reading and mature strategy instruction. Janice used to worry about this; however, throughout the semester she came to realize that it is okay to be at Point 3. Strategy teachers grow and develop just as readers do. Point 3 is a necessary step along the way in such growth.

In his staff development project, Duffy (1993b) did not provide such direct information to his teachers, and for years Janice would not provide her students with such information. She felt they needed to experience the ambiguity that accompanies authentic strategy use, and she was uncomfortable with the limitations of identifying specific indications of declarative, procedural, and conditional knowledge for strategies. However, she also has become acutely familiar with the affective dimension that accompanies strategy instruction. It can be a very painful growth process that, when coupled with the pressure that comes from being enrolled in a graduate course, can become debilitating and demoralizing. Duffy's (1993b) teachers were volunteers involved in a 5-year staff development project. They had time to grow and develop. The teachers in Janice's class enrolled in the course as an elective; however, the finite nature of a 15-week course and the added pressure of grading made this learning environment more intense than a staff development project.

Although Janice assured the teachers repeatedly that their final grade would be based on their individual growth rather than comparisons with other students, they still had an intense desire to excel. Thus, she celebrated the teachers' insights regarding the declarative, procedural, and conditional knowledge associated with individual strategies. Their collaborative discussion helped them understand these concepts more fully, and, in turn, they began to incorporate these critical aspects of strategy instruction into their lessons. Rather than remaining paralyzed by the complexity of strategy instruction, mapping the declarative, procedural, and conditional knowledge onto specific strategies enabled them to "try out" and experiment with strategy instruction. Their experiments eventually led many of them far beyond Point 3. One teacher commented in her final portfolio:

> I am not fully confident that I understand declarative, procedural, and conditional knowledge. I do know that I have really grown in this area. At first I never heard

of these terms before and by the end of the semester I was successfully using them in my lessons. The funny thing is I now find myself thinking about these terms and using them daily in other subject areas. . . . I need to help equip my students with the "know-how" of what to do when reading breaks down. At first I found myself focusing on making sure my students knew each individual strategy. I now realize one must also have an overall idea of what it means to be strategic. This also proves why declarative, procedural, and conditional knowledge are crucial to strategy instruction.

Many other teachers also noted that understanding declarative, procedural, and conditional knowledge was one of their greatest areas of growth. Including all three aspects into explicit instruction is a hallmark of teaching strategic processing. Given the difficulty of including such information in lessons, many successful teachers develop anchor charts to post in the classroom (see Figure 8.1). Anchor charts such as this serve two purposes: (1) They remind teachers to include all three types of knowledge (declarative, procedural, and conditional knowledge) in their instruction; and (2) they remind their students of what a given strategy is, the steps in how to use the strategy, and when, where, and why they should use it.

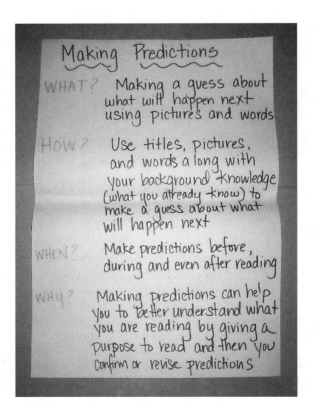

FIGURE 8.1. Reminders to include declarative, procedural, and conditional knowledge in instruction: A sample prediction anchor chart. Photo courtesy of Keli Garas-York.

Modeling Strategic Processing and Providing Opportunity for Guided Practice

Similar to the results of many studies, the teachers in Janice's course initially had difficulty modeling their own cognitive processes for students via think-alouds and demonstrations, and they had difficulty understanding how to provide appropriate guided practice. Often teachers did not include modeling or thinking aloud in their lessons at all. Sometimes they merely engaged the student in an activity and did not provide any strategic instruction. They believed that simply telling students what to do or how to perform a strategy was sufficient. Some teachers initially felt uncomfortable thinking aloud, which may have inhibited them; however, in time, they began to model their cognitive thought processes while reading and using strategies for their students. Other teachers felt strongly that implicit instruction could achieve similar results with struggling readers. Janice encouraged these teachers to try both types of instruction and reflect on the results. In his final portfolio reflection, one of these teachers noted:

> In the process of developing these lessons, I came to the realization (after some lengthy introspection) that I am an implicit learner. This was just one of many insights I was to acquire on the path to self-discovery, but this little bit of knowledge opened my eyes to the importance of concrete scaffolding when working with a struggling reader. Many of the things that I took for granted as easily absorbed through the process of observation had to be taught in a much more explicit manner. And so, I learned a valuable lesson, the basic premise being, that you can never start out too concrete in your instruction, and that once the base knowledge has been established you can then start to remove the scaffolding.

Explicit instruction bothered this teacher. He thought of it as stifling and narrow. Once Janice demonstrated lessons that allowed for open-ended thinking and also included elements of explicit instruction, he began to experiment with this type of instruction and found that, although it may not suit *his* style of learning, it did suit his student's needs.

Guided practice also was difficult for the teachers to understand. They saw it as a quick opportunity for students to practice the strategy they had been taught. Once this guided practice had occurred, they felt that instruction could proceed. However, as they observed their students' independent strategy use in varied contexts, they realized that their students were not approaching text in the strategic manner that had been taught and modeled. Often, the guided practice the teachers provided was in a much less scaffolded context than the original instruction, and their students were unable to implement the instruction. For example, if the original instruction occurred in a highly scaffolded context in which the teacher modeled strategy use during an event or while reading a wordless picture book together (i.e., Points 1–3 of Figure 6.2), but the guided practice required them to use the same strategies while reading a text independently (i.e., Point 35 of Figure 6.2), the guided practice was too far removed from that explicit instruction (however excellent it may have been), and students were unable to use the strategies.

Many found that their students needed a great deal of scaffolded support in order to think strategically at all. In her fifth reflective memo, one student wrote: "I also need to slow down and realize that the process is what I want [the student] to learn. I sometimes feel rushed to have him work independently. I need to provide enough support and guidance so that when I am not there, he has enough background [knowledge] to utilize the strategy independently." The teachers also found that they were able to understand their students' difficulties better by comparing them to their own learning in the course. One student wrote:

> I feel that I have just made a major discovery both as a teacher and learner. As a teacher I would get very frustrated at my students when it was time for them to work independently and they could not do it. I would think to myself, "I just spent 30 minutes [teaching them], and they still do not understand it." This has become a pet peeve of mine. Hopefully, I have never let my students know how much [their failure to understand] bothers me. Unfortunately, I can remember myself saying, "I don't think you were paying attention." Now as a learner I find the same thing happening to myself. In class everything makes sense; it is not until Thursday night when I start to work independently I have difficulty. . . . This has really hit home with me and made a lasting impression.

When Janice read this comment, she immediately identified with this teacher. She had been thinking the exact same thing about her graduate students. She knew that she had taught them a lot about strategy instruction; yet they acted as if they had never heard about it before. Janice even altered her teaching style and the nature of the course but still had the same feeling. She now realizes, as mentioned above, that learning to teach strategic processing takes a great deal of time and must be practiced in a variety of contexts, under a variety of conditions, before various aspects of this complex process are understood, let alone integrated. Her graduate students would often say, "Can't you just show us a video of someone teaching strategies?" She would think, "Yes, I could. I showed you one last semester in the Childhood Literacy Methods class. Obviously you weren't paying attention." She was ready to take them to a higher level of understanding regarding strategy instruction; however, they were not at that point. It was not that they did not pay attention in the previous class, nor was it that they did not understand it. They understood it at one level—a level appropriate for an introductory course in literacy instruction. Now that they had to put strategy instruction into practice with a real student, across a whole semester, it took on a completely different perspective. They needed to hear explanations of terms repeatedly, see demonstration lessons again, and watch videos of strategy instruction several times. Embarrassed, Janice often thought, "Well, I don't really have that many videos to share. They've already seen the ones I have."

She pondered these difficulties for years but did not share them with her graduate students until the spring of 2000. When she finally shared her own instructional insecurities with the teachers, they responded unanimously: "We *want* to see the same videos again. We *want* you to do the same demonstration lessons again. Now we understand so much more. We'll view them completely differently. If you showed us different videos, then we'd be starting at square one again. This way, we have some background knowledge, and we can begin watching with a more informed eye." And so we did. We reviewed videos of Patty DiLaura George's comprehension monitoring lesson, Janice retaught basic "how to" elements of strategy instruction, and she did demonstration lessons again. Where she had intended to begin the course on a "higher" level, in which she focused on research and theory, she found that she was focusing on many of the same basic aspects of strategy instruction that she had already taught most of them in a previous course. And they got it. What was different?—the type of guided practice Janice expected of them. They now had a reason for understanding. Rather than writing a lesson plan only for her to read, they had to meet, face to face, with a struggling reader and plan instruction for at least 1 hour every week. They found that they could not look into the eyes of those children and teach them without understanding the underlying concepts. One student expressed the importance of modeling and guided practice in her last reflective memo:

> After working with [the student] over the course of the semester, I also realize the importance in constant modeling and guided practice. I observed throughout all the lessons that [the student] was much better able to utilize strategies when [I provided] constant modeling and opportunities for guided practice along with the declarative, procedural, and conditional explanations. I believe that without the modeling and guided practice these strategies would have meant nothing to her. I have discovered that not only do students . . . need to apply what they have learned in different contexts, I also need to apply what I have learned in different contexts in order to have a much better idea about how to engage in explicit instruction because this is the way we have been taught in class. In my opinion, having the opportunities for guided practice by actually working with a student is the best way to learn how to teach reading strategies.

It is the same with children. We must provide opportunities for guided practice that are meaningful, authentic, and important to *them*. Using strategies without authentic purpose does not produce the same level of understanding. Thus, not only must guided practice be meaningful, it also must be appropriate and at the right level. After teaching her fourth lesson, one teacher was able to make links between her reading of Paris et al.'s (1983) article and her student's behavior:

> As I reviewed the Paris, Lipson, and Wixson article entitled "Becoming a Strategic Reader" (1983), I came to a section that I highlighted. It said that, "If they [the students] do not judge the behavior as significant or useful, it is unlikely that they would pursue it in the absence of external directives or incentives" (p. 800). I kept flipping back, rereading my highlighted portions, and read, "Without conditional knowledge regarding why it is a useful procedure, it might only be executed in compliance with a teacher's request" (p. 798). These quotes in particular made me reflect very hard on [the student's] performance, both in our one-on-one sessions and in a small group. Although [the student] often rushes to complete her work, she always wants to please me, and does not usually complain when I ask her to complete a task. She is never resistant to scaffolding, especially using questioning to assist her in coming to her own conclusions. However, she does not appear to be ready to use these strategies independently. She still requires quite a bit of questioning and support. This leads me to believe that [the student] may be using strategies because she knows that I want her to, not because she thinks that they are important to use.

This teacher's insights are revealing and instructive. First, they show the amount of effort and reflection that she put into her instruction and planning. She read and reread course readings in an effort to try to understand the behaviors she was observing in her student. She worked diligently to make connections between theory and what she was seeing in practice. This is a dedicated teacher. Her reflections also reveal that she is beginning to see that strategy instruction must be meaningful to the student. Although this teacher was not yet at the point of designing completely authentic reading and writing events, in which students would see the need to learn and use strategies to accomplish their goals, she gave evidence of being well on her way.

Reducing Processing Demands

Janice's graduate students also had difficulty understanding the notion of reduced processing. Given that the previous section included information about their difficulties providing appropriate levels of scaffolding, this discussion focuses on their difficulty providing concrete instruction. Their difficulty in this area arose from two sources: (1) they did not initially "buy in" to the notion that concrete examples and concrete texts would be necessary or make a difference in their instruction, and (2) they had difficulty thinking of ways to make strategy instruction more concrete.

The teachers seemed to understand the theory underlying the strategy of reduced processing; however, their inexperience prevented them from including it in their planning. Because they were all successful readers, they could not understand just *how* concrete instruction needed to be in order to make it possible for less proficient readers to approach text strategically. In her last reflective memo, one teacher noted:

> I have learned that so many of the little things that I take for granted are big things to struggling readers. It seems like common sense, and I thought that I knew this fact all along, but it took sitting down with a student and watching her struggle with what I had given her, for me to realize just how true everything that I have been reading over the course of this school year is concerning the absolute necessity of reducing processing demands, modeling, and repetition. While I thought I knew this, putting it into practice both with [the student] and with the students in the schools in which I substitute teach this semester has given me an entirely new perspective on how concrete I need to be in order to successfully teach.

This same teacher noted that her earlier lessons put too much pressure on her student, who withdrew in response and exhibited decreased motivation. When she reduced processing by using semiotic texts, such as pictures and photographs, to elicit strategic thinking, her student "laughed and smiled throughout the entire lesson" and was able to use strategies independently to make sense of those texts.

Another teacher noted that using concrete examples helped her as well as her student:

> While [the student] has been learning different ways to improve his comprehension, I have learned many significant lessons about both my instruction and my learning. Using a concrete example to introduce a concept is much more important than I realized. Not only did it help [the student] grasp the idea that I would be teaching him, but it also helped to solidify the abstract nature of the strategy in *my* mind. It gave me a foundation to base my instruction on, and my lessons began to flow more and build on one another.

Another teacher aptly summed up the importance of concrete instruction as follows:

> Through our readings and class discussions, I have come to see how critical concrete beginnings are to the successful introduction of reading strategies. By building our foundation upon the concrete, we allow students to make connections to what

they already know. This linkage to prior knowledge will help students to see the applicability of the strategy being taught in relationship to a process they already understand. Therefore, the inclusion of this strategy into students' schema for reading is more likely to occur.

As the teachers experimented with incorporating concrete events and experiences into their instruction, they began to see the value. However, one of their difficulties in getting to that point was thinking of ways to make their instruction concrete. Many of the teachers expressed their frustration about having to think so creatively. One third-grade teacher noted that it was challenging to think of ways to make her instruction concrete, but she was also struggling to accept the notion because she felt that if we reduced processing, we would not set high expectations for our students. In class Janice explained that we *must* set high expectations and goals for *all* of our students, but it is our job first to meet them where *they* are, take them by the hand, and lead them to those same high expectations. We cannot expect students to meet us where we are, or where the "average" student is. It is up to teachers to meet each student where he or she is. After considering these ideas, the same teacher noted:

> During these sessions with [the student] I have become increasingly aware of the importance to start off using concrete examples so that the student is able to link these to the more abstract ideas or concepts that I am trying to teach. I think that coming up with concrete ways to help [the student] understand what is being taught has been one of the biggest challenges that I had to face in planning the lessons. The chart that you introduced us to in class [Figure 6.2] helped me to see how much [of] a strain I am really putting on my student when I ask her to grasp something very abstract at the beginning of a session. This also fits in with the reduction of processing demands, which I really think has been one of the main reasons for [the student's] recent progress. . . . In the past couple of weeks I have come to learn the importance of removing obstacles so that the student can tackle one problem at a time and experience success.

Other teachers expressed similar frustrations and shared how they were able to think about instruction in new ways. One experienced second-grade teacher had taken the Childhood Literacy Methods course with Janice previously and had already begun trying to use concrete events and experiences to teach strategies to her second graders. She noted that one of Janice's demonstration lessons in class (a vicarious concrete experience) had created a "lasting impression":

> I could not wait to use this idea of moving from the concrete to abstract gradually through events, read-alouds, wordless picture books, and texts. Implementing this model, however, would involve a new way of thinking. "How can I create an 'aha' experience linked to a particular comprehension strategy?" At first it took me awhile to think in such a way, but eventually it became easier. Rather than going to the text first, as I was accustomed to doing, I thought of ways to make such abstract concepts . . . more concrete.

This teacher tried out these new concepts in her classroom, and when Janice applied the same notion to word recognition strategies, she noted that she had another "aha" experience in which she now tried to think of ways to make word recognition strategies more concrete:

> With this revelation, along with considering [the student's] strengths and needs, I had to create an event for him to understand how to use context to assist with words. As noted in my previous reflective discovery memo, since verbalization serves as a key assessment component in lessons, I needed something that would captivate him along with fostering discussion. Immediately, using a puzzle came to mind. While [the student] assembled an unfinished Clifford puzzle, I asked him to explain his thinking [as he] put it together. Such thoughts as "I knew this piece went here because his eyes are at the top" and "I'll put this piece back for later" were shared. Unknown to me at the time of planning my lesson was that his comments would serve as a springboard to analogize this process of putting a puzzle together with using context clues.

After the concrete lesson was linked to using context cues to recognize unknown words, this teacher found that her student was able to begin applying the strategy, in conjunction with other strategies, on his own while reading:

> While reading *Harry and Willy and Carrothead* (Caseley, 1991) [the student] came across the word *cooed*. At first he used a Post-it note to indicate it was a CLUNK word—a word he could not say; however, he later removed the Post-it when he reached the end of the sentence. When asked how he got the word, [the student] replied, "It looked like *cooled*, but it doesn't have the *l* and it wouldn't make sense, 'He cried and *cooled* and waved his arms like any baby.'"

In this example, the student demonstrated that he was able to recognize when he encountered an unfamiliar word, and he was able to verbalize the strategic processes he used to recognize it. In this case, he used a combination of letter–sound cues and context cues to decode the word strategically.

While Janice's class discussions and demonstration lessons helped these teachers see the importance of reduced processing and gave them an overall view of how reduced processing looks during instruction, they found that the opportunity to share ideas with one another in class stimulated their thinking and helped them as well. The professional exchange of ideas is essential for strategy teachers, who often feel alienated and alone in their planning. Teachers typically rely on manuals, textbooks, publisher materials, and kits to gain new instructional ideas. However, as Brown (2008) noted, strategy instruction is not, and cannot be, prepackaged, scripted, or rigid—which is what makes it so difficult. In this circumstance the support that came from professional relationships and networks became especially critical for teachers.

Focused Lessons

It took the teachers a long time to begin to realize that "less is more." Many of their lessons were overly ambitious and included lots of objectives that Janice knew could never be attained within 1 hour of instruction. For example, one teacher's lesson had five primary objectives for her student and eight secondary objectives. All of these objectives were appropriate and would be ideal if the student could actually integrate all of these strategies; however, it was an overwhelming amount of new information to introduce at one time. Some of the primary objectives included being able to use prediction to aid comprehension, relating background knowledge to text, improving word recognition strategies, increasing self-monitoring, and being self-directed in using strategies. These are all fine objectives, but there is no viable way a student who has never heard of, or used, any of these strategies could digest all of this new information in 1 hour.

In the margins next to these long lists of objectives, Janice would note: "These are all fine objectives, but this is a lot to do in one lesson." Some of the teachers' reflective memos that followed these "powerhouse" lessons did not acknowledge their enormity, nor did they seem to notice whether their students were able to digest all of this new information. It took about five or six lessons before the teachers noticed their students beginning to succumb to information overload. After teaching her sixth lesson, in which she focused her lesson more and reduced processing by teaching strategy use with pictures, this same teacher noted in her reflective memo: "In our previous sessions, I think the learning context that I created for [the student] was a bit overwhelming for her, and thus her motivation was just to get the 'right answers.' Today the pressure was off of her, and she seemed to enjoy herself, and as a result, performed much better." Other teachers were able to recognize that they were trying to do too much in their lessons, and they subsequently began to focus their instruction more. One teacher was able to recognize this misdirection after her third lesson:

> I think that the first mistake that I made was that I expected my student to remember and be able to use right away the prediction strategy that I taught during our last lesson. I still cannot figure out why I thought that. Most of the time when you are teaching, the student cannot remember what was taught the day before, let alone a few days before. I think that in the future, I need to keep this in mind. Since we only have to meet five more times, I need to focus on just one thing and try to keep working on that rather than doing lots of different things. I feel like I am muddling my way through and that I am trying to do too many things at once and therefore am rushing. . . . I remember thinking that an hour is a long time to be working one on one, but I am now finding out that it is not.

The teachers noted several reasons for their ambitious planning. One reason was that they assumed their students would be able to handle this much new information. This misconception seemed to be a product of just getting to know their students. One teacher, who had tried to teach her student how to use prefixes, suffixes, and root words to recognize unfamiliar words all in one lesson, noted:

> This lesson did not go as planned. I think I tried to give way too much information at one time. Since I still do not know the child's abilities, I assumed that he would not have a problem with this lesson. . . . By trying to give direct instruction on prefixes, suffixes, and root words the demands on cognitive processing were too demanding. This in turn did not create a safe environment. . . . During the assessment, I realized that the lesson was not a success. He could not tell me what a root word is. I also did not relate the lesson to an authentic text so it was probably meaningless to the student.

These are very painful, but necessary, lessons to learn. Although Janice knew she had explained, demonstrated, and modeled very focused lessons for these students before they embarked on their own lessons, her demonstration lessons were only that—demonstrations. Authentic contexts provide more meaningful learning. Such lessons are poignant and motivating reminders of just how complex strategy instruction is.

One of the students noted that she overplanned because she was afraid she might "run out of material to cover in our hour lesson. I thought it was better for me, and it would give me more confidence, if I was overprepared, than underprepared." This is a very reasonable and understandable explanation. This same teacher noted that she felt especially anxious because it was the first lesson in which she was on her own without any support or guidance from class to help her plan. We had spent a great deal of time preparing for their initial sessions with their students; however, after those initial sessions, each teacher had his or her own unique circumstances for which to plan, making it difficult to spend as much time helping each individually. In essence, Janice had done precisely what her graduate students had difficulty with: She had provided a lot of scaffolded support in class initially and then removed most of the scaffolds too quickly, expecting her students to be able to stand on their own. Teaching people to think strategically is difficult at *all* levels.

Planning Coherent Lessons

The teachers described another common difficulty: providing coherence within and across their lessons. Particularly in the beginning, some of their lessons stated one objective, but their instruction focused on another. For example, one objective stated: "The student will learn to organize important information from a text." This statement gave Janice the impression that the lesson was going to focus on identifying or summarizing those ideas that are most important in a text; however, the actual lesson involved using a K-W-L chart. Clearly, this teacher selected an activity to "do" first and tried to think of an objective to match it later. Neither the objective nor the lesson was focused on the student's needs or on strategy instruction. It was just an activity.

At other times teachers' assessments did not match their instruction; they taught one area and assessed a completely different area. Usually this type of intralesson incoherence was more evident in the initial lessons with their students, when the teachers had little information on which to base their lessons. After pointing out the incoherence in their lesson plans and encouraging them to plan lessons around students' needs rather than a "neat idea" or an activity, this type of intralesson incoherence subsided quickly. From there, however, the teachers began to have difficulty planning *across* lessons. Because they believed that one form of guided practice was sufficient to help a student understand strategy use, they expected their students to understand and use strategies much more quickly than is actually possible. Perhaps because most of the teachers were at the "trying out" point on Duffy's (1993b) continuum of progress, they often taught multiple strategies in one lesson or taught a different strategy every lesson. In time, they found that their students were not retaining or transferring any of the information they had been taught. In the reflective memo after her seventh lesson, one teacher noted:

> I also think I am having a difficult time providing [the student] with opportunities to practice strategies that he is learning. As I look back, I have thrown a different strategy at him every lesson. I think I should have only done a couple of these

strategies, or possibly only one and found many different ways of teaching it, which in turn would give him much more practice with the strategy. Garner (1987) states in chapter seven that guided practice is the key in teaching readers to be strategic: "Learners come to use strategies concurrently and semi-automatically through temporally distributed practice. To ensure that students practice strategies, teachers must allocate some school time to the activity. . . . This sort of practice must be guided. Teachers must intersperse practice with more direct instruction and must give substantive feedback about strategy use during practice sessions" (p. 136). I wish this were something I realized at the beginning of all these lessons because now looking back, I wonder if [the student] and myself would have been more successful in our journey together. If we took small steps, with lots of modeling, practice, and scaffolding, the outcome might be different than what it is with one lesson left.

This teacher was not alone. Many of her peers mistakenly thought that they needed to teach as much as possible, as quickly as possible. They had difficulty understanding that strategic processing needed to be taught as an overall process that continued from one lesson to the next and from one context to the next. Many of the teachers came to this awareness near the end of their teaching experience. One teacher noted in a reflective memo after her seventh lesson: "[The student] was visibly pleased to learn that our lesson was going to be a continuation of last time! Again, I realize in hindsight that a slower pace in the beginning would have benefited him. He needs more time to let these complicated ideas settle in his head."

Distinguishing between Skills, Strategies, and Activities

Many of the teachers struggled to understand the difference between instruction that was skill-like and that which was strategic. Although they tried to incorporate the basic elements of strategy instruction into their lessons, some still designed instruction that focused on narrow skills taught apart from authentic reading and writing experiences. For example, one of the teachers knew that his student had difficulty recognizing unfamiliar words, particularly polysyllabic words. Therefore, he decided to teach his student how to recognize prefixes in words. His lesson began by presenting the student with index cards that had the prefixes *un-*, *re-*, *in-*, and *dis-* printed on them, along with their meanings. The teacher pronounced each prefix and explained its meaning, and showed the student a list of root words. The teacher pronounced each root word, then added one of the prefixes to the beginning of each word. Next the student repeated each word and recited its meaning. They read a text together that had words with prefixes in it; however, contextualized instruction regarding how to use this procedure as a strategy to help the student read unfamiliar words never occurred. The lesson was devoid of any strategic language or explicit instruction related to strategy use. It was a skills lesson on prefixes.

Another experienced teacher struggled with the same confusion. In her final portfolio reflection, she noted:

At first, I was very confused about what strategies were. How was this different from what I already do in my classroom? I honestly thought at first that strategy instruction was just a different way of doing the same activities. For example, with my student, I worked on prediction. Of course I have my students predict in reading group on a regular basis. Of course they know how to do it. However, they did not know *why* they were doing it, nor *when* they should do it on their own. In essence, they had procedural knowledge, but not declarative or conditional knowledge. It took me most of the semester to realize that what I was teaching were specific *skills*, not *strategies*.

Some teachers found themselves providing students only with the opportunity to "do" an activity rather than teaching them how to be strategic as they read. In her sixth reflective memo, one teacher noted: "I was more caught up in the teaching of the activity than the actual strategy. For example, although I knew that I wanted [the student] to learn the importance of prediction and using what he knows to understand what he does not know, I began to focus my instruction on the K-W-L chart and how *it* is used rather than the actual strategy." This teacher was beginning to see that strategy instruction involved teaching students to approach reading as a problem-solving situation.

Several teachers did not evidence any sort of difficulty distinguishing between skills and strategies in their lesson plans but noted in their final portfolio reflections that understanding the difference was a struggle for them. These teachers were able to mechanically design "strategy-like" lessons but did not fully understand the nature of strategy instruction even as they implemented it. One teacher wrote:

This semester I have also learned the difference between a strategy versus skill. I have now realized after several of our assigned classroom readings, that strategies are distinct from skills. Students perform skills the same way every time. Traditional skill instruction relies on drill and practice techniques. Duffy (1993b) states that strategies do not replace skills. Strategies are plans for solving problems. Unlike skills, these plans cannot be automatic because the uniqueness of each text requires readers to modify strategies. Pressley (1989) [Pressley, Goodchild, et al., 1989] states a "good strategy user" uses sets of strategies and shifts strategies when appropriate. After reading these articles and listening to class discussions, I realize that good strategy users try something else when they are not successful. This is where my role as a teacher comes to play. I need to make sure I help equip my students with the "know-how" of what to do when reading breaks down.

These self-realizations did not come easily. The teachers worked diligently to make sense of difficult readings, and they worked hard to make sense of their own instruction. Like some of the teachers at Points 1 and 2 on Duffy's (1993b) continuum, these teachers wanted Janice to tell them what to do to make their instruction strategic rather than skill-like. One teacher, in particular, struggled with how to make word recognition a strategic process. She felt that her student would benefit from lessons on diphthongs and consonant blends. Immediately Janice knew that her focus was on skills rather than teaching the student to approach unknown words strategically. Janice's comments on her lesson plans pointed out that she wanted her to try to make her lessons more strategic rather than focusing on isolated skills. She e-mailed Janice, noting that she felt frustrated: "At first I was defeated by reading your comments on my lessons 2 and 3. I was assessing [the student's] needs and trying to create lessons that would help her. I worked hard and thought I was on the right track, but obviously I wasn't. I'm not crying yet!" She went on to ask Janice to help her make her lessons more strategic rather than skill-like. Janice responded:

The major point of my comments is that your lessons are seemingly focused on skills rather than strategies. Now, I can tell you what to do, but that will really defeat the purpose of the course, for this is a course on learning how to be reflective as a teacher—only you can do such reflection—not me. I think that a good place for you to begin would be to review the readings and class notes on what the differences are between a strategy and a skill, then reflect upon these readings/class notes, your lessons, and my comments. Think about questions such as:

- What are the primary differences between strategies and skills?
- What makes a reader strategic?
- How does [the student] fit into the good strategy user model described in class?
- What phase of word reading development is she in and what code cueing strategies would help her move to the next phase?
- What am I doing in my previous lessons that reflect skills-based instruction?
- What could I do to make my lessons focus more on strategies?

I know this is not the response for which you had hoped, but as a professor, my goal must be to push you to think on your own. You are a very bright and energetic woman—I *know* that you can figure this out. I will be here to support you all the way—by asking you hard questions, by pushing your thinking, and by reacting to your reflections.

This way of responding is not what any of us would hope to receive when we are seeking *answers*, not more questions. However, this teacher took the challenge. She described herself as a "mature learner" who was "not easily discouraged or overwhelmed." Janice knew that she possessed these traits and that she could push her with this challenge. Her lessons did indeed become more strategic, and in her final portfolio reflection, she noted, in three different places, that her "greatest single moment of growth came when Dr. Almasi would not answer my question via e-mail of how to change my lessons from being skill-based to being strategy-based instruction." Ambiguity makes strategy instruction very difficult. Learning to teach strategically requires an intense amount of reflection and effort from teachers. Often the learning is painful. These teachers, like good strategy users, were able to see, firsthand, that their intense efforts paid off. However, they were discouraged at the end of the semester when they began thinking about who would teach their student next. One first-grade teacher was so pleased with the progress she had made with her student that she began teaching her entire class to be strategic as they read. In her final reflective memo, she noted:

After implementing a strategic program in my own class, I am 100% positive that reading strategies work. It has been so amazing to see my first-grade students using these strategies and using the terms that go along with them. I have had several parents comment on some of the words that they had heard their child say. One parent mentioned to me recently that she heard their first grader tell an older sibling that the sibling forgot to activate his prior knowledge before reading. I also had to take a day off from work due to my father-in-law's surgery, and when I got back there was a note from the substitute mentioning how impressed she was with the reading ability and reading terminology of my students. The substitute also mentioned how well behaved my class was. I think that goes along with the fact that the students are taking an active part in their learning. By doing so they are too busy to get into trouble. I am looking forward to next school year when I can implement these strategies right from the beginning of the school year. The only thing that bothers me is my class this year will be going to a teacher who does not use this in her classroom. I have discussed this with her, and she thinks it is way too much work.

This teacher clearly saw the value and benefit of her efforts, and she was willing to continue working hard to understand and implement strategy instruction. Janice's response to her final comment was, "Yes, it is [too much work]. I guess it depends on whether you think the children are worth it or not." In the end, despite all of the hard work, the frustrations, and the difficulties that they endured throughout the semester, Janice's graduate students decided that children *are* worth it. It is difficult to imagine any greater insight.

IN THEIR OWN WORDS

As Janice planned the first edition of this text, she thought that this chapter would be "fun" to write. But after reading, rereading, and reliving her students' emotional experiences repeatedly, it somehow did not seem fun at all. Theirs are stories of struggle filled with emotions such as confusion, pain, agony, and despair. At times their stories are hopeful, but that hope always seemed to be tinged with doubt—for they sensed that, although the semester had come to a close, they themselves were not "finished." There was much more to learn about teaching strategic processing, and although they were exhausted, they knew they were not done learning. As Janice analyzed their final portfolios, she found that they characterized their growth in one of four ways: (1) as a journey, (2) as a maturing process, (3) as a puzzle to be solved, or (4) as raw emotion. Each type of growth is described briefly followed by samples from their portfolio reflections.

Strategies Instruction as a Journey

Those teachers who described their growth as a journey often used the analogy of a road trip. They tried to capture the notion that roads are sometimes bumpy, sometimes smooth, and sometimes nearly impassable. Some used road signs to indicate various "road" conditions. Some used the notion of packed suitcases to represent the knowledge they brought with them on the journey and souvenirs to represent the knowledge they gained along the way. Like Rachel Brown in her 2008 article in *The Reading Teacher* describing TSI teachers' instructional practices, some used poetry, such as Robert Frost's "The Road Not Taken," or song lyrics such as "The Long and Winding Road" by the Beatles, to characterize their journeys. Being on this same journey herself, Janice identified and empathized with her students and their struggles when she read these poems and lyrics. She knew from the moment they entered the course what they would face, and she tried to prepare them for it. In fact, she tried to prepare herself for it. However, when she thinks about how hard these teachers worked, and when she read the lyrics to "The Long and Winding Road" a teacher had written on the last page of her portfolio, she couldn't help but wonder whether these journeys should be so difficult.

This teacher struggled to digest and implement the course information, and although she experienced successes and triumphs amid her frustrations, in the end she realized that this type of learning is a lifelong process.

Figure 8.2 depicts a similar but more lighthearted journey, using maps from different ages as a metaphor for the journey of personal growth and development. The teacher who created this visual display described his journey in the following manner:

> The use of maps represents my personal voyage of discovery and how at times the course and direction of which were not easily discernible. The often-used term in early navigation maps "there be monsters here" was frequently appropriate when describing the unseen perils of wading into strategy instruction, especially when dealing with struggling readers. My journey began with a map that was as incomplete as the early seafaring charts of the ancient mariners. As I was later to learn, I was not alone in my uncertainty. This approach to strategy instruction was new to most of us. We all thought we knew what strategy instruction was, but invariably we were confusing skills with strategies. Based on the often-misleading information in print, it is apparently a common mistake.

When she read his portfolio, Janice wanted to think that the "seasoned guides" and "trained navigators" to whom the student refers in the first and second maps referred to her guidance and instruction; however, she knows that, in his efforts to understand strategy instruction, he went far beyond course requirements and sought experienced teachers and administrators to help him. He interviewed and sought advice from other teachers, and he requested that administrators observe and critique his teaching, even though the district in which he tutored did not employ him. Despite the heavy burdens of the course requirements, these teachers read and reread over 100 class readings, they sought additional reading from outside sources, and they often interviewed and discussed strategy instruction with other professionals. These are extraordinary teachers who undertook an extraordinary journey.

Strategies Instruction as a Maturing Process

Those teachers who viewed strategy instruction as a slow and gradual maturing process used analogies of a maturing tree or the life cycle of a butterfly to depict their growth. One teacher likened most of the semester to the long "cocoon" stage, in which she actually "hid" from strategy instruction. This is an apt analogy in that many students choose to avoid it when frustrated and confused by the complexity of strategy instruction, rather than doing the hard thinking required to understand it. It would be similar to what would happen to a caterpillar that, knowing the process of maturing into a butterfly involved considerable change, decided that it would be more comfortable to remain a caterpillar. My student described her analogy in the following manner:

> In the last few months I have learned a lot about myself as a teacher and as a person in general. I wish that I could say that throughout this process of change, everything was wonderful, but I cannot. I struggled and became frustrated with myself over instances that I was in control of and decided that I was overwhelmed. I like to compare myself to the life cycle of a butterfly. This creature in its beginning stages of

Every journey begins with a plan or map, but even with a good chart we often get lost in unfamiliar waters.
Even a seasoned traveler can become disoriented without the help of a guide who knows the route.
The use of fanciful monsters to delineate the unknown areas on early seafaring charts was a way of expressing
this uncertainty. That is why I chose these maps, to symbolize the uncertain beginnings of my venture into the
daunting realm of strategy instruction. Thank God for seasoned guides who help us through these unfamiliar waters.

In the beginning, there where many monsters, and obstacles impedeing my path to becoming a teacher of stratagies.
Without the help of a trained navigator all would be lost.

(cont.)

FIGURE 8.2. Growth as a teacher of strategic processing depicted as a journey.

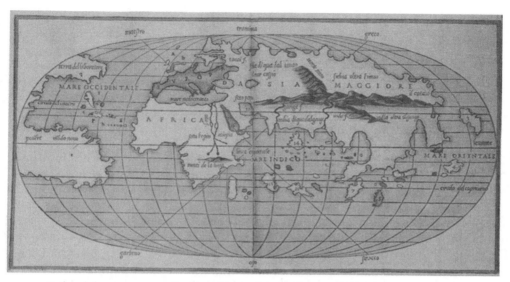

Each week the map got more complete, less uncharted reefs, less monsters, more confidence in my knowledge as an instructor of strategies. This is not ot say that I've called off the watch for unforseen obstacles, it's just that I don't have to be quite so diligent about it. Which means I now sleep a little more soundly.

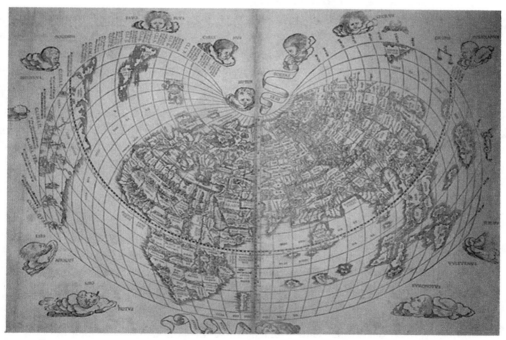

Maps like educators need to be updated if they are to remain useful. There is no branch of knowledge that is ever truly stagnant. Therefore, as educators we must be diligent in our efforts to stay abreast of the changes that will affect our students.

FIGURE 8.2. *(cont.)*

life is a caterpillar, which is eager to crawl around and explore new experiences, as I was at the beginning of the course. I was excited to try new strategy instruction and learn about the student I was going to be working with. The caterpillar then makes a cocoon and hides in this cocoon until it is ready to mature. After a few lessons in implementing strategy, or sometimes by error, skill instruction, I closed myself off, just as a caterpillar is hidden within a cocoon. I was not exactly sure where to go with my instruction, but one thing I knew for sure is that I wanted to help the child I was working with become a better reader. The caterpillar then emerges from the cocoon as a beautiful butterfly after some time. This is the way I feel now. I feel that I have emerged into a better teacher with greater understanding of what strategy instruction entails. After hitting a wall and feeling that I was not succeeding, I grew into someone different.

This type of development is particularly painful to watch because the "dormant" phase, if left too long, can lead to low self-esteem, lack of motivation, and despair. Like Duffy (1993b), Janice felt that genuine and lasting growth and development as a teacher of strategies must come from within. However, as noted earlier, the parameters of a 15-week graduate course often meant that she had to gently prod and poke the "cocoon" to awaken the butterfly within it.

Strategies Instruction as a Puzzle/Mystery

Whereas some teachers characterized the difficult aspects of strategy instruction as "road obstacles" or "monsters," other teachers saw these difficulties as puzzle pieces to be put together, or a mystery to be solved. Those who made an analogy between their growth as a strategy teacher and that of an investigator probing a mystery sought "clues" and "evidence" in their lesson plans, reflective memos, and their students' work. Those who viewed their growth as a puzzle used the analogy not just to represent the "puzzling" nature of strategy instruction but to also represent the manner in which they were able to "piece together" their understanding. Figure 8.3 depicts one teacher's experience of her growth and development. In her description she likens her growth to the declarative, procedural, and conditional knowledge she struggled so hard to understand. Another teacher described her puzzle analogy in this manner:

This has been an interesting course. Since it was the last course in my reading specialist program, and I had already completed the clinical practicum experiences, I thought eight tutoring sessions would not hold much challenge. I soon found, however, that things I thought I had learned had pieces to them I had not before considered. The assignments, lesson plans, and readings were all pieces of a puzzle that I attempted to fit into my picture of teaching reading. Some of them fit easily, some I had to figure out, and I am still wrestling with a few. I think this is a good way to finish my program. I have learned a great deal in all of my courses, and I feel qualified to be a beginning reading teacher, but this course has reminded me how important it is to keep growing and to never think of professional development as "finished." I believed this before, but this course has given me specific questions and goals to pursue. It has made me aware of more puzzle pieces that I need to fit in, and more that I need to find. Because of this, I chose a puzzle to represent my work for this course.

**DECLARATIVE KNOWLEDGE:
PIECES OF THE PUZZLE**

At first I struggled with the concept of the different types of knowledge. I now feel that coming into this class, I possessed some of the declarative pieces (individual pieces scattered around) about reading. I knew about a few strategies and reading concepts when I first began, but I had not yet started to make connections with or between them. Now I feel that my declarative knowledge has grown, and that I am starting to make connections to ideas that I have learned in the past.

**PROCEDURAL KNOWLEDGE:
STARTING TO KNOW
HOW TO PUT THE PIECES TOGETHER**

I still have a ways to go in this area. While I have learned new strategies . . . there are still questions that I have. I am beginning to understand the steps needed to do and teach the strategies, but I still want and need to learn more. I have only recently started to make the links between the major concepts and their smaller components.

**CONDITIONAL KNOWLEDGE:
STILL MISSING A FEW PIECES**

Although some of the pieces have recently started to fall into place for me, I still have a long way to go before I will actually feel confident in knowing what I am doing. For me, the conditional piece of the puzzle is knowing why and when to teach a student a specific strategy. I still feel very unsure in this area, but I think that with time and experience, I will become better at doing it. While I feel like I am still missing some of the pieces needed to be a successful reading specialist, I do feel like I am on my way.

FIGURE 8.3. Growth as a teacher of strategic processing depicted as a puzzle.

The puzzle/mystery analogy worked on multiple levels for these teachers. It served as a concrete depiction of their struggle to understand strategy instruction, and it served as a symbol of that same problem-solving process.

Strategies Instruction as Raw Emotion

Although each teacher had unique students with unique reading difficulties, and each teacher had his or her own way of approaching learning and depicting growth, they all experienced similar emotions: They initially approached strategy instruction with vigor and excitement; they tried out new ideas and soon became confused and frustrated; during this frustration period, they reflected deeply and sought answers by reading, rereading, discussing, observing, and taking risks. Throughout this process they authored their own learning. They grew in many ways and were able to attribute their growth to their own efforts. In the end they realized that their growth was not complete and that they still had more to learn. This humbling realization can be overwhelming. It is these raw emotions that came through in several teachers' depictions of their growth and development.

One teacher's final portfolio reflection described, in painful detail, the emotions that she experienced while trying to understand strategy instruction. Her story is a poignant one, in which she came to understand her student's struggle to learn to read by comparing it to her own struggle to learn to teach strategic processes:

> This course has been by far, the most difficult course I have ever taken. It is also one of the few more memorable ones that has left a lasting impression on me as a teacher, student, and future reading specialist. I would not say that I ever had a conflict with this class or its instructor. I would say that I had an event that lasted for the first two and a half months of class. When I enrolled in this class, I expected to learn about strategies in the form of a lecture. I thought that the information would be presented in such a way that "if the child you are working with can't do _____, then you should _____." As the semester went on (actually it wasn't until the last 6 weeks) I found that teaching reading is not quite that simple. I guess that it was my lack of experience or that I was one of those people who thought that a student who is struggling can be "fixed" using a certain formula. The experience that I had with [the class] and the student that I worked with, quickly changed my view of reading to it probably being the most difficult and challenging process to teach.
>
> I think that I learned more from my student than she did from me. This class forced me to take on the perspective of a struggling student. I did not handle this role very well. In the beginning and up until the very end, I had several feelings and emotions that I went through—mainly confusion, frustration, apathy, anger, despair, hopelessness, and finally persistence. Many, if not all, of these emotions are felt by a student who is struggling with reading. To hear about them is one thing, but to actually go through it is quite another. I personally do not feel that you can truly understand the students you are working with (as a reading specialist/teacher) unless you are put into a situation that mirrors their own. My lack of motivation and the feelings that I had about this class affected every aspect of this class as well as my life. I would not speak out in class; rather I took on the role of a quiet and

passive learner. Rather than going and trying to talk to the instructor, I went to my advisor and tried to find an easier way out. Her response was, "You can either change your attitude or you are going to fail." That was it. That was all she said. However, in many ways that was all she had to say. I couldn't and wasn't going to fail this class. So I took the words of the instructor on the first day of class ("If you're at the bottom, you can only go one way—up") and I picked myself up and met with the instructor. Once I realized that she was approachable and that I could actually talk to her about what I was going through (creating a safe environment), I felt a renewed hope since she seemed to understand and said I still stood a chance of passing the class.

Each time Janice reads this reflection, even now 10 years later, she can see this teacher's face. She still sees the blank, emotionless, apathetic face that stared at her throughout the first two-thirds of the semester. Her face never responded, and her hands never turned in any lesson plans or reflections. At the beginning of each class, she passed out the students' name tags and usually tried to say something personal to each student. Knowing that this teacher was struggling, Janice always asked whether everything was "okay" or how things were going. This student always nodded slightly and said "okay" through tightly pursed lips. With her (and one or two other students) in mind, Janice reassured the class that they could make an appointment to talk with her or meet with her at any time. She never came. Finally, after the meeting with her advisor, the student met with Janice. After greeting her warmly Janice asked her to share what was on her mind. Janice listened carefully and then shared situations in which she felt the same way as a teacher and learner, and she helped the student rethink some of the issues she was pondering about strategy instruction. Together they plotted a way for her to submit her lessons and reflective memos in the few remaining weeks of the semester. As a result of this meeting, Janice began to see a face that smiled, and she saw a face that had eyes that squinted and eyebrows that furrowed as they tried to make sense of the environment. The blank, emotionless face that had dared Janice to teach was gone. Another one had made it over "the wall."

Another teacher depicted her growth simply in terms of the feelings she experienced throughout the semester. Her growth followed the familiar pattern of many of her peers—confidence, followed by confusion and frustration, culminating in a sense of renewed hope. Figure 8.4 displays the faces that she chose to depict her emotions. In these depictions she included excerpts from her reflective memos, her most recent reflections, and prose to describe her growth and development.

Many of the teachers seemed to be at Points 3 and 4 on Duffy's (1993b) continuum of teacher progress. That is, they taught strategies individually, and this instruction was often the primary focus of their lessons. Because of the overwhelmingly complex nature of strategy instruction, Janice heeded the advice of Pressley, Woloshyn, et al. (1995), and of Brown (2008), who recommended that strategy teachers begin by selecting only a few strategies to teach at a time—perhaps even only one. Although Janice knew this type of instruction did not fully represent the nature of authentic strategy use, she encouraged it to reduce processing demands. The students' emotional reactions show that even this form of strategy instruction initially was arduous to understand. In time, Janice challenged her graduate students to try to think of strategy instruction as an overall process. They read the research on teacher development described earlier in this chapter and were

CONFIDENT

When I first was given this project, I felt extremely confident. I thought I knew exactly how I would teach a child to learn. In fact, my overconfidence led me to believe that I would learn new reading activities to add to my current teaching style in my classroom. What I came to realize is that I was overconfident, and I needed to change my thinking in order to become a strategic teacher!

SURPRISED

Much to my surprise, I have discovered I made a misjudgment about a student's capabilities in my classroom. Working with him on an individual level is very helpful for me to better my instruction techniques. Plus, it makes me want to take the time to work in small groups with all my other students. Prior to these last few lessons, I did not see the need to have small-group reading instruction. At this point I have always taught whole-group reading. I can't believe I did not see the benefits prior to this grad class! I am glad that I am struggling because I am learning about myself as a teacher.

CONFUSED

I am beginning to question myself!! What was I thinking when I thought all I needed to learn was some new reading activities to use in my classroom. I am beginning to feel VERY CONFUSED about what it means to be a strategic reading teacher. I did not understand that I need to alter my approach in teaching! BUT how do I DO that?? I hope I'll learn as I read more and teach more lessons!!

OVERWHELMED

I practiced giving directions and modeling the behavior of a good reader. This was a difficult task for me. Sometimes I feel overwhelmed trying to think about myself as a reader. Reading is always so easy for me! I ask myself, "Am I making sense? Am I doing this right?" I don't know how I can become more aware of my students' needs. In fact, I am shocked at the attitude I had when I first began this project. Boy, did I have a lot to learn!

(cont.)

FIGURE 8.4. Growth as a teacher of strategic processing depicted through raw emotion.

FRUSTRATED

Feeling upset—I don't know what I'm doing!
Really feel like screaming
Understanding this stuff is TOUGH
Struggling to learn
Temper is rising
Run and HIDE
Attempting new teaching = STRESSED
Trying to get past the wall
Encounter emotions of pain
Doing a think-aloud for the first time makes me feel awkward

HOPEFUL

It has taken me five lessons to adapt to strategy instruction, adjust my teaching, and think quickly on my feet. This implies that I am learning how to "modify my instruction in order to enhance literacy" (Walker, 2000, p. 44). I feel more comfortable modifying my instruction. I am hopeful that I will be able to share some knowledge about strategies to a group of students. I am beginning to adjust my thinking as a teacher, and I must remember that I need to model how to be a strategic reader. If I approach reading instruction this way, my students will be more successful.

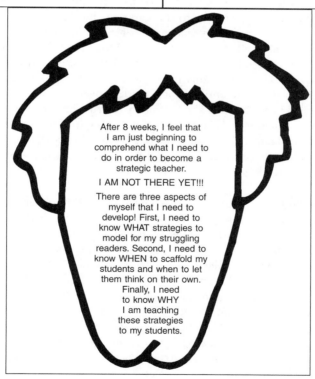

After 8 weeks, I feel that I am just beginning to comprehend what I need to do in order to become a strategic teacher.

I AM NOT THERE YET!!!

There are three aspects of myself that I need to develop! First, I need to know WHAT strategies to model for my struggling readers. Second, I need to know WHEN to scaffold my students and when to let them think on their own. Finally, I need to know WHY I am teaching these strategies to my students.

FIGURE 8.4. *(cont.)*

encouraged to reflect on their own growth in relation to that of the teachers in those research studies. One teacher described her growth in the following manner:

> It is also clear just from reading my memos that my understanding of strategy instruction increased. In the beginning of the semester I was very confused about what it is we were actually expected to do with our students. By my last three memos I had developed a purpose and clarity regarding my goals as I worked with my student. I finally understood that strategic reading means more than simply knowing some strategies, and that in order to teach students to read this way, we need to encourage independence.
>
> I still feel that I need to work on how to integrate different strategies. I have a handle on how to teach a few of them, but not on how to get kids to use all of them interchangeably. This seems to be a common problem, as Duffy (1993b) wrote; students in many instructional situations are more aware of isolated strategies than of an overall plan to be strategic. This is something I would like to pursue in my future work with students.
>
> I do not feel badly about my progress in strategic reading instruction during this semester. Knowing that teachers who did it full time for a year still were not comfortable with strategy instruction (El-Dinary & Schuder, 1993) makes me realize that any progress I've made is impressive. Considering that I started out having never taught and knowing very little about reading instruction, I feel that just getting to Point 4, Modeling Process into Content (Duffy, 1993b), is an accomplishment. I am not positive that I fit precisely into this category, but I know that I was here to some extent. I attempted to put my student in control of his strategy use, and I tried to always use authentic texts to teach strategies. I also used think-alouds to model my strategy use for my student. I do not feel that I made it over "the wall" because my student was not exhibiting totally independent strategy use, which did not happen in Duffy's (1993b) study until teachers made it over "the wall." The most significant thing I feel I have learned about strategy instruction is that it involves much more than simply teaching kids how to predict or how to "chunk." Walker (2000) discussed the many factors that contribute to a reader's strategy use. Teachers need to encourage students to be independent, active readers and to develop a concept of themselves as good readers.

At the conclusion of the course the teachers suggested that perhaps future teachers should read about strategy teachers' development first. They felt that, had they known that all teachers experience similar feelings as they struggled to teach strategic processes, they would have felt better about themselves at various points in the process. This is an excellent suggestion—one that Janice planned to try herself. Each time Janice taught this course in teaching strategic reading processes, she struggled with the fact that although she had taught most of these same teachers in the prerequisite course on childhood literacy methods, they did not seem to retain any of the information regarding strategic processing. She often blamed her own teaching or the students for their lack of transfer. As Janice closely watched her own and her students' growth during the semester, she learned that teaching strategic processing is a process in itself. Her students helped her understand that their learning, like that of an emergent reader, is a developmental process that must be handled with care and gently nurtured.

SUMMARY

Becoming a successful teacher of strategic processing is a difficult process that takes many years. Teachers' evolution often proceeds as a pattern in which they begin by seeking routines and answers to implement rigidly. In time they begin to experiment with their instruction and eventually become flexible in their approach and feel comfortable in the process. Graduate students initially had difficulty in five areas: (1) including the basic elements of explicit instruction in their lessons (i.e., declarative/procedural/conditional knowledge, modeling, and guided practice); (2) reducing processing demands; (3) creating focused lessons; (4) planning coherently within and across lessons; and (5) distinguishing between skills, strategies, and activities. In time they were able to master these elements and were consistently successful in creating a safe environment for their students, maintaining an open mind and flexibly adjusting their instruction to meet students' needs. These teachers experienced a range of emotions as they learned how to implement strategy instruction. An initial (and brief) period of excitement was followed by confusion, frustration, and anguish. Teachers found that persistence and tenacity enabled them to reach a deeper level of insight and to feel hopeful that they would eventually become successful teachers of strategic processing.

CHAPTER NINE

Conclusions
Putting It All Together

In this book we have discussed what it means to be strategic, what is involved in strategic reading processes, what good strategy users do, and what poor strategy users don't do. We've talked about a specific model of strategies instruction—*critical elements of strategies instruction (CESI)*—and examined its elements. Much attention in reading instruction, particularly for struggling readers, has shifted to interventions, as in response to interventions (RTI), so it seemed imperative to discuss what sound intervention instruction that incorporates strategies instruction might look like. We've presented a variety of assessment tools and procedures that will enable reading professionals to carefully assess readers' strategic processing. Strategy instruction that supports comprehension and word recognition was examined in two chapters along with a number of lesson examples. Finally, we shared many of the reflections and comments of teachers who are in varying stages of development as "strategies teachers."

PUTTING IT ALL TOGETHER: STRATEGIES INSTRUCTION ACROSS A DAY AND ACROSS THE WEEK

One of the most difficult aspects of teaching readers to be strategic is thinking about how to plan for this approach across a whole day in an elementary classroom. In this section we focus on answering several questions that we are often asked. These questions form the basis for the information shared in the remainder of this chapter.

- When do I teach strategies?
- How do I organize my instruction?
- What does this instruction look like across a day or a week?
- Do I focus on strategies one at a time, maybe one per week, and then move on to another one that seems important?
- What do I need to put in place to get started?
- How can I improve my practice as a strategies teacher?

When Do I Teach Strategies?

Teaching readers to be strategic should occur in every lesson every day. This sounds impossible, given that we have an overcrowded curriculum and so much assessment, but in order for students to truly learn to *be strategic*, they must see how we use strategies in a variety of contexts and settings. The ideas that follow will help you see how to weave strategies instruction into all aspects of your curriculum.

How Do I Organize My Instruction? What Does This Instruction Look Like across a Day or a Week?

Typical instructional schedules in upper elementary classrooms focus on three areas: (1) a literacy block, (2) a mathematics block, and (3) a content block. The literacy block ideally would range between 2.5 to 3 hours in length and would include instruction related to all literacy processes (e.g., reading, writing, listening/speaking). The mathematics block would be 1.5 hours; the content block would range from 1 to 1.5 hours and would include science and social studies (30–45 minutes for each). How long each block is and whether each is a coherent block of time or split depend on many factors, including when lunch, recess, and specials (e.g., physical education, music, art) occur. As an overview, Figure 9.1 depicts a typical daily schedule in an upper elementary classroom. Please note that although this text is focused on reading, we have included guided, shared, and independent writing in our sample schedule, so that readers will see where writing instruction would fit into the schedule. We do not discuss guided, shared, or independent writing, as that is beyond the scope of this text.

As you plan across a day or week, you might want to begin by selecting a focal strategy on which to center your instruction.

Literacy Block

Within the literacy block five literacy practices should be included: (1) teacher read aloud(s), (2) shared reading/writing, (3) small-group strategies lessons and guided reading/writing, (4) independent reading/writing, and (5) presenting. You may not be able to fit each of these literacy practices in every day, but you should plan to incorporate each across a week. Your students can be encouraged to be strategic during all five literacy practices.

Teacher read-alouds provide a wonderful opportunity for teachers to embed the explanation and modeling/think-aloud phases of explicit instruction related to strategies. You might choose to do these read-alouds with your whole class or with a small group. As part of the read-aloud you can provide initial explanation of the declarative, procedural, and conditional knowledge related to a particular strategy (see Table 6.1 for knowledge related to comprehension strategies and Table 7.3 for knowledge related to word recognition strategies) and then model how you would use a particular strategy by thinking aloud as you read the book to the students. The lesson that Eileen Ludwig designed, related to generating predictions while reading (Figure 6.6), is an example of a read-aloud lesson in which the teacher provided explanation of the declarative, procedural, and conditional knowledge related to generating predictions. She then used another critical element from the CESI model and reduced processing demands by relating the notion of predicting while reading to trying to guess what is in an overnight bag. She models the thoughts that

Time	Activity		
9:00–11:30	**Literacy Block**		
	Teacher Read-Aloud • Ideal for explanation and modeling of any strategic process • Teacher can lead whole class or small group	*Sample Lessons in This Text* • Figure 6.6 lesson on generating predictions while reading (What's in the Bag?) • Figure 6.11 lesson on identifying narrative text structure (Pizza/Story Parts) • Figure 6.21 lesson on creating mental images (Imagine It!) • Figure 7.6 lesson on recognizing words using letter–sound cues (Letter–Sound Cues) • Figure 7.9 lesson on recognizing words using analogy (Analogizing)	
	Shared Reading/Writing • Ideal for explanation and modeling of strategic processes • Teacher can lead whole class or small groups • Ideal for focusing on fluency	*Sample Lessons in this Text:* • Figure 7.5 lesson on recognizing words by sight	
	Small-Group Reading/ Writing Instruction • Ideal for explanation, modeling, and guided practice of any strategic process • Teacher meets with small groups or individuals	*Comprehension Strategies* • Activating prior knowledge • Setting purposes • Predicting • Visualizing • Identifying text structure • Monitoring comprehension	*Sample Lessons in This Text* • Figure 6.1 lesson on using prior knowledge (Pack Your Bags!) • Figure 6.4 lesson on activating prior knowledge/setting purposes (Grocery Shopping) • Figure 6.10 lesson on generating predictions while reading (VLP) • Figure 6.20 lesson on identifying expository text structure (Grocery Story/Department Store) • Figure 6.22 lesson on monitoring comprehension while reading (Stop/Go)
		Word Recognition Strategies • Using letter–sound cues • Analogizing • Chunking • Using context cues	*Sample Lessons in This Text* • Figure 7.10 lesson on recognizing words using structural analysis (Chunking) • Figure 7.11 lesson on using context cues to recognize words (Puzzle)
		Writing Strategies • Planning • Drafting • Revising • Editing	*For Varied Purposes and Audiences* • Descriptive writing • Narrative writing • Persuasive writing • Informative/explanatory writing • Creative writing (e.g., poems)

(cont.)

FIGURE 9.1. Sample daily schedule for an upper elementary classroom.

Time	Activity
9:00–11:30 (cont.)	*Independent Reading/Writing* • Ideal for student to use/try out strategic processes independently • Teacher can use this time to conduct observations/assessments of individual students or meet with small groups for strategies instruction
	Presenting/Sharing • Ideal time for reader's chair, author's chair, or thinker's chair where students share their responses to books they have read, writing they have done (or would like feedback on before polishing), and thinking they have done about reading/writing • Students might share orally, use PowerPoint, share digital storybooks, share visual representations, share dramatic renditions of texts they have read/written
11:30	Special (art, music, physical education)
12:00	Lunch
12:30	Recess
1:00–2:30	**Math Block**
	Mathematics Strategies That Are Similar to Reading Strategies • Monitor and evaluate progress (similar to monitoring comprehension) • Looking for patterns (similar to identifying text structure in comprehension and chunking and analogizing in word recognition) • Analyzing data to make conjectures and estimations (similar to making inferences and predictions) • Visualize or make visual representations of solutions (similar to visualizing/imagery and using graphic organizers while reading to visually represent structure of text)
2:30–3:30	**Content Block**
	Science / Social Studies (see below)
3:30	Dismissal

Science
Sample Lessons in This Text
• Setting purposes (Figure 6.4)
• Identifying text structure (Figure 6.20)

Strategic Processes Related to the Scientific Method That Are Similar to Reading:
• Ask a question (similar to setting a purpose)
• Do background research (similar to activating prior knowledge)
• Hypothesizing (similar to predicting)
• Test your hypothesis by doing research (similar to verifying/updating/revising predictions)
• Analyze your data and draw a conclusion (similar to making inferences)
• Communicate your results

Social Studies
Sample Lessons in This Text
• Setting purposes (Figure 6.4)
• Identifying text structure (Figure 6.20)

Strategic Processes Related to Historical Thinking That Are Similar to Reading:
• Seeking multiple accounts and perspectives (similar to reading as a transactional event in which readers may have different and even conflicting interpretations of the same text)
• Ask questions (similar to monitoring comprehension)
• Sourcing/analyzing primary documents (similar to making predictions/inferences and critically analyzing information across one text or across multiple texts)
• Contextualizing/understanding historical context (similar to making predictions/inferences, critically analyzing and evaluating information)
• Close reading (obviously similar to critical reading and evaluation)
• Corroborating/claim–evidence connections (similar to monitoring comprehension and analyzing evidence and making inferences)

FIGURE 9.1. *(cont.)*

go through her mind as she makes predictions about the items pulled out of the overnight bag. After modeling, she encourages students to verbalize their own thinking about how they make predictions as other items are pulled out of the bag. Next, she uses this same modeling/thinking-aloud procedure related to making predictions as she begins reading the book *Ira Sleeps Over* by Bernard Waber (1975). Eileen's prediction lesson would be a perfect one with which to begin the week because it combines the concrete activity with the overnight bag and a read aloud in one lesson. Figure 9.1 lists other sample read-aloud lessons provided in the text.

During *shared reading* students can see and follow along with the text as it is being read. Reading is typically done in unison. Students should not be expected to read aloud alone during shared reading, nor should they be expected to read without having practiced. Texts used during shared reading are typically those that have some form of repetitious or predictable pattern. There are many types of predictable books: (1) repetitious word/phrase (words or phrases are repeated, as in Bill Martin's (1992) *Brown Bear, Brown Bear*); (2) pattern stories (scenes within the story are repeated, as in Paul Galdone's (2001) *The Little Red Hen*); (3) familiar sequences (story is organized by a recognizable sequence such as months, days of the week, or numbers, as in Maurice Sendak's (1962) *Chicken Soup with Rice*); (4) cumulative patterns (each time a new event occurs all previous events are repeated, as in Simms Taback's (1997) *There Was an Old Lady Who Swallowed a Fly*); (5) chain or circular story (the plot is linked so that the ending leads back to the beginning, as in Laura Numeroff's (1985) *If You Give a Mouse a Cookie*); (6) rhymes/poems (any rhymes or poems that have refrains or patterns); and (7) songs that have repetitive refrains or patterns.

Texts used in shared reading are read repeatedly via activities such as shared book experience, choral reading, Readers' Theatre, language experience approach, and buddy/partner reading. After the initial reading, during which strategic processing might be explained and modeled, repeated readings provide more opportunities for applying strategic processes to learning and developing fluency. Thus, the nature of shared reading may lend itself better to developing sight-word recognition and fluency as demonstrated in the sample lesson in Figure 7.5.

Small-group strategies instruction provides an obvious opportunity to incorporate explicit strategy instruction and guided practice to small groups of students. Explicit instruction, as described in Chapter 2, should include (1) an explanation related to the declarative, procedural, and conditional knowledge of strategies; (2) modeling and thinking aloud; (3) guided practice; and (4) independent practice. All four aspects of instruction should be included, and the format makes it ideal for teaching strategies. As Almasi, Garas-York, and Hildreth (2007) noted, the first step in planning small-group instruction is to assess students. Chapter 4 of this text provided guidelines for observing and assessing students to determine their strengths and challenges. Those strengths and challenges can be used to form initial hypotheses about the type of instruction that will help students progress to higher levels (see sample STAIR hypotheses in Figure 4.11 and at the beginning of each sample lesson in Chapters 6 and 7). Once you have identified hypotheses for your students, you can form small groups to accommodate various instructional needs. These groups should not be static; you should form and reform them based on emerging instructional goals. Sample lessons from Chapters 6 and 7 that would fit well in small-group strategies instruction are identified in Figure 9.1.

Key to small-group strategies instruction is providing each student with instruction that is tailored to meet his or her needs. Although the explanation and modeling of strategies are critical, Dewitz et al. (2010) found that the five major core reading programs used in the United States encourage teachers to *only explain declarative knowledge*. They found that published core reading programs provide little direction to teachers related to procedural and conditional knowledge of strategies. As noted in previous chapters, if teachers followed these programs with 100% fidelity, it would mean that students would never learn *how* to perform strategies or *when, where*, and *why* they are important to use. These two critical aspects of explanation—indeed the aspects that are the hallmarks of *being a strategic reader*—are often omitted from instruction and core reading programs. In addition, the guided practice aspect of explicit instruction also falls short. Guided practice tends to be either minimal or nonexistent in core reading programs (Dewitz et al., 2009). The gradual release of responsibility from teacher to student is foundational to comprehension strategies instruction (Dewitz et al., 2009). Without guided practice, the transfer of strategy use from teachers to students is unlikely to occur. To overcome this problem, in this text we have introduced a lesson planning grid (Figure 6.2) to plan for the gradual release of responsibility from teacher to students across lessons. The lesson planning grid helps you plan a series of lessons so that your instruction starts off by reducing processing demands for students. Instructional lessons and guided practice designed to fit within the upper left quadrant of the lesson planning grid (e.g., Points 1, 2, 8, and 9 of Figure 6.2) provide reduced levels of cognitive responsibility and cognitive activity for students, and there is also more scaffolding by teachers in the form of explicit instruction, explanation, modeling/thinking aloud, etc. Instructional lessons and guided practice in the middle of the lesson planning grid (e.g., Points 17, 18, 24, and 25 of Figure 6.2) begin to transfer responsibility from the teacher to the students. These lessons feature more cognitive responsibility for students in terms of thinking and verbalizing. As well, there is more cognitive activity required to use and engage in strategic behaviors while reading linguistic texts. Instructional lessons and guided practice designed to fit into the lower right quadrant of the lesson planning grid (e.g., Points 27, 28, 34, and 35 of Figure 6.2) require a great deal of cognitive effort on the part of students to use strategies independently while reading. If the responsibility for such thinking is not gradually released through a series of lessons, then students will become frustrated and may not be successful.

Thus, the goal is to plan a series of lessons in which you gradually release the responsibility for using strategies to the students. Figure 9.2 displays a planning guide that might help you lay out a series of lessons to gradually release responsibility to your students. As an example, a series of comprehension monitoring lessons is depicted in Figure 9.2. The first lesson on Monday might be a very concrete event conducted with the whole class. The lesson might be similar to that described in Chapter 2 in which Liz Graffeo and Summer Sciandra designed a lesson in which the very large spider hanging from the ceiling in their classroom was missing. They used this concrete event as a springboard for teaching their students about what it feels like to monitor. That is, when the students noticed the missing spider, they said things like, "Oh my gosh, what happened?" and "Where's our spider?" They noticed that something was missing, and they went on a search to find it. They asked questions and they searched for clues to locate the missing spider. The process of noticing that something is missing or does not make sense is what comprehension monitoring is all about. This event provides students with a concrete experience of comprehension monitoring. Figure 9.3 depicts this missing spider lesson at Point 1 of the lesson planning grid.

On Tuesday, Wednesday, and Thursday strategies lessons can occur with small groups. For each group you might plan to use different texts that are at their instructional

Strategy	Concrete Experiences/ Events	Film/Video	Wordless Picture Books	Books for Read-Aloud	Picture Books
Predicting					
Thinking about Prior Knowledge (Making Connections)					
Setting Purposes					
Picturing Things in Your Mind (Visualizing)					
Monitoring/ Questioning (Stop/Go)	Monday: Missing Spider lesson (see Chapter 2) (Point 1 of lesson planning grid)		Tuesday: Good Dog Carl Stop/Go lesson (Transcript in Chapter 2; lesson plan in Figure 6.22) (Point 10 of lesson planning grid)	Wednesday: Model/think-aloud lesson to demonstrate how to write stop/ go sticky notes while reading	Thursday: Review declarative, procedural, and conditional knowledge of how to monitor comprehension while reading and have students make stop/ go sticky notes in text while reading
Identifying Text Structure (Narrative or Informational)					
Summarizing While Reading					

FIGURE 9.2. Planning for the gradual release of responsibility by reducing processing demands: A sample comprehension monitoring lesson sequence.

Amount of Cognitive Activity Required by Text

		Events/ Experiences (enactive)	Movies/ Videos	Wordless Picture Books	Read-Alouds	Shared Reading	Picture Books	Texts (symbolic)
Less	Teacher/ Whole Class	1 Mon.	2	3	4	5	6	7
	Small Group	8	9	10 Tues.	11	12	13 Wed.	14 Thurs.
	Trios	15	16	17	18	19	20	21
	Pairs	22	23	24 Tues.	25	26	27 Wed.	28
More	Individual	29	30	31	32	33	34	35 Thurs.

Less Cognition Concrete (semiotic) ⟷ *More Cognition Abstract (linguistic)*

Amount of Student's Cognitive Responsibility

FIGURE 9.3. Lesson planning grid: Planning for strategy instruction across a week.

level. In the example in Figure 9.2 the stop/go lesson that Patty DiLaura George designed (Figure 6.22) for use with Alexandra Day's (1997) wordless picture book *Good Dog Carl* would be ideal for those struggling readers who are having difficulty with monitoring. The lesson offers explanation of the declarative, procedural, and conditional knowledge associated with comprehension monitoring. It also provides students with the opportunity to see the teacher model and think aloud before they begin monitoring their comprehension using the stop and go tags. The lesson creates a very safe environment for strategy use and helps students learn to verbalize their thoughts about whether the text "makes sense" or not. This small-group lesson would be located at Point 10 of the lesson planning grid in Figure 9.3. After the lesson you might provide guided practice by having students in that group pair up and practice using their stop and go tags to monitor their comprehension with other wordless picture books, such as Molly Bang's (1980) *The Gray Lady and the Strawberry Snatcher*, Raymond Brigg's (1978) *The Snowman*, Tomie dePaola's (1978) *Pancakes for Breakfast*, and Emily Arnold McCully's *Picnic* (2003) or *First Snow* (2004). Each pair of students would buddy-read the wordless picture book, stopping after each page to turn their stop/go tags and talk with one another about whether that page made sense to them or not. As pairs read and monitor their comprehension, they should be encouraged to explain their thinking about what makes sense in the text and what does not. This guided practice follow-up is depicted in Figure 9.3 by the dashed line leading from Point 10 to Point 24 of Figure 9.3. The follow-up provides students with guided practice with a partner to engage in the same strategic behaviors that were modeled in the larger group. This type of guided practice gradually releases responsibility for the same strategic behaviors from the teacher to the students.

To move students further toward independence on Wednesday, our goal will be to model the use of stop/go sticky notes while reading a picture book. The goal here is to move from using the stop/go tags to teaching students how to use sticky notes while reading to note when text does and does not make sense. This might be accomplished during a read-aloud or small-group instruction. We have depicted it as part of small-group instruction at Point 13 of the lesson planning grid in Figure 9.3. During this lesson you would select a picture book that is at the group's instructional reading level. Then you might remind students of the declarative, procedural, and conditional knowledge related to monitoring comprehension, noting that we also monitor our understanding when we read any kind of book. Then demonstrate how to monitor your comprehension while reading the book by placing premade stop and go sticky notes at places in the book that make sense or do not make sense to you. Of course you would model and think aloud about the thoughts in your head as you monitor. As guided practice, pairs of students could buddy-read a portion of the picture book (as they did the previous day with the wordless picture book) and place their stop and go sticky notes at places in the book to indicate when the text did or did not make sense. As they place their sticky notes, the pairs should be encouraged to verbalize the thoughts in their heads to explain why the text either did or did not make sense to them. This small-group strategies lesson (at Point 13 of the lesson planning grid), followed by guided practice at Point 27 of the lesson planning grid, helps move students closer to independence. As guided practice continues, be sure to take anecdotal notes of students' progress to determine whether they are ready to move on or whether you might need to reteach.

By Thursday, if students are ready to move on, they should be familiar with the declarative, procedural, and conditional knowledge associated with monitoring, but they should still be reminded of that knowledge. In this small-group strategies instruction you might select a different text at students' instructional reading level. We would recommend selecting text from a different genre. If you have been using narrative text, then you might want to select an expository text. Follow the same procedure as Wednesday by demonstrating and modeling how to monitor your comprehension by placing stop and go sticky notes in the text to indicate whether it made sense or not. Again, you will want to model for several pages. For guided practice students can read the next portion of the text on their own and place stop and go sticky notes as they read. You may want to direct students to read a particular number of pages and then either meet with the group to have a small-group discussion of those aspects of the text that made sense and those that did not, or ask them to have a peer discussion of the text regarding those aspects that did and did not make sense. If time does not permit peer discussion on Thursday, it might occur on Friday as part of the presentation/sharing part of the literacy block.

A sample of the type of dialogue that might occur during peer discussion as students share aspects of the text that did not make sense to them is taken from a first-grade peer discussion of Nan Gregory's (2002) *How Smudge Came*. In the story, a young woman with Down syndrome finds a puppy to love but is unable to keep it at the home where she lives. These first graders have difficulty understanding why the young woman would not be allowed to keep the puppy in her room at the home. The students had placed sticky notes at points in the text to indicate places that did not make sense to them. In the discussion they use the phrase "I don't get it" as their way of indicating that the text did not make sense—a sign that they were monitoring their comprehension:

STACY: I think in this . . . (*paging through the book*) I don't get it on this page. (*Shows the page to Maggie.*)

MAGGIE: (*Pages through the book.*)

NOAH: (*Stops Maggie at the right spot in the book.*)

MAGGIE: I don't get it either.

COURTNEY: Oh, you know what? She was wondering real bad what happened to that puppy. Her brain told her hands to not drop the dog. Because your brain is the boss of your whole body. So maybe her brain was sleeping and her hands started to shake or something and maybe she went like this or something and woke it up.

MAGGIE: Noah, go ahead.

NOAH: Maybe the dog opened the food and he ate it all and they didn't have any food left.

MAGGIE: I didn't understand why she got her dog to her room because he probably had a key to her room just in case there was something like an emergency and then they would unlock the door.

COURTNEY: Or maybe the dog would have got the girl in trouble or like make a fight in the room 'cause dogs can do that.

MAGGIE: And he could have messed up her dog. He could have kept bumping into it trying to get out and he will.

STACY: Or if she left the dog in her room and locked the door, the dog will be sad and he will howl. Then he will figure it out.

Collaborative peer discussions of this nature are part of the speaking and listening standards in the Common Core State Standards for all grades. Although specifics vary slightly for each grade level, anchor standard 1 of the speaking and listening for comprehension and collaboration standard states that students should be able to "prepare for and participate effectively in a range of conversations and collaborations with diverse partners, building on others' ideas and expressing their own clearly and persuasively" (Common Core State Standards, *www.corestandards.org/the-standards/english-language-arts-standards/anchor-standards/college-and-career-readiness-anchor-standards-for-speaking-and-listening*). Thus, providing time for students to engage in dialogic discussion of the texts they read is critical.

The small-group strategies lesson and guided practice described above would take students from Point 14 on the lesson planning grid to Point 35. At this point you will want to monitor their progress closely to see if they are able to monitor their comprehension or if it is too difficult to do on their own. If students struggle with the task, you would go back to the lesson planning grid and design more lessons at earlier points in the grid to provide more scaffolding.

Independent reading provides students with time to read texts that are self-selected or texts that are part of small-group reading instruction. It is critical that the texts used for independent reading are those at either a student's independent reading level (when self-selecting texts) or at an instructional level (if the student has already had explicit instruction using the text). It is critical that students do not read texts at their frustrational level because they will not have any scaffolded support during this time. The goal during small-group reading instruction (guided reading lessons or strategies lessons) is to provide students with time to read texts independently and to use the strategies they have been taught. Some schools and teachers have found it difficult to find time for independent reading. One way to find time is to reserve 10–15 minutes each day for whole-class independent reading, or independent reading can occur for some students while others are receiving small-group reading instruction with the teacher.

Presenting and sharing is an important part of the literacy block that enables students to share their reading, writing, and thinking with others. *Sharing* might mean informal discussions among students (as in a peer discussion) or more formal presentations. This time might be envisioned as a "reader's chair" or "author's chair" or "thinker's chair" in which students are able to share and reflect on what they have been reading, writing, and thinking throughout the week. Time for sharing might be set aside on Fridays, or it might be worked into the rotational schedule of small-group instruction. That is, as one small group meets with the teacher, another group might be engaged in independent reading and writing, while members of another group present and share their reading/writing/thinking with one another.

Like discussion, presenting and sharing information is one of the Common Core State Standards' anchor standards for speaking and listening. Anchor standard 4 relates to the presentation of knowledge and ideas and states that students should be able to "present information, findings, and supporting evidence such that listeners can follow the line of reasoning and the organization, development, and style are appropriate to task, purpose, and audience." Anchor standard 5 states that students should be able to "make strategic use of digital media and visual displays of data to express information and enhance understanding of presentations." Thus, the presentation and sharing part of the literacy block will provide an opportunity for you to help your students make progress toward these standards.

Presentations might involve an informal sharing of responses and reactions to texts that have been read and written by students. As well, students may create more formal presentations using PowerPoint, visual arts, or digital media to represent and share their reading and writing throughout the week. These presentations offer students opportunities to share their responses and reactions to the reading as well as what they have learned as a result of their reading.

Mathematics Block

Strategies instruction can occur in the mathematics block by helping students see that some of the same strategies they use when they read are similar to those used in math (see Figure 9.1). For example, just as readers must monitor their reading and evaluate their progress, so must mathematicians. They must continually ask whether their solutions to problems "make sense," just as readers must do. Just as readers look for clues to the underlying structure of the texts and words they are reading, so do mathematicians look for clues to identify patterns in numbers. When we identify text structure, we are looking for cue words and patterns in the sentences—which is similar to the process of looking for number patterns. Likewise, when we use word recognition strategies such as analogizing and chunking, we are looking for patterns. The ability to make predictions and inferences by observing the clues in the text and making links to prior knowledge is similar to the process of analyzing numerical data and making conjectures or estimations about the solution. Finally, just as good readers might visualize while they read or make a diagram to help them visually represent the information in a text, so to do mathematicians.

Content Block

Science and social studies provide overlap in terms of the strategic processes used as well. The steps involved in the scientific method are very similar to the strategic processes we use in reading. Figure 9.1 notes that when we ask questions or design an inquiry in science, it is similar to setting purposes in reading. Scientists then typically do background research about the question, which not only involves actually reading but also is similar to the strategic process of activating prior knowledge about a topic before we read. After gathering information, scientists make hypotheses about what they think will happen. This is nearly identical to the process of predicting in reading. We make an educated guess about what will happen based on the evidence we have observed and gathered, and we connect it with our prior knowledge (or research) to make a hypothesis about what will happen in the experiment. The hypothesis is tested by actually conducting the experiment and gathering the resulting data. This experimental process is similar to verifying, updating, and revising predictions while reading. That is, as we read, we gather the incoming information and "test" it against our prediction to see whether it is verified or whether it needs to be updated or revised based on that information. Once the experiment is finished, the data need to be analyzed in the scientific method. This process is similar to making inferences in reading. We must look across various pieces of data (in reading across sentences and paragraphs), analyze that information, and make connections between the data and theory (our prior knowledge in reading) to arrive at an interpretation of the data. Finally, scientists communicate their results either orally, in writing, or visually. This is similar to the notion of presenting and sharing our reading, writing, and thinking, described earlier in the literacy block.

Strategic processes are also involved in historical thinking in social studies (e.g., Wineburg, 1991). The notion of historical thinking involves reading across multiple texts, analyzing the claims and the evidence, and drawing conclusions. Thus, the process as a whole is reading. But, on a smaller scale, the process is similar to what we do when we make predictions and inferences. We observe and gather evidence, we examine it critically and make connections to our prior knowledge to make predictions, inferences, and draw conclusions. During the process of historical thinking, historians seek information from multiple accounts and perspectives so that they can weigh and analyze conflicting evidence. This is similar to the interpretive process in reading. Historical thinking views history as an interpretive process in much the same way as we defined comprehension as a transactional process in Chapter 5. Just as historians view history as a process of thinking rather than memorizing, we have described reading comprehension as a strategic process rather than a product comprising literal details and facts that are recalled from memory. The process of sourcing that historians use involves studying primary source documents from different perspectives and asking critical questions about the author and how the document was created. This process is similar to the questioning we do when we read and monitor our comprehension. We continually think about whether the text makes sense. As well, sourcing uses critical thinking and evaluation that involve analyzing information from multiple documents, which is similar to the process of making inferences and critically evaluating the information. Contextualizing is used by historians as a way of thinking critically about the setting (e.g., time, place) in order to situate the primary source documents. Situating the primary source documents enables historians to think critically and evaluate the information to make inferences about its credibility. Historians then engage in close reading in which they read all sources carefully and critically evaluate them. This is followed by corroboration, in which historians weigh all of the claims and evidence they have gathered, consider the veracity and credibility of each, and then draw conclusions about the historical event. Because the process involves a great deal of inference, different historians may view and interpret events in different ways. This entire process is very similar to the reading process.

Do I Focus on Strategies One at a Time, Maybe One per Week, and Then Move On to Another One That Seems Important?

Although our ultimate goal is to be able to teach students to *be strategic* by modeling how to use all strategies as a flexible set, consider beginning by focusing on teaching strategies one at a time, as recommended by Brown (2008) and Shanahan et al. (2010). This will make the shifts in instruction a bit easier to manage. As well, you will want to set goals for your strategy instruction.

What Do I Need to Put in Place to Get Started?

Figure 9.4 describes 10 tips for getting started. The first tip suggests, as noted above, to select a focal or target strategy. We recommend that this process should be informed by observations and evidence derived from assessments as described in Chapter 4. However, if it is the beginning of the year and little assessment has been completed, we recommend beginning with comprehension monitoring. This is at the heart of all strategic processes, since all students must be able to monitor in order to actually *be* strategic.

Second, select one element of the good strategy user (GSU) model described in Chapter 1 (Figure 1.5) on which to focus. Each student in your class will have different combinations of GSU elements available to him or her. For example, some students may have declarative and procedural knowledge about a variety of strategies. However, they may not have conditional knowledge of where and when to use them, or they may not be motivated to use them. Thus, observations and assessments will determine which GSU elements merit the most attention for different individuals in your class. With younger students we find that, as a whole, they lack declarative and procedural knowledge of strategies or tend to rely on the same strategies repeatedly, even if they do not work. This suggests the need to teach students a variety of strategies, how to analyze the task so that they know when to use a given strategy, and the conditional knowledge associated with using each one so that they know when and where to use different strategies.

When teaching upper elementary students, the former example may be true. That is, students know about strategies but fail to use them. This would require focusing on motivation, which ultimately means creating a safe and risk-free environment in the CESI model.

Tip	How Do I Do It?	Sample
1. Select a focal strategy for the week (see Figure 1.8). • Comprehension strategies • Fix-up strategies • Word recognition strategies	Use evidence from observations, assessments, and STAIR hypotheses (see Chapter 4).	My students are word callers and show no evidence that reading should make sense. I will focus on comprehension monitoring this week.
2. Select a focal good strategy user element (Figure 1.5) based on students' needs. • Knowledge of strategies (declarative, procedural, conditional) • Motivated to use strategies • Metacognitive • Analyze the task • Possess a variety of strategies	Use evidence from observations, assessments, and STAIR hypotheses (see Chapter 4).	My students lack knowledge about comprehension monitoring. So, I will focus on teaching declarative, procedural, and conditional knowledge of comprehension monitoring.
3. Plan instruction across the week to gradually release reponsibility to students.	Think about how you might introduce monitoring in a concrete way using an event or experience. Then plan instruction to use different types of texts across the week to demonstrate strategy use with varied texts.	Figures 9.2 and 9.3 provide tools for planning your weekly instruction that enable transfer to occur.
4. Select a range of authentic texts to use in lessons.	Gather a variety of authentic texts. • Narrative text structure • Expository text structure • Variety of readabilities • Semiotic texts (events, film, music, art, etc.) • Linguistic texts (picture books, chapter books, online text, etc.)	The Cooperative Children's Book Center at the School of Education, University of Wisconsin–Madison, provides a variety of booklists for children of all ages particularly for comprehension strategies: *www.education.wisc.edu/ ccbc/books/detailListBooks. asp?idBookLists=201.*
5. Annotate your lesson plans. • CESI model (Figure 2.1) • Good strategy user model (Figure 1.5)	Plan your lesson carefully at first by writing a full lesson plan and annotating it so that you are sure you are including all four CESI elements and considering the five aspects of the good strategy user model.	See sample lessons in Chapters 6 and 7.
6. Use anchor charts to remind your students (and yourself) of knowledge related to strategies.	Use the information in Table 6.1 for knowledge related to comprehension strategies and Table 7.3 for knowledge related to word recognition strategies to construct an anchor chart.	See Figure 9.5 for a sample anchor chart related to sight words. Figure 8.1 provides a sample anchor chart related to predicting.

(cont.)

FIGURE 9.4. Ten tips for starting strategies instruction.

Tip	How Do I Do It?	Sample
7. Set a pedagogical goal: Identify one CESI element to work on to improve your instructional practice (see Figure 2.1).	Think about and identify which CESI element might be easiest for you to try to implement first. Focus primarily on that element as you plan your lessons. After each lesson reflect on its effectiveness and things that went well, things you struggled with, and things you would like to try. Use the action plan in Figure 9.6 to help you reflect and plan.	See Figure 9.6 for a sample action plan. Sample goals might include: • Focus on creating a safe environment. • Focus on explicit instruction. • Focus on reducing processing in order to gradually release responsibility to students. • Focus on creating opportunities for students to verbalize.
8. Plan for responsive/ differentiated instruction.	Use the guidelines in Chapter 3.	See Chapter 3.
9. Plan for ongoing assessment to monitor students' progress.	Begin with the classwide assessments of strategy use and motivation discussed in Chapter 4. Use those assessments to identify students who may lack knowledge of strategies or may lack motivation. Begin to do more focused observation and running records with those students. Develop STAIR hypotheses for each of those struggling students based on the more focused individual assessments. As instruction proceeds based on STAIR hypotheses, engage in ongoing assessment to monitor student progress.	See Chapter 4 for samples of assessments (Table 4.1) and STAIR hypotheses (Figures 4.10, 4.11).
10. Evaluate progress toward meeting you own pedagogical goals.	Reflect on your own instruction or have a colleague who is a "critical friend" come and observe your instruction. Follow up with a constructive conversation.	Use observation protocols to guide observation notes (see Figure 9.7).

FIGURE 9.4. *(cont.)*

Third, plan instruction across a week to gradually release responsibility from teacher to students. Gradually releasing responsibility means that we are reducing processing demands for students. This was described in a detailed example in the small-group reading section above. You may want to use the planning guides in Figures 9.2 and 9.3 to assist in planning.

Fourth, it is important to select a range of authentic texts to use in instruction. Students do not learn to be strategic when they are not engaged in authentic reading. The worry here is that many classroom activities in literacy focus on reading isolated words, pseudo words, or small paragraphs to "practice" using skills or strategies. We cannot stress enough that students will not learn to be strategic if guided practice does not occur in the authentic context in which you ultimately expect students to succeed. In short, if teachers teach students to use comprehension strategies using contrived segments of text, and if they teach students to use word recognition strategies using isolated words and pseudo words, instruction *will not* transfer! The Cooperative Children's Book Center in the School of Education at the University of Wisconsin maintains a website with excellent booklists for a variety of teaching purposes. One of their lists identifies books to use for teaching various comprehension strategies (*www.education.wisc.edu/ccbc/books/detail-ListBooks.asp?idBookLists=201*).

Our fifth recommendation is to develop full lesson plans and annotate them, as illustrated in all of the sample lesson plans in Chapters 6 and 7. Although this is a tedious process, we recommend it as you begin learning to teach strategic processing because the process is so complicated. Many teachers have difficulty remembering to include all of the various components of the CESI model and the GSU model. If you plan ahead, you will be more likely to remember to include all instructional elements. Readers are strategic when the reading process is difficult; we must heed the same advice. Strategies instruction is complex and difficult and requires that we are planful and deliberate in our instruction—just as readers are planful and deliberate when they use strategies.

To help in this process, some teachers find it useful to create anchor charts for strategy instruction (Tip 6). Anchor charts not only remind students about what strategies are (i.e., declarative knowledge), the steps in using a strategy (i.e., procedural knowledge), and where, when, and why to use them (i.e., conditional knowledge), but they also remind teachers to incorporate declarative, procedural, conditional knowledge into their explanations during explicit instruction. Figure 9.5 provides a sample anchor chart that is annotated to remind the teacher to include declarative, procedural, and conditional knowledge as part of an explanation of sight words.

As a seventh tip we suggest identifying one element of the CESI model to work on or improve. As noted in Chapter 7, teachers in the reading clinic found it easier to focus on creating a safe and risk-free environment, so that may be one element to focus on early. The teachers found it more difficult to incorporate and plan all aspects of explicit instruction, and they found it difficult to learn how to plan lessons over time that reduced processing demands and gradually released responsibility from teachers to students. It may be easier to begin by focusing on portions of each as progress continues in your development as a strategies teacher. Figure 9.6 provides a sample action plan to identify things that are going well in terms of the CESI model, things that are difficult to understand or frustrating, and things that you would like to try. This action plan can form the basis for reflecting on your accomplishments and your next steps as a strategies teacher.

As noted throughout Chapter 3, sound strategies instruction depends on a teacher's ability to respond to students and to provide differentiated instruction. Thus, our eighth tip is that, at some point, one pedagogical goal should be to truly examine and reflect on your practice to be more responsive to your students' strengths and needs.

Our ninth tip will help you become more responsive, but it is also labor intensive in that it involves engaging in ongoing assessment and monitoring of students' progress. As discussed in Chapter 4, the goal of assessment should be to inform instruction. Thus, the STAIR system of generating and revising hypotheses about your students described in Chapter 4 will be very helpful in providing an organized means of tracking and documenting students' progress. Realistically, you should only need to use STAIR for those students who are of most concern. It is not necessary to generate and maintain STAIR

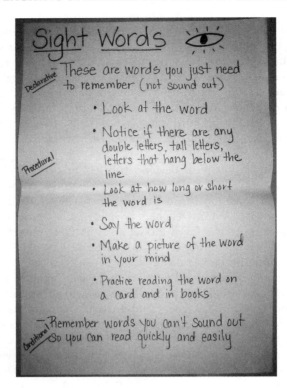

FIGURE 9.5. Sample anchor chart to remind students and teachers of declarative, procedural, and conditional knowledge. Photo courtesy of Keli Garas-York.

hypotheses for students who are making satisfactory progress. However, the STAIR system will be very beneficial for students who are struggling to make progress.

Our final tip is to evaluate your own progress toward your pedagogical goals periodically. Engaging in ongoing reflection on your own practice is critical to becoming an effective strategies teacher. The type of deep reflection that is helpful is evident throughout the text in teachers' reflective memos about their lessons. As well, it is evident in Chapter 7 in the teachers' portfolios.

How Can I Improve My Practice as a Strategies Teacher?

The 10 tips for starting strategies instruction is a good place to begin. We also recommend, as in Tip 10, that you find colleagues who are interested in strategies instruction and begin a study group in which you might read and discuss texts such as this one, plan and share lesson ideas, and reflect deeply and critically on the strategies instruction process. One idea that some teachers have found helpful is to observe one another's lessons. If your schedule does not permit you to observe each other in person, it is helpful to digitally record your lessons. Recorded lessons can provide a starting point for your own reflection and for a study group's discussion. Figure 9.7 provides a sample observation protocol that you and your colleagues may find useful as you observe yourself and one another. The protocol provides reminders of each element of the CESI model and GSU

Critical Elements of Strategy Instruction			
	Create a Safe Environment for Motivated Strategy Use	Reduce Processing Demands	Provide Explicit Instruction (Declarative, Procedural, Conditional Knowledge)	Provide Opportunities for Students to Verbalize Thinking
Things I tried that were successful				
Things I struggle to understand				
Things I'd like to try				

By our next meeting my goal is to:

I will know I have attained my goal if:

319

FIGURE 9.6. Individual action plan for teaching strategic processing.

models that are central to successful strategies instruction. It also provides reminders of sample classroom activities and behaviors that might contain evidence of the CESI and GSU elements. Your personal action plan in Figure 9.6, combined with the observation protocol in Figure 9.7, will give you some beginning tools to enable you and your colleagues to observe and reflect on your progress. We wish you the best as you begin your journey!

Summary

This chapter provided a set of tools for "putting together" the complexities of strategies instruction in your classroom. We described the process of planning and organizing strategies instruction across a day and a week. The chapter then described 10 tips for getting started with strategies instruction and concluded by sharing tools to help teachers reflect on and improve their own practice as a strategies teacher.

Teacher Name: _____

School: _____

Observer: _____

Date of Observation: _____

1. As you observe in a colleague's classroom, look for the following elements, all of which are essential for excellent strategies instruction:

    A. Evidence that elements of the critical elements of strategy instruction (CESI) model (this volume) are present in the lesson

    B. Evidence that features of the good strategy user model (Pressley, Goodchild, et al., 1989) are present

    C. Evidence of responsive/differentiated instruction

    D. Evidence that ongoing assessment/data collection on student progress is maintained

2. You might find evidence in three places:

    A. *Environmental evidence* will be evident in student work or instructional artifacts posted around the room, on bulletin boards, or in the hallway. Environmental evidence may also include texts being used during instruction, available on bookshelves, or on display in the classroom.

    B. *Observational evidence* will be evident during observations of instructional lessons.

    C. *Verbal evidence* may be obtained via informal or formal interviews with students, teachers, literacy coaches, or administrators.

3. Try to determine which level of scaffolded support was provided during explicit instruction (circle in black on the chart) and during guided practice (circle in another color on the chart). Think about whether the distance between the two is sufficient to lead to growth but not too great to lead to frustration.

Scaffolded Instructional Support for Strategic Processing (this volume)

Amount of Cognitive Activity Required by Text

Less Cognition Concrete (semiotic) →→→ More Cognition Abstract (linguistic)

	Events/ Experiences (enactive)	Movies/ Videos	Wordless Picture Books	Read-Alouds	Shared Reading	Picture Books	Texts (symbolic)
Teacher/ Whole Class	1	2	3	4	5	6	7
Small Group	8	9	10	11	12	13	14
Trios	15	16	17	18	19	20	21
Pairs	22	23	24	25	26	27	28
Individual	29	30	31	32	33	34	35

Amount of Student's Cognitive Responsibility (Less → More)

(cont.)

FIGURE 9.7. Teaching strategic processing observation protocol.

A. Evidence of Critical Elements of Strategy Instruction (CESI) Model Present

CESI Element	Classroom Activities	Environmental Evidence	Observational Evidence	Verbal Evidence (Interview)
1. *Creates a safe and risk-free environment for motivated strategy use.*	• Teacher's instructional language lets students know it is okay when text doesn't make sense. • Instructional materials/texts are not at a frustrational level for students. • Teacher reduces processing demands by using concrete events, experiences, and texts to initially teach students about strategies. • Teacher attempts to relate strategy to other tasks from everyday life or other domains.			
2. *Reduces processing demands during instruction.*	• Teacher uses concrete events, tasks, experiences, or "texts" during instruction. • Teacher uses manipulatives in lesson to make learning more concrete (strategy toolbox, stop/go tags, etc.). • Teacher relates strategy to a concrete task. • Teacher reduces processing demands by using semiotic text (video clips, movie excerpts, commercials, photos, etc.)			

FIGURE 9.7. *(cont.)*

322

(cont.)

CESI Element	Classroom Activities	Environmental Evidence	Observational Evidence	Verbal Evidence (Interview)
3. *Provides explicit strategies instruction.*	• Teacher explains what the strategy is (declarative knowledge). • Teacher explains steps for how to perform the strategy (procedural knowledge). • Teacher explains where and when students can use the strategy (conditional knowledge). • Teacher explains how the strategy will be helpful to students (conditional knowledge). • Teacher uses think-alouds and/or modeling to demonstrate how to do the strategy. • Students are involved in modeling. • Teacher provides guided practice for students that is close in proximity to the type of scaffolding offered in the lesson. • Teacher provides guided practice for students that promotes transfer of strategy use to authentic contexts.			

(cont.)

FIGURE 9.7. *(cont.)*

CESI Element	Classroom Activities	Environmental Evidence	Observational Evidence	Verbal Evidence (Interview)
4. *Creates opportunities for verbalization.*	• Teacher provides opportunity for students to talk about how/when/where they used the strategy. • Teacher provides opportunity for students to share/discuss varied ways in which they used the strategy as they read. • Teacher provides opportunity for students to share/discuss different ways to "do" a strategy. • Teacher provides opportunities for students to explain their thinking. • Teacher provides opportunities for students to explain how they arrived at a particular thought, prediction, etc. • Teacher provides opportunities for students to share/discuss why strategies may or may not have worked. • Opportunities for verbalization are in a context that is safe of chastisement, criticism, or ill-mannered remarks (from teacher and other peers) about the child's thoughts.			

(cont.)

FIGURE 9.7. *(cont.)*

324

B. Teacher Awareness of Features of Good Strategy Users (GSU)

GSU Feature	Classroom Activities	Environmental Evidence	Observational Evidence	Verbal Evidence (Interview)
1. *Makes sure students possess a variety of strategies for comprehending texts and identifying words.*	• Students learn about a variety of strategies that have a sound research base. • Students learn that they have cognitive "toolboxes" containing many strategies to help them as they read. • Students learn to use strategies flexibly. • Students learn to use strategies in authentic contexts.			
2. *Makes sure students are able to analyze the reading task to plan and select strategies when needed.*	• Students learn to analyze the reading task to know which strategies might be helpful under particular conditions. • Students learn to analyze the task to know whether a particular strategy might be helpful or not. • Students learn how to recognize problems while reading and resolve them on their own. • Students learn how to make adjustments while reading if something goes "wrong."			

(cont.)

FIGURE 9.7. *(cont.)*

GSU Feature	Classroom Activities	Environmental Evidence	Observational Evidence	Verbal Evidence (Interview)
3. *Makes sure students are motivated to employ strategies while reading.*	• Teacher helps students realize that their own efforts make them successful using strategies. • Teacher helps students understand a strategy's value. • Teacher creates a safe and risk-free environment. • Teacher helps students set goals for strategy use. • Teacher provides opportunity for students to evaluate their efforts (rating sheets, every pupil response, etc.). • Teacher provides opportunity for students to chart their progress using strategies. • Teacher reinforces student progress steadily and consistently. • Teacher provides specific, detailed, and constructive feedback related to students' efforts to use strategies.			

(cont.)

FIGURE 9.7. *(cont.)*

326

GSU Feature	Classroom Activities	Environmental Evidence	Observational Evidence	Verbal Evidence (Interview)
4. *Makes sure students are taught the appropriate knowledge to use strategies (declarative, procedural, conditional).*	• Teacher explains what the strategy is (declarative knowledge). • Teacher explains steps for how to perform the strategy (procedural knowledge). • Teacher explains where and when students can use the strategy (conditional knowledge). • Teacher explains how the strategy will be helpful to students (conditional knowledge).			
5. *Makes sure students use metacognitive factors to regulate and monitor comprehension.*	• Teacher assesses students' metacognitive ability. • Teacher provides explicit instruction related to metacognition and comprehension monitoring. • Teacher explains metacognition using concrete lessons. • Students learn to monitor their comprehension and recognize when they do not understand. • Students learn to use fix-up strategies when they do not understand.			

FIGURE 9.7. *(cont.)*

327

(cont.)

C. Evidence of Responsive/Differentiated Instruction

Domain	Classroom Activities	Environmental Evidence	Observational Evidence	Verbal Evidence (Interview)
Differentiation of instruction	• Generates/revises hypotheses regarding individual student strategy use habits (GSU model). • Small-group instruction provided. • One-on-one instruction provided. • Use of different levels of texts/materials. • Different work displayed for each student (on walls, in folders). • Different lesson plans created for different students or groups of students.			

(cont.)

FIGURE 9.7. *(cont.)*

D. Evidence of Ongoing Assessment/Data Collection

Domain	Classroom Activities	Environmental Evidence	Observational Evidence	Verbal Evidence (Interview)
Ongoing assessment/ data collection	• *Observation* and *conversation* used to generate hypotheses, assess GSU progress, and plan instruction. • *Think-aloud* data used to generate hypotheses, assess GSU progress, and plan instruction. • Self-report data from *metacognitive interviews* and *text interviews* used to generate hypotheses, assess GSU progress, and plan instruction. • Data from *informal reading inventories/miscue analysis* used to generate hypotheses, assess GSU progress, and plan instruction. • Student *self-evaluations* used to chart progress. • Every pupil response techniques used as informal/quick assessments of student awareness and metacognition.			

FIGURE 9.7. *(cont.)*

329

References

Adams, M. J. (2011). The relation between alphabetic basics, word recognition, and reading. In S. J. Samuels & A. E. Farstrup (Eds.), *What research has to say about reading instruction* (4th ed., pp. 4–24). Newark, DE: International Reading Association.

Afflerbach, P. (1990). The influence of prior knowledge and text genre on readers' prediction strategies. *Journal of Reading Behavior, 22*(2), 131–148.

Afflerbach, P. (1993). STAIR: A system for recording and using what we observe and know about our students. *The Reading Teacher, 47,* 260–263.

Afflerbach, P. (2007). *Understanding and using reading assessment K–12.* Newark, DE: International Reading Association.

Afflerbach, P., & Cho, B. (2011). The classroom assessment of reading. In M. L. Kamil, P. D. Pearson, E. B., Moje, & P. P. Afflerbach (Eds.), *Handbook of reading research* (Vol. IV, pp. 487–514). New York: Routledge.

Afflerbach, P., & Johnston, P. (1984). Research methodology: On the use of verbal reports in reading research. *Journal of Reading Behavior, 16*(4), 307–322.

Afflerbach, P. P., Pearson, P. D., & Paris, S. G. (2008). Clarifying differences between reading skills and reading strategies. *The Reading Teacher, 61*(5), 364–373.

Alexander, P. A., Graham, S., & Harris, K. K. (1998). A perspective on strategy research: Progress and prospects. *Educational Psychology Review, 10*(2), 129–154.

Alexander, P. A., & Jetton, T. L. (2000). Learning from text: A multidimensional and developmental perspective. In M. L. Kamil, P. B. Mosenthal, P. D. Pearson, & R. Barr (Eds.), *Handbook of reading research* (Vol. III, pp. 285–310). Mahwah, NJ: Erlbaum.

Allington, R. L. (2008). *What really matters in response to intervention: Research-based designs.* Boston: Allyn & Bacon.

Allington, R. L., & Johnston, P. H. (2002). *Reading to learn: Lessons from exemplary fourth grade classrooms.* New York: Guilford Press.

Allington, R. L., & McGill-Franzen, A. (1988). *Coherence or chaos? Qualitative dimensions of the literacy instruction provided low-achievement children.* lbany: State University of New York at Albany.

Allington, R. L., Steutzel, H., Shake, M., & Lamarche, S. (1986). What is remedial reading?: A descriptive study. *Reading Research and Instruction, 26,* 15–30.

Almasi, J. F. (1991). Helping students deal effectively with comprehension failure. *Literacy: Issues and Practices, 8,* 59–66.

Almasi, J. F. (1993). *The nature of fourth graders' sociocognitive conflicts in peer-led and teacher-led discussions of literature.* Unpublished doctoral dissertation, University of Maryland, College Park, MD.

Almasi, J. F. (1995). The nature of fourth graders' sociocognitive conflicts in peer-led and teacher-led discussions of literature. *Reading Research Quarterly, 30*(3), 314–351.

Almasi, J. F. (1996). A new view of discussion. In L. B. Gambrell & J. F. Almasi (Eds.), *Lively discussions!: Fostering engaged reading* (pp. 2–24). Newark, DE: International Reading Association.

Almasi, J. F. (2002). Peer discussion. In B. Guzzetti (Ed.), *Literacy in America: An encyclopedia* (Vol. 2, pp. 420–424). New York: ABC.

Almasi, J. F., Edwards, P., & Hart, S. (2011, December). *Waiting for special education: Intended and unintended influences of RTI on literacy instruction.* Paper presented at the annual meeting of the Literacy Research Association, Jacksonville, FL.

Almasi, J. F., Garas-York, K., & Hildreth, L.-A. (2007). *Teaching literacy in third grade.* New York: Guilford Press.

Almasi, J. F., & Hart, S. J. (2011). Best practices in comprehension instruction. In L. M. Morrow & L. B. Gambrell (Eds.), *Best practices in literacy instruction* (4th ed., pp. 250–275). New York: Guilford Press.

Almasi, J. F., O'Flahavan, J. F., & Arya, P. (2001). A comparative analysis of student and teacher development in more and less proficient discussions of literature. *Reading Research Quarterly, 36*(2), 96–120.

Almasi, J. F., Palmer, B. M., Madden, A., & Hart, S. (2011). Interventions to enhance narrative comprehension. In R. Allington & A. McGill-Franzen (Eds.), *Handbook of reading disability research* (pp. 329–344). New York: Routledge.

Alvermann, D. E., Smith, L. C., & Readence, J. E. (1985). Prior knowledge activation and the comprehension of compatible and incompatible text. *Reading Research Quarterly, 20*, 420–435.

Anderson, L. M., Brubaker, N. L., Alleman-Brooks, J., & Duffy, G. (1985). A qualitative study of seatwork in first-grade classrooms. *Elementary School Journal, 86*(2), 123–140.

Anderson, R. C., & Pearson, P. D. (1984). A schema–theoretic view of basic processes in reading. In P. D. Pearson, R. Barr, M. L. Kamil, & P. B. Mosenthal (Eds.), *Handbook of reading research* (Vol. I, pp. 255–291). New York: Longman.

Anderson, R. C., Pichert, J. W., & Shirey, L. L. (1983). Effects of the reader's schema at different points in time. *Journal of Educational Psychology, 75*(2), 271–279.

Anderson, R. C., Reynolds, R. E., Schallert, D. L., & Goetz, E. T. (1977). Frameworks for comprehending discourse. *American Educational Research Journal, 14*(4), 367–381.

Anderson, T. H. (1980). Study strategies and adjunct aids. In R. J. Spiro, B. C. Bruce, & W. F. Brewer (Eds.), *Theoretical issues in reading comprehension* (pp. 483–502). Hillsdale, NJ: Erlbaum.

Anderson, V. (1992). A teacher development project in transactional strategy instruction for teachers of severely reading-disabled adolescents. *Teaching and Teacher Education, 8*, 391–403.

Anderson, V., & Roit, N. (1993). Planning and implementing collaborative strategy instruction for delayed readers in grades 6–10. *Elementary School Journal, 94*(2), 121–137.

Andreassen, R., & Bråten, I. (2011). Implementation and effects of explicit reading comprehension instruction in fifth-grade classrooms. *Learning and Instruction, 21*, 520–537.

Armbruster, B. B., Anderson, T. H., & Ostertag, J. (1987). Does text structure/summarization instruction facilitate learning from expository text? *Reading Research Quarterly, 22*, 449–457.

Armbruster, B. B., Anderson, T. H., & Ostertag, J. (1989). Teaching text structure to improve reading and writing. *The Reading Teacher, 43*(2), 130–137.

August, D. L., Flavell, J. H., & Clift, R. (1984). Comparison of comprehension monitoring of skilled and less skilled readers. *Reading Research Quarterly, 20*, 39–53.

Baker, L. (1984). Spontaneous vs. instructed use of multiple standards for evaluating comprehension: Effects of age, reading proficiency, and type of standard. *Journal of Experimental Psychology, 38*, 289–311.

Baker, L., & Anderson, R. I. (1982). Effects of inconsistent information on text processing: Evidence for comprehension monitoring. *Reading Research Quarterly, 17,* 281–294.

Baker, L., & Beall, L. C. (2009). Metacognitive processes and reading comprehension. In S. E. Israel & G. G. Duffy (Eds.), *Handbook of research on reading comprehension* (pp. 373–388). New York: Routledge.

Baker, L., & Brown, A. L. (1984). Metacognitive skills and reading. In P. D. Pearson, R. Barr, M. L. Kamil, & P. B. Mosenthal (Eds.), *Handbook of reading research* (Vol. I, pp. 353–394). New York: Longman.

Baker, L., & Stein, N. (1981). The development of prose comprehension skills. In C. M. Santa & B. L. Hayes (Eds.), *Children's prose comprehension: Research and practice* (pp. 7–43). Newark, DE: International Reading Association.

Bandura, A. (1989). Human agency in social cognitive theory. *American Psychologist, 44*(9), 1175–1184.

Bandura, A. (2001). Social cognitive theory: An agentic perspective. *Annual Review of Psychology, 52,* 1–26.

Bandura, A. (2006). Toward a psychology of human agency. *Perspectives on Psychological Science, 1*(2), 164–180.

Bartlett, F. C. (1932). *Remembering.* London: Cambridge University Press.

Beach, R., & Hynds, S. (1991). Research on response to literature. In R. Barr, M. L. Kamil, P. B. Mosenthal, & P. D. Pearson (Eds.), *Handbook of reading research* (Vol. II, pp. 453–489). New York: Longman.

Bean, R. M., Cooley, W. W., Eichelberger, R. T., Lazar, M. K., & Zigmond, N. (1991). Inclass or pullout: Effects of setting on the remedial reading program. *Journal of Reading Behavior, 23*(4), 445–464.

Bear, D. R., Invernizzi, M., Templeton, S., & Johnston, F. (2012). *Words their way: Word study for phonics, vocabulary, and spelling instruction* (5th ed.). Upper Saddle River, NJ: Pearson.

Beck, I. L., & McKeown, M. G. (1991). Conditions of vocabulary acquisition. In R. Barr, M. L. Kamil, P. B. Mosenthal, & P. D. Pearson (Eds.), *Handbook of reading research* (Vol. II, pp. 789–814). New York: Longman.

Bereiter, C., & Bird, M. (1985). Use of thinking aloud in identification and teaching of reading comprehension strategies. *Cognition and Instruction, 2*(2), 131–156.

Berliner, D. (1988, February). *The development of expertise in pedagogy.* Paper presented at the meeting of the American Association of Colleges for Teacher Education, New Orleans, LA. Retrieved from *www.eric.ed.gov/ERICWebPortal/detail?accno=ED298122*

Berninger, V. W., Vermeulen, K., Abbott, R. D., McCutchen, D., Cotton, S., Cude, J., et al. (2003). Comparison of three approaches to supplementary reading instruction for low-achieving second-grade readers. *Language, Speech, and Hearing Services in Schools, 34*(2), 101–116.

Biancarosa, G., Bryk, A. S., & Dexter, E. R. (2010). Assessing the value-added effects of Literacy Collaborative professional development on student learning. *Elementary School Journal, 111*(1), 7–34.

Blachman, B. A. (2000). Phonological awareness. In M. L. Kamil, P. B. Mosenthal, P. D. Pearson, & R. Barr (Eds.), *Handbook of reading research* (Vol. III, pp. 483–502). Mahwah, NJ: Erlbaum.

Black, P., Harrison, C., Lee, C., Marshall, B., & Wiliam, D. (2004). Working inside the black box: Assessment for learning in the classroom. *Phi Delta Kappan, 86*(1), 8–21.

Black, P., & Wiliam, D. (1998). Inside the black box: Raising standards through classroom Assessment. *Phi Delta Kappan, 80*(2), 139–48.

Blanton, W. E., Wood, K. D., & Moorman, G. B. (1990). The role of purpose in reading instruction. *The Reading Teacher, 43*(7), 486–493.

Bleich, D. (1978). *Subjective criticism.* Baltimore: Johns Hopkins University Press.

Block, C. C., & Israel, S. E. (2004). The ABCs of performing highly effective think-alouds. *The Reading Teacher, 58*(2), 154–167.

Borkowski, J. G., Carr, M., Rellinger, E., & Pressley, M. (1990). Self-regulated cognition: Interdependence of metacognition, attributions, and self-esteem. In B. F. Jones & L. Idol (Eds.), *Dimensions of thinking and cognitive instruction* (pp. 53–92). Hillsdale, NJ: Erlbaum.

Boulineau, T., Fore, C., Hagan-Burke, S., & Burke, M. D. (2004). Use of story-mapping to increase the story-grammar text comprehension of elementary students with learning disabilities. *Learning Disability Quarterly, 27*(2), 105–121.

Bransford, J. D., & Johnson, M. K. (1972). Contextual prerequisites for understanding: Some investigations of comprehension and recall. *Journal of Verbal Learning and Verbal Behavior, 11,* 717–726.

Bransford, J. D., & Johnson, M. K. (1973). Considerations of some problems of comprehension. In W. Chase (Ed.), *Visual information processing* (pp. 383–438). New York: Academic Press.

Brown, A. L. (1980). Metacognitive development and reading. In R. Spiro, B. Bruce, & W. Brewer (Eds.), *Theoretical issues in reading comprehension* (pp. 453–481). Hillsdale, NJ: Erlbaum.

Brown, J., Goodman, K., & Marek, A. (Eds.). (1996). *Studies in miscue analysis: An annotated bibliography.* Newark, DE: International Reading Association.

Brown, J. S., Collins, A., & Duguid, P. (1989). Situated cognition and the culture of learning. *Educational Researcher, 18*(1), 32–42.

Brown, R. (2008). The road not yet taken: A transactional strategies approach to comprehension instruction. *The Reading Teacher, 61*(7), 538–547.

Brown, R., & Coy-Ogan, L. (1993). The evolution of transactional strategies instruction in one teacher's classroom. *Elementary School Journal, 94*(2), 221–233.

Brown, R., Pressley, M., Van Meter, P., & Schuder, T. (1996). A quasi-experimental validation of transactional strategies instruction with low-achieving second-grade readers. *Journal of Educational Psychology, 88*(1), 18–37.

Bruner, J. S. (1966). *Toward a theory of instruction.* Cambridge, MA: Belknap Press.

Butkowsky, I. S., & Willows, D. M. (1980). Cognitive–motivational characteristics of children varying in reading ability: Evidence for learned helplessness in poor readers. *Journal of Educational Psychology, 72*(3), 408–422.

Cain, K., & Oakhill, J. V. (1999). Inference-making ability and its relation to comprehension failure in young children. *Reading and Writing: An Interdisciplinary Journal, 11,* 489–503.

Cain, K., & Oakhill, J. V. (2006). Profiles of children with specific reading comprehension difficulties. *British Journal of Educational Psychology, 76,* 683–696.

Cain, K., Oakhill, J. V., Barnes, M. A., & Bryant, P. E. (2001). Comprehension skill, inference-making ability, and their relation to knowledge. *Memory and Cognition, 29*(6), 850–859.

Cain, K., Oakhill, J. V., & Bryant, P. (2000). Phonological skills and comprehension failure: A test of the phonological processing deficit hypothesis. *Reading and Writing: An Interdisciplinary Journal, 13,* 31–56.

Calfee, R., & Hiebert, E. (1991). Classroom assessment of reading. In R. Barr, M. L. Kamil, P. Mosenthal, & P. D. Pearson (Eds.), *Handbook of reading research* (Vol. II, pp. 281–309). New York: Longman.

Cartwright, K. B. (2010). *Word callers: Small-group and one-to-one interventions for children who "read" but don't comprehend.* Portsmouth, NH: Heinemann.

Cazden, C. (1986). Classroom discourse. In M. C. Wittrock (Ed.), *Handbook of research on teaching* (3rd ed., pp. 432–463). New York: Macmillan.

Chall, J. S. (1983). *Stages of reading development.* New York: McGraw-Hill.

Chan, L. K. S., Cole, P. G., & Morris, J. N. (1990). Effects of instruction in the use of a visual-imagery strategy on the reading-comprehension competence of disabled and average readers. *Learning Disabilities Quarterly, 13*(1), 2–11.

Clay, M. M. (1966). *Emergent reading behavior.* Unpublished doctoral dissertation, University of Auckland, Auckland, NZ.

Clay, M. M. (1979). *Reading: The patterning of complex behavior* (2nd ed.). London: Heinemann.

Clay, M. M. (1982). *Observing young readers: Selected papers*. Portsmouth, NH: Heinemann.

Clay, M. M. (1985). *The early detection of reading difficulties* (3rd ed.). Auckland, NZ: Heinemann.

Clay, M. M. (1987). Learning to be learning disabled. *New Zealand Journal of Educational Studies, 22*, 155–173.

Clay, M. M. (1991). *Becoming literate: The construction of inner control*. Portsmouth, NH: Heinemann.

Clay, M. M. (1993). *Reading Recovery: A guidebook for teachers in training*. Portsmouth, NH: Heinemann.

Clay, M. M. (1998). *By different paths to common outcomes*. York, ME: Stenhouse.

Clay, M. M. (2001). *Change over time in children's literacy development*. Portsmouth, NH: Heinemann.

Clay, M. M. (2005). *Literacy lessons designed for individuals: Part two. Teaching procedures*. Portsmouth, NH: Heinemann.

Clay, M. M. (2006). *An observation survey of early literacy achievement*. Portsmouth, NH: Heinemann.

Clay, M. M., & Cazden, C. B. (1990). A Vygotskian interpretation of Reading Recovery. In L. C. Moll (Ed.), *Vygotsky and education: Instructional implications and applications of sociohistorical psychology* (pp. 206–222). Cambridge, UK: Cambridge University Press.

Coiro, J., & Dobler, E. (2007). Exploring the online comprehension strategies used by sixth-grade skilled readers to search for and locate information on the Internet. *Reading Research Quarterly, 42*, 214–257

Collins, A., Brown, J., & Larkin, J. (1980). Inference in text understanding. In R. Spiro, B. Bruce, & W. Brewer (Eds.), *Theoretical issues in reading comprehension* (pp. 385–407). Hillsdale, NJ: Erlbaum.

Costello, K. A., Lipson, M. Y., Marinak, B., & Zolman, M. F. (2010). New roles for educational leaders: Starting and sustaining a systemic approach to RTI. In M. Y. Lipson & K. K. Wixson (Eds.), *Successful approaches to RTI: Collaborative practices for improving K–12 literacy* (pp. 231–260). Newark, DE: International Reading Association.

Davey, B. (1983). Think aloud: Modeling the cognitive processes of reading comprehension. *Journal of Reading, 27*(1), 44–47.

Davey, B. (1988). The nature of response error for good and poor readers when permitted to reinspect text during question-answering. *American Educational Research Journal, 25*(3), 399–414.

Derry, S. J. (1990). Learning strategies for acquiring useful knowledge. In B. F. Jones & L. Idol (Eds.), *Dimensions of thinking and cognitive instruction* (pp. 347–379). Hillsdale, NJ: Erlbaum.

Dewey, J. (1991). *How we think*. Buffalo, NY: Prometheus Books. (Original work published 1910)

Dewitz, P., Carr, E. M., & Patberg, J. P. (1987). Effects of inference training on comprehension and comprehension monitoring. *Reading Research Quarterly, 22*(1), 99–121.

Dewitz, P., Jones, J., & Leahy, S. (2009). Comprehension strategy instruction in core reading programs. *Reading Research Quarterly, 44*(2), 102–126.

Dewitz, P., Leahy, S., Jones, J., & Sullivan, P. M. (2010). *The essential guide to selecting and using core reading programs*. Newark, DE: International Reading Association.

Diakidoy, I. N., Mouskounti, N. T., & Ioannides, N. C. (2011). Comprehension and learning from refutation and expository texts. *Reading Research Quarterly, 46*(1), 22–38.

Diener, C. I., & Dweck, C. S. (1978). An analysis of learned helplessness: Continuous changes in performance, strategy, and achievement cognitions following failure. *Journal of Personality and Social Psychology, 36*(5), 451–462.

Diener, C. I., & Dweck, C. S. (1980). An analysis of learned helplessness: II. The processing of success. *Journal of Personality and Social Psychology, 39*(5), 940–952.

Dinsmore, D. L., Alexander, P. A., & Loughlin, S. M. (2008). Focusing the conceptual lens on metacognition, self-regulation, and self-regulated Learning. *Educational Psychology Review, 20,* 391–409.

Dole, J. A., Brown, K. J., & Trathen, W. (1996). The effects of strategy instruction on the comprehension performance of at-risk students. *Reading Research Quarterly, 31*(1), 62–88.

Dole, J. A., Duffy, G. G., Roehler, L. R., & Pearson, P. D. (1991). Moving from the old to the new: Research on reading comprehension instruction. *Review of Educational Research, 61*(2), 239–264.

Dole, J. A., Nokes, J. D., & Drits, D. (2009). Cognitive strategy instruction. In S. E. Israel & G. G. Duffy (Eds.), *Handbook of research on reading comprehension* (pp. 347–372). New York: Routledge.

Dorn, L. J., & Henderson, S. C. (2010). A comprehensive intervention model: A systems approach to response to intervention. In M. Y. Lipson & K. K. Wixson (Eds.), *Successful approaches to RTI: Collaborative practices for improving K–12 literacy.* Newark, DE: International Reading Association.

Dorn, L. J., & Schubert, B. (2008). A comprehensive intervention model for reversing reading failure: A response to intervention approach. *Journal of Reading Recovery, 7*(2), 29–41.

Dorn, L. J., & Soffos, C. (2012). *Interventions that work: A comprehensive intervention model for preventing reading failure in grades K–3.* Boston, MA: Pearson.

Duffy, G. G. (1993a). Rethinking strategy instruction: Four teachers' development and their low achievers' understandings. *Elementary School Journal, 93*(3), 231–247.

Duffy, G. G. (1993b). Teachers' progress toward becoming expert strategy teachers. *Elementary School Journal, 94*(2), 109–120.

Duffy, G. G. (2009). *Explaining reading: A resource for teaching concepts, skills, and strategies* (2nd ed.). New York: Guilford Press.

Duffy, G. G., Roehler, L. R., Meloth, M. S., Polin, R., Rackliffe, G., Tracy, A., et al. (1987). Developing and evaluating measures associated with strategic reading. *Journal of Reading Behavior, 19,* 223–246.

Duffy, G. G., Roehler, L. R., Meloth, M. S., Vavrus, L. G., Book, C., Putnam, J., et al. (1986). The relationship between explicit verbal explanations during reading instruction and student awareness and achievement: A study of reading teacher effects. *Reading Research Quarterly, 21*(3), 237–252.

Duffy, G. G., Roehler, L. R., & Rackliffe, G. (1986). How teachers' instructional talk influences students' understanding of lesson content. *Elementary School Journal, 87*(1), 3–16.

Duffy, G. G., Roehler, L. R., Sivan, E., Rackliffe, G., Book, C., Meloth, M. S., et al. (1987). Effects of explaining the reasoning associated with using reading strategies. *Reading Research Quarterly, 22*(3), 347–368.

Duke, N. K. (2000). 3.6 minutes per day: The scarcity of informational text in first grade. *Reading Research Quarterly, 35,* 202–224.

Duke, N. K., & Carlisle, J. (2011). The development of comprehension. In M. L. Kamil, P. D. Pearson, E. B. Moje, & P. P. Afflerbach (Eds.), *Handbook of reading research* (Vol. IV, pp. 199–228). New York: Routledge.

Duke, N. K., & Pearson, P. D. (2002). Effective practices for developing reading comprehension. In A. E. Farstrup & S. J. Samuels (Eds.), *What research has to say about reading instruction* (pp. 205–242). Newark, DE: International Reading Association.

Duke, N. K., & Pearson, P. D. (2008). Effective practices for developing reading comprehension. *Journal of Education, 189*(1/2), 107–122.

Durkin, D. (1978/79). What classroom observations reveal about reading comprehension instruction. *Reading Research Quarterly, 14*(4), 481–533.

Dweck, C. S. (2000). *Self-theories: Their role in motivation, personality, and development.* Philadelphia: Psychology Press/Taylor & Francis.

Edmonds, M. S., Vaughn, S., Wexler, J., Reutebuch, C., Tackett, K. K., & Schnakenberg, J. W.

(2009). A synthesis of reading interventions and effects on reading comprehension outcomes for older struggling readers. *Review of Educational Research, 79*(1), 262–300.

Ehri, L. C. (1991). Development of the ability to read words. In R. Barr, M. L. Kamil, P. B. Mosenthal, & P. D. Pearson (Eds.), *Handbook of reading research* (Vol. II, pp. 383–417). New York: Longman.

Ehri, L. C. (1994). Development of the ability to read words: Update. In R. B. Ruddell, M. R. Ruddell, & H. Singer (Eds.), *Theoretical models and processes of reading* (4th ed., pp. 323–358). Newark, DE: International Reading Association.

Ehri, L. C. (1998). Grapheme–phoneme knowledge is essential for learning to read words in English. In J. L. Metsala & L. C. Ehri (Eds.), *Word recognition in beginning literacy* (pp. 3–40). Mahwah, NJ: Erlbaum.

Ehri, L. C. (2005). Learning to read words: Theory, findings, and issues. *Scientific Studies of Reading, 9*(2), 167–188.

Ehri, L. C., Satlow, E., & Gaskins, I. W. (2009). Grapho-phonemic enrichment strengthens keyword analogy instruction for struggling readers. *Reading and Writing Quarterly: Overcoming Learning Difficulties, 25*, 162–191.

El-Dinary, P. B., & Schuder, T. (1993). Seven teachers' acceptance of transactional strategies instruction during their first year using it. *Elementary School Journal, 94*(2), 207–219.

Eldredge, J. L., Reutzel, D. R., & Hollingsworth, P. M. (1996). Comparing the effectiveness of two oral reading practices: Round-robin reading and the shared book experience. *Journal of Literacy Research, 28*, 201–225.

Englert, C. S., & Hiebert, E. H. (1984). Children's developing awareness of text structures in expository materials. *Journal of Educational Psychology, 76*, 65–74.

Fall, R., Webb, N. M., & Chudowsky, N. (2000). Group discussion and large-scale language arts assessment: Effects on students' comprehension. *American Educational Research Journal, 37*(4), 911–941.

Federal Register. (2006, August 14). *Assistance to states for the education of children with disabilities and preschool grants for children with disabilities: Final rule.* Retrieved July 22, 2011, from *edocket.access.gpo.gov/2006/pdf/06–6656.pdf*

Fielding, L. G., & Pearson, P. D. (1994). Reading comprehension: What works. *Educational Leadership, 51*, 62–68.

Fitzgerald, J., & Teasley, A. B. (1986). Effects of instruction in narrative structure on children's writing. *Journal of Educational Psychology, 78*(6), 424–432.

Flanigan, K. (2007). A concept of word in text: A pivotal event in early reading acquisition. *Journal of Literacy Research, 39*(1), 37–70.

Flaro, L. (1987). The development and evaluation of a reading comprehension strategy with learning disabled students. *Reading Improvement, 24*, 222–229.

Flavell, J. H. (1979). Metacognition and cognitive monitoring: A new area of cognitive–developmental inquiry. *American Psychologist, 34*, 906–911.

Fleisher, L. S., Jenkins, J. R., & Pany, D. (1979). Effects on poor readers' comprehension of training in rapid decoding. *Reading Research Quarterly, 15*(1), 30–48.

Fletcher, J. M., Lyon, G. R., Barnes, M., Stuebing, K. K., Francis, D. J., Olson, R. K., et al. (2002). Classification of learning disabilities: An evidence-based evaluation. In R. Bradley, L. Danielson, & D. P. Hallahan (Eds.), *Identification of learning disabilities: Research to practice* (pp. 185–262). Mahwah, NJ: Erlbaum.

Forbes, S., Poparad, M. A., & McBride, M. (2004). To err is human; to self-correct is to learn. *The Reading Teacher, 57*(6), 566–572.

Fountas, I. C., & Pinnell, G. S. (1996). *Guided reading: Good first teaching for all children.* Portsmouth, NH: Heinemann.

Fountas, I. C., & Pinnell, G. S. (2006). *Teaching for comprehending and fluency: Thinking, talking, and writing about reading, K–8.* Portsmouth, NH: Heinemann.

Fox, B. J. (2000). *Word identification strategies: Phonics from a new perspective* (2nd ed.). Upper Saddle River, NJ: Merrill.

Fox, E. (2009). The role of reader characteristics in processing and learning from informational text. *Review of Educational Research, 79*(1), 197–261.

Frith, U. (1985). Beneath the surface of a developmental dyslexia. In K. Patterson, J. Marshall, & M. Coltheart (Eds.), *Surface dyslexia: Neuropsychological and cognitive studies of phonological reading* (pp. 301–330). London: Erlbaum.

Fuchs, D., & Fuchs, L. S. (2006). Introduction to response to intervention: What, why, and how valid is it? *Reading Research Quarterly, 41*(1), 93–99.

Fullerton, S. K. (2001). Achieving motivation: Guiding Edward's journey to literacy. *Literacy Teaching and Learning, 6*(1), 43–71.

Fullerton, S. K., & Dunston, P. J. (2010, December). *Teacher decision-making and reflection: The intersection of assessment, texts, tasks, and talk*. Paper presented at the annual meeting of the Literacy Research Association, Fort Worth, TX.

Fullerton, S. K., & Quinn, M. P. (2002). Teacher research as professional development: A study of teaching and learning. In E. Rodgers & G. S. Pinnell (Eds.), *Learning from teaching in literacy education* (pp. 119–134). Portsmouth, NH: Heinemann.

Gallant, P., & Schwartz, R. (2010). Examining the nature of expertise in reading instruction. *Literacy Research and Instruction, 49*(1), 1–19.

Gallimore, R., & Tharp, R. (1990). Teaching mind in society: Teaching schooling and literate discourse. In L. C. Moll (Ed.), *Vygotsky and education: Instructional implications and applications of sociohistorical psychology* (pp. 175–205). Cambridge, UK: Cambridge University Press.

Gambrell, L. B., & Almasi, J. F. (1996). (Eds.). *Lively discussions!: Fostering engaged reading*. Newark, DE: International Reading Association.

Gambrell, L. B., & Bales, R. J. (1986). Mental imagery and the comprehension-monitoring performance of fourth- and fifth-grade poor readers. *Reading Research Quarterly, 21*(4), 454–464.

Gambrell, L. B., & Jawitz, P. (1993). Mental imagery, text illustrations, and children's story comprehension and recall. *Reading Research Quarterly, 28*, 264–276.

Gambrell, L. B., Palmer, B. M., Codling, R., & Mazzoni, S. A. (1996). Assessing motivation to read. *The Reading Teacher, 49*(7), 518–533.

Gambrell, L. B., Wilson, R. M., & Gantt, W. N. (1981). Classroom observations of task-attending behaviors of good and poor readers. *Journal of Educational Research, 74*(6), 400–404.

Gamse, B.C., Jacob, R.T., Horst, M., Boulay, B., & Unlu, F. (2008). *Reading First impact study final report executive summary* (NCEE 2009-4039). Washington, DC: National Center for Education Evaluation and Regional Assistance, Institute of Education Sciences, U.S. Department of Education.

Garner, R. (1980). Monitoring of understanding: An investigation of good and poor readers' awareness of induced miscomprehension of text. *Journal of Reading Behavior, 12*, 55–63.

Garner, R. (1987). *Metacognition and reading comprehension*. Norwood, NJ: Ablex.

Garner, R. (1990). When children and adults do not use learning strategies: Toward a theory of settings. *Review of Educational Research, 60*(4), 517–529.

Garner, R., & Kraus, C. (1981). Good and poor comprehender differences in knowing and regulating reading behaviors. *Educational Research Quarterly, 6*(4), 5–12.

Garner, R., & Reis, R. (1981). Monitoring and resolving comprehension obstacles: An investigation of spontaneous text lookbacks among upper-grade good and poor readers. *Reading Research Quarterly, 16*(4), 569–582.

Gaskins, I. W. (2011). Interventions to develop decoding proficiencies. In A. McGill-Franzen & R. L. Allington (Eds.), *Handbook of reading disabilities* (pp. 289–306). New York: Routledge.

Gaskins, I. W., Anderson, R. C., Pressley, M., Cunicelli, E. A., & Satlow, E. (1993). Six teachers' dialogue during cognitive process instruction. *Elementary School Journal, 93*, 277–304.

Gay, G. (2002). Preparing for culturally responsive teaching. *Journal of Teacher Education, 53*(2), 106–116.

Gee, J. P. (1992). Socio-cultural approaches to literacy (literacies). In W. A. Grabe (Ed.), *Annual review of applied linguistics* (Vol. 12, pp. 31–48). New York: Cambridge University Press.

Gee, J. P. (2000). Discourse and sociocultural studies in reading. In M. L. Kamil, P. B. Mosenthal, P. D. Pearson, & R. Barr (Eds.), *Handbook of reading research* (Vol. III, pp. 195–207). Mahwah, NJ: Erlbaum.

Gentry, J. R. (1987). *Spel . . . is a four-letter word*. Portsmouth, NH: Heinemann.

Gersten, R., & Carnine, D. (1986). Direct instruction in reading comprehension. *Educational Leadership, 43*(7), 70–78.

Gersten, R., Compton, D., Connor, C. M., Dimino, J., Santoro, L., Linan-Thompson, S., et al. (2008). *Assisting students struggling with reading: Response to intervention and multi-tier intervention for reading in the primary grades. A practice guide* (NCEE 2009-4045). Washington, DC: National Center for Education Evaluation and Regional Assistance, Institute of Education Sciences, U.S. Department of Education. Retrieved from *ies.ed.gov/ncee/wwc/publications/practiceguides*.

Gersten, R., & Dimino, J. A. (2006). RTI (response to intervention): Rethinking special education for students with reading difficulties (yet again). *Reading Research Quarterly, 41*(1), 99–107.

Gersten, R., Fuchs, L. S., Williams, J. P., & Baker, S. (2001). Teaching reading comprehension strategies to students with learning disabilities: A review of research. *Review of Educational Research, 71*(2), 279–320.

Gillett, J. W., & Temple, C. (1994). *Understanding reading problems: Assessment and instruction*. New York: HarperCollins.

Goatley, V. J., Brock, C. H., & Raphael, T. E. (1995). Diverse learners participating in regular education "book clubs." *Reading Research Quarterly, 30*(3), 352–365.

Goldman, S. R., & Rakestraw, J. A. (2000). Structural aspects of constructing meaning from text. In M. L. Kamil, P. B. Mosenthal, P. D. Pearson, & R. Barr (Eds.), *Handbook of reading research* (Vol. III, pp. 311–335). Mahwah, NJ: Erlbaum.

Goodman, K. S. (1965). Cues and miscues in reading: A linguistic study. *Elementary English, 42*, 639–643.

Goodman, K. S. (1973). Miscues: Windows on the reading process. In K. S. Goodman (Ed.), *Miscue analysis: Applications to reading instruction* (pp. 3–14). Urbana, IL: ERIC Clearinghouse on Reading and Communication Skills and the National Council of Teachers of English.

Goodman, K. S. (2009). Making sense of written language: A lifelong journey. *Journal of Literacy Research, 37*(1), 1–24.

Goodman, Y. M. (1971). *Longitudinal study of children's oral reading behavior*. Washington, DC: U.S. Department of Health, Education and Welfare, Office of Education, Bureau of Research.

Goodman, Y. M., & Burke, C. L. (1972). *Reading miscue inventory manual: Procedures for diagnosis and evaluation*. New York: Macmillan.

Goodman, Y. M., Watson, D. J., & Burke, C. L. (1987). *Reading miscue inventory: Alternative procedures*. New York: Richard C. Owen.

Goodman, Y. M., Watson, D. J., & Burke, C. (2005). *Reading miscue inventory: From evaluation to instruction*. New York: Richard C. Owen.

Goswami, U., & Bryant, P.E. (1990). *Phonological skills and learning to read*. Hillsdale, NJ: Erlbaum.

Goswami, U., & Mead, F. (1992). Onset and rime awareness and analogies in reading. *Reading Research Quarterly, 27*(2), 152–162.

Graesser, A. C. (2007). An introduction to strategic reading comprehension. In D. S. McNamara (Ed.), *Reading comprehension strategies: Theories, interventions, and technologies* (pp. 3–26). New York: Erlbaum.

Graesser, A. C., McNamara, D. S., & Louwerse, M. M. (2003). What do readers need to learn in order to process coherence relations in narrative and expository text? In A. P. Sweet & C. E. Snow (Eds.), *Rethinking reading comprehension* (pp. 82–98). New York: Guilford Press.

Greene, S., & Ackerman, J. M. (1995). Expanding the constructivist metaphor: A rhetorical perspective on literacy research and practice. *Review of Educational Research, 65,* 383–420.

Guthrie, J. T., Taboada, A., & Coddington, C. S. (2007). Engagement practices for strategy learning in concept-oriented reading instruction. In D. S. McNamara (Ed.), *Reading comprehension strategies: Theories, interventions, and technologies* (pp. 241–266). New York: Erlbaum.

Guthrie, J. T., Van Meter, P., McCann, A., Wigfield, A., Bennett, L., Poundstone, C. C., et al. (1996). Growth of literacy engagement: Changes in motivations and strategies during concept-oriented reading instruction. *Reading Research Quarterly, 31*(3), 306–332.

Guthrie, J. T., & Wigfield, A. (1999). How motivation fits into a science of reading. *Scientific Studies of Reading, 3*(3), 199–205.

Guthrie, J. T., & Wigfield, A. (2000). Engagement and motivation in reading. In M. L. Kamil, P. B. Mosenthal, P. D. Pearson, & R. Barr (Eds.), *Handbook of reading research* (Vol. III, pp. 403–422). Mahwah, NJ: Erlbaum.

Guthrie, J. T., Wigfield, A., Barbosa, P., Perencevich, K. C., Taboada, A., Davis, M. H., et al. (2004). Increasing reading comprehension and engagement through concept-oriented reading instruction. *Journal of Educational Psychology, 96*(3), 403–423.

Hacker, D. J. (2004). Self-regulated comprehension during normal reading. In R. B. Ruddell & N. J. Unrau (Eds.), *Theoretical models and processes of reading* (5th ed., pp. 755–779). Newark, DE: International Reading Association.

Hall, G. E., & Hord, S. M. (1987). *Change in schools: Facilitating the process.* Albany: State University of New York Press.

Halliday, M. A. K., & Hasan, R. (1976). *Cohesion in English.* New York: Longman.

Hartman, D. K., & Hartman, J. A. (1993). Reading across texts: Expanding the role of the reader. *The Reading Teacher, 47*(3), 202–211.

Hiebert, E. H., Englert, C. S., & Brennan, S. (1983). Awareness of text structure in recognition and production of expository discourse. *Journal of Reading Behavior, 15*(4), 63–79.

Hiebert, E. H., Winograd, P. N., & Danner, F. W. (1984). Children's attributions of failure and success in different aspects of reading. *Journal of Educational Psychology, 76*(6), 1139–1148.

Holdaway, D. (1979). *The foundations of literacy.* Sydney, Australia: Ashton-Scholastic.

Hoover, W. A., & Gough, P. (1990). The simple view of reading. *Reading and Writing: An Interdisciplinary Journal, 2,* 127–160.

Idol, L. (1987). Group story mapping: A comprehension strategy for both skilled and unskilled readers. *Journal of Learning Disabilities, 20*(4), 196–205.

Idol, L., & Croll, V. J. (1987). Story-mapping training as a means of improving reading comprehension. *Learning Disability Quarterly, 10,* 214–229.

Individuals with Disabilities Education Improvement Act of 2004, Public Law 108-466.

International Reading Association. (2010). *Response to Intervention: Guiding principles for educators from the International Reading Association.* Newark, DE: Author. Retrieved from *www.reading.org/Libraries/Resources/RTI_brochure_web.sflb.ashx.*

International Reading Association & National Council of Teachers of English. (2010). *Standards for the assessment of reading and writing.* Newark, DE: Author. Retrieved from *www.reading.org/general/currentresearch/standards/assessmentstandards.aspx.*

Ivey, G., Johnston, P., & Cronin, J. (1999, April). *Process talk and children's sense of literate competence and agency.* Paper presented at the annual meeting of the American Educational Research Association, Montreal, Canada.

Johns, J. (1993). *Basic reading inventory* (8th ed.). Dubuque, IA: Kendall-Hunt.

Johnson, P., & Keier, K. (2010). *Catching readers before they fall: Supporting readers who struggle, K–4.* Portland, ME: Stenhouse.

Johnston, P. H. (2004). *Choice words: How our language affects children's learning.* Portland, ME: Stenhouse.

Johnston, P. H. (2010a). A framework for Response to Intervention in Literacy. In P. H. Johnston (Ed.), *RTI in literacy: Responsive and comprehensive* (pp. 1–9). Newark, DE: International Reading Association.

Johnston, P. H. (2010b). An instructional frame for RTI. *The Reading Teacher, 63*(7), 602–604.

Johnston, P. H. (2011). Response to intervention in literacy: Problems and possibilities. *Elementary School Journal, 111*(4), 511–534.

Johnston, P. H., Allington, R., & Afflerbach, P. (1985). The congruence of classroom and remedial reading instruction. *Elementary School Journal, 85*(4), 465–477.

Johnston, P. H., & Winograd, P. N. (1985). Passive failure in reading. *Journal of Reading Behavior, 17*(4), 279–301.

Juel, C. (1988). Learning to read and write: A longitudinal study of 54 children from first through fourth grades. *Journal of Educational Psychology, 80*(4), 437–447.

Juel, C. (1991). Beginning reading. In R. Barr, M. L. Kamil, P. B. Mosenthal, & P. D. Pearson (Eds.), *Handbook of reading research* (Vol. II, pp. 759–788). New York: Longman.

Kamil, M. L., Borman, G. D., Dole, J., Kral, C. C., Salinger, T., & Torgesen, J. (2008). *Improving adolescent literacy: Effective classroom and intervention practices—a practice guide* (NCEE 2008-4027). Washington, DC: National Center for Education Evaluation and Regional Assistance, Institute of Education Sciences, U.S. Department of Education. Retrieved from *ies.ed.gov/ncee/wwc.*

Kendeou, P., & van den Broek, P. (2007). The effects of prior knowledge and text structure on comprehension processes during reading of scientific texts. *Memory and Cognition, 35*(7), 1567–1577.

King, S. D. (1990). *Combining a story structure strategy with the vocabulary language prediction strategy.* Unpublished manuscript.

Kintsch, W. (1998). *Comprehension: A paradigm for cognition.* New York: Cambridge University Press.

Kintsch, W., & Kintsch, E. (2005). Comprehension. In S. G. Paris & S. A. Stahl (Eds.), *Children's reading comprehension and assessment* (pp. 71–104). Mahwah, NJ: Erlbaum.

Klenk, L., & Almasi, J. F. (1997). School-based practicum in reading disabilities. *Language and Literacy Spectrum, 7,* 73–79.

Klingner, J. K., & Edwards, P. E. (2006). Cultural considerations with response to intervention models. *Reading Research Quarterly, 41*(1), 93–99.

Klingner, J. K., Vaughn, S., & Schumm, J. S. (1998). Collaborative strategic reading during social studies in heterogeneous fourth-grade classrooms. *Elementary School Journal, 99*(1), 3–22.

Koskinen, P., & Blum, I. (2002, August). *Supporting the comprehension development of diverse learners: Book access, shared reading, and audio models.* Paper presented at the 19th World Congress on Reading, Edinburgh, UK.

Kress, G. (2000). Design and transformation. In B. Cope & M. Kalantzis (Eds.), *Multiliteracies: Literacy learning and the design of social futures* (pp. 153–161). New York: Routledge.

Kucan, L., & Beck, I. L. (1997). Thinking aloud and reading comprehension research: Inquiry, instruction, and social interaction. *Review of Educational Research, 67*(3), 271–299.

LaBerge, D., & Samuels, S. J. (1974). Toward a theory of automatic processing in reading. *Cognitive Psychology, 6*(2), 293–323.

Langer, J. A. (1985). Children's sense of genre: A study of performance on parallel reading and writing tasks. *Written Communication, 2*(2), 157–187.

Leach, J. M., Scarborough, H. S., & Rescorla, L. (2003). Late-emerging reading disabilities. *Journal of Educational Psychology, 95*(2), 211–224.

Leslie, L., & Caldwell, J. S. (2011). *Qualitative Reading Inventory–5.* Boston: Pearson.

Leu, D. J., Jr., Coiro, J., Castek, J., Hartman, D. K., Henry, L. A., & Reinking, D. (2008). Research on instruction and assessment in the new literacies of online reading comprehension. In C. C.

Block & S. R. Parris (Eds.), *Comprehension instruction: Research-based best practices* (2nd ed., pp. 321–346). New York: Guilford Press.

Li, Y., Anderson, R. C., Nguyen-Jahiel, K., Dong, T., Archodidou, A., Kim, I., et al. (2007). Emergent leadership in children's discussion groups. *Cognition and Instruction, 25*(1), 75–111.

Lipson, M. Y. (1983). The influence of religious affiliation on children's memory for text information. *Reading Research Quarterly, 18,* 448–457.

Lipson, M. Y. (1996). Conversations with children and other classroom-based assessment strategies. In L. R. Putnam (Ed.), *How to become a better reading teacher: Strategies for assessment and intervention* (pp. 167–179). Englewood Cliffs, NJ: Merrill.

Lipson, M. Y., Mosenthal, J. H., Mekkelsen, J., & Russ, B. (2004). Building knowledge and fashioning success one school at a time. *The Reading Teacher, 57*(6), 534–542.

Lipson, M. Y., & Wixson, K. K. (2008). *Assessment and instruction of reading and writing difficulties: An interactive approach* (4th edition). Boston: Allyn & Bacon.

Lose, M. K. (2007). A child's response to intervention requires a responsive teacher of reading. *The Reading Teacher, 6*(3), 276–279.

Lyons, C. A. (1994). Constructing chains of reasoning in Reading Recovery demonstration lessons. In D. Leu & C. Kinzer (Eds.), *Multidimensional aspects of literacy research, theory, and practice: Forty-third yearbook of the National Reading Conference* (pp. 276–286). Chicago: National Reading Conference.

Lyons, C. A., & Pinnell, G. S. (2001). *Systems for change in literacy education: A guide to professional development.* Portsmouth, NH: Heinemann.

Magliano, J. P., & Millis, K. K. (2003). Assessing reading skill with a think-aloud procedure and latent semantic analysis. *Cognition and Instruction, 21*(3), 251–283.

Maloch, B. (2002). Scaffolding student talk: One teacher's role in literature discussion groups. *Reading Research Quarterly, 37*(1), 94–112.

Maloch, B. (2004). On the road to literature discussion groups: Teacher scaffolding during preparatory experiences. *Reading Research and Instruction, 44,* 1–20.

Mandler, J. M., & Johnson, N. S. (1977). Remembrance of things parsed: Story structure and recall. *Cognitive Psychology, 9,* 111–151.

Markman, E. M. (1977). Realizing that you don't understand: A preliminary investigation. *Child Development, 48,* 986–999.

Marshall, J. (2000). Research on response to literature. In M. L. Kamil, P. B. Mosenthal, P. D. Pearson, & R. Barr (Eds.), *Handbook of reading research* (Vol. III, pp. 381–402). Mahwah, NJ: Erlbaum.

Martin, N. M., & Duke, N. K. (2011). Interventions to enhance informational text comprehension. In A. McGill-Franzen & R. L. Allington (Eds.), *Handbook of reading disability research* (pp. 345–361). New York: Routledge.

Masonheimer, P. E., Drum, P. A., & Ehri, L. C. (1984). Does environmental print identification lead children into reading? *Journal of Reading Behavior, 16,* 257–271.

Mathes, P. G., Denton, C. A., Fletcher, J. M., Anthony, J. L., Francis, D. J., & Schatschneider, C. (2005). The effects of theoretically different instruction and student characteristics on the skills of struggling readers. *Reading Research Quarterly, 40,* 148–182.

Mathes, P. G., Howard, J. K., Allen, S. H., & Fuchs, D. (1998). Peer-assisted learning strategies for first-grade readers: Responding to the needs of diverse learners. *Reading Research Quarterly, 33*(1), 62–94.

McEneaney, J. E., Lose, M. K., & Schwartz, R. M. (2006). A transactional perspective on reading difficulties and response to intervention. *Reading Research Quarterly, 41*(1), 117–128.

McKoon, G., & Ratcliff, R. (1992). Inference during reading. *Psychological Review, 99,* 440–466.

McMaster, K. L., Fuchs, D., Fuchs, L.S., & Compton, D. L. (2005). Responding to nonresponders: An experimental field trial of identification and intervention methods. *Exceptional Children, 71,* 445–463.

McNamara, D. S. (2001). Reading both high-coherence and low-coherence texts: Effects of text sequence and prior knowledge. *Canadian Journal of Experimental Psychology, 55*(1), 51–62.

McNaughton, S. & Lai, M. K. (2010). The learning schools model of school change to raise achievement in reading comprehension for culturally and linguistically diverse students in New Zealand. In P. H. Johnston (Eds.), *RTI in literacy: Response and comprehensive* (pp. 313–335). Newark, DE: International Reading Association.

Mehan, H. (1979). *Learning lessons.* Cambridge, MA: Harvard University Press.

Meichenbaum, D. (1977). *Cognitive behavior modification.* New York: Plenum.

Meichenbaum, D., Burland, S., Gruson, L., & Cameron, R. (1985). Metacognitive assessment. In S. R. Yussen (Ed.), *The growth of reflection in children* (pp. 3–30). Orlando, FL: Academic Press.

Mesmer, A. E., & Griffith, P. L. (2005–2006). Everybody's selling it: But just what is explicit, systematic phonics instruction? *The Reading Teacher, 59*(4), 366–376.

Meyer, B. J. F. (1975). Identification of the structure of prose and its implications for the study of reading and memory. *Journal of Reading Behavior, 7,* 7–48.

Meyer, B. J. F., Brandt, D. M., & Bluth, G. J. (1980). Use of top-level structure in text: Key for reading comprehension of ninth-grade students. *Reading Research Quarterly, 16,* 72–103.

Meyer, B. J. F., & Rice, G. E. (1984). The structure of text. In P. D. Pearson, R. Barr, M. L. Kamil, & P. B. Mosenthal (Eds.), *Handbook of reading research* (Vol. I, pp. 319–351). New York: Longman.

Meyer, K. E., & Reindl, B. L. (2010). Spotlight on the comprehensive intervention model: The case of Washington School for Comprehensive Literacy. In M. Y. Lipson & K. K. Wixson (Eds.), *Successful approaches to RTI: Collaborative practices for improving K–12 literacy* (pp. 121–133). Newark, DE: International Reading Association.

Miller, S. D. (2003). Partners-in-reading: Using classroom assistants to provide tutorial assistance to struggling first-grade readers. *Journal of Education for Students Placed at Risk, 8,* 333–349.

Miller, S. D., & Faircloth, B. S. (2009). Motivation and reading comprehension. In S. E. Israel & G. G. Duffy (Eds.), *Handbook of research in reading comprehension* (pp. 307–322). New York: Routledge.

Millis, K., Magliano, J. P., & Tadaro, S. (2006). Measuring discourse-level processes with verbal protocols and latent semantic analysis. *Scientific Studies of Reading, 10*(3), 225–240.

Mokhtari, K., & Reichard, C. A. (2002). Assessing students' metacognitive awareness of reading strategies. *Journal of Educational Psychology, 94,* 249–259.

Moshman, D. (1982). Exogenous, endogenous, and dialectical constructivism. *Developmental Review, 2*(4), 371–384.

Murray, B. A., Stahl, S., & Ivey, G. M. (1996). Developing phonemic awareness through alphabet books. *Reading and Writing: An Interdisciplinary Journal, 8,* 307–322.

Myers, M., & Paris, S. G. (1978). Children's metacognitive knowledge about reading. *Journal of Educational Psychology, 70,* 680–690.

Nation, K. (2005). Children's reading comprehension difficulties. In M. J. Snowling & C. Hulme (Eds.), *The science of reading: A handbook* (pp. 248–266). Malden, MA: Blackwell.

Nation, K., & Snowling, M. J. (1999). Developmental differences in sensitivity to semantic relations among good and poor comprehenders: Evidence from semantic priming. *Cognition, 70,* B1–B13.

National Center for Education Statistics. (2009). *The nation's report card: Reading 2009* (NCES 2010-458). Washington, DC: Institute of Education Sciences, U.S. Department of Education.

National Center on Response to Intervention. (2011). *Screening tools chart.* Retrieved from *www. rti4success.org/screeningTools.*

National Reading Panel. (2000). *Teaching children to read: An evidence-based assessment of the scientific research literature on reading and its implications for reading instruction* (Report of the Subgroups). Washington, DC: U.S. Department of Health and Human Services, Public Health Service, National Institutes of Health, and the National Institute of Child Health and Human Development.

New London Group. (2000). A pedagogy of multiliteracies. In B. Cope & M. Kalantzis (Eds.), *Multiliteracies: Literacy learning and the design of social futures* (pp. 9–37). New York: Routledge.

Oakhill, J. V., Cain, K., & Bryant, P. E. (2003). The dissociation of word reading and text comprehension: Evidence from component skills. *Language and Cognitive Processes, 18*(4), 443–468.

O'Connor, R. E. (2000). Increasing the intensity of intervention in kindergarten and first grade. *Learning Disabilities Research and Practice, 15*, 43–54.

Ogle, D. M. (1986). K-W-L: A teaching model that develops active reading of expository text. *The Reading Teacher, 39*(6), 564–570.

Ohlhausen, M. M., & Roller, C. M. (1988). The operation of text structure and content schemata in isolation and in interaction. *Reading Research Quarterly, 23*(1), 70–88.

Oster, L. (2001). Using the think-aloud for reading instruction. *The Reading Teacher, 55*(1), 64–69.

Paivio, A. (1986). *Mental representations: A dual coding approach.* New York: Oxford University Press.

Palincsar, A. S. (2003). Collaborative approaches to comprehension instruction. In A. P. Sweet & C. E. Snow (Eds.), *Rethinking reading comprehension* (pp. 99–114). New York: Guilford Press.

Palincsar, A. S., & Brown, A. L. (1984). Reciprocal teaching of comprehension-fostering and comprehension-monitoring activities. *Cognition and Instruction, 1*, 117–175.

Palincsar, A. S., & Brown, A. L. (1989). Instruction for self-regulated reading. In L. B. Resnick & L. E. Klopfer (Eds.), *Toward the thinking curriculum: Current cognitive research* (pp. 19–39). Alexandria, VA: Association for Supervision and Curriculum Development.

Palincsar, A. S., David, Y. M., Winn, J. A., & Stevens, D. (1991). Examining the context of strategy instruction. *Remedial and Special Education, 12*(3), 43–53.

Pappas, C. C. (1991). Young children's strategies in learning the "book language" of information books. *Discourse Processes, 14*, 203–225.

Paris, S. G., Byrnes, J. P., & Paris, A. H. (2009). Constructing theories, identities, and actions of self-regulated learners. In B. J. Zimmerman & D. H. Schunk (Eds.), *Self-regulated learning and academic achievement* (2nd ed., pp. 253–287). New York: Routledge.

Paris, S. G., Cross, D., & Lipson, M. Y. (1984). Informed strategies for learning: A program to improve children's reading awareness and comprehension. *Journal of Educational Psychology, 76*, 1239–1252.

Paris, S. G., & Hamilton, E. E. (2009). The development of children's reading comprehension. In S. E. Israel & G. G. Duffy (Eds.), *Handbook of research on reading comprehension* (pp. 32–53). New York: Routledge.

Paris, S. G., & Jacobs, J. E. (1984). The benefits of informed instruction for children's reading awareness and comprehension skills. *Child Development, 55*, 2083–2093.

Paris, S. G., Lipson, M. Y., & Wixson, K. K. (1983). Becoming a strategic reader. *Contemporary Educational Psychology, 8*, 293–316.

Paris, S. G., & Myers, M. (1981). Comprehension monitoring, memory, and study strategies of good and poor readers. *Journal of Reading Behavior, 13*, 5–22.

Paris, S. G., & Oka, E. R. (1986a). Children's reading strategies, metacognition, and motivation. *Developmental Review, 6*, 25–56.

Paris, S. G., & Oka, E. R. (1986b). Self-regulated learning among exceptional children. *Exceptional Children, 53*(2), 103–108.

Paris, S. G., Wasik, B. A., & Turner, J. C. (1991). The development of strategic readers. In R. Barr, M. L. Kamil, P. Mosenthal, & P. D. Pearson (Eds.), *Handbook of reading research* (Vol. II, pp. 609–640). New York: Longman.

Paris, S. G., & Winograd, P. (2001). *The role of self-regulated learning in contextual teaching: principles and practices for teacher preparation.* Commissioned paper for the project Preparing Teachers to Use Contextual Teaching and Learning Strategies to Improve Student Success in and beyond School. Washington, DC: U.S. Department of Education.

Pearson, P. D. (1996). Reclaiming the center. In M. F. Graves, P. van den Broek, & B. M. Taylor (Eds.), *The first R: Every child's right to read* (pp. 259–274). Newark, DE: International Reading Association.

Pearson, P. D., & Dole, J. A. (1987). Explicit comprehension instruction: A review of research and a new conceptualization of instruction. *Elementary School Journal, 88*(2), 151–165.

Pearson, P. D., & Fielding, L. (1991). Comprehension instruction. In R. Barr, M. L. Kamil, P. B. Mosenthal, & P. D. Pearson (Eds.), *Handbook of reading research* (Vol. II, pp. 815–860). New York: Longman.

Pearson, P. D., & Gallagher, M. C. (1983). The instruction of reading comprehension. *Contemporary Educational Psychology, 8*, 317–344.

Pearson, P. D., Hansen, J., & Gordon, C. (1979). The effect of background knowledge on young children's comprehension of explicit and implicit information. *Journal of Reading Behavior, 11*(3), 201–209.

Perkins, D. N., & Salomon, G. (1989). Are cognitive skills context-bound? *Educational Researcher, 18*, 16–25.

Pilonieta, P. (2010). Instruction of research-based comprehension strategies in basal reading programs. *Reading Psychology, 31*(2), 150–175.

Pinnell, G. S. (1989). Reading Recovery: Helping at-risk children learn to read. *Elementary School Journal, 90*, 161–183.

Pinnell, G. S. (2002). The guided reading lesson: Explaining, supporting, and prompting for comprehension. In C. C. Block, L. B. Gambrell, & M. Pressley (Eds.), *Improving comprehension instruction: Rethinking research, theory, and classroom practice* (pp. 106–134). San Francisco: Jossey-Bass.

Pinnell, G. S., Lyons, C. A., DeFord, D. E., Bryk, A. S., & Seltzer, M. (1994). Comparing instructional models for the literacy education of high-risk first graders. *Reading Research Quarterly, 29*(1), 9–39.

Poplin, M. S. (1988). The reductionistic fallacy in learning disabilities: Replicating the past by reducing the present. *Journal of Learning Disabilities, 21*, 401–416.

Prawat, R. S. (1989). Promoting access to knowledge, strategy, and disposition in students: A research synthesis. *Review of Educational Research, 59*(1), 1–41.

Prensky, M. (2001). Digital natives, digital immigrants, Part 1. *On the Horizon, 9*(5), 1–6.

Pressley, M. (1986). The relevance of the good strategy user model to the teaching of mathematics. *Educational Psychologist, 21*, 139–161.

Pressley, M. (2000). What should comprehension instruction be the instruction of? In M. L. Kamil, P. B. Mosenthal, P. D. Pearson, & R. Barr (Eds.), *Handbook of reading research* (Vol. III, pp. 545–561). Mahwah, NJ: Erlbaum.

Pressley, M. (2006). *Reading instruction that works: The case for balanced teaching* (3rd ed.). New York: Guilford Press.

Pressley, M., & Afflerbach, P. P. (1995). *Verbal protocols of reading: The nature of constructively responsive reading.* Hillsdale, NJ: Erlbaum.

Pressley, M., Borkowski, J. G., & Schneider, W. (1989). Good information processing: What it is and how education can promote it. *International Journal of Educational Research, 13*, 857–867.

Pressley, M., Brown, R., El-Dinary, P. B., & Afflerbach, P. P. (1995). The comprehension instruction that students need: Instruction fostering constructively responsive teaching. *Learning Disabilities Research and Practice, 10*(4), 215–224.

Pressley, M., El-Dinary, P. B., Gaskins, I., Schuder, T., Bergman, J. L., Almasi, J., et al. (1992). Beyond direct explanation: Transactional instruction of reading comprehension strategies. *Elementary School Journal, 92*(5), 513–555.

Pressley, M., Goodchild, F., Fleet, J., Zajchowski, R., & Evans, E. D. (1989). The challenges of classroom strategy instruction. *Elementary School Journal, 89*, 301–342.

Pressley, M., Harris, K. R., & Marks, M. B. (1992). But good strategy instructors are constructivists! *Educational Psychology Review, 4*(1), 3–31.

Pressley, M., Johnson, C. J., Symons, S., McGoldrick, J. A., & Kurita, J. A. (1989). Strategies that improve children's memory and comprehension of text. *Elementary School Journal, 90*(1), 3–32.

Pressley, M., Schuder, T., SAIL Faculty and Administration, Bergman, J., & El-Dinary, P. B. (1992). A researcher–educator collaborative interview study of transactional comprehension strategies instruction. *Journal of Educational Psychology, 84*, 231–246.

Pressley, M., Symons, S., Snyder, B. L., & Cariglia-Bull, T. (1989). Strategy instruction comes of age. *Learning Disability Quarterly, 12*, 16–30.

Pressley, M., Wharton-McDonald, R., Allington, R., Block, C. C., Morrow, L., Tracey, D., et al. (2001). A study of effective first-grade literacy instruction. *Scientific Studies of Reading, 5*(1), 35–58.

Pressley, M., Wharton-McDonald, R., Mistretta-Hampston, J., & Eschevarria, M. (1998). Literacy instruction in 10 fourth and fifth grade classrooms in upstate New York. *Scientific Studies of Reading, 2*(2), 159–194.

Pressley, M., Woloshyn, V., & Associates (1995). *Cognitive strategy instruction that really improves children's academic performance* (2nd ed.). Cambridge, MA: Brookline Books.

Proctor, C. P., Carlo, M. S., August, D., & Snow, C. E. (2005). Native Spanish-speaking children reading in English: Toward a model of comprehension. *Journal of Educational Psychology, 97*, 246–256.

RAND. (2006). *RAND research brief: Developing an R&D program to improve reading comprehension.* Retrieved from *www.rand.org/pubs/research_briefsRB8024/index1.htm*

Recht, D. R., & Leslie, L. (1988). Effect of prior knowledge on good and poor readers' memory of text. *Journal of Educational Psychology, 80*(1), 16–20.

Reutzel, D. R., & Cooter, R. B. (2011). *Strategies for reading assessment and instruction: Helping every child succeed.* Boston: Pearson.

Reutzel, D. R., Smith, J. A., & Fawson, P. C. (2005). An evaluation of two approaches for teaching reading comprehension strategies in the primary years using science information texts. *Early Childhood Research Quarterly, 20*, 276–305.

Reyna, V. F., & Brainerd, C. J. (2011). Dual processes in decision making and developmental neuroscience: A fuzzy-trace model. *Developmental Review, 31*, 180–206.

Richards, I. A. (1929). *Practical criticism.* New York: Harcourt, Brace and World.

Riddle Buly, M., & Valencia, S. W. (2002). Below the bar: Profiles of students who fail state reading assessments. *Educational Evaluation and Policy Analysis, 24*(3), 219–239.

Roberts, B. S. (1992). The evolution of the young child's concept of word as a unit of spoken and written language. *Reading Research Quarterly, 27*(2), 125–138.

Rodgers, E. M. (2004). Interactions that scaffold reading performance. *Journal of Literacy Research, 36*(4), 501–532.

Rodgers, E. M., Fullerton, S. K., & DeFord, D. (2002). Making a difference with professional development. In E. Rodgers & G. S. Pinnell (Eds.), *Learning from teaching in literacy education* (pp. 52–62). Portsmouth, NH: Heinemann.

Rogoff, B. (1990). *Apprenticeship in thinking: Cognitive development in social context.* New York: Oxford University Press.

Romeo, L. (2002). At risk students: Learning to break through comprehension barriers. In C. C. Block, L. B. Gambrell, & M. Pressley (Eds.), *Improving comprehension instruction: Rethinking research, theory, and classroom practice* (pp. 354–369). San Francisco: Jossey-Bass.

Rosemary, C. A., Roskos, K. A., & Landreth, L. K. (2007). *Designing professional development in literacy: A framework for effective instruction.* New York: Guilford Press.

Rosenblatt, L. M. (1978). *The reader, the text, the poem: The transactional theory of the literary work.* Carbondale, IL: Southern Illinois University Press.

Rosenblatt, L. M. (1988). Writing and reading: The transactional theory. *Reader, 20,* 7–31.

Rosenblatt, L. M. (1991). Literature—S.O.S! *Language Arts, 68,* 444–448.

Rovane, C. A. (1998). *The bounds of agency: An essay in revisionary metaphysics.* Princeton, NJ: Princeton University Press.

Rowe, D. W., & Rayford, L. (1987). Activating background knowledge in reading comprehension assessment. *Reading Research Quarterly, 22*(2), 160–176.

Rumelhart, D. E. (1980). Schemata: The building blocks of cognition. In R. J. Spiro, B. C. Bruce, & W. F. Brewer (Eds.), *Theoretical issues in reading comprehension* (pp. 33–58). Hillsdale, NJ: Erlbaum.

Rumelhart, D. E., & Ortony, A. (1977). The representation of knowledge in memory. In R. C. Anderson, R. J. Spiro, & W. E. Montague (Eds.), *Schooling and the acquisition of knowledge* (pp. 99–135). Hillsdale, NJ: Erlbaum.

Sadoski, M. (1983). An exploratory study of the relationships between reported imagery and the comprehension and recall of a story. *Reading Research Quarterly, 19,* 110–123.

Sadoski, M. (1985). The natural use of imagery in story comprehension and recall: Replication and extension. *Reading Research Quarterly, 20,* 658–667.

Sadoski, M., Goetz, E. T., & Kangiser, S. (1988). Imagination in story response: Relationships between imagery, affect, and structural importance. *Reading Research Quarterly, 23*(3), 320–336.

Sailors, M., & Price, L. R. (2010). Professional development that supports the teaching of cognitive reading strategy instruction. *Elementary School Journal, 110*(3), 301–322.

Samuels, S. J. (2004). Toward a theory of automatic information processing in reading, revisited. In R. B. Ruddell & N. J. Unrau (Eds.), *Theoretical models and processes of reading* (5th ed., pp. 1127–1148). Newark, DE: International Reading Association.

Santa, C. M., & Høien, T. (1999). An assessment of Early Steps: A program for early intervention of reading problems. *Reading Research Quarterly, 34*(1), 54–79.

Scanlon, D. M., Gelzheiser, L. M., Vellutino, F. R., Schatschneider, C., & Sweeney, J. M. (2008). Reducing the incidence of early reading difficulties: Professional development for classroom teachers vs. direct interventions for children. *Learning and Individual Differences, 18,* 346–359.

Scanlon, D. M., & Sweeney, J. M. (2008). Response to intervention: An overview—new hope for struggling learners. *Educator's Voice, 1,* 16–29. Retrieved from *www.nysut.org/educators-voice_10025.htm*

Scanlon, D. M., Vellutino, F. R., Small, S. G., Fanuele, D. P., & Sweeney, J. M. (2005). Severe reading difficulties—can they be prevented?: A comparison of prevention and intervention approaches. *Exceptionality, 13*(4), 209–227.

Schmitt, M. C. (1990). A questionnaire to measure children's awareness of strategic reading processes. *The Reading Teacher, 43*(7), 454–461.

Schunk, D. H., & Pajares, F. (2005). Competence perceptions and academic functioning. In A. J. Elliott & C. S. Dweck (Eds.), *Handbook of competence and motivation* (pp. 85–104). New York: Guilford Press.

Schunk, D. H., & Rice, J. M. (1987). Enhancing comprehension skill and self-efficacy with strategy value information. *Journal of Reading Behavior, 19,* 285–302.

Schwartz, R. M. (1997). Self-monitoring in beginning reading. *The Reading Teacher, 51*(1), 40–48.

Schwartz, R. M. (2005). Decisions, decisions: Responding to primary students during guided reading. *The Reading Teacher, 58*(5), 436–443.

Seligman, M. E. P., & Maier, S. F. (1967). Failure to escape traumatic shock. *Journal of Experimental Psychology, 74*(1), 1–9.

Shanahan, T., Callison, K., Carriere, C., Duke, N., Pearson, P. D., Schatschneider, C., et al. (2010). *Improving reading comprehension in kindergarten through 3rd grade: A practice guide* (NCEE 2010–4038). Washington, DC: National Center for Educational Evaluation and Regional Assistance, Institute of Education Sciences, U.S. Department of Education. Retrieved from *whatworks.ed.gov/publications/practiceguides*

Shelton, N. R. (2010). Program fidelity in two reading mastery classrooms: A view from the inside. *Literacy Research and Instruction, 49*, 315–333.

Short, E. J., & Ryan, E. B. (1984). Metacognitive differences between skilled and less skilled readers: Remediating deficits through story grammar and attribution training. *Journal of Educational Psychology, 76*, 225–235.

Sipe, L. R., & Brightman, A. E. (2009). Young children's interpretations of page breaks in contemporary picture storybooks. *Journal of Literacy Research, 41*(1), 68–103.

Smith, A. B. (2011). *A case study of teacher responsivity in one-on-one and small-group lessons conducted by teachers trained in Reading Recovery.* Doctoral dissertation, University of Kentucky, Lexington, KY.

Snow, C. E., & Sweet, A. P. (2003). Reading for comprehension. In A. P. Sweet & C. E. Snow (Eds.), *Rethinking reading comprehension* (pp. 1–11). New York: Guilford Press.

Spectrum K12/Council of Administrators of Special Education. (2008). *Response to intervention (RTI) adoption survey.* Retrieved from *www.spectrumk12.com/rti/the_rti_corner/ rti_adoption_report.*

Spectrum K12 School Solutions. (2011). *Response to intervention: Adoption survey 2011.* Retrieved from *www.spectrumk12.com/rti/the_rti_corner/rti_adoption_report.*

Speece, D. L., Mills, C., Ritchey, K. D., & Hillman, E. (2003). Initial evidence that letter fluency tasks are valid indicators of early reading skill. *Journal of Special Education, 36*(4), 223–233.

Spivey, N. N., & King, J. R. (1989). Readers as writers composing from sources. *Reading Research Quarterly, 24*, 7–26.

Stahl, S. A. (1992). Saying the "p" word: Nine guidelines for exemplary phonics instruction. *The Reading Teacher, 45*, 618–626.

Stanovich, K. E. (1986). Matthew effects in reading: Some consequences of individual differences in the acquisition of literacy. *Reading Research Quarterly, 21*, 360–407.

Stauffer, R. G. (1969). *Directing reading maturity as a cognitive process.* New York: Harper & Row.

Stauffer, R. G. (1970). *The language experiences approach to the teaching of reading.* New York: Harper & Row.

Stein, N. L., & Glenn, C. G. (1979). An analysis of story comprehension in elementary school children. In R. Freedle (Ed.), *New directions in discourse processing* (pp. 53–120). Norwood, NJ: Ablex.

Sternberg, R. J., & Horvath, J. A. (1995). A prototype view of expert teaching. *Educational Researcher, 24*(6), 9–17.

Taft, M. L., & Leslie, L. (1985). The effects of prior knowledge and oral reading accuracy on miscues and comprehension. *Journal of Reading Behavior, 17*(2), 163–179.

Taylor, B. M. (1980). Children's memory for expository text after reading. *Reading Research Quarterly, 15*(3), 399–411.

Taylor, B. M., Pearson, P. D., Clark, K., & Walpole, S. (2000). Effective schools and accomplished teachers: Lessons about primary grade reading instruction. *Elementary School Journal, 101*(2), 121–165.

Taylor, B. M., Pearson, P. D., Peterson, D., & Rodriguez, M. C. (2003). Reading growth in high-poverty classrooms: The influence of teacher practices that encourage cognitive engagement in literacy learning. *Elementary School Journal, 104*(1), 3–28.

Taylor, B. M., Pearson, P. D., Peterson, D. S., & Rodriguez, M. C. (2004). The CIERA school change framework: An evidence-based approach to professional development and school reading improvement. *Reading Research Quarterly, 40*(1), 40–60.

Taylor, B. M., Peterson, D. S., Pearson, P. D., & Rodriguez, M. C. (2002). Looking inside classrooms: Reflecting on the "how" as well as the "what" in effective instruction. *Reading Teacher, 56*(3), 270–280.

Tompkins, G., & McGee, L. (1993). *Teaching reading with literature: Case studies to action plans*. New York: Merrill.

Turner, J. C. (1995). The influence of classroom contexts on young children's motivation for literacy. *Reading Research Quarterly, 30*(3), 410–441.

Valencia, S. W. (2007). Inquiry-oriented assessment. In J. R. Paratore & R. L. McCormack (Eds.), *Classroom literacy assessment: Making sense of what students know and do* (pp. 3–20). New York: Guilford Press.

Valencia, S. W. (2011). Reader profiles and reading disabilities. In A. McGill-Franzen & R. L. Allington (Eds.), *Handbook of reading disability research* (pp. 25–35). New York: Routledge.

Van den Branden, K. (2000). Does negotiation of meaning promote reading comprehension?: A study of multilingual primary school classes. *Reading Research Quarterly, 35*(2), 426–443.

Van Keer, H. (2004). Fostering reading comprehension in fifth grade by explicit instruction in reading strategies and peer tutoring. *British Journal of Educational Psychology, 74*, 37–70.

Van Ryzin, M. J. (2011). Motivation and reading disabilities. In A. McGill-Franzen & R. L. Allington (Eds.), *Handbook of reading disability research* (pp. 242–252). New York: Routledge.

Vaughn, S., Linan Thompson, S., & Hickman, P. (2003). Response to instruction as a means of identifying students with reading/learning disabilities. *Exceptional Children, 69*, 391–409.

Vellutino, F. R., & Scanlon, D. M. (2002). The interactive strategies approach to reading intervention. *Contemporary Educational Psychology, 27*, 573–635.

Vellutino, F. R., Scanlon, D. M., Sipay, E. R., Small, S. G., Pratt, A., Chen, R., et al. (1996). Cognitive profiles of difficult-to-remediate and readily remediated poor readers: Early intervention as a vehicle for distinguishing between cognitive and experiential deficits as basic causes of specific reading disability. *Journal of Educational Psychology, 88*, 601–638.

Vellutino, F. R., Scanlon, D. M., Small, S. G., & Fanuele, D. P. (2006). Response to intervention as a vehicle for distinguishing between reading disabled and non-reading-disabled children: Evidence for the role of kindergarten and first-grade intervention. *Journal of Learning Disabilities, 39*(2), 157–169.

Vogt, M., & Shearer, B. A. (2011). *Reading specialists and literacy coaches in the real world*. Boston: Allyn & Bacon.

Vygotsky, L. S. (1978). *Mind in society*. Cambridge, MA: Harvard University Press.

Wade, S. E. (1990). Using think-alouds to assess comprehension. *The Reading Teacher, 43*(7), 442–451.

Wagoner, S. A. (1983). Comprehension monitoring: What it is and what we know about it. *Reading Research Quarterly, 18*(3), 328–346.

Wagstaff, J. M. (1997–1998). Building practical knowledge of letter–sound correspondences: A beginner's word wall and beyond. *The Reading Teacher, 51*(4), 298–304.

Walker, B. J. (2000). *Diagnostic teaching of reading: Techniques for instruction and assessment* (4th ed.). New York: Pearson.

Walker, B. J. (2012). *Diagnostic teaching of reading: Techniques for instruction and assessment* (7th ed.). Upper Saddle River, NJ: Pearson.

Wanzek, J., & Vaughn, S. (2007). Research-based implications from extensive early reading interventions. *School Psychology Review, 36*(4), 541–561.

Wasik, B.A., & Slavin, R. E. (1993). Preventing early reading failure with one-to-one tutoring: A review of five programs. *Reading Research Quarterly, 28,* 179–200.

Weaver, C. A., & Kintsch, W. (1991). Expository text. In R. Barr, M. L. Kamil, P. B. Mosenthal, & P. D. Pearson (Eds.), *Handbook of reading research* (Vol. II, pp. 230–245). New York: Longman.

Weekes, B. S., Hamilton, S., Oakhill, J. V., & Holliday, R. E. (2008). False recollection in children with reading comprehension difficulties. *Cognition, 106,* 222–233.

Weiner, B. (1979). A theory of motivation for some classroom experiences. *Journal of Educational Psychology, 71,* 3–25.

Weiner, B. (1985). An attributional theory of motivation and emotion. *Psychological Review, 92*(4), 548–573.

Weiner, B. (1990). History of motivational research in education. *Journal of Educational Psychology, 82*(4), 616–622.

Westra, J., & Moore, D. (1995). Reciprocal teaching of reading comprehension in a New Zealand high school. *Psychology in the Schools, 32*(3), 225–232.

Whaley, J. F. (1984). Story grammars and reading instruction. *The Reading Teacher, 34,* 762–771.

Wharton-McDonald, R., Pressley, M., & Hampston, J. M. (1998). Literacy instruction in nine first-grade classrooms: Teacher characteristics and student achievement. *Elementary School Journal, 99*(2), 101–128.

Wharton-McDonald, R., & Swiger, S. (2009). Developing higher order comprehension in the middle grades. In S. E. Israel & G. G. Duffy (Eds.), *Handbook of research on reading comprehension* (pp. 510–530). New York: Routledge.

White, T. G., Power, M. A., & White, S. (1989). Morphological analysis: Implications for teaching and understanding vocabulary growth. *Reading Research Quarterly, 24,* 283–304.

White, T. G., Sowell, J., & Yanagihara, A. (1989). Teaching elementary students to use word-part clues. *The Reading Teacher, 42,* 302–308.

Wigfield, A., & Guthrie, J. T. (1997). Relations of children's motivation for reading to the amount and breadth of their reading. *Journal of Educational Psychology, 89*(3), 420–432.

Wigfield, A., Guthrie, J. T., Tonks, S., & Perencevich, K. C. (2004). Children's motivation for reading: Domain specificity and instructional influences. *Journal of Educational Research, 97,* 299–309.

Wilkinson, I. A. G., Soter, A. O., & Murphy, P. K. (2010). Developing a model of quality talk about literary text. In M. G. McKeown & L. Kucan (Eds.), *Bringing reading research to life* (pp. 142–169). New York: Guilford Press.

Wineburg, S. (1991). Historical problem solving: A study of the cognitive processes used in the evaluation of documentary and pictorial evidence. *Journal of Educational Psychology, 83*(1), 73–87.

Winne, P. H., & Marx, R. W. (1982). Students' and teachers' views of thinking processes for classroom learning. *Elementary School Journal, 82*(5), 493–518.

Winograd, P., & Johnston, P. (1982). Comprehension monitoring and the error-detection paradigm. *Journal of Reading Behavior, 14,* 61–74.

Wixson, K. (2011). A systemic view of RTI research: Introduction to the special issue. *Elementary School Journal, 111*(4), 503–510.

Wixson, K. K., Lipson, M. Y., & Johnston, P. H. (2010). Making the most of RTI. In M. Y. Lipson & K. K. Wixson (Eds.), *Successful approaches to RTI: Collaborative practices for improving K–12 literacy* (pp. 1–19). Newark, DE: International Reading Association.

Wood, D., Bruner, J., & Ross, S. (1976). The role of tutoring in problem-solving. *Journal of Child Psychology and Psychiatry, 17,* 89–100.

Wood, D., & Wood, H. (1996). Vygotsky, tutoring and learning. *Oxford Review of Education, 22*(1), 5–16.

Wood, K. D., & Robinson, N. (1983). Vocabulary, language, and prediction: A prereading strategy. *The Reading Teacher, 36,* 392–395.

Wylie, R. E., & Durrell, D. D. (1970). Teaching vowels through phonograms. *Elementary English, 47,* 787–791.

Yuill, N., & Oakhill, J. (1988). Effects of inference awareness training on poor reading comprehension. *Applied Cognitive Psychology, 2,* 33–45.

Yuill, N., & Oakhill, J. (1991). *Children's problems in text comprehension: An experimental investigation.* Cambridge, UK: Cambridge University Press.

Zimmerman, B. J. (2000). Attaining self-regulation: A social cognitive perspective. In M. Boekaerts, P. R. Pintrich, & M. Zeidner (Eds.), *Handbook of self-regulation* (pp. 13–39). Burlington, MA: Elsevier Academic Press.

Children's Literature

Aardema, V. (1983). *Bringing the rain to Kapiti plain: A Nandi tale.* New York: Penguin.

Arnosky, J. (1999). *All about deer.* New York: Scholastic.

Bang, M. (1980). *The gray lady and the strawberry snatcher.* New York: Simon & Schuster.

Brett, J. (1989). *The mitten.* New York: Penguin Putnam Books for Young Readers.

Briggs, R. (1978). *The snowman.* New York: Random House.

Buckley, M. (2007). *The fairytale detectives.* New York: Amulet Books.

Caseley, J. (1991). *Harry and Willy and Carrothead.* New York: Greenwillow Books.

Cowley, J. (1996). *Along comes Jake.* New York: Wright Group/McGraw-Hill.

Day, A. (1985). *Good dog Carl.* New York: Aladdin.

Deming, A. (1993). *Who is tapping at my window?* New York: Penguin Putnam.

dePaola, T. (1978). *Pancakes for breakfast.* New York: Harcourt, Brace.

Flournoy, V. (1985). *The patchwork quilt.* New York: Dell Books for Young Readers.

Fowler, A. (1996). *Spiders are not insects.* New York: Children's Press.

Galdone, P. (2001). *The little red hen.* New York: Clarion Books.

Gibbons, G. (1995). *Planet Earth inside/out.* New York: William Morrow & Co.

Ginsburg, M. (1988). *The chick and the duckling.* New York: Simon & Schuster.

Ginsburg, M. (1991). *Mushroom in the rain.* In D. Alvermann, C. A. Bridge, B. A. Schmidt, L. W. Searfoss, P. Winograd, & S. G. Paris (Eds.), *My best bear hug* (pp. 144–154). Lexington, MA: Heath.

Gregory, N. (2002). *How Smudge came.* New York: Fitzhenry & Whiteside.

Hepworth, C. (1996). *Antics: An alphabetical anthology.* New York: William Morrow.

Kalan, R. (1981). *Jump, frog, jump!* New York: Greenwillow Books.

Kalman, B., & Everts, T. (1994). *Frogs and toads.* New York: Crabtree.

Kellogg, S. (1987). *Chicken Little.* New York: HarperCollins.

Kuskin, K. (1958). "Spring" from *In the middle of the trees.* New York: Harper & Row.

Lobel, A. (1970). *Frog and toad are friends.* New York: HarperCollins.

MacLachlan, P. (1985). *Sarah, plain and tall.* New York: HarperCollins.

Martin, B. (1992). *Brown bear, brown bear, what do you see?* New York: Henry Holt.

McCully, E. A. (2003). *Picnic.* New York: HarperCollins.

McCully, E. A. (2004). *First snow.* New York: HarperCollins.

Melser, J. (1998). *My home.* New York: Wright Group/McGraw-Hill.

Mooser, S. (1978). *The ghost with the Halloween hiccups.* New York: William Morrow.

Most, B. (1986). *There's an ape behind the drape.* New York: William Morrow.

Most, B. (1992). *There's an ant in Anthony.* New York: HarperCollins.

Numeroff, L. (1985). *If you give a mouse a cookie.* New York: HarperCollins.

Peck, R. N. (1986). *Soup's new shoes*. In V. A. Arnold & C. B. Smith (Eds.), *Winning moments* (pp. 276–286). New York: Macmillan.

Peppe, R. (1985). *The house that Jack built*. New York: Delacourte.

Pilgrim, E. B. (2000). *Curse of the Red Cross ring*. St. John's, NL: Flanker Press.

Sendak, M. (1962). *Chicken soup with rice*. New York: HarperCollins.

Shaw, N. E. (1988). *Sheep in a jeep*. New York: Houghton Mifflin Harcourt.

Silverstein, S. (1974). *Where the sidewalk ends*. New York: HarperCollins.

Steig, W. (1969). *Sylvester and the magic pebble*. New York: Aladdin.

Taback, S. (1997). *There was an old lady who swallowed a fly*. New York: Viking.

Waber, B. (1975). *Ira sleeps over*. New York: Houghton Mifflin.

Willems, M. (2003). *Don't let the pigeon drive the bus*. New York: Hyperion Books for Children.

Yolen, J. (1987). *Owl moon*. New York: Philomel Books.

Index

Page references in italic refer to figures and tables.